Kenkoku University and the Experience of Pan-Asianism

SOAS Studies in Modern and Contemporary Japan features scholarly books on modern and contemporary Japan, showcasing new research monographs as well as translations of scholarship not previously available in English. Its goal is to ensure that current, high quality research on Japan, its history, politics and culture, is made available to an English speaking audience.

Published:

Women and Democracy in Cold War Japan, Jan Bardsley
Christianity and Imperialism in Modern Japan, Emily Anderson
The China Problem in Postwar Japan, Robert Hoppens
Media, Propaganda and Politics in 20th Century Japan, The Asahi Shimbun
Company (translated by Barak Kushner)
Contemporary Sino-Japanese Relations on Screen, Griseldis Kirsch
Debating Otaku in Contemporary Japan, edited by Patrick W. Galbraith,
Thiam Huat Kam and Björn-Ole Kamm
Politics and Power in 20th-Century Japan, Mikuriya Takashi and
Nakamura Takafusa (translated by Timothy S. George)
Japanese Taiwan, edited by Andrew Morris
Japan's Postwar Military and Civil Society, Tomoyuki Sasaki
The History of Japanese Psychology, Brian J. McVeigh

Kenkoku University and the Experience of Pan-Asianism

Education in the Japanese Empire

Yuka Hiruma Kishida
Bridgewater College, USA

BLOOMSBURY ACADEMIC
LONDON • NEW YORK • OXFORD • NEW DELHI • SYDNEY

BLOOMSBURY ACADEMIC
Bloomsbury Publishing Plc
50 Bedford Square, London, WC1B 3DP, UK
1385 Broadway, New York, NY 10018, USA

BLOOMSBURY, BLOOMSBURY ACADEMIC and the Diana logo
are trademarks of Bloomsbury Publishing Plc

First published in Great Britain 2020

Cover image: Students at Chien kuo University (1938–1945) in
Hsinking (Changchun), Manchukuo, by Toyoji Minagawa, published in December 1939
(© public domain, from Wikimedia commons)

A catalogue record for this book is available from the British Library.

A catalog record for this book is available from the Library of Congress.

ISBN: HB: 978-1-3500-5785-2
         ePDF: 978-1-3500-5786-9
         eBook: 978-1-3500-5787-6

Typeset by Integra Software Services Pvt. Ltd.
Printed and bound in Great Britain

To find out more about our authors and books visit www.bloomsbury.com
and sign up for our newsletters.

To the light of hope

Contents

Tables

Acknowledgments

It has been a truly wonderful experience working with Bloomsbury's editorial team, Rhodri Mogford, Laura Reeves, Beatriz Lopez, and Emma Goode. I would like to extend my special thanks to Christopher Gerteis, Series Editor, for his encouragement and moral support. The book has greatly benefitted from insightful feedback of anonymous reviewers.

At the University of Iowa, I received indispensable guidance, critique, advice, encouragement, and support from my teachers and colleagues. I would like to thank Dr. Jennifer Sessions, Dr. Shuang Chen, Dr. Paul Greenough, Dr. Sonia Ryang, Dr. David Arkush, Dr. Elizabeth Heineman, Dr. Michaela Hoenicke Moore, Dr. Glenn Penny, Dr. Scott Schnell, Dr. Alyssa Park, Dr. Jacki Rand, Dr. Sarah Hanley, Pat Goodwin, Sheri Sojka, Mary Strottman, Jean Aikin, Dongwang Liu, and Min Tian. Assistance provided by Japanese Studies Librarian Chiaki Sakai was indispensable to this research. Finally, becoming a student of Dr. Stephen Vlastos has been one of the greatest fortunes that I have had. Ever since reading his publication as an undergraduate student in California, he has been an inspiration to me. He is the greatest role model for me not only as a historian but also as an enthusiastic and dedicated educator. I am forever grateful to Stephen for his advice, guidance, and the warm support and encouragement he and Mary Ann have given me.

A number of people have read early drafts of parts of this book and offered helpful feedback and advice. I would like to extend my special thanks to the participants of the Midwest Japan Seminar held at Niagara University in April 2015 and the Yale InterAsia Connections Conference in February 2016. I would also like to thank Leander Seah, Phillip Guingona, Jamyung Choi, Woyu Liu, Josh Cochran, and Gabi von Roedern. My special thanks are extended to the colleagues and students of Bridgewater College's Department of History and Political Science.

This research has benefitted from Bridgewater College Faculty Research Grants, University of Iowa's Crossing Borders Summer Travel Scholarships, the Stanley Graduate Award for International Research, the Laurence Lafore Fellowship, the Center for Asian and Pacific Studies' Graduate Dissertation Grants, and the Graduate College's Summer Fellowship.

I would like to express my gratitude to Kenkoku University alumni and their family members whom I met in Tokyo and Osaka in 2010 and 2011: Mr. Fujimori Kōichi, Mr. Matsumoto Hirokazu, Ms. Matsumoto Misao, Mr. Shiokawa Shigeya, Mr. Nakamura Masazō, Mr. Ochi Michiyo, Mr. Ishii Gen, Mr. Shiotsuki Genshi, and Mr. Murase Yoshikazu. Upon learning of my research interest, all of them willingly shared their opinions and stories about their alma mater with me. In addition, both the Alumni Association and individual alumni members offered me a number of variable sources. I hope I have fulfilled their expectation of constructing Kendai's history from the perspectives of not only Japanese but also other Asian students.

I would also like to dedicate this book to all of the wonderful teachers and friends I met throughout long years at school in Japan and the United States. Teachers at Ikaruga Nishi Elementary School taught me the joy of learning. Teachers at Kansai Soka Junior and Senior High Schools opened my eyes to various new things and have continued to give me warm encouragement as if I am their own sister or daughter. The school brass band, to which I belonged for six years, taught me the preciousness of friendship and the importance of daily effort. At Soka University of America, I was able to study with great professors and friends. I am forever grateful to Dr. Dongyoun Hwang for showing me how interesting and important Asian History is and for encouraging me to pursue further studies in the United States. Finally, I would like to express my utmost appreciation to my mentor in life, Dr. Daisaku Ikeda, the founder of Soka schools I attended, and a leader of a grassroots international movement to actualize world peace through education and culture based on Buddhist philosophies. In 2001, he gave me a book with a word of encouragement, "学は光なり (learning brings the light to life)," written on the title page. It is my vow as his disciple to embody this word in my historical research and teaching and live a contributive life.

Lastly, I would like to express my very great appreciation to my family in Japan, the Netherlands, and the United States. I owe so much to their continuous support and cheers, especially that of my mother. To my wonderful partner, Hide, words cannot express my gratitude and love to you. Thank you so much for being who you are. Being with such a sincere person makes me want to better myself each day. Hikari, thank you for choosing us as your parents. You are the light of hope for us.

When introducing students enrolled at Kenkoku University, I add their class names following their names. In accordance with the institutional convention, their class names are based on the order of their matriculation at the university.

Table A1 Entering Classes and their Matriculation Years

Entering Class	Category of Applicant	Year of Matriculation
First entering class	All	1938
Second entering class	All	1939
Third entering class	All	1940
Third entering class under a new admission rule	*nikkei*	1941
Fourth entering class	*mankei*	1941
	nikkei	1942
Fifth entering class	*mankei*	1942
	nikkei	1943
Sixth entering class	*mankei*	1943
	nikkei	1944
Seventh entering class	*mankei*	1944
	nikkei	1945
Eighth entering class	All	1945

In the admission process, the university categorized applicants into two groups. Those who received education in the Manchukuo school system were called the *mankei* ("of Manchurian descent"). The applicants who went through the Japanese school system in Japan, Korea, and Taiwan were called the *nikkei* ("of Japanese descent"). The admission criteria, such as required minimum age, differed between the two groups to accommodate different backgrounds of prior education under the two systems.

Starting in 1941, the *mankei* applicants were admitted into a longer program than the *nikkei* applicants, as shown in the table.

Abbreviations

CCP	Chinese Communist Party
GMD	Guomindang or Chinese Nationalist Party
ISNSC	The Institute for the Study of the National Spirit and Culture (*kokumin seishin bunka kenkyūjo*)
JTB	Japan Tourist Bureau
Kendai	Kenkoku University ("Nation-Building University")
KURI	Kenkoku University Research Institute
KURIMJ	*Kenkoku University Research Institute Monthly Journal*
PRC	People's Republic of China
ROK	Republic of Korea
SCAP	Supreme Commander for the Allied Powers
SMR	South Manchuria Railway

Notes on romanization

Japanese terms and names are romanized according to the Hepburn system, including the use of macrons for longer vowels. However, macrons for well-known terms such as Tokyo and Osaka were omitted. Most of the Chinese terms and names are romanized according to the pinyin system, except for certain names that are well-known to English speakers differently romanized (e.g. Chiang Kai-shek and Sun Yat-sen). Korean terms and names are romanized according to the Revised Romanization of Korean.

Following East Asian conventions, Japanese, Chinese, Korean, and Taiwanese names appear in the order of a surname followed by a first name, except for the authors of contemporary books and articles. Those scholars' names appear in the order of a first name followed by a surname, to be consistent with the names of other authors.

1

Introduction

Kenkoku University (Nation-Building University, abbreviated as Kendai) was the university founded in 1938 by the Kwantung Army, the Japanese Army of occupation of the northeastern provinces of China commonly designated Manchuria. After the Manchurian Incident (1931), the Kwantung Army established Manchukuo (1932), which proclaimed itself as an independent state. The state's founding principles, rule by the "kingly way (ōdō)"[1] to realize "ethnic harmony (minzoku kyōwa),"[2] ostensibly presented Manchukuo as a utopian state that would pioneer Japan's Pan-Asianist endeavor of creating a new order in East Asia. In reality, however, the establishment of Manchukuo only furthered Japan's informal colonial control of the region where Japan acquired footholds after its victory in the Russo–Japanese War, 1904–5. Within Manchukuo, Kendai had a special institutional significance. It was the only institution of higher learning that was administered directly by the Manchukuo's governing authority, the State Council. Other schools were placed under the Ministry of Culture and Education. The State Council, which was dominated by Japanese military and civilian officers, clearly regarded Kendai as a distinct institution tasked to spearhead Manchukuo's ideological propaganda effort. At the same time, as the top university of Manchukuo, Kendai enjoyed a high degree of autonomy. The university recruited male students of Japanese, Chinese, Korean, Taiwanese, Mongolian, and Russian backgrounds, and aimed to train the generation of leaders who would actualize the goal of "ethnic harmony." About 1,400 male students enrolled at this institution between 1938 and 1945 were truly the cream of the crop, not only from Manchukuo but from different corners of the Japanese Empire. Kendai's institutional commitment to the Pan-Asianist ideal was reflected in its arrangement of student residences in which students of different cultural, ethnic, and national backgrounds shared a living space. In addition, the recruitment of non-Japanese faculty members and the fact that the students were allowed to use non-Japanese languages outside class indicate the university's commitment to the equalitarian conception of Pan-Asianism. These practices make Kendai not only unique within the Japanese Empire but also set it in sharp contrast with the brutality of the Japanese invading forces in China as epitomized in the Nanjing Massacre of 1937. Thus, in the midst of Japan's expansion and war, Kendai served as a vehicle of Pan-Asianism, a rare space for the transnational exchange of ideas, and for historians today, an ideal institutional site to interrogate the praxis of Pan-Asianism, a highly ambiguous ideology.

This book examines the perceptions of Pan-Asianism that were expressed by diverse groups in the University: the Kendai administration, faculty members and, most importantly, by students—both Japanese and non-Japanese. In light of Japan's rapid territorial expansion, especially after 1931 and through the early 1940s, it is easy to dismiss Japan's wartime discourse of Pan-Asianism as just another empty rationale for the domination of subject peoples by an imperial power, akin to the Anglo-American "white man's burden." The book complicates this picture through careful examination of both institutional and individual experiences of the ideology at Kendai.

Manchuria and Manchukuo

Japan had established informal colonial control in southern Manchuria through two footholds gained as a result of victory in the Russo–Japanese War in 1905. First, Japan occupied and administered the Liaodong peninsula, which Japan designated the Kwantung Leased Territory. Second, Japan had acquired the Russian-built South Manchuria Railway, which ran from Harbin to Lushun (Port Arthur), and its adjacent areas called the South Manchuria Railway (SMR) Zone. This railway and the SMR zone were administered by the South Manchuria Railway Company, a semi-public Japanese corporation. Although the Japanese government encouraged its citizens to emigrate to Manchuria and settle in this region to strengthen Japanese control, Japanese residents remained a small minority. In 1930, the Japanese population in the SMR zone and the Kwantung Leased Territory was at most 240,000, while the Chinese population in Manchuria reached 30,000,000.[3] By the late 1920s, the Japanese community in Manchuria faced two threats: the growing expression of nationalism by the Chinese people and the Soviet Union's re-assertion of power in the Far East.

It was at this crucial time that Ishiwara Kanji, one of the protagonists in this book, arrived in Manchuria as Operations Officer of the Kwantung Army. Later,

I will discuss his involvement in Kendai as the initiator of its foundation; here, Ishiwara comes into focus for his prominent role in the expansion of Japanese interest in Manchuria, a resource-rich and contested region. Believing secure control of Manchuria to be essential to Japan's preparation for the coming war with the United States, which he believed was imminent, Ishiwara orchestrated military actions that led to Japan's occupation of the whole of Manchuria in late 1931. Meticulous planning started in March 1929. He not only travelled throughout Manchuria to study the topography and deployment of Chinese military forces but also secretly negotiated with the Imperial Army Korea Command for support in case of military conflict in Manchuria.[4] By the summer of 1931, Ishiwara felt that the time was ripe for military action, as no single foreign power seemed prepared to challenge Japan in a land war in northeast Asia. The Soviet Union was in the middle of its five-year plan; the United States and Western Europe had not yet fully recovered from economic depression; and Nationalist China was struggling to consolidate its control south of the Great Wall.[5] What followed was the Manchurian Incident of September 18, 1931, in which Kwantung Army officers blew up a section of the South Manchuria Railway in Mukden, blamed it on the Chinese and used it as a pretext for launching a general military offensive against Chinese forces. Although Ishiwara's specific role in this incident is unknown, he had initiated long-term planning for direct military action. Moreover, following the initial incident, Ishiwara engineered the ensuing expansion of military operations, repeatedly defying orders from the cabinet and central command in Tokyo, as well as the Kwantung Army Commander, General Honjō Shigeru, not to advance. By 1932 the Kwantung Army had occupied the whole of Manchuria, which the Tokyo government ultimately accepted as a *fait accompli* and the Japanese public celebrated wildly.

Concurrently with planning for military action, ever since his arrival in Manchuria in 1928 Ishiwara was involved in the Kwantung Army's state-building initiatives. The idea of separating Manchuria from China proper originated in the interactions between the former Qing royalists and the Kwantung Army.[6] Wishing to restore Manchu rule by gaining regional autonomy in the Three Eastern Provinces (Liaoning, Jilin, and Heilongjiang), Qing royalists had maintained connections with the Kwantung Army after the 1911 revolution that deposed the Qing Dynasty and formally established China as a republic. In August and September 1927, and again in August 1929, attendants of the last Qing emperor, Puyi, visited Kwantung Army officers to recommend the enthronement of Puyi in Manchuria. Ishiwara and Itagaki Seishirō, Senior Staff Officer, welcomed this proposal. They seized on this idea as the perfect opportunity to sever Manchuria from China proper on the pretext of acting on behalf of an oppressed minority—ethnic Manchus—seeking self-determination. In addition, the enthronement of Puyi proved effective in incorporating the Inner Mongolian independence movement activists in the Kwantung Army's state-building operation. Historic ties between the Qing court and Mongolian leaders predating the Qing conquest of China brought the two peoples closer in opposition to Han Chinese control.[7] On March 1, 1932, Manchukuo proclaimed its foundation as a putatively independent state. Incorporating the four northeastern Chinese provinces of Fengtian, Jilin, Heilongjiang, and Rehe, the new state declared independence from China proper and established a federation of the "people of Manchuria and Mongolia," or, more commonly, Manchukuo.[8]

Declaration of Manchukuo's independence was, thus, by and large, a result of Japan's accumulated interest in Manchuria, which was meshed with the aspirations of Manchu and Mongolian nationalists. The League of Nations did not recognize Manchukuo as a legitimate state; instead, the international community supported the Chinese Nationalist government's view that Manchukuo was a puppet-state established by the Japanese. Historians have agreed that Manchukuo was indeed a part of Japan's bigger imperial and expansionist project. Yet, Manchukuo differed from Japan's formal colonies such as Taiwan and Korea. By assuming the form of a sovereign state with an ethnically diverse population, Manchukuo provided a unique political space to put into practice the idealistic aspects of Japan's Pan-Asianism, as epitomized in its founding principles of rule by the "kingly way" to realize "ethnic harmony."

Manchukuo's use of the principle of rule by the "kingly way" originated in Japanese Sinologist Tachibana Shiraki's response to Sun Yat-sen's famous speech in Kobe, Japan, in 1924.[9] Sun, a Chinese hero of the republican revolution, urged his Japanese audience to choose whether to become "a cat's-paw of the West's Despotic Way (*seihō hadō*) or a bastion of the East's Kingly Way (*tōhō ōdō*)."[10] Though these Confucian terms, "kingly way" and "despotic way," had been used by many in China, Sun's speech made them famous among Japanese contemporary thinkers. Drawing the term "kingly way" from an ancient Chinese philosopher, Mencius, Sun promoted the principle of governance by virtue based on Eastern, or more specifically, Confucian, tradition, which presented a direct contrast to the Western "despotic way" or governance through force.[11] Tachibana, a paid researcher in the Research Department of the SMR Company, concurred on Sun's framing of East–West opposition. In his article on Chinese nationalism, published in 1925, Tachibana advocated Japan's role to support Chinese nationalist efforts to transform society from within.[12] Unlike his contemporary Japanese Sinologists, whose thoughts were confined to Japan's national interests and disdain for China, Tachibana found potential in Chinese peasants. Tachibana argued that Japan had better "win friends" among the rural Chinese, whose cooperation was essential for bringing about social reform in China.[13] His positive belief in the Chinese rural masses led Tachibana to advocate Japanese rule of Manchuria by the "kingly way" that would replace authoritative, feudalistic, and militaristic control by warlords.

Once employed by the Manchukuo government in 1932, however, the principle of the "kingly way" served to legitimize the Japanese dominant position in the state. The State-Founding Proclamation of Manchukuo declared that the "[g]overnment will be based on the Way, and the Way is rooted in heaven. The principle for the creation of the new state is uniformly to lay emphasis on following the Way of heaven and bringing peace to the people."[14] On the surface, the document appears consistent with Sun's conception of the "kingly way," as an Asian theory of governance that could lead Asia to regional solidarity against Western imperialism. Nevertheless, this state-founding document left the words "the Way" undefined, and, as the non-Japanese Manchukuo population later learned to their disappointment, this open-ended term meant the Japanese "imperial way" (*kōdō*) in actuality. Indeed, the non-Japanese Manchukuo population never enjoyed the same rights as Japanese residents. In the end, the principle of the "kingly way" betrayed its original meaning and would lose much of its idealistic appeal at the hands of the Japanese civil and military bureaucrats who dominated Manchukuo politics.

Likewise, the principle of "ethnic harmony," which is often called "harmony of five peoples (*gozoku kyōwa*)" among Han Chinese, ethnic Manchus, Mongolians, Japanese, and Koreans, did not correspond to the reality either.[15] The early Japanese discourses about "ethnic harmony" reveal the pragmatic use of the concept in the Japanese settler community. One of the strong advocates of the principle was the Manchurian Youth League (*Manshū seinen renmei*), a Japanese settlers' organization that was initiated by the Dairen Newspaper Company. In lobbying for the secession of Manchuria from China proper in the 1920s, the League's members promoted the idea of creating a multi-ethnic state. Under the slogan of building a harmonious relationship among diverse peoples, they sought to protect their rights in the region from the anti-Japanese agitation that was rampant in and around Manchuria.[16]

Such a pragmatic use of the principle of "ethnic harmony" can also be found in the State-Founding Proclamation of Manchukuo. The document stated:

the people who now reside on the terrain of the new state make no distinctions among races or between superiors and inferiors. In addition to the Han, Manchu, and Mongolian peoples who were originally from this region and the Japanese and Koreans—that is, people from other lands—those who wish to reside here in perpetuity shall enjoy equal treatment. The rights they receive shall be protected and shall not be violated in the least.[17]

While appearing to promote equality and harmonious coexistence of all peoples, this statement clearly reflected the longstanding Japanese concern about their rights in Manchuria, as expressed by the Manchurian Youth League. In that sense, Manchukuo's founding document's emphasis on ethnic equality was directed against the growing Chinese anti-Japanese activities rather than establishing ethnic equality as the state's governing principle. Indeed, the Manchukuo government did not develop any particular policy to actualize the idealistic vision of "ethnic harmony." Rather, the Japanese army and civil officials who dominated the government authorized institutionalized discrimination by segregating and differentiating people based on their ethnicities in education, conscription, the court, and other aspects of public life.[18] Although local leaders were initially appointed as the prime minister, the heads of ministries and various offices, or governors, many of these positions were replaced by Japanese vice-ministers, vice-governors, or assistant directors-general, on the explanation of "placing the right man in the right place."[19] Or, those non-Japanese officials assumed key positions in name only, while their Japanese colleagues in vice positions exercised actual administrative authority. Thus, not only did Japanese occupy 45.8 percent of all positions in central and local governments but they wielded the real administrative power.[20] Likewise, Puyi, even though he became the chief executive of Manchukuo and later ascended to become emperor, had no meaningful official business to conduct other than affixing his name on already completed documents. In the end, the Japanese rule of Manchukuo betrayed its founding document's promise of ethnic equality.

A brief discussion is needed on the term *minzoku* used in the principle of "ethnic harmony" (*minzoku kyōwa*). Although the slogan has often been translated as "racial harmony" or "inter-racial harmony," these English translations do not convey the precise meaning of the original Japanese term. As Kevin M. Doak has lucidly shown, the Japanese term *minzoku* as used in this context was not a purely biological concept of race. In terms of race, or *jinshu*, the official discourse of wartime Japan claimed that there was only one race in East Asia. Meanwhile, wartime Japan perceived its empire as a multi-ethnic empire, based on "a culturally defined ethnic concept of nationality."[21] Hence,

Manchukuo's founding principle concerned harmonious coexistence of ethnic nations, or the peoples of different ethnic and national identities. Throughout the book, I use "ethnic harmony" as a translation for *minzoku kyōwa*, with the understanding that *minzoku* under discussion refers to ethnic nations, ethnicities, or more broadly, peoples, and not a biological concept of race.

While earlier works on the history of this contested region, Manchuria, have provided solid knowledge on Japan's geopolitical and economic interests in Manchuria and demonstrated exploitative motives behind its development projects, their national focus on Japan has inevitably drawn a line between the colonizer and the colonized.[22] By examining the relations between Japanese and non-Japanese in political and economic terms, those works tended to endorse binary narratives of non-Japanese people's experience as resistance to or collaboration with Japanese imperialism. Recent research on the region has broken from a nation-centric view of Manchuria and incorporated a plurality of experiences into analysis. Rejecting the national scope of Japanese imperialism, Prasenjit Duara (2003) has examined the origins of Manchukuo's ideological construct in a broader context of the emerging discourse of Asianism—both perceived by Japanese and Chinese.[23] Authors in Mariko Asano Tamanoi's *Crossed History* (2005) have focused on non-governmental actors as subjects of study and called into question the assumption of necessary opposition and even clear-cut boundaries between the colonizer and the colonized.[24] Louise Young (1998) and Emer O'Dwyer (2015) have expanded the scope of the Japanese experience by incorporating civil society into their studies.[25] Furthermore, Rana Mitter (2000), Hyun Ok Park (2005), and Norman Smith (2007) have challenged a dichotomist characterization of the Chinese and Korean experiences as collaboration or resistance.[26] Hence, building on the earlier political and economic research, the recent literature on Manchuria has broadened the scope of research, incorporated non-Japanese and non-governmental actors into focus, and suggested a more complicated picture of relations among the diverse population.[27]

Building upon these recent works, this book seeks to add further dimensions to the field's understanding of Manchuria by examining the institution that constituted a centrepiece of Manchukuo's program of ideological propaganda. As the top educational institution of Manchukuo, Kendai was tasked with coming up with an ideal practice of the state's Pan-Asianist principle of "ethnic harmony." The fact that the State Council continued to allocate ample budget to the university attests to the political significance it held within the Manchukuo state. However, the large majority of individual members of the Kendai campus community did not belong to the political elite. Students were aware of their career prospect of serving the state as government officials. At the same time, they were deeply cognizant that the raison d'être of Kendai lay in bringing changes to the current practice and making the Pan-Asianist ideal a true reality. With that understanding, Kendai faculty and students assumed the role of critics of the current Manchukuo policy. As intellectuals and as future leaders of the state, they carved out a space for themselves to carry out open exchange of ideas as equal partners in this endeavor, amid Japan's intensifying war.[28]

Japan's Pan-Asianism

Like Anglo-American empires' sense of mission that was expressed as "the white man's burden" and the French vision of an "Algerian melting pot," Pan-Asianism was an important part of the Japanese Empire.[29] Japan's Pan-Asianism took a variety of forms—a broad vision of Asian unity, call for Japan–China collaboration, the Greater East Asia Co-Prosperity Sphere, as well as the ideological construct of Manchukuo. On one hand, Japan's Pan-Asianism differs from the idealistic visions of Western empires, because it originated in the nation's experience of Western menace in the nineteenth century. In other words, Japan's Pan-Asianist thinking began in an effort to position the nation in the perilous world to which it had just entered. On the other hand, Japan's Pan-Asianism is similar to its Western counterparts in the sense that the bona fides of its idealistic claims are in question.

Japan's Pan-Asianism emerged as an influential idea among the political elites in the early Meiji era, when the nation was forming its new identity after more than 200 years of "national seclusion" policy. Concurring with Fukuzawa Yukichi's call for "escaping from Asia (*datsu-a*)," the Meiji leaders hurriedly built a nation state and adopted imperialist diplomacy following the Western model, believing that it was vital for national survival. In that context, Pan-Asianism provided an idealistic alternative to "joining the West." It advocated "remaining in Asia," uniting with Asian neighbors and fighting against Western encroachment. In the following decades, the Pan-Asianist call to unite with Asian neighbors gained support from a wide spectrum, including liberal internationalists, leftists, rightists, and military expansionists. Behind this intellectual trend in Japan was a growing sense of confidence as a new modern state as well as continuing frustration with Western contempt for Japan. Victories in two wars, against Qing China (1894–95) and Russia (1904–5), funneled confidence and pride as a rising world power. Nonetheless, the Japanese continued to feel their non-white race deterred Western powers from truly embracing Japan as their equal, which became especially apparent through the racial equality debate at the Paris Peace Conference (1919) and the US anti-Japanese Immigration Act (1924). Meanwhile, the context of Western colonialism and Japan's seeming success with modernization made Pan-Asianism appealing to anti-colonial nationalists in Asia. Indeed, the early twentieth century through the late 1920s observed some transnational dialogue and cooperation among Pan-Asianists throughout Asia.[30] There were also some prominent Asian nationalists who continued to put their faith in Japan-sponsored Pan-Asianism.[31] Pan-Asianist discourses became incorporated into Japan's foreign policy by the late 1920s and came to serve as a tool for legitimizing Japanese expansion and military aggression in Asia during the 1930s and the early 1940s.

We owe much of our understanding of Japan's Pan-Asianism to earlier research in the form of biographies of political elites and key theorists. Mark R. Peattie's biography of Ishiwara Kanji (1975) highlighted the fundamental contradiction of the prominent militarist thinker's Pan-Asianism.[32] Joshua A. Fogel's two biographies of Japanese Sinologists Naitō Kōnan (1984)[33] and Nakae Uchikichi (1989)[34] demonstrated two different types of scholarship that concerned Japan's relations with China.[35] Lincoln Li's intellectual biography of Tachibana Shiraki (1996) showed how this prominent Sinologist developed a new ideology that combined leftist sympathy toward Chinese nationalism and the rightist imperialist dream of rallying Asia against the West.[36]

Besides these intellectual biographies, works that concern the cultural aspects of the Japanese Empire have examined Pan-Asianism and race as important subject matters.[37] Concentrating on the years of the Pacific War (1941–45), John W. Dower (1986) investigated the role of race in Japan's wartime policy.[38] In his thesis on the prominent role played by race in igniting and intensifying war hatred on both sides—Japan and the Anglo-American allies—one finds the author's discussion of Japan's race-based Pan-Asianism. In analyzing the wartime reports written by governmental bureaucrats, Dower identified the concept of the "proper place" as the key to the Japanese racial view of the world. Based on the idea of the racial purity of the Japanese, whose emperor supposedly descended from the Sun Goddess, the Japanese official ideology held that the Japanese were destined to dominate other peoples in Asia who belonged to lower places within a new Pan-Asianist order.[39]

Gerald Horne (2004) similarly highlighted the vital role that race-based Pan-Asianism played in Japan's initial military success in the war against the allies.[40]

He has shown how Japanese propaganda efforts utilized the local reality—Southeast Asian people's strong resentment at white supremacist racism under Western colonial rule—to construct a Pan-Asianist message that Japan was a liberator of Asians.[41] This strategy proved effective, as Japanese troops were able to gain support from the nationalists of each country. Such race-based collaborations against white colonial regimes occurred throughout Southeast Asia—in Indochina (under French rule), Singapore, Malaya, and Burma (under British rule), Indonesia (under Dutch rule), New Guinea (under Australian rule), and the Philippines (under American rule).[42] Thus, Horne demonstrated how Japanese policymakers were keenly aware of Western racism and used racialized Pan-Asianist propaganda to tap into the anti-Western nationalist sentiments of peoples in the region.

More recently, Eri Hotta (2007) brought Pan-Asianism into central focus in her examination of Japanese policy making.[43] She has argued that the ideology shaped Japan's national policy throughout the Fifteen-Year War. More specifically, Hotta demonstrated that Pan-Asianism functioned as "a consensus-building tool for an otherwise divided government" throughout the years between 1931 and 1945.[44] At crucial moments in Japan's war, such as the Manchurian Incident of 1931, the outbreak of the Second Sino–Japanese War in 1937, and the Pearl Harbor attack of 1941, Hotta contends, the catchall nature of Pan-Asianism brought internationalists, imperialists, bureaucrats, and literary elites together in support of the empire.

A point of agreement among Hotta and the works on Japanese elite Pan-Asianists is that the dominant perception of Pan-Asianism by the 1930s was Japan-centered. Hotta has called this thread of idea Meishuron Pan-Asianism—*meishu*, or leader, referring to Japan. Representing this line of thinking, ultranationalist and expansionist organizations such as Kokuryūkai (Amur River Society) and Gen'yōsha (Dark Ocean Society) insisted that Japan had "an active role to play in transforming China and other Asian nations in the image of Japan."[45] Hence, the scholarship on Japan's Pan-Asianism that concerns the elites and the ideology's impact on Japan's policy has established the supremacy of Meishuron Pan-Asianism in wartime Japanese politics during the 1930s and 1940s.

This book does not intend to refute this claim; rather, by bringing into focus Japanese and non-Japanese scholars and students of Kendai, who remained outside of the political elite circle, this book suggests that there continued to be a wide variety of conceptions and practices of the ideology through Japan's intensifying war among the peoples below the level of the political elite. In that sense, this book extends the effort made by recent works on Pan-Asianism to complicate the field's knowledge about this topic by identifying multiple and competing articulations of the ideology while re-examining its reception by subject populations.

Cemil Aydin (2007) took a global approach to Anti-Westernism by comparing Pan-Islamism and Pan-Asianism.[46] Both Masafumi Yonetani (2006)[47] and an edited volume by Sven Saaler and J. Victor Koschmann (2007)[48] focused mainly on Japanese Pan-Asianist theorists but examined a variety of conceptions articulated by progressive thinkers such as Rōyama Masamichi and Miki Kiyoshi, feminist internationalist Inoue Hideko, Confucian scholar Yasuoka Masahiro, and a religious organization, Ōmotokyō. More recently, Sven Matthiessen (2016) presented a case study of Japanese Pan-Asianism in formation, implementation, and reception in the Philippines, and demonstrated that the ideology continued to find diverse articulations even into the 1930s and 1940s.[49] Thus, these recent works have greatly expanded the field's understanding of Pan-Asianism.

One point that distinguishes this book from these recent works on Pan-Asianism is that its examination of the historical experiences of Pan-Asianism is firmly grounded in one unique institution. Rather than finding multiple and competing articulations of this ideology in different places within the Japanese Empire, the book aims to recreate an institutional experience of Pan-Asianism and lively exchange of ideas among its constituents. The ambiguity inherent in the ideology and its expression in the goal of "ethnic harmony" led to diverse discourses, both overlapping with and diverging from the official conception of Meishuron Pan-Asianism. Furthermore, the university's institutional objective of fostering a generation of leaders who would actualize those Pan-Asianist dreams and its institutional dedication to the principle of ethnic equality among the students created a rare space for young men of different ethnic and cultural backgrounds to engage in open dialogue. Among these idealists, an egalitarian conception of Pan-Asianism continued to exercise considerable appeal even late into the Second World War, even as at the institutional level, mobilization for war intensified contradictions between ideal and practice.

Structure

Following the Introduction, Chapter 2 presents an institutional history that describes Kendai's origin, planning period, and the school curriculum. Drawing on Manchukuo's government records and institutional records of the university, the chapter shows how the Japanese elites who made up Kendai's planning committee struggled to put Pan-Asianist ideals into practice in the educational setting. One finds that divergent perceptions of Pan-Asianism were incorporated into the physical plant and curriculum of Kendai and thus caused contradictions such as encouraging free discussion on one hand and imposing Japanese customs and values on the other. Among the sources I use in this chapter is *Kenkoku Daigaku nenpyō [The chronological timetable of Nation-Building University]*, which was compiled by one of the former Japanese students, Yuji Manzō in 1981.[50] Unlike a conventional chronology, this thick tome contains testimonies by planning committee members, faculty members, and students as well as Kendai's institutional records. Chapter 2 also analyzes the scholarly writings authored by Kendai's Japanese and non-Japanese faculty members and shows the patterns of their Pan-Asianist thinking. The Manchukuo government regarded Kendai as a vital organ within the administrative machinery of Manchukuo, particularly in its efforts in ideological propaganda. Indeed, the university established Kenkoku University Research Institute in September 1938, which was ordained by an Imperial Ordinance with the seal of Manchukuo Emperor Puyi. However, the examination of Kendai faculty members' publications does not point to a clearly defined, uniform conception of Pan-Asianism. The contemporary writings of Kendai faculty, the majority of whom were Japanese but included some scholars from Korea and China, reveal the variety of ways they constructed the historical meaning of "Asia" as a civilization.[51] I argue that while Japanese members tended to represent Japan's role as central in forging an Asian unity, they presented differing explanations for Japan's relationship with Asia and the motives of Asian participation in the Pan-Asian crusade against the West. Some saw a teacher–pupil relationship emphasizing Japan's quick modernization and mission to guide others. Others took it for granted that Asian peoples would voluntarily cooperate with a Japan-led project of constructing a new Asian order, highlighting the shared experience of Western menace. Meanwhile, although Kendai's non-Japanese faculty did not oppose the Japanese Empire in their writings, their articles presented subtle challenges to the central position of Japan in the ongoing Pan-Asianist endeavor.

While Kendai faculty members explored and expounded their conceptions of Pan-Asianism in their research, students experimented with and contemplated the meaning of Pan-Asianism in their daily lives on campus. Chapters 3 to 5 focus on Kendai students' experiences and their perceptions of and relationships with Pan-Asianism. Chapter 3 concerns Japanese students, Chapter 4 Korean and Taiwanese students, and Chapter 5 Chinese students. Due to limited records regarding Russian and Mongolian students, their experiences do not form a chapter; but we will encounter some of them in Chapter 6. Chapters 3, 4, and 5 examine students' motives for attending Kendai, their initial reactions to the school, their interactions with their fellow classmates and teachers, and their evaluations of Kendai, Manchukuo, and the Japanese Empire.

For Chapter 3, which analyzes the experiences of the Japanese students, I rely mostly on their contemporary writings—diaries they kept during school days. Numerous entries are compiled in the aforementioned chronology. In addition, a few other Japanese alumni published their diaries with varying degrees of edit. What these sources reveal is that the cross-cultural interactions on the Kendai campus had two different effects on the Japanese students. Some Japanese students matriculated at Kendai full of imperial idealism, and their encounters inside and outside the classroom led to serious critique of Japanese imperialism and disillusionment. One even finds growing sympathy toward Chinese and Korean students' ethnic nationalist sentiments. For other Japanese students, their experiences solidified their sense of Japan's superiority and commitment to the hierarchical notion of Japanese as the guiding nation of Asia. The chapter features four Japanese students' experiences at Kendai to demonstrate a variety in their youthful struggle to find the meanings of their lives and the role that Pan-Asianism played in such struggle.

Chapter 4 focuses on the experiences of students from Korea and Taiwan, who as residents of Japan's formal empire possessed the dual identity of the colonized other and Japanese imperial subjects, with many—though not all—the rights of Japanese citizens. Japan annexed Taiwan in 1895 after winning the Sino–Japanese War (1894–95). Korea had been Japan's protectorate since 1905 when Japan defeated Russia in the Russo–Japanese War (1904–5), and had subsequently been annexed in 1910. Students from these formal colonies grew up under Japan's assimilation policy. Indeed, some of them had Japanese or Japanized names, and all were officially acknowledged as Japanese imperial subjects. Moreover, many of them were highly proficient in Japanese. In reconstructing their experiences, I rely on their memoirs.[52] First, *Kankirei—manshū kenkoku daigaku zaikan dōsō bunshū [Kankirei: collection of memoirs written by alumni in Korea]* (2004)[53] contains twenty-one essays written by Korean alumni residing in South Korea and were translated into Japanese. Second, one of the contributors to this collection also published a book-length memoir titled *Hankyore no sekai: aa nihon [The world of my countrymen: Ah, Japan]* in 1999.[54] Third, the only substantial writing authored by Taiwanese alumni is Li Shuiqing's memoir *Dongbei banian huigulu [Memory about the eight years that I lived in Dongbei]*

(2007).[55] These memoirs show that whether or not they had embraced Japan's assimilation policy in their home countries before matriculating at Kendai, these students became awakened to their identity as Korean or Taiwanese as they interacted with other Asian students on campus. Furthermore, one finds evidence of their support for an egalitarian conception of Pan-Asianism, which could coexist with their emerging sense of ethnic nationalism. Cutting across the clear border of collaboration and resistance, their experiences complicate the picture of colonial subjects' experiences within the multi-ethnic empire.

The central source in Chapter 5 is an anthology of former Chinese students' recollections *Huiyi weiman jianguo daxue [Recollections of Bogus Manchukuo Nation-Building University]* (1997).[56] This source, published in the People's Republic of China (PRC), presents problems of how to read the narratives that were produced under political constraints. In light of the authorized narrative of the Second Sino–Japanese War (1937–45) in the PRC and the risk of guilt by association with Japanese militarism, it is not surprising that the Chinese memoirs emphasize the negative aspects of their experiences of Kendai and represent it as a vehicle of Japanese imperialism. There are, however, a limited number of memoirs written by former Chinese students that were published in Japanese in Japan. Reading the former texts against the latter allows for a more nuanced interpretation of the Chinese students' experiences. One finds subtle differences in their views of Pan-Asianism and Kendai's practice of it. We also learn about the arrest of a group of Kendai's Chinese students for their involvement in secret anti-Japanese activities and the administration's response to it.

While the chapters thus far separately examine the institution and faculty, and students of different ethnic and cultural backgrounds, Chapter 6 aims to bring those campus community members, particularly the students, more closely together. It analyzes the three volumes of *Kenkoku: kenkoku daigaku juku zasshi [Nation-Building: Kenkoku University Juku Journal]*,[57] a student-run periodical published by the university's *juku* (student residences) organization, seven issues of *Kenkoku daigaku juku geppō [Kenkoku University Juku Monthly]*,[58] and a couple of other student-run periodicals' extant issues.[59] These periodicals, which were bilingual in Japanese and Chinese, served as a print forum for students to express their everyday concerns as well as their perspectives on Manchukuo society and the ongoing war. As such, these materials, while not previously analyzed in existing research on Kendai, provide a perfect window into the university's institutional experience of Pan-Asianism. It is on the pages of these student-run periodicals that one finds the liveliest interchanges of ideas among the diverse students of Kendai. Contemplating the meaning of "ethnic harmony" in their everyday life, Kendai students tackled a difficult question of whether their emerging sense of ethnic nationalism and Pan-Asianism could coexist.

The Epilogue describes the lives of Kendai students after the closing of the university in August 1945, following the capitulation of Japan and the dissolution of Manchukuo. Due to their associations with Kendai, many former students had a difficult time adjusting themselves to their respective societies. For instance, during the Allies' occupation of Japan, former Kendai faculty members and students were removed from public offices. Some former Chinese students were persecuted during the Cultural Revolution. Meanwhile, since its establishment in Tokyo in 1953, the Kenkoku University Alumni Association has published memoirs and other sources regarding the school, held meetings in and outside Japan, and forged exchanges among former Kendai students across national borders. The association's fifty-seventh and final general meeting, held in Tokyo in June 2010, was attended by approximately 120 members, all in their 80s and 90s.[60] The association's decades of lively activities is a legacy of a Pan-Asian partnership that Kendai students nurtured through open discussions at the difficult time of war and colonialism.

Dreaming big about Pan-Asianist education: Kenkoku University's origins, planning period, school curriculum, and faculty

On July 7, 1937, the Marco Polo Bridge Incident occurred near Beijing, which triggered the Second Sino–Japanese War (1937–45). Just as this minor and yet historically significant clash between Chinese and Japanese armies erupted to the south of Manchukuo, a group of twelve Japanese and three Chinese officials and academics were holding a meeting in Shinkyō, the capital of Manchukuo, to finalize plans to establish Manchukuo's leading institution of higher learning.[1] As one of the participants later recalled, they reacted to the news of the fighting with surprise and recognized that it was "a serious matter" but without any apprehension this was the opening battle of an all-out war between China and Japan.[2] The meeting proceeded as planned and approved the Imperial Ordinance on Kenkoku University, which would be issued on August 5, 1937 under the name of Manchukuo Emperor Puyi. The document boldly declared: "Kenkoku University aims to nurture a generation of talented young men who embody the essence of (Manchukuo's) founding principles, master the depth of learning that informs their actions, and become pioneering leaders who will construct a world of high moral."[3] This mission statement was as abstract as it was grandiose, and the school's administration, faculty, and students would subsequently interpret it in diverse ways. Nevertheless, as this chapter shows, the conception of Kendai's institutional mission as conceived by the planning committee's core members was based on a Japan-centered ideology of *kōdō*, or the imperial way. This ideology's central tenet was belief in the unbroken and sacred lineage of the Japanese emperor, which paradoxically was transposed to the "empty space" of Manchuria to actualize the state's unique mission of creating "ethnic harmony" among its diverse population.

Just as the Kendai planning committee was feverishly finalizing its plan in Shinkyō, Major General Ishiwara Kanji was in Tokyo frantically trying to stop the military conflict that was unfolding in North China. Within central headquarters, opinion was sharply divided over how to respond: whether to expand or contain the conflict. Ishiwara, Chief of the Operations Division of the Japanese Army, argued that Japan must avoid a war with China at all costs. Although he eventually yielded to the opinion of the majority and authorized mobilization for the battle near Beijing, Ishiwara continued to advocate a policy of cooperation with China, for, in his mind, the Soviet Union was a greater menace than the strident nationalism of Chiang Kai-shek's Nanjing government. Furthermore, he regarded the development of Manchukuo and a cooperative relationship among Japan, Manchukuo, and China as a precondition for successful prosecution of an eventual war with the United States, which he held was unavoidable.[4]

It was with this vision of Pan-Asianism—a strategic alliance of Japan, Manchukuo, and China—that Ishiwara initiated the foundation of Manchukuo's leading institution of higher education in the fall of 1936. He envisioned the school becoming the center of Pan-Asian unity not just among the diverse peoples residing in Manchukuo but also among all Asian peoples. In the end, he did not have the final say in key decisions due to the nature of his assignments during the crucial phase of Kendai's planning.[5] He did not attend the planning committee meeting in Shinkyō that approved a plan that diverged substantially from Ishiwara's original vision. Nevertheless, the idea of creating a university that would be not just another overseas Japanese institution of higher learning but a radically different kind of institution with a Pan-Asianist mission sprang from Ishiwara's thought.

This chapter first examines the origin of Kendai in Ishiwara Kanji's geopolitical conception of East Asia and the actual planning process as it was implemented by the committee led by four Japanese academics. By exploring Ishiwara's initial vision and the extent of its actual realization in Kendai's curriculum and structure, I will demonstrate that Kendai as an institution incorporated variant articulations of its unique mission. While sharing the commitment to Kendai's idealistic mission—putting the Pan-Asianist ideal of "ethnic harmony" into practice—Ishiwara and the planning committee defined the central concept differently. Ishiwara emphasized the necessity of forging a cooperative relationship between Japan and China, in which Manchukuo would play a crucial bridging role. In contrast, the four key academics on the planning committee viewed Japan as the moving force and rightful leader of

Pan-Asian unity. In addition, although Ishiwara and the planning committee shared the determination to create a unique institution of higher learning, very different from Japan's imperial universities, they frequently disagreed over how to achieve this goal. Such conflicts of ideas continued to shape Kendai, which I will show by examining the school curriculum and selected academic writings of Kendai faculty, including Japanese, Chinese, and Korean. As a whole, Kendai's administration and faculty provides valuable insight into the variety of conceptions of Pan-Asianism in circulation in the discourse on empire in Japanese-occupied Manchuria during the Second Sino–Japanese War and Japan's war with the Allies.

Forging an East Asian League to prepare for the Final War: Ishiwara Kanji's perception of Pan-Asianism

Ishiwara Kanji (1889–1949) was a philosopher as well as a high-ranking military officer. Though excelling at school and successfully rising within the army to become part of the military elite, Ishiwara was nonetheless known for his fearless defiance of his superiors. While attending the Central Military Preparatory School and subsequently the Military Academy in Tokyo, Ishiwara gave undivided attention to his studies. Besides delving deep into philosophy, literature, religion, and world civilization, he visited prominent thinkers such as Tokutomi Sohō, Nogi Maresuke, and Ōkuma Shigenobu, seeking guidance.[6]

Ishiwara developed his Pan-Asianism in the early twentieth century. During this period, following Japan's victory in the Russo–Japanese War (1904–5), Pan-Asianism—especially the idea that Japan must lead an Asian crusade against the West—gained popularity not only in Japan but also in Asia.[7] This articulation of Pan-Asianism arose from growing confidence in Japan as a model for indigenous modernization that had rapidly advanced since the Meiji Restoration. In contrast, Ishiwara's perception of Pan-Asianism was rooted in a sober conviction that militarism was essential to the future of Japan. He developed this idea through his critical evaluation of Japan's victory over Russia. In his judgment, Japan won the war out of luck; he believed that Russia would have prevailed if the war was protracted, because Japan had no clear plan for a prolonged war.[8]

Ishiwara's next concern was the rising US power in Asia, which he thought would eventually clash with Japan. This apprehension led him to develop a theory of Final War. According to this theory, the Japan–US confrontation was to be the final world war that would divide the globe into two: the East led by Japan and the West led by the United States. Ishiwara's study of the Russo–Japanese War taught him that Japan must prepare for this coming conflict, which he predicted would be a prolonged war. How should Japan prepare? For Ishiwara, Pan-Asian unity was the answer. He argued that Japan must expand its control over Manchuria and China proper to strengthen its position geopolitically and to power its economic expansion.

Such strategic concern was linked to Ishiwara's genuine belief in Japan's global mission as world savior. Initially, Ishiwara could not find significance in the *kokutai* ideology that the Japanese state had used to define the nation since the Meiji Restoration. *Kokutai* ("national polity") defined Japan's polity as centered in Japan's imperial institution whose essential feature was the unbroken lineage believed to trace back to Japan's mythological founder, the Sun Goddess. To Ishiwara, this definition of *kokutai* based on Japan's state religion, Shinto, seemed particularistic. He was not persuaded by the use of *kokutai* as the evidence of Japanese superiority and justification of Japanese mission to save the world. However, through Tanaka Chigaku's school of Nichiren Buddhism, Ishiwara was able to find broader meaning in the *kokutai* ideology. Tanaka's Nichirenism was a religious and nationalist ideology that connected Nichiren Buddhism of the thirteenth century and Japanese nationalism of the early twentieth century. Tanaka broadly interpreted Nichiren's personal commitment to save Japan, enunciated at the time of the Mongol invasions, to advocate that Japan as a nation possessed the sacred mission to save the world because of its *kokutai*. As explained by historian Mark Peattie, this was not the original teaching of Nichiren. Nevertheless, Tanaka's rendering of Nichiren Buddhism convinced Ishiwara that Japan was destined to fulfill its sacred task of world renovation by leading Asian countries in the Final War.

As discussed in the Introduction, Ishiwara, as Operations Officer of the Kwantung Army, played a prominent role in the expansion of Japanese interest in Manchuria through the Manchurian Incident of 1931. Concurrently, he was actively involved in the state-building scheme that culminated in the foundation of Manchukuo on March 1, 1932. While Ishiwara's involvement in both of these military and political operations flowed from his strategic calculation of the essential role Manchuria would play in Japan's Final War, his vision of Manchukuo was based on his Pan-Asianist idealism. Ishiwara believed that the period of Japanese military administration must be kept as short as possible. Once hostilities ceased and order was restored, he argued, Manchukuo must develop through the cooperative efforts of its own diverse population. In Peattie's summation of Ishiwara's vision, such cooperation involved a division of labor in which "the Japanese were to manage heavy industry and those enterprises requiring special technological abilities; the Chinese were to develop the small businesses of the region; and the Koreans in Manchuria were to devote their efforts to paddy farming."[9] Thus, Ishiwara's conception of Pan-Asianism was hierarchical; while recognizing ethnic and cultural differences, he viewed the Japanese as most advanced, and thus most suitable for the leading position.

Ishiwara did not see a contradiction between a hierarchy of civilization and realization of harmonious relationships, which he enthusiastically supported. In April 1932, he encouraged Japanese residents of Manchukuo to establish the Concordia Association (Kyōwakai), a civic organization whose goal was to promote a sense of nationhood in Manchukuo and which aimed to make the ideal of "ethnic harmony" a reality.[10] To Ishiwara, developing a strong civic organization to shape politics appeared to provide an alternative to the Japanese military-controlled Manchukuo government nominally headed by Puyi. He insisted that this association, with grass-root support, should assume the role of political leadership in the new state functioning as a single party dictatorship that would reflect the people's will. Together with the association's members, Ishiwara called for equal pay for government employees regardless of ethnic nationality and proposed Japan's voluntary surrender of leaseholds of Kwantung Territory and the SMR Zone to the new state.[11]

In addition, Ishiwara developed his broader vision of an East Asian League, a federation of Japan, Manchukuo, China, and other Asian nations based on cooperation in preparation for the Final War. Manchukuo would serve as the model of Ishiwara's envisioned alliance of Asian peoples. In a speech delivered in 1940 but reflecting his early conviction of the necessity of a Pan-Asian alliance against the West, he summarized four principles. First, in terms of military defense, Japan, Manchukuo, and China will "cooperate and protect East Asia against the white race."[12] Second, the three countries will "integrate their economies as one ... to achieve co-prosperity and co-existence in a real sense."[13] Third, the three countries will "maintain ... their political independence and will not meddle in with each other's internal affairs."[14] Finally, they will "form a partnership based on the spirit of kingly way (ōdō)."[15]

In 1940 Ishiwara's vision appears to be a case of willful refusal to confront reality, as the speech was delivered three years into the Japan–China war fought in large part over Japan's insistence on Manchukuo's "independence" from China. Yet, prior to the Marco Polo Bridge Incident, Ishiwara's evocation of the "spirit of kingly way," a conception of benevolent governance that originated in Confucianism and had taken root in Asian cultures, at least held out the possibility of an alliance that was not simply top-down and in which relations between member states were not dictated by military imperatives.

Ishiwara's radical vision of an East Asian League and his strong advocacy of "ethnic harmony" were not easily squared with the Kwantung Army's mentality as an army of occupation. By the time Ishiwara left Manchukuo in August 1932 to take up a new assignment in Japan, he was dispirited by the direction of the new state in which he had invested so much of his energy and dreams. The Kwantung Army controlled the machinery of state administration to the exclusion of meaningful participation in governance by civilian officials representing the different ethnic groups of the new state. The Concordia Association had lost much of its initial idealism and grassroots character and increasingly functioned as a propaganda and intelligence gathering tool of the Kwantung Army. Most importantly, a sense of Manchukuo nationhood showed no signs of taking root, especially among ethnic Han Chinese, who comprised the vast majority of the population.

When he returned to Manchukuo as the Vice Chief of Staff of the Kwantung Army in September 1937, Ishiwara found himself even more disappointed than he had been five years earlier. Japanese military bureaucrats dominated all aspects of Manchukuo society.[16] The goal of "ethnic harmony" was far from a reality. The Japanese resided in segregated urban enclaves; and the salary gap continued to exist among different groups in society. Furthermore, the Japanese-dominated government of Manchukuo sought to integrate this new state into the Japanese Empire by adopting Japan's political system and laws and granting the Japanese government administrative authority over military affairs and Shinto shrines.[17] No sooner had he returned to Manchukuo than Ishiwara began criticizing the military bureaucrats who were running the country behind the scenes. He also proposed reforms—but to no avail. Ishiwara, a fearless dissident, again left Manchukuo in August 1938, utterly disappointed.

Visions of Pan-Asianist education: Ishiwara Kanji, Planning Committee, and the four professors

While often omitted in the narratives of Ishiwara's involvement in Manchuria, Kenkoku University was his brainchild.[18] The impetus was his growing disillusionment with the Concordia Association. After leaving Manchukuo in August 1932, he corresponded with Kwantung Army officials and discussed with them the possibility of establishing a "governmental university (*seiji daigaku*)" that would help making the principle of "ethnic harmony" a reality.[19] Initially, he called the university "*ajia daigaku*," or Asia University, which reflected Ishiwara's vision that Manchukuo would become the showcase of Pan-Asian unity and a model for the political alliance, the East Asian League, of Asian nations against the West.

In the fall of 1936, Ishiwara proposed the founding of a university to Kwantung Army officials through Kwantung Army Captain Tsuji Masanobu, who lost no time in recruiting staff for a planning committee. The committee, which maintained its offices in Tokyo and Sinkyō (modern Changchun), the capital of Manchukuo, consisted of army officers (of both the Kwantung Army and Imperial Army headquarters in Tokyo), Manchukuo's government officials, and prominent Japanese academics. Membership of the committee was fluid during the planning period, and the sources are not entirely consistent on the matter of membership, but as many as twenty-eight people were at some point involved in the planning process.[20] Almost all were Japanese and, not surprisingly, male.

Apparently, the Japanese-dominated planning committee at least sought to represent itself as a multi-ethnic group. One of the committee members, Tsutsui Kiyohiko, indicates that as of July 1937 the fifteen committee members included three "*mankei*" members.[21] The term "*mankei*," which can be translated as "of Manchu decent," was widely used by the Japanese in Manchukuo to refer to the Chinese-speaking population. Another such term was *manjin*, or "Manchurians." These terms in actuality included not only ethnic Manchu but also Han Chinese, Hui, and sometimes Mongolian people.[22] No other source lists *mankei* persons in Kendai's planning committee. Nor do these three *mankei* members' names appear in sources regarding Kendai's planning in any significant way. One of them, Zhang Jinghui, Manchukuo's Prime Minister, was later appointed Kendai's President; however, the actual administrative tasks were entrusted to Vice President Sakuta Sōichi, a Japanese academic.[23] Luo Zhenyu and Yuan Jinkai were both Chinese politicians in the Manchukuo government, but other Kendai-related sources do not mention their names. It appears that these *mankei* members did not have a meaningful role in the committee.

The planning committee entrusted the detailed planning to four Japanese academics. These men—often referred to as the "four professors (*yon hakase*)"—developed a curriculum and institutional structure that was quite different from Ishiwara's original idea. Even the name of the university changed. In the spring of 1937, the planning committee changed the name from Asia University to Kenkoku University ("Nation-Building" University), to emphasize the institution's mission to train government officials of the new state.[24]

We know the essential features of Ishiwara's vision from a memo drafted by Major General Mishina Takayuki following Tokyo committee members' meeting with Ishiwara in May 1937.[25] According to the memo, Ishiwara insisted that the university had to be radically different from existing Japanese universities. In Ishiwara's mind, change must begin with the faculty themselves, who were "not to be cut from the same old mold (of Japan's university professors)."[26] Kendai's ideal education, Ishiwara insisted, would emerge through cooperative research by its students and the pioneers who had lived in Manchuria and contributed to the making of Manchukuo since its establishment.[27] For this reason, Ishiwara did not expect the Kendai faculty to assume a strong directive role. Ishiwara told the planning members that after three years of study at the university, students "should go into the real society (of Manchukuo) and sweat blood. They should then bring back what they learned from their actual experiences (to Kendai), discuss them over and over to develop theories on politics, economics, culture, and philosophy, and teach that knowledge to (Kendai) students."[28]

According to Mishina's notes on the meeting, Ishiwara believed that "the fundamental purpose in establishing the University was to realize the ethnic harmony."[29] In Ishiwara's formulation, this endeavor was not something to be limited to Manchukuo but was to be extended throughout Asia. Ishiwara told the committee: "What Asian countries, beginning with Manchukuo, need is a new culture of economics, politics and philosophy rooted in the ideal of ethnic harmony."[30] Kendai, Ishiwara believed, could be the incubator of this new Pan-Asianist culture. According to another committee member, Tsutsui Kiyohiko, Ishiwara urged that this new culture would be based on *ōdō*, the spirit of the kingly way.[31] His use of this concept, which originated in Confucianism, further distinguished Ishiwara's vision of Pan-Asianist education from existing Japanese universities. Mishina's memo also shows that Ishiwara insisted on "the total equality for the students of different backgrounds, in the content of education, means of instruction, campus life, and all other aspects."[32] Ishiwara made two concrete proposals on how the university could promote the ideal of unity on the basis of equality: integrated student residences and recruitment of non-Japanese scholars to serve on the faculty.

Mishina's memo vividly conveys Ishiwara's enthusiasm about Kendai's integrated student residences as follows:

> Let students take their meals together, study together, and argue among themselves—in Japanese, Korean, Mongolian, or whatever language they speak. This definitely is the way to go. It shouldn't be Japanese students attending the

lectures of Japanese instructors and *mankei* students being instructed in their native language.[33]

Only on the basis of equality among the diverse student body, Ishiwara believed, could students have the honest exchange of ideas and opinions that would ultimately lead to genuine bonding among Asian youths. This emphasis on equality and recognition of differences reveals the idealistic aspect of Ishiwara's Pan-Asianism. He believed that students interacting as equals would eventually reconcile the difference of their ethnic national outlooks and cultural values and achieve a harmonious whole.

Ishiwara also proposed the recruitment of non-Japanese intellectuals. He urged the planning committee to invite not only prominent scholars of Asia but also revolutionary leaders from around the world. One passage from Ishiwara's essay "Kokubō seiji ron" discloses his rationale for the unconventional proposal. In the essay published five years later but articulating his early commitment to genuine and wide ranging intellectual inquiry, Ishiwara wrote:

> I also suggested studying the history of Japanese rule of Taiwan and Korea as well as the history of (Western) rule of India, Vietnam, the Philippines, and Outer Mongolia. This was to understand why the Taiwanese and Korean peoples' feelings (about Japanese rule) were still recalcitrant despite the fact that the Japanese rule since the Meiji period had brought them great improvement and happiness. Also, a comparative study of western colonial policy (and that of Japanese) can provide lessons for the politics of Manchukuo.[34]

This passage reveals that Ishiwara somewhat naïvely believed that progress in the form of economic and social modernization under Japanese rule should have brought "happiness" to the peoples of Taiwan and Korea. While he recognized the failure of Japanese colonial regimes to win the hearts and minds of many Taiwanese and Koreans, he had no doubt about the validity of Japan's colonization per se. At the same time, Ishiwara appears to have recognized that learning from past mistakes was necessary to overcome the obstacles to gaining Asian peoples' support for Japanese-led Pan-Asian unity. To this end he suggested that Kendai seek to recruit various revolutionary leaders, including but not limited to those who were involved in anti-Japanese movement in Manchukuo, and critics of Japanese expansionism.[35] In this context, we must see his idea of inviting Mohandas Gandhi and Subhas Chandra Bose from India, Leon Trotsky from the Soviet Union, and Pearl Buck from the United States not as the sign of his cosmopolitanism but as derived from his attempt at reforming the Japanese Empire.[36]

The planning committee members shared Ishiwara's determination to create a brand new university and his commitment to the ideal of "ethnic harmony." However, they had different ideas of how to realize these goals. The four professors, as the key members of the planning committee, were responsible for much of the detailed planning, and one of them was later selected as Kendai Vice President. Not surprisingly, these four Japanese academics' visions had a great influence on the institution's foundation.

When ordered by Ishiwara to form the Kendai planning committee, Kwantung Army Captain Tsuji Masanobu first contacted a renowned history professor at Tokyo Imperial University, Hiraizumi Kiyoshi.[37] He was a chief theorist of *kōkoku shikan*, a view of history based on a Shintoistic belief in the unbroken sacred lineage of the Japanese imperial family.[38] Hiraizumi had close connections with Japanese state and military officials through his involvement in the Institute for the Study of the National Spirit and Culture (*kokumin seishin bunka kenkyūjo*; ISNSC).[39] The ISNSC was established by the Education Ministry of Japan in August 1932 in an effort to counter the influence of radical student movements both leftist and rightist.[40] Promoting *kōdō*, or the imperial way, as the central principle, this statist organ criticized Japanese universities for engaging in Western-style abstraction rather than practical research. Historian Miyazawa rightly argues that the Japan-centered ideology of the ISNSC influenced the planning of Kendai because the four professors were all from this institute. Hiraizumi believed that Kendai should establish its own academic program that was distinct from existing Japanese universities, which, he lamented, had received too much influence from the West. In Hiraizumi's words, the new academic culture at Kendai should "depart from the Western influence, base itself on Asian—particularly Japanese—philosophy and learning, and contribute to the development of scholarship and culture of the world."[41]

Based on this belief, Hiraizumi recommended three other ISNSC scholars: Kakei Katsuhiko (professor of constitutional law at Tokyo Imperial University), Sakuta Sōichi (professor of economics at Kyoto Imperial University), and Nishi Shin'ichirō (professor of philosophy at Hiroshima Bunri University).[42] All three fit Hiraizumi's criteria. Within their respective fields of studies, Kakei and Sakuta focused on Shintoism and *kōdō*, and Nishi sought to establish a practical philosophy by combining Kantianism and Eastern philosophies such as Confucianism and Daoism.[43] The scholarship of these four professors was infused with Japanese values such as Shintoism and *kōdō*, though Nishi's emphatic emphasis on Eastern values was the exception. This strong element of Shinto-based imperial ideology within the scholarship of the four professors demonstrates a problem that existed from the early stage of Kendai's institutional planning: although the institution originated in Ishiwara's commitment to create a university based on an expansive conception of Pan-Asianism, the core planning members' perceptions of Pan-Asianism were in fact Japan-centered.

Differences between Ishiwara's and the four professors' visions appeared as early as February 1937 when the four professors joined the planning committee. One of the committee members, Tsutsui Kiyohiko, recalls that Ishiwara's emphasis on the principle of the kingly way and the Japan-centered ideology of the four professors were incommensurable from the beginning.[44] It all comes down to the difference between the principles of the kingly way, *ōdō*, and the imperial way, *kōdō*. For Ishiwara, who regarded Manchukuo as the driving force of an East Asian League, the Confucian concept of the kingly way ought to be the guiding principle for achieving cross-cultural cooperation. He believed that unlike the broadly shared Confucian concept of the kingly way, Japan's imperial way was too particularistic for this purpose. In contrast, the four professors saw the imperial way as the fundamental philosophy because they believed that Japan, not Manchukuo, must lead Pan-Asian cooperation. These differing ideas about Pan-Asianism led to divergent expectations for the university. Ishiwara envisioned it to be Asia University that would train leaders not only for Manchukuo but also for a federation of Asian countries aligned against the West, his ideal of an East Asian League. The four professors, on the other hand, sought to foster talented individuals who would contribute to the nation-building of Manchukuo, thus calling the school Kenkoku ("Nation-Building") University. They believed that Japan would be a more appropriate place to build a type of school that Ishiwara called Asia University because Japan, as the rightful leader of Asia, was responsible for forging unity among Asian nations. On April 20, 1937, the planning committee decided that the new university would be called Kenkoku University.[45]

Just as the four professors began detailed planning of the university in Tokyo, the planning committee in Shinkyō was searching for a site for the Kendai campus. Kida Kiyoshi, Nemoto Ryūtarō, and Tsuji Masanobu opened a map of Shinkyō City and selected a tract of vacant land on the outskirts.[46] It was approximately 2.15 square kilometers, on a hill and several kilometers south of Shinkyō's city center. Named Kankirei in Japanese, it had political significance, as the starting point for the geological survey of Manchukuo begun in 1933, and was thus regarded as an inaugural moment of the state.[47] Tsuji selected this location for Kendai campus, hoping that the university would similarly become the origin of Manchukuo's pioneering leaders.[48]

The campus infrastructure reflected the political orientation of the core planning members. At Tsuji's insistence, university facilities on the vast campus were laid out to represent the concept of *hakkō ichiu*.[49] The concept, which first appeared in the eighth-century Japanese classics *Nihonshoki*, literally means "the entire world under a single roof" and was used in the twentieth century by the advocates of empire to justify Japan's territorial expansion. Needless to say, the "single roof" in the latter context signified Japan's world hegemonic position. Accordingly, Kendai's six *juku* (student residences) buildings, the cafeteria, classroom building, Research Institute, and gymnasium called *yōseidō* ("nurture justice hall") were constructed around a central plaza to form a semicircle. This highly symbolic layout had a major disadvantage when it came to steam heating, which was an essential feature of construction for Manchuria's severe winter. Circulation of heated air through the central pipeline was extremely inefficient, and some *juku* buildings did not receive sufficient heat. Some students even had to wear overcoats while sleeping in their *juku* rooms.[50] In the planning process, Tsuji insisted on this arrangement over objections of other committee members and even in the presence of a famous architect, Kishida Hideto.[51] His tenacity on this matter reveals that Tsuji strongly believed in the symbolic importance of *hakkō ichiu* as a foundational concept for Kendai's establishment. As we have seen, this articulation of the ideal of "ethnic harmony" was hierarchical, with Japan assuming the leading position.

Despite the strong influence of Japan-centered Pan-Asianism on Kendai planning, the committee developed an educational system that was distinct from existing Japanese universities. After a short period of heated discussion, the committee came up with the following structure described in "Guidelines for the Establishment of Kenkoku University (*kenkoku daigaku sōsetsu yōkō*)," which was issued on August 5, 1937. Kendai would admit approximately 150 male students each year. Although there was no stated quota system for student admission, each year's ratio of students' ethnicities remained almost the same as in the first year. The first entering class consisted of seventy-five Japanese, fifty Chinese, and twenty-five students of Korean, Mongolian, and Russian ethnicities. These designations were ambiguous. The "Chinese students" included those from Taiwan as well as Chinese-speaking non-Han peoples. In addition, the "Japanese students" included both those who were born and raised in Japan and those who had lived in Manchuria.[52] Students came from virtually all prefectures of Japan, Taiwan, Korea, Karafuto (Sakhalin), the Kwantung Leased Territory, and Manchukuo. Tuition and living expenses were covered by the Manchukuo government.[53] In addition, every student received a monthly spending allowance of five yen.[54] The generous financial aid system was one of the main factors that attracted a large number of applicants—in fact, 10,000 applied for the first admission.[55]

The qualifications for admission differed slightly for Japanese and non-Japanese applicants. According to the "Guidelines for Applicants (*kenkoku daigaku yoka daiikki seito senbatsu yōkō an*)" issued on June 9, 1937, Japanese applicants must be twenty years old or younger and have or will have graduated from middle schools (*chūtō gakkō*), which enrolled students aged twelve to seventeen.[56] "Manchu, Mongolian, and Russian" applicants must be twenty-one years old or younger, have or will have graduated from middle schools in Japan or Manchukuo (*kōkyū chūtō gakkō*) and must be single.[57] The requirement of graduating from Japanese or Manchukuo middle schools seems to indicate that the admission committee targeted young people who had already been acculturated to the Japanese educational system. The difference in the age qualification was due to the different school systems in Japan, Korea, and Taiwan on one hand, and Manchukuo on the other. It is unclear, though, why only non-Japanese had to be single.[58] Here, again, the categorization of applicants' ethnicities was ambiguous. In this document, "Manchu" seems to include both ethnic Manchus and Han Chinese. "Japanese" appears to include Koreans and Taiwanese. What is unclear is whether those who had resided in Manchukuo were considered as "Manchu" or categorized according to their ethnic backgrounds.

Admission was based on a written exam and an interview. Competence in Chinese, English, French, Russian, or German was required for Japanese applicants, and Japanese language was required for non-Japanese candidates. The interview weighed heavily in the admission decision. The admission committee consisted of the planning committee members for the first year and the administrators and faculty in the subsequent years. One of the admission committee members, Kida Kiyoshi, enumerated the desired personalities of candidates as "good health, a strong will, not necessarily the so-called the brainy kids, but excellent students who can translate words into action, and exercise strong leadership."[59] The emphasis on action and strength of mind originated in Kendai's perceived function as a training ground of the state leaders who would contribute to nation-building in Manchukuo. Given the male-dominant politics both in prewar Japan and the Japanese Empire, it is not surprising that Kendai's admission criteria emphasized such masculine traits. However, with the vision of Manchukuo as the empire's frontier, Kendai sought for a particular type of masculinity in its prospective students. That is, the "good health" and "strong will" with which they could carry out the pioneering works in the vast land of Manchuria. In addition, this vision of student excellence derived from the admission committee's critical review of the existing Japanese universities that prioritized exam scores. Kida says that the admission committee had numerous heated arguments over which applicant possessed such potential. Mishina Takayuki, who also observed the interviews for the first year of admissions, recalls that the committee members seriously considered visiting some candidates' elementary school teachers or village elders in order to better understand the candidates' personalities.[60] The emphasis on personalities distinguished Kendai's admission process from that of Japanese universities, which the planning members criticized as elitist.

The academic program consisted of two levels of study, and each was three years long. The courses during the first level included general education, theory of Kenkoku ("nation-building") spirit, two languages, military training, labor service, and martial arts as compulsory subjects. The academic standard of the first level was the equivalent of Japanese higher middle schools (*kōtō gakkō*), which represented the elite, pre-university track in the prewar educational system. The content of the rigorous physical training was distinctively Japanese. Kendai required training courses on *kendō, jūdō,* and *aikido*—all were Japanese martial arts.[61] Here, we see that the masculine image of strong body and mind was shaped by the Japanese model and not a Pan-Asian or multicultural one. Chinese language study was required for Japanese students and Japanese language for non-Japanese students. In addition, all students selected a second foreign language from among Mongolian, Russian, French, German, and English.[62] These first three years were to prepare students for the second level that offered university-level courses such as law and politics, economics, ethics, philosophy and history, in addition to military training and labor service. Students chose one of three majors. The numbers of students in each major are available only for the first, second, and third entering classes. Of those students, 55.9 percent majored in Political Science, 32.3 percent in Economics, and 11.8 percent in Humanities.[63] Except for the language courses, all courses were taught in Japanese.

Overall, Kendai's curriculum was based on the principle of "*chikō gōitsu,*" or "oneness of knowledge and practice," and emphasized the equal importance of learning, military training, and labor service.[64] The use of the principle also reflected the university's critical stance against Japan's elitist education. Kendai expected students to apply knowledge to contribute to society. The fact that the Kendai curriculum did not require written exams reveals the institution's emphasis on practical learning and cultivation of the mind rather than memorization of facts. The principle of *chikō gōitsu* continued to shape Kendai's curriculum that aimed to nurture leaders of Manchukuo. After completing six years of education at Kendai, students were guaranteed positions in the Manchukuo government and other public sector jobs.[65] Before its closure in August 1945, Kendai officially graduated 288 students of the first three entering classes. Seventy-two of them were conferred diplomas early because they were drafted into the armed forces. Besides them, seventy-three graduates, the largest number, landed government and public sector jobs, forty-eight worked in higher education, twenty-six obtained positions at the Concordia Association, four at banks, and three at companies. Fifty-three graduates of the third entering class were undertaking training to become governmental officials when Manchukuo dissolved in August 1945.[66] Thus, in its short history, Kendai produced cohorts of young leaders in the public sector and education in Manchukuo, fulfilling its institutional mission.

While the aforementioned academic curriculum was enough to distinguish Kendai from Japanese universities, its high level of commitment to the principle of "ethnic harmony" made the institution unique. This aspect of Kendai was conspicuous, especially in the context of Manchukuo society, where the ideal of harmonious relationships contradicted the reality of people's life. Outside of the Kendai campus, discrimination and tensions among different ethnic groups prevailed, and Japanese and non-Japanese residents generally did not intermingle. By contrast, Kendai's integrated *juku* (student residences) system signified the school's dedication to making "ethnic harmony" a reality. It required all students to live in on-campus dorms together with other students and faculty members, who were called *jukutō* or *juku* headmasters. The planning members expected *juku* to be a place for students to share all aspects of life with students of different ethnic and cultural backgrounds and grow into capable leaders through friendly competition. Students were allowed to speak their own languages in *juku* buildings, and this tolerance was remarkable when contrasted with Japan's compulsory assimilation policy in Korea and Taiwan. Mishina Takayuki later commented that, although many of Ishiwara's ideas were not actualized in the end, the inter-cultural interactions through dormitory life did become a reality to a certain degree, and this aspect was the most remarkable and unique feature of Kendai's curriculum.[67]

Unlike other Japanese universities that called their dorms "*ryō*" or dormitory, Kendai referred to it as "*juku*," which could be translated as "private academy." Kendai's *juku* was not only a place for residing but also an organization of students and *jukutō* to carry out life-based training. Each entering class of about

150 students was divided into several ethnically integrated *juku* organizations, each consisted of about twenty-five students and one *jukutō*. *Juku* buildings had study rooms and a recreation room in which students enjoyed board games, music, and so on.[68] It is not clear how many students shared bedrooms, but it appears that a large number of students slept in a big Japanese-style room with *tatami* mats. The *juku* life was highly regimented. Students woke up at 5:30 a.m. and gathered at the athletic field for the morning meeting to start their day. Before going to bed at 9:30 p.m., each *juku* held a close of the school day meeting where the *jukutō* gave guidance to students. Besides, students spontaneously held roundtable discussion meetings (*zadankai*) and freely exchanged opinions on a variety of topics such as *juku* rules, academic culture of the institution, politics, and current issues. Thus, Kendai's *juku* offered a place for life-based discipline as well as interactions among students of diverse backgrounds.[69]

Despite the ethnic and cultural diversity of *juku* members, the required life style incorporated numerous Japanese customs and rituals. At the morning meeting, in addition to light physical exercise and recitation of Manchukuo's founding principles, students had a daily flag-raising ceremony where they hoisted not only the Manchukuo flag but also the Japanese flag. Moreover, students were required to bow deeply facing east—the direction of the Imperial Palace in Tokyo—to show respect for the Japanese Emperor. Before breakfast, students had to recite an ancient Japanese poem that expressed gratitude to *Amaterasu* or the Shinto Sun Goddess. At the meeting at the close of the school day, students were expected to sit on the floor in the distinctively Japanese style, which many non-Japanese students found painful.[70] These Japanese customs and rituals were forced on all students regardless of their ethnic, cultural, and ideological differences.

Besides the ethnic composition of the student body and the *juku*-centered education, the institutional commitment to the ideal of "ethnic harmony" can also be seen in its efforts to recruit non-Japanese scholars for faculty. In the autumn of 1937, Ishiwara ordered members of the planning committee to approach Chinese and Korean scholars and invite them to teach at Kendai. This mission was entrusted to Nemoto Ryūtarō, two other Japanese academics who had resided in Manchukuo and later joined the Kendai faculty, and Gu Cixiang, a Chinese politician with a position of the Assistant Manager at Manchukuo's Management and Coordination Agency.[71] Initially, Gu, who spoke both Chinese and Japanese, was to head the mission to Beijing. However, he asked Nemoto to lead the group instead, arguing that

[i]f we Chinese go to Beijing and speak to Chinese scholars, they would dismiss us as running dogs of the Japanese and discussions would go nowhere ... On the other hand, if you take the lead and I serve as an interpreter, they would be more likely to trust us. So, I'd like you to perform that role of the front man.[72]

In Nemoto's account, Gu's advice was genuine and evidence of his desire to cooperate. However, we cannot rule out the possibility that Gu was hoping to avoid making an official appearance as a Manchukuo government agent in Beijing.

Leaving aside Gu's real intention, the mission, now headed by Nemoto, succeeded in contracting three prominent figures: Bao Mingqian and Su Yixin from China and Choe Nam-Seon from Korea.[73] Bao, a graduate of Qinghua University in China and Johns Hopkins University, and Su, a graduate of Columbia University, were both specialists in politics and well-known political activists who played leading roles in the May Fourth Movement of 1919 and subsequent anti-Japanese activities in China. Choe, too, was known as a nationalist activist in Korea. After dropping out of Waseda University in Japan, he became involved in the March First Independence Movement of 1919. In fact, he was one of the authors of the declaration of Korean independence from Japan that was issued in that movement.[74] The three scholars were not only renowned intellectuals but also genuine nationalist movement activists.

In an address to a group of Chinese scholars in Beijing, Nemoto explained why Kendai wanted to invite non-Japanese intellectuals to join the faculty:

Kenkoku University is an educational and research institution whose true mission is the creation of "ethnic harmony" in Manchukuo. Indeed, we are building the University based on this principle not as a mere theory but as a philosophy of actual practice. This is why we are inviting scholars who are veterans of real nationalist movements.[75]

Bao was impressed by this speech and agreed to teach at Kendai. He then persuaded Su to join him.[76] Later, Choe also decided to join Kendai, believing that Manchukuo recognized Koreans as a distinct people, unlike in Korea where the Japanese colonial regime was carrying out the assimilation policy.[77] Because of these intellectuals' affiliations with nationalist movements, some of the commanders of the Japanese Army in China and Korea opposed their appointments, and Tōjō Hideki, the Kwantung Army Chief of Staff, was furious. Nevertheless, Ishiwara and Nemoto insisted and managed to overcome the opposition of these senior military officers.[78]

Besides these three intellectuals, fourteen scholars from China, Korea, and Germany joined the Kendai faculty by 1941. However, the seventeen non-Japanese represented only a small portion in the Kendai faculty, which included 191 Japanese members as of 1941, including affiliated faculty.[79] Sakuta, one of the four professors serving on the planning committee, explains this imbalance as follows:

> Although we (the administration) recruited those Manchurian and Korean persons of erudition as Professor Emeritus, we hired predominantly Japanese for the actual teaching positions for *juku*, academic courses and trainings … For one reason, there were not many strong candidates. Furthermore, because Kendai aimed to carry out a new vision of education that was distinct from the existing system, (we) speculated that (non-Japanese scholars) would not be suitable.[80]

Sakuta also cited the difficulty of recruiting Chinese academics due to the tense relations between China and Japan. This passage generates more questions than it explains the rationale behind the imbalance in faculty's ethnicities. If Kendai was to become a university "distinct from the existing system" of Japanese higher education, and if it was committed to the Pan-Asianist ideal of harmonious relationships, one would assume non-Japanese faculty members were to play vital roles. Indeed, that was Ishiwara's intention when he proposed that Kendai recruit a number of non-Japanese scholars and activists. Why did Sakuta, who was later selected to become Kendai's Vice President, the top academic administrator, think the non-Japanese scholars were "not suitable" for the task of creating a new education for Kendai? He must have considered the "new vision of education" as essentially a Japanese idea. From his perspective, even if non-Japanese scholars were welcomed, they were thought to play a secondary role. By extension, this seems to suggest that Sakuta regarded the project of forging Pan-Asian unity to be essentially Japan's endeavor. Or, he may have doubted the genuineness of non-Japanese cooperation for that dream and thus wanted to keep their involvement to a minimum.[81] Even so, the presence of non-Japanese faculty—especially Bao, Su, and Choe, who were famous for their roles in nationalist movements in China and Korea—must have appealed to prospective students from these countries. Later in this chapter, I will discuss the academic works of selected Japanese and non-Japanese faculty members.

On August 10, 1937, Kendai started its student recruitment for the first entering class. In late September 1937, when Ishiwara returned to Manchukuo, this time as Kwantung Army Vice Chief of Staff, it was clear that many of

Ishiwara's ideas for the institution had not been implemented. Ishiwara and Sakuta had held discussions in July 1937 but failed to resolve the difference between their visions.[82] Immediately after Ishiwara arrived in Manchukuo, he was so dissatisfied with the current Kendai plan that he asked the administration to suspend admissions of the first entering class. Eventually, he yielded to the planning committee and sought modest but symbolically significant changes, such as the recruitment of more non-Japanese scholars, which led to the recruitment of Bao, Su, and Choe. In the end, *juku*-centered education was Ishiwara's only idea that was fully actualized at Kendai.[83]

Ishiwara's discontent continued even after May 2, 1938, when Kendai opened its doors and welcomed the first class of about 150 students. When he visited the campus on July 7 that year to deliver a lecture to commemorate the first anniversary of the Marco Polo Bridge Incident, Ishiwara frankly shared his discontent with Manchukuo in front of the newly enrolled Kendai students. A student from Taiwan, Li Shuiqing, vividly recalls in his memoir that as soon as Ishiwara stood at the podium, he shouted to the audience: "unless people go mad, there can be no war" between Japan and China.[84] Although Ishiwara was one of the key players in the Manchurian Incident of 1931 and the creation of Manchukuo, he opposed the China–Japan war. To him, the realization of "ethnic harmony" was more important than enlarging the land of occupation through war. According to Li, Ishiwara blamed the Japanese for escalating hostilities as well as for failing to make harmonious relationships a reality. Ishiwara shared his indignation that the principle of "ethnic harmony" was not materializing in Manchukuo "because the Japanese are acting from a sense of superiority and dominating the peoples of other ethnicities."[85] Then, Ishiwara asked the students in the audience: "Aren't you acting in the same way?"[86] Clearly, he directed this question at the Japanese students of Kendai. To this, Li's close friend in his *juku*, a Japanese student, Yoneda Masatoshi, replied in a loud voice: "No, we're not like that!"[87] "It doesn't help if only one person acts differently," said Ishiwara, who apparently was relieved by Yoneda's response, and began his lecture on his theory of the world's Final War, which was to be his first and last lecture at Kendai.[88]

Li's recollection of this occasion, the only discussion of the event by Kendai's non-Japanese students that one can find, provides a glimpse into the reception of Ishiwara's lecture by the first entering class. At that time, there was no consensus within the Japanese Army on what to prioritize: solidifying Japan's current territorial holding in Manchukuo, preparing for the Soviet Union's possible attack, or expanding the territories further into the north provinces of China. In contrast to these purely territorial and military concerns, Ishiwara emphasized strengthening Manchukuo as a state through cooperation among Manchukuo's diverse residents. Ishiwara's frank criticism of the Manchukuo and the Japanese government and military must have come as a shock to Kendai students, especially those of non-Japanese backgrounds. While Li does not provide further details of the content of the lecture, he writes that the talk convinced Kendai students that Ishiwara "opposed the incident of July 7 (Marco Polo Bridge Incident) and its expansion into the war."[89] Moreover, Ishiwara's talk showed that "the principle of 'ethnic harmony' was not a mere slogan but a goal that [Ishiwara] was determined to realize."[90] Li stresses that this was not just his own impression but "was likely shared by most other students on campus."[91]

Based on interviews with the members of the first entering class, Yamada Shōji, a Japanese student of the eighth entering class concurs with Li on the students' impression on Ishiwara's lecture. Regarding the impact of Ishiwara's lecture, Yamada notes that not only Japanese but also non-Japanese students started openly discussing the concept of "ethnic harmony."[92] Li's and Yamada's accounts, taken together, show that the significant effect of Ishiwara's talk was that it inspired Kendai students to develop an atmosphere of free discussions. This is remarkable considering the fact that thought control was severe in Japan; Japan was at war with China; Korea and Taiwan were military-occupied colonies; and Manchukuo was a sovereign state in name only.

In August 1938, Ishiwara submitted a proposal for far-reaching reforms, whose aim was to terminate the Kwantung Army's control of Manchukuo politics. His proposal called for the establishment of a new university to be called Kyōwa ("Concordia") University, which would serve as "the core of policy making" in Manchukuo.[93] Kyōwa University would fulfill Ishiwara's initial expectation for Kendai, which, as we have seen, was grandly ambitious: nothing less than to create new theories of culture, economics, politics, and philosophy based on the ideals of the "kingly way" and "ethnic harmony." Kendai, he recommended, should be merged with Daidō Gakuin (Daidō Institute), Manchukuo's government clerk training academy.[94] Ishiwara emphasized that the Japanese students at Kendai and the Japanese government clerks in Manchukuo must be recruited from the Japanese population who resided in Manchukuo and not from Japan. Underlying these proposals was Ishiwara's disappointment at the current state of Kendai and his determination to "complete the independence of Manchukuo."[95]

Ishiwara's proposal of August 1938 had virtually no effect on Kendai or on Manchukuo politics. As mentioned earlier, his radical proposals encountered opposition and were rejected by the military bureaucrats who dominated Manchukuo politics. At the top of this group of military bureaucrats was Tōjō

Hideki, Kwantung Army Chief of Staff and Ishiwara's immediate supervisor. Ishiwara's career in Manchukuo ended abruptly when he left for Japan in August 18, 1938, and resigned his position soon afterwards.[96] By January 3, 1942, Ishiwara regarded Kendai as a total failure. In his speech before the members of the Association for an East Asian League (Tōa renmei kyōkai) in Tokyo, Ishiwara spoke disparagingly of the University: "though it has some admirable scholars, [Kendai] had come to resemble Japanese universities or even falling below their levels."[97] The division between Ishiwara and the four professors represented in this speech would have a lasting effect on Kendai.

Indeed, disagreement was rife during Kendai's planning period. The four professors may have united in opposition to Ishiwara, but many more disagreements occurred even among the four professors. According to Tsutsui Kiyohiko, a planning committee member, Sakuta and Kakei once had an intense argument over their different perspectives on China. Tsutsui also remembers that Nishi and Sakuta were somewhat sympathetic toward Ishiwara's idealism, while Hiraizumi and Kakei directly opposed it.[98] As many scholars joined its faculty and as Kendai opened its doors to students of diverse backgrounds, those new members of the campus community brought even more divergent perceptions of Pan-Asianism. It would not be an exaggeration to say that serious disagreements over virtually any topic for discussion became an integral part of the intellectual life of the institution. Within the faculty, for instance, three Japanese Associate Professors who served as *jukutō* during the institution's first year resigned from their positions, left campus for a certain period of time, and later returned to the faculty, due to their discontent with the administration. Ehara Fushinosuke, Ishinaka Kōji, and Fujita Matsuji had all been recruited by Ishiwara Kanji to serve the institution as *jukutō*. Being supporters of the vision of an East Asian League and believing in the importance of ethnic equality among students, these three *jukutō* maintained strong mentorship and developed deep bonds with their students, as testified by both Japanese and Chinese students, who credit them for the early success of the *juku* training at Kendai.[99]

Before we turn to Kendai faculty members' scholarly writings about Pan-Asianism as examined in the following sections, a brief discussion of the university's Research Institute is essential to understanding the institutional significance of Kendai in Manchukuo. The Manchukuo government regarded Kendai as a very important organ within the administrative machinery of the state, particularly in its efforts in ideological propaganda. Thus, when the Kendai administration submitted a budget proposal regarding the establishment of a university-affiliated research institute, the government swiftly approved it without reservations. Soon, on September 1, 1938, the plan of founding Kenkoku University Research Institute

(KURI) was ordained by an Imperial Ordinance with the seal of Manchukuo Emperor Puyi.[100] A document attached to the ordinance identified the ultimate objective of the institute as the construction of the "*manshū kokugaku*," which literally means "the studies of Manchukuo" and refers to a new interdisciplinary academic discipline that focuses on Manchukuo.[101] The document also stated that the KURI would engage in "critical examination of various philosophies and doctrines found in [Manchukuo] and outside world."[102] Interestingly, about one year earlier, Kendai's planning committee had defined the KURI's mission in a different way. At the meeting on June 20, 1937, the University's planning committee approved a document that outlined the committee's vision for the Research Institute. This document stipulated that the institute's objective was "to create a new culture by integrating the cultures of various ethnic groups with that of the Yamato people (the Japanese) as the central pillar."[103] This earlier vision thus reflects the academic inclination of the four professors: a Japan-centered approach to Pan-Asianism. This approach likely met opposition from the faculty members who joined the Kendai and its further planning of the KURI, resulting in the more expansive language used in the Imperial Ordinance's iteration of the institute's mission. Thus, one finds evidence of a debate over the KURI's mission among the planning committee, administration, and faculty.

During the eight years of Kendai's short history from 1937 to 1945, a total of 295 faculty members served the University as educators, researchers, and administrators. Approximately forty-five members were non-Japanese.[104] Although some Kendai scholars' publications have been preserved, they represent only a portion of the whole faculty's output. Most of what has been preserved is research reports and articles that were published by the KURI. Next I examine seven Japanese and two non-Japanese Kendai faculty members' writings from the late 1930s and early 1940s that appeared in KURI's monthly newsletters and other publications. I chose their writings not only because of their relevance to the topic of Pan-Asianism but also for their varying articulations of the ideology and its relationship with Manchukuo.

Kenkoku University Japanese faculty members' conceptions of Pan-Asianism

Japanese Kendai faculty members' conceptions of Pan-Asianism varied among individuals and yet shared the general characteristics of contemporary Japanese Pan-Asianism in the early 1940s. On one hand, writing in the late 1930s and early

1940s in Manchukuo, the cornerstone of the Japanese imperial project at that time, Japanese Kendai intellectuals appeared to have been influenced by Japan's increasingly aggressive foreign policy in Asia. On the other hand, through their involvement in the idealistic endeavor of Kendai's Pan-Asianist education, these intellectuals' writings reflected some universalistic aspects of the ideology.

Strong criticisms of the West drove historian Mori Katsumi to develop a hierarchical conception of Asian unity under Japanese leadership in an article published in 1942. Mori, Associate Professor of History, described the long history of Western imperialism in Asia, from the fifteenth-century Portuguese arrival in India, the sixteenth-century Spanish conquest of the Philippines, and the subsequent interventions of the Netherlands, Great Britain, France, and the United States. He also cited the Russian expansion southward since the sixteenth century. In terms of Western aggression against China, Mori recognized that Great Britain and the United States had taken the lead—the British Opium Wars (1839–42 and 1856–60) laid a ground for China's semi-colonial fate, while at the turn of the century the United States advanced imperialist competition over China by the Open Door policy. Mori described the contemporary situation regarding China as follows: "the United States and Britain, the fox and raccoon, are now wiping away their past evil deeds and eagerly backing Chiang Kai-shek, the betrayer of the Asian peoples, as if they were the saviors of the Chinese. That is what I call the comedy of the century."[105] Not surprisingly, Mori did not mention Japan's participation in this scramble for China.

Associate Professor of Economics Matsuyama Shigejirō echoed Mori's anti-Western theme but concentrated his critique on Western individualism and economic liberalism. In an essay published in 1942, Matsuyama argued that these two features of Western civilization formed the current world order, in which Western imperialists enjoyed material wealth at the cost of other peoples' misery. In such a world, "countries came together only for the shared interests or under the American and British plutocratic authority"; Matsuyama continued, "such despotic unity of nations would ... surely dissolve when national interests conflict or the subordinated countries' economy exceeds that of the domineering states."[106] Matsuyama insisted that the new order, which would replace this failing model of international relations, must apply the "principle of 'ethnic harmony' based on morality and comradery."[107]

Assuming that the world was shifting from one era to another, Mori and Matsuyama stressed Japan's special mission in leading Asia's march into the new era. The previous era, which they called "*kindai*," denoted the period when the West exercised imperialistic control over the East and other parts of the world.

Highlighting the common suffering that Asian peoples had borne, Mori and Matsuyama explained that Japan was destined to become Asia's leader because it had achieved preeminent modernization among Asian countries. Mori asserted that Japan's triumph in the Russo–Japanese War (1904–5) "had revealed Japan's historical mission of liberating Asian peoples from the shackles of the United States, Great Britain, and Netherlands, and recuperating the viability inherent in Asia itself."[108] For Matsuyama, Japan's initiative in establishing Manchukuo proved Japan's capacity to cleave a path to a new era in which Asian peoples would live harmoniously.[109]

Mori's and Matsuyama's historical explanations for Japan's legitimate leadership led them to assume that Asian peoples would voluntarily cooperate with Japan in creating the new order. Such an assumption is evident in Matsuyama's assertion that "creating the Greater East Asia Co-Prosperity Sphere is the historical mission of the billions of Asian peoples."[110] Because all Asians were historic victims of Western imperialism, the ongoing Pan-Asianist project was a task that was the charge of all Asians, not just of the Japanese. In addition to the shared experience of Western imperialism, Mori identified the long history of the East as a cultural bloc as an important foundation for the Co-Prosperity Sphere. He stated:

> before the sixteenth century, the East formed an independent world with a single cultural bloc ... The currently advocated "the Greater East Asia Co-Prosperity Sphere", though the term itself is new, is by no means concocted rhetoric of opportunism and sheer expediency but is grounded on the cultural bloc that emerged as a natural outcome of the shared historical experiences of Eastern peoples.[111]

In short, Mori's and Matsuyama's rationale was as follows—because Japan had emerged as the political center of Asia in the midst of Asian peoples' experience of Western oppression, and because Japan shared the common Eastern historical culture of other Asian countries, Japan was now in the position to provide leadership for Asia.

While Mori and Matsuyama assumed Asian peoples' voluntary cooperation in the creation of the Co-Prosperity Sphere, Nakano Sei'ichi, Professor of Law, and Ono Kazuhito, Associate Professor of History, argued that Japan could legitimately impose unity on Asians. Behind this dissimilarity were subtle differences in Pan-Asianist theorists' understandings of the origins of Japanese leadership in Asia. As seen previously, Mori's and Matsuyama's rendering of world history stressed the shared historical experiences among Asian peoples, including Japanese, in validating Japan's guiding position. By contrast, Nakano and Ono, emphasizing the superiority of Japan and its long-lasting efforts to modernize and protect Asia from Western imperialism, argued that Japan was uniquely capable of leading Asia's modernization. In other words, they regarded Japan's central position in the Co-Prosperity Sphere as the historical legacy of Japan's arduous but successful march to modernity. Nakano explained that Japan had endeavored since Meiji "to catch up with the West economically, culturally, and militarily so that it could eventually produce a pivotal political power (Japan) to East Asia."[112] Ono emphasized the contrast between Japan, the first and only Asian nation that correctly understood the Western threat, and "the various regions of East Asia that had remained asleep and dormant."[113] Japan, Ono continued, had no choice but to stand up to ensure "the survival of the whole of East Asia in the midst of the Western [threat]."[114]

Assuredness about Japanese supremacy over Asia enabled Nakano and Ono to justify Japan's imposing cooperation upon Asian peoples whom they recognized as not necessarily willing participants in the Japanese imperial project of uniting Asia. Unlike Mori and Matsuyama, who assumed "voluntary" participation of Asians in the Japanese-led Pan-Asianism, Ono clearly recognized other Asian peoples' opposition to Japan's leading role. He lamented that "the unawakened East Asian peoples had mistaken Japan as another imperialistic latecomer capitalist" even though Japan had fought for the sake of Asian survival.[115] Among those "unawakened" peoples, Ono specifically blamed Qing China, which "failed to understand in good faith" the true intent of Japan, and the succeeding Republic of China, which "continued to offer resistance in desperation at the instigation of the countries like United States and Great Britain."[116] Ono argued, however, that the leadership of Asia was a destined and inescapable mission given to Japan, the only Asian nation with the capacity to counter the West. Hence, Ono insisted that Asia must unite under Japanese leadership. An important omission, which weakens his argument, is the sheer brutality of Japan's invading forces in China.

Nakano's belief in Japan's supremacy over Asia was reflected in his vision of a three-level hierarchy in Asia with Japan at the top. In his conception, the top place in the hierarchy belonged to those nations that possessed advanced technology and military power and thus were "in the position of guiding the others."[117] Second place belonged to independent Asian nations that required guidance to achieve further development. In third place were Asian peoples within East and Southeast Asia who suffered from western colonial rule. Nakano claimed that Japan was in the first position, responsible for guiding the second group and freeing the third group from the shackles of Western imperialism, and establishing peace and order within the Co-Prosperity Sphere. He further stated: "each nation's equal sovereignty must not contradict the tutoring relationship among the nations."[118] Thus, Nakano, as a member of the guiding nation, imposed this three-level hierarchy despite "equal sovereignty" within the "tutoring relationship" on Asian peoples. In short, Nakano and Ono were more assertive about Japan's role of guiding other Asian peoples because they regarded them as ignorant, vulnerable, and inferior to Japan.

While the aforementioned four intellectuals envisioned a hierarchical Asian order with Japan at the top, Murai Tōjūrō and Sakuta Sōichi assigned the leading role to both Japan and Manchukuo. Murai, Professor of Politics, claimed that "*daitōa* (Greater East Asia) is not only objectively capable of and has good reasons for uniting as one—due to its shared world historical mission (to revolutionize the Western dominated world), and geographical, economic, and cultural reasons—but also is destined to unite due to its shared historical experiences and culture."[119] In Murai's conception, the shared "destiny" and moral principles were the key to a new form of Asian unity, which must replace the Western nations' unity, which was based on each constituent nation's "self-centered utilitarianism."[120] Murai believed that the Japan–Manchukuo bond must lead to new Asian unity because "Japan is the only *dōgi kokka* (ethical nation) that has embraced morality since the country's birth" and because "the Japan–Manchukuo alliance was as strong as that between blood-related brothers."[121] He also likened the relationship between Japan and Manchukuo to that of a parent and a child.[122] Hence, while placing both Japan and Manchukuo at the center of a new order, Murai clearly posited Japan's superiority.

Sakuta, Honorary Professor of Economics and Kendai's Vice President, agreed with Murai on the importance of the Japan–Manchukuo alliance. Sakuta's Pan-Asianist vision was based on the Japanese concept of *hakkō ichiu*, with Japan and Manchukuo as its center.[123] In his view, the two countries had different yet equally important complementary roles in the creation of a new order. Japan was the only country capable of creating the multi-ethnic community of Asia, while Manchukuo was expected to offer a working model as an embodiment of the principle of "ethnic harmony." Sakuta asserted:

> The true purpose of the establishment of Manchukuo as an Asian state that was created under the guidance of the Heaven is to firmly establish the integrity (as a state), unite its peoples, cooperate with Japan, build the foundation of the state so its peoples will enjoy stable life, administer the state, become the continental fortress for reviving Asia, and to contribute to the global project of *hakkō ichiu* and the creation of the harmonious world.[124]

Entrusting this unique mission to Manchukuo, Sakuta placed Manchukuo in the pivotal position in the ongoing Pan-Asianist project. Unlike Nakano and Ono, Sakuta did not indicate a clear tutoring relationship among Asian peoples. For, in Sakuta's understanding, if Manchukuo could showcase the ideal of Pan-Asian utopia, peoples throughout Asia would naturally cooperate with Japan and Manchukuo in freeing themselves from the West's subordination. Hence, both Murai and Sakuta emphasized the need for cooperation between Japan and Manchukuo as motors of change, while differing from each other as to the nature of the relationship between the two.

Honorary Professor of Philosophy Nishi Shin'ichirō's communal vision of Pan-Asianism adds further variety to the conceptions of Pan-Asianism expressed by Kendai faculty members. Considering all peoples living in Manchukuo as the "Emperor's children," Nishi emphasized the equality of all residents under the imperial family's benevolent rule.[125] However, as seen in the following passage, Nishi argued that imperial loyalty came first:

> Rather than attempting to create an ideal society by harmonizing the peoples of five different ethnicities, Manchukuo people must nurture loyalty to their Emperor whose benevolence impartially reaches out everyone without fail. Only then, can peoples of different backgrounds nurture companionship and prosper together as the Emperor's children.[126]

In this statement, it should be noted that Nishi referred to Puyi, the Manchukuo Emperor, not Japan's. In that sense, he regarded Manchukuo as an independent polity. Nevertheless, he added that the Manchukuo Emperor's sovereignty only existed when he was embraced by the Japanese imperial order. In the last analysis, although Nishi's conception of Manchukuo's harmonious relationships was communal rather than hierarchical, it ultimately hinged on the centrality of the Japanese imperial order. This tendency could be extended to his conception of Pan-Asianism because he believed Manchukuo could offer a model for the Greater East Asia Co-Prosperity Sphere.

Despite differences, there were three overall commonalities in these seven Japanese Kendai intellectuals' conceptions of Pan-Asianism. First, they fundamentally rejected the contemporary world order of Western imperialism. Second, they assumed the history had reached a turning point away from the Western dominated "*kindai*" to a new era of change. Third, they concurred that Japan should play a special role in the ongoing world-wide transition. In other words, they all emphasized Japan's centrality—Japan was situated at the top of the hierarchy, at the center of *hakkō ichiu* or at the special position as the home of the Emperor, the father of all Asian peoples. These common characteristics of Pan-Asianist thinking were reflected in their perceptions of Manchukuo as well because these scholars regarded Manchukuo as part of the bigger project of creating the Greater East Asia Co-Prosperity Sphere. It followed that Manchukuo, as an integral part of Japan's imperial project, must also be guided by Japan or cooperate closely with Japan.

Kenkoku University non-Japanese faculty members' conceptions of Pan-Asianism

Despite Ishiwara's recommendation that Kendai invite scholars and anti-colonial activists from around Asia, non-Japanese instructors constituted a small minority within the faculty. Although as many as forty-five non-Japanese members were affiliated with Kendai at some point, KURI's monthly newsletters show that only a handful of them actively participated in research and teaching at Kendai. Moreover, among their publications through the KURI, only three documents extant today record their views of Pan-Asianism—one by a Chinese scholar, Li Songwu, and two by the Korean nationalist Choe Nam-Seon.[127]

Li Songwu joined the Kendai faculty in 1938 as Research Associate and became Associate Professor in the following year. After graduating from Beijing University with a degree in History in 1933, Li worked for Beijing University's Law School as a researcher focusing on the economic history of China. He moved to Kendai by invitation but was not proficient in Japanese. All three articles he wrote for KURI's monthly newsletters were written and published in Chinese. Nonetheless, language apparently did not overly hinder collegiate relations. He wrote that he made a research trip to Japan with a few other Kendai faculty members who helped him communicate in Japanese. He also met many Japanese scholars in Kyoto and Tokyo who were fluent in Chinese.[128] There was a long tradition of East Asian peoples communicating with each other through written words in the absence of a commonly spoken language.[129] It is notable that Li and other Chinese-speaking faculty members had the option of publishing their writing in Chinese. It may show the cultural tolerance of KURI. On another level, however, the institute valued the use of Chinese as a means of fulfilling one of its missions: producing materials for mass education in Manchukuo. In fact, KURI was undertaking a project of translating some of its research results into Chinese and publishing them for the "young generation of *mankei*, especially new government clerks."[130] The planned publication date was

June 1943; however, the outcome is not certain. As seen below, Li's pro-Japanese perspective served perfectly for such purpose.

The largest piece of Li's contribution to KURI's monthly newsletters was full of praise for the Japanese Empire. Titled "Cultural and Intellectual History of Manchuria," and published in December 1943, well into Japan's war with the Allies, it reads like a polemic in giving enthusiastic support for Japan. After describing the changes in culture in Manchuria from nomadic and agricultural to the current state of civilization, Li stated that currently Manchuria's culture was flourishing under the Manchukuo government. "Not only agriculture but also industry and business were simultaneously developing; and, both urban cities and rural villages were prospering."[131] He then praised "our beloved Japanese people … who gave us all of these things."[132] In return, he continued, "we must give our all to further develop Manchukuo's culture as a whole and bring together the different cultures of various peoples and all of our efforts so we could definitely win the sacred war."[133]

Li also defended Japan's war effort and identified the United States and Great Britain as the enemies of Asia. "We must think about it. We are living comfortably behind the battle lines. Who gave this life to us? Was it the heaven? Was it something we had achieved on our own? We owe all of this happy life to our beloved imperial army (of Japan)."[134] After this emotional statement, Li argued that the situation would have been disastrous at the hands of the United States and Great Britain and again insisted that "the imperial army was fighting the sacred war, killing enemies, and trying to drive out Americans and British from East Asia for the sake of our future, development, liberation, and survival."[135] Here, Li omitted any mention of China as the enemy of the imperial army, although China had been a crucial member of the Allies, and the bulk of Japan's army was deployed in China. Furthermore, Li ignored the fact that China had been at full-blown war with Japan since 1937.

Like Kendai's Japanese faculty members, Li viewed Japan as the central force in the ongoing Pan-Asianist project of realizing "ethnic harmony" and the Greater East Asia Co-Prosperity Sphere. However, Li's understanding of the relationship between Manchukuo and Japan slightly differed from that of his Japanese colleagues. The central message in his article was that the peoples of Manchukuo must work hard to create a new culture. "We, the peoples of Manchukuo, relied upon our beloved nation Japan for its support, guidance, and assistance to found a new country. Now, isn't it we who must change, prepare for anything, exert efforts, cultivate our minds, train ourselves, and overall, spiritually reform?"[136] This passage implies that Japan had fulfilled its role by founding the Manchukuo state and that the peoples of the new independent country now had to assume responsibility for its future. While positing a mentoring relationship between Japan and Manchukuo, Li stressed the necessity of the peoples of Manchukuo taking the initiative.

What should Manchukuo's peoples do to create the new culture of "ethnic harmony"? It is in his attempt to answer this question that one can detect slight but important divergence from the Japan-centered Pan-Asianism expounded by his Japanese colleagues. That is, Li clearly expected that Chinese culture and people would play a decisive role in the nation-building of Manchukuo. Throughout his article, Li drew heavily from Confucius and Mencius. By copiously citing these ancient Chinese philosophers, Li appears to believe that the diverse population of Manchukuo could all learn lessons from China's past. As seen previously, it is notable that when Li used the words "we" and "us," he appears to include the non-Japanese population of Manchukuo. In the passages cited he established a clear-cut distinction between "we," the peoples of Manchukuo, and the Japanese. The majority of Manchukuo's population was Han Chinese or other Chinese-speaking minorities. If we see Li's article as targeting the Chinese-speaking population, the use of Confucius and Mencius appears unexceptional. However, publishing in KURI's newsletter, Li must have been aware of another audience: his fellow Kendai researchers, including Japanese colleagues who could read Chinese. Thus, if we see this article as Li's message to his colleagues at Kendai, the extensive use of ancient Chinese philosophers could be interpreted as his subtle way of claiming the centrality of Chinese culture in the ongoing Pan-Asianist endeavor.

One does not find the pro-Japanese outlook of Li's work in Choe Nam-Seon's research. As we have seen, Choe was one of the three academics whom Kendai invited to join the faculty on Ishiwara's recommendation. It appears that the other two—Bao Mingqian and Su Yixin from China—were not involved in Kendai's teaching and research in any meaningful way by the time KURI's monthly newsletters began to publish issues in 1940. Their names do not appear on the lists of instructors of courses offered on campus; nor do we find publications or any other evidence of their research activities as Kendai scholars.[137] By contrast, Choe actively engaged in his historical research while at Kendai between 1938 and 1943. Through KURI, he published two articles on the ancient religious cultures of Manchuria and northeast Asia. Moreover, he apparently was an active participant in the institute. KURI's monthly newsletters show that Choe belonged to at least three research groups between April 1941 and August 1942—groups that focused on the issue of *minzoku* ("ethnic nationality"), Eastern languages, and Manchurian-Mongolian culture. He was a leader of the last group, which consisted of six other scholars, all Japanese.[138]

His active participation in academic research in collaboration with Japanese scholars had actually started before his arrival at Kendai. In Korea, after being imprisoned for his involvement with the March First Independence Movement, Choe began to work with the Government-General of Korea on academic projects. For this reason, Choe has often been discredited as a collaborationist of Japan who abandoned his earlier Korean nationalist aspiration.[139] However, as historian Chizuko T. Allen shows, and as demonstrated in his publications through the KURI, Choe's wartime scholarly writings cannot be simply branded as collaborationist service to Japanese imperialism.

The thrust of Choe's research offers an alternative perspective on Asia. Put more directly, Choe challenged the Japan-centered view of Asia endorsed by the Kendai faculty. He accepted the premise that Asians share many things in common but provided a different idea of what those commonalities were. As we have seen, for some of Kendai's Japanese scholars, it was the historic experience of the Western encroachment that Asians shared and this served as a ground for Pan-Asian unity. By highlighting the common enemy, they sought to validate Japan's dominant position in Asia, as they believed that Japan with its modernized state and military was the only capable leader. By contrast, Choe looked back to religious customs of earlier centuries to find commonalities among the societies of northeast Asia. In his 1939 piece, he examined various names of a mountain in Manchuria, contemporaneously called *chōhakusan*, or Long White Mountain. He found that this mountain had been named differently by peoples residing in the surrounding areas but was equally seen as a sacred place. Among those peoples Choe introduced were the Jurchens of the Jin Dynasty (1115–1234), the Manchus of the Qing Dynasty (1644–1912), the Han Chinese of the preceding dynasties, Koreans, and Mongolians.[140] Despite the differences in language, culture, and time, these societies all held great reverence for the sun, regarding it synonymous with the heaven, gods, and the sovereign, and saw the mountain as the sacred dwelling place of the sun. In tribute to one of the ancient names of Long White Mountain, Choe proposed designating northeast Asian culture "Purham" culture.[141] In his view, this cultural zone covered northeast Asia centered on Manchuria. However, it is interesting to note that he did not mention the Japanese in his explanation of the shared religious worship of Long White Mountain within what he termed the "Purham" cultural zone.[142] Indeed, the Japanese, separated by the sea, had had no contact with this mountain until the beginning of the twentieth century. Choe thus was indirectly emphasizing the non-Japanese past of the culture that existed in this region.

Choe's thesis also challenges the very foundation of *kōdō* ("imperial way")—the idea that Japan was a unique nation with its divine emperor who was the direct descendant of the sun goddess. Choe's article shows that many societies had linked their sovereign and the sun god. His list of examples included not just the societies of the "Purham" cultural zone but also from ancient India and Rome.[143] After stating that such tendency was "universal at a global level," he stressed that reverence for the sun had been particularly strong and prevalent in northeast Asia.[144] Choe then added that "the idea that Japan's imperial family had descended from the sun goddess ... falls into the shared tradition of this cultural zone."[145] By emphasizing the universality of this religious tradition, Choe was refuting the uniqueness of the Japanese imperial leadership with which the Japanese state legitimated its rule over Asia.

Choe's challenge to the Japan-centered perspective appeared again in his 1941 publication, in which he went so far as to highlight the Korean past of Manchuria. He began by noting how the wind had been deified in various cultures, including China, India, and Japan. After thus placing Japan's religious tradition in a broader context, he expounded on his main topic: *sui no kami*, the highest god in Goguryeo (37 BC–668), an ancient kingdom that ruled the northern part of the Korean peninsula and Manchuria. While the national identity of Goguryeo continued to spur debates, Choe assumed it was a Korean kingdom.[146] He had found mention of the god *sui no kami* in the *Book of Wei* of the *Records of the Three Kingdoms*, a Chinese historical text that was compiled in the third century. However, according to Choe, this text did not make clear what exactly *sui no kami* was. Choe's etymological investigation of the god's name led him to conclude that *sui no kami* referred to the god of the east wind that signified the arrival of spring to Manchuria.[147] Moreover, he found that Manchuria's god of wind had originated from an ancient Korean kingdom. By extension, Choe, as a Korean scholar, appears to have staked a claim to Manchuria's past.

In 1941, Choe was assigned to teach a course on the culture of Manchuria and Mongolia to the first entering class.[148] Although no records of his course survive, there are references, which are not entirely consistent, in two former Korean students' memoirs. Jin Won-Jung did not have an opportunity to attend Choe's lecture as he was a member of the third entering class. But, based on what he heard from fellow Korean students, Jin writes that Choe expounded his theory of "Purham" culture. Jin implies that Choe taught the course for one year.[149] A member of the second entering class, Hong Chun-Sik, gives a different account of the length of Choe's course. According to Hong, Choe delivered a lecture only once, as the Kendai administration removed him from the instructor's position after the first day of class. Hong explains that it was because Choe directly opposed the view of Manchurian history advocated by a Japanese Kendai faculty member, Inaba Iwakichi. Hong writes: "[w]hile Professor Inaba taught us that Goguryeo was a kingdom of ethnic Manchus and not of Koreans, [Professor Choe] told a story that … Koreans originated in Manchuria, gradually migrated southward, and found Japan."[150] Unfortunately, there is no official record that explains what actually happened to Choe's course. What we do know from these accounts is that Choe did not hesitate to share his alternative perspective on the history of Manchuria and Asia with his students and that the administration intervened at some point.

Choe's career at Kendai reveals that while not absolute, Kendai's academic culture was perhaps uniquely open compared to that of the wartime Japanese homeland. As seen in his articles, Choe did not explicitly defy the Japanese Empire. Nevertheless, written in proficient and sophisticated Japanese, his argument comes across clearly. The implication of his thesis—that he was challenging the Japan-centered view of Asia—must have been clear to any Japanese scholars who read these pieces. The fact that Choe could publish these works and remain on the faculty shows the degree of academic freedom allowed at Kendai. Furthermore, even after publishing these articles, he was selected by the administration to teach a course in 1941. This appointment seems to indicate that the Kendai regime, at least at the beginning of 1941, was willing to expose its students to the alternative view of Asia that Choe was putting forth. Even after the administration's subsequent intervention in his course, Choe remained on the Kendai faculty. As discussed in Chapter 4, he continued to hold informal "lectures" at his residence for Kendai's Korean students. In addition, he continued to lead one of the research groups at the KURI until February 1943 when he resigned his position for an unknown reason.

Conclusion

Although the four professors shared Ishiwara's obsession with creating a unique university, they developed a curriculum and structure that were "unique" in a different sense. Unlike Ishiwara's initial proposal to create a new philosophy and culture for Asia, Kendai was designed to establish a new scholarship based on Japanese values such as *kōkoku shikan* and Shintoism, which, in the four professors' perspectives, had not been fully realized in Japanese academia. For the four professors, who were disappointed that the imperial universities in

Japan had been influenced by Western bodies of thought such as materialism and Marxism, Kendai offered a rare opportunity to actualize a new education distinct from that of Japan. The ethnic imbalance of the faculty and the imposition of Japanese customs and rituals in the *juku* training demonstrate that the four professors understood "ethnic harmony" as a unity of different ethnic groups under Japanese leadership. The abstractness of the term "ethnic harmony" enabled the four professors to use the rhetoric of utopian idealism for validating their enterprise to the non-Japanese participants, while pursuing their ethnocentric vision of Pan-Asianism. In other words, while they appealed to non-Japanese scholars and students with the call for actualizing "ethnic harmony" through education, their conceptions of "ethnic harmony" were based on an ethnocentric version of Pan-Asianism that envisioned harmony of Asia under Japanese leadership. Reflected in the university's curriculum and structure, the four professors' slanted understandings of Kendai's unique mission had a strong influence on the institution.

However, the Kendai faculty, who were charged with the task of creating a new theory of Pan-Asianism, seemed to have had their own agenda. The resulting discourse on Pan-Asianism and Manchukuo in the Kendai faculty allowed differences rather than establishing a single theory even amidst Japan's war. Variation of views among Japanese faculty members was less impressive. One essential agreement was the central role that Japan must play in the ongoing Pan-Asianist endeavor; but, their writings also exhibited slight differences. Most Japanese scholars imagined Asian unity to be a hierarchical order led by the Japanese and insisted that Asian peoples must cooperate under Japanese leadership. Others clung to the egalitarian idealism and envisioned a communal order in Asia in which Asian peoples' participation in the creation of the Greater East Asia Co-Prosperity Sphere would be voluntary. Still, Japanese members' views more or less conformed to the general trend of Japan's official discourse of Pan-Asianism in the early 1940s.

Non-Japanese scholars' writings added a greater variety to the Kendai faculty's discussion of Pan-Asianism. Li's emphasis on the Chinese initiative was obviously compatible with the official pronouncement of Japan-led Asian unity. At the same time, by highlighting what the Chinese people with their rich culture could contribute, Li appeared to lay claim for the Chinese population to play an expanded role in Manchukuo. Unlike Li's subtle departure from Japan-centered conceptions, Choe's writings defied the official line of thinking more explicitly. He contextualized and refuted the Japanese claim to unique, divine imperial rule—not once but twice in KURI publications. He also freely put forth his argument that Manchuria had been home to Korean people in the ancient past. It is clear that Choe was not wielding a pen in service of the empire. Under the limitation of the colonial setting, he—and to a certain degree, one can argue Li, too—managed to exercise intellectual freedom to express ideas that diverged from the ethnocentric Pan-Asianism prevalent in Japan's official pronouncements.

The Kendai faculty's effort of creating a new theory of Pan-Asianism certainly had limitations. The ethnic imbalance of the faculty body betrayed the school's pronounced commitment to Pan-Asian unity on the basis of equality. In addition, many of the Japanese faculty members were prone to the wartime need of supporting the chauvinistic rhetoric of Japan's official Pan-Asianism. Nonetheless, it is notable that the school administration allowed its faculty to express different perspectives—although with obvious limits, as seen in the removal of Choe from the classroom. As shown in the chapter, the variation among the Kendai faculty members' conceptions of Pan-Asianism and Manchukuo suggests that Kendai as an institution allowed interchanges of ideas among Asian intellectuals. In that sense, Kendai faculty members were not merely replicating the official version of Pan-Asianism as an imperial ideology. At least some of them were exploring different meanings for the ideal of Pan-Asian unity, and the faculty body endorsed those differences by including them in its Research Institute's newsletters.

3

Exploring the meaning of Pan-Asia: Japanese students' experiences at Kenkoku University

While it was easier for Kendai's faculty members to theorize about the Pan-Asianist ideal of "ethnic harmony" in academic writings, it was an emotionally difficult and life-changing experience for young Japanese students to explore the meaning of Pan-Asianism through day-to-day interactions with their non-Japanese classmates. Observing cultural differences and non-Japanese students' ethnic nationalist and even anti-Japanese sentiments, Kendai's Japanese students quickly realized how difficult it was to live out the ideal of "ethnic harmony" in real life. Their responses call into question the stereotypical image of wartime Japanese youths as obedient and hyper patriotic. Some Kendai students did contest the disconnect between the stated ideals of Kendai as an institution and proclamations of Manchukuo's status as a sovereign nation state on the one hand and, on the other, the reality that they encountered on the ground. They were able to do so in part because of the openness of Kendai's educational environment and, more importantly, the unique opportunity of seeing firsthand Kendai's non-Japanese students' reactions to Japan's policy in Manchukuo and elsewhere in East Asia. Their experiences of going to Manchukuo, attending an educational institution whose purpose was to train government functionaries of the new state, and sharing their living space with non-Japanese students led the Japanese students to develop divergent understandings of Pan-Asianism. In Japanese students' experiences, we find examples of extreme responses: from a strengthened sense of their superiority as Japanese to utter rejection of Japan's official version of Pan-Asianism that positioned Japan securely at the top of the hierarchy of Asian peoples.

Whether one maintained an ethnocentric approach to Pan-Asianism or developed a growing sympathy toward non-Japanese peoples' sufferings, Kendai's Japanese students exhibited an overwhelming sense of mission that distinguished their experiences from that of other groups on campus. Seeing themselves as pioneers undertaking the construction of Manchukuo and a new order in East Asia, the Japanese students often expressed their determination to devote the rest of their lives to Manchukuo, becoming *manshūkokujin*, or "the citizen of Manchukuo." There is no surprise that Kendai's Pan-Asianist education, which had started as a Japanese enterprise, found the most enthusiastic responses from Japanese students. What the Kendai administration perhaps did not anticipate was that these young pioneers developed divergent understandings as to what their mission entailed.

The main sources of this chapter are the diaries kept by some of the Japanese students enrolled at Kendai. I will introduce those specific diaries later; here, I will briefly discuss the Japanese practice of diary keeping as part of the school curriculum. Diary keeping in Japanese society is not necessarily a private practice, unlike the English word "diary," which more often than not connotes a private document. In effect, diary keeping continues to be an integral part of the Japanese school curriculum, especially in elementary schools. Often, students are required to keep a diary and occasionally submit it to the teacher, who returns it with comments. Even in secondary education, each class often has a class diary, in which students take turns keeping a day-by-day record of the group's activities along with some reflections, which is submitted to the homeroom teacher. Historian Samuel Hideo Yamashita explains that such a "public" diary had a particularly important function in wartime Japanese elementary education. He states that compulsory diary keeping "created a record of the children's thoughts, feelings, and activities for their supervisors" and also gave those children "a way to police themselves as they were being transformed into willing subjects."[1] At Kendai, too, occasionally students were required to submit their diaries to the *jukutō*, or *juku* headmasters; hence, their diaries need to be read as documents that were produced by young adults well aware of the possible consequences of expressing "wrong" ideas in their diaries. Nonetheless, available entries from Kendai students' "public" diaries express a surprising degree of variation in their responses to Manchukuo and Kendai, and various perceptions of Pan-Asianism.[2]

Choosing an alternative path and going to the frontier of the Japanese Empire

As indicated in Chapter 2, for Japanese students to qualify for admission to Kendai, they had to successfully complete middle schools (*chūtō gakkō*).[3] This admission requirement narrowed the applicant pool to top-ranking students.

In prewar Japanese society, not only Kendai but higher education in general was reserved for a competitively selected minority. A series of school edicts issued by the Meiji and Taisho governments established a two-tier school system—one aiming to foster an elite and the other to produce skilled workers. Henry DeWitt Smith provides useful statistical data that shows how steep the educational ladder from elementary to higher education was. Of all male graduates of elementary schools (age six to twelve) in 1920, 34 percent went onto either higher elementary schools or lower vocational schools, which represented the lower-tier of the education system. On the higher-tier, middle schools accepted only 10 percent of elementary school graduates who passed competitive exams. After the five-year secondary education at middle schools (age twelve to seventeen), 40 percent of its graduates attended three-year terminal colleges specialized in professional training such as medicine and engineering. Ten percent of middle school graduates were admitted to private universities (age seventeen to twenty-three), which first offered a three-year college preparatory course and then a three-year college-level course. Often the top 10 percent of middle school graduates attended three-year higher schools (age seventeen to twenty), which was the public equivalent of the college preparatory course offered at private colleges. After graduation, all higher school graduates were admitted to Imperial Universities, the most prestigious of all schools in Japan.[4] The Japanese students whom we encounter in this book chose an alternative path that was equally competitive: the highest seat of learning of Manchukuo.

Although a small number of Japanese students were born and raised in Manchuria by Japanese immigrant parents, the majority of the Japanese students had lived their entire lives in Japan before matriculating at Kendai. For many of these Japanese youths, attending Kendai involved adventure—leaving their hometowns for the first time and going to a foreign country that had a special significance to the Japanese Empire they had known since birth. Since 1905, when Japan acquired the rights over the South Manchurian Railway, the adjacent railway zones, and the Kwantung Leased Territory from Russia, the Japanese state had encouraged its farming population to emigrate to Manchuria. By 1931 the Japanese population in Manchuria was 233,320.[5] Many more groups—government and military clerks, entrepreneurs and intellectuals—followed, pursuing the "Manchurian dream" of new opportunities.[6] Furthermore, in the context of the war fever that had gripped Japan since the Manchurian Incident of 1931, Manchuria became a popular site for Japan's burgeoning Asian tourism industry.[7] As will be seen in this chapter, the Japanese students who moved from

Japan often exhibited a typical tourist-like reaction to Manchuria. Moreover, some were shocked to discover the extent of the gap between the stated ideal of "ethnic harmony" and the reality they encountered.

The diary of Nishimura Jūrō (second entering class) provides evidence of the competitiveness of the application process and the allure Kendai held for many of Japan's adolescents. When he expressed his desire to apply to Kendai in 1938, his parents initially objected. Nishimura was the eldest son in a family with six sons. It was the common expectation in prewar Japan that the eldest son would stay at home to become the next household head, which makes Nishimura's parents' objection to his going to Manchukuo unsurprising. However, as he later wrote, Nishimura persuaded his parents to let him take the exam by telling them that he could not possibly pass the extremely competitive entrance exam that had an acceptance rate of 1 percent.[8] To his and his parents' surprise, Nishimura did pass the exam, fulfilling his dream. The news of his acceptance made his parents so proud that they reversed their earlier opposition and allowed him to attend Kendai. It appears that for both Nishimura and his parents, gaining admission to Kendai was an honorable alternative to attending the prestigious *kōtō gakkō* (higher schools) that guaranteed a place in Japan's Imperial Universities or attending *kōtō senmon gakkō* (higher technical colleges) in Japan.[9]

Morisaki Minato (fourth entering class) chose to attend Kendai for somewhat different reasons, but like Nishimura he viewed Kendai as an attractive career path. For Morisaki, an ambitious young man raised for much of his childhood in an economically hard-pressed family, enrolling in Kendai offered obvious financial incentives. He was not alone; Japanese students most frequently cite the university's generous financial scholarships as a key deciding factor. To Morisaki, however, Kendai held out other attractions as well. His diary from his last year in middle school shows his deep dissatisfaction with the educational system in Japan. In his diary entry of July 30, 1941, Morisaki vented his frustration: "Can (a middle school) fulfill its mission merely by cramming a lot of information into students' heads?"[10] Rather than keeping them busy preparing for the higher schools' entrance exams, Morisaki continued, "the most effort should go to 'disciplining the will' and nurturing 'self-control.'"[11] Kendai, which placed equal emphasis on learning and physical and spiritual cultivation, likely caught Morisaki's attention and appealed to him as an alternative to Japan's narrowly academic education system he so disliked.

Moreover, the mere idea of traveling to Manchukuo appears to have excited Morisaki, a young idealist. As Mariko Asano Tamanoi lucidly shows, Morisaki held a firm belief in Japan's leading role in constructing Asia for Asians.[12] On

November 3, 1941, while waiting to hear whether he had been accepted at Kendai, Morisaki wrote that the cooperation between Japan and Manchukuo alone would not be enough for the grand task of "constructing eternal peace in the East," which was the proclaimed justification for Japan's war in China after 1937.[13] For that purpose, he claimed, "on the basis of Japan–Manchukuo unity ... peaceful cooperation with *shina* (a condescending term commonly used in prewar Japan to refer to China) must be achieved."[14] Hence, Morisaki regarded going to Manchukuo as only the first step in realizing his grand vision of Pan-Asianism. For him, Kendai would offer an opportunity to meet Chinese youths in person, nurture friendships, and thus put his ideal into practice. Soon afterwards, he received an acceptance letter from Kendai.

All students arriving from Japan were required to participate in a pre-matriculation orientation program. The program, which initially lasted a month, took place in several cities in Japan, Korea, and Manchukuo, as the group travelled from Tokyo to Shinkyō, Manchukuo's capital city and home to the Kendai campus.[15] The itinerary included visits to several Shinto shrines, museums, and tourist spots, as well as spiritual training through *misogi*, Shinto's ascetic practice that aims at the purification of the body by bathing in cold streams or standing under a waterfall. Also included were meetings with dignitaries of the War Ministry and the Embassy of Manchukuo, a send-off party with Japanese political VIPs, and lectures by Kendai's professors. Looking at this itinerary, one cannot help but notice the high expectations placed upon Kendai by the Manchukuo and Japanese governments. The university administration's choice to include not one but multiple activities related to Shinto reminds us of the Japan-centered approach that the school planning committee maintained. After Japan entered the war with the Allies in December 1941, Kendai's orientation program was modified to address the exigencies of total war by including more practical training. For instance, the program in 1942 that Morisaki participated in began with one week of military training in Toyohashi City, Aichi Prefecture, before embarking for Manchuria. Thus, the first instruction that Morisaki received as a prospective student at Kendai was how to handle a rifle. Even the orientation lectures were geared towards Japan's war effort. For instance, Morisaki noted in his diary that he attended a lecture "Training behind the Current Military Achievements of the Imperial Troops" by Captain Matsumoto Kazuo from the Army News Service.[16] Morisaki apparently did not notice the contradiction between Kendai's stated position as the highest educational institution of Manchukuo and the fact that its pre-matriculation orientation itinerary was shaped by Japan's war effort.

The Japanese students' diaries reveal diverse outlooks and expectations as prospective Kendai students. Nishimura's experience resonates with that of typical Japanese visitors to the Asian continent, where Manchukuo was a popular tourist destination.[17] When Nishimura completed his pre-matriculation orientation program and departed Japan from Kōbe on April 4, 1939, around thirty people, including his entire family, relatives, and friends, saw him off. It was apparently a grand, joyous occasion for his family and friends; the group accompanied Nishimura on the train, and he passed the time chatting with them while holding a young cousin on his lap.[18] In his diary, Nishimura recorded what he observed during his trip, much as any tourist would do. He commented on the scenery in Busan, Korea, which reminded him of "the exotic atmosphere of Kōbe (his hometown)."[19] He made a note of "strange" things such as the low platforms in train stations, double windows on trains, mountains without trees, and snow in April.[20] His tourist-like enthusiasm momentarily abated when Nishimura encountered armed guards on the Korea–Manchukuo border, the sight of which "gave [him] a jolt."[21] When he arrived at Shinkyō, Nishimura felt at ease with the broad streets and modern buildings that reminded him of his hometown. During the few days between his arrival on campus and the start of the semester, he attended several orientation events at school and went to the downtown to check things out. One experience, however, the first agricultural training on campus, prompted him to affirm his sense of mission as a new Kendai student. "Under the direction of Professor Fujita," he wrote on April 10, 1938, "we worked the earth of Manchuria with shovels and tilled the soil. My mind was stirred by the idea that I am partaking in the nation-building of Manchuria."[22]

Meanwhile, Fujimori Kōichi, who entered Kendai in 1939, the same year as Nishimura, experienced shock when he arrived in Manchukuo. Unlike Nishimura, who took comfort in seeing Japanese influence in a foreign land, Fujimori was disappointed to observe that Manchukuo cities were "completely modeled after the Japanese style."[23] While this reaction appears not atypical of imperial travelers of Japanese and Western empires, who often exhibited fascination with things exotic, the following entry by Fujimori separates him from those travelers. Fujimori was struck by the separation of residential areas for Japanese and non-Japanese and the sharp contrast between the two. He wrote:

> The nice-looking areas are exclusively for Japanese residents. It looks like the Japanese have the nice places all to themselves … We can never realize genuinely harmonious relationships if we go on like this. What should I do?—I have

no idea. This is something that I must ponder from now on. I'm sure that the way Japanese are behaving now isn't at all a happy experience for *manjin* ("Manchurians"). I must do something.[24]

Here Fujimori is commenting on the contrast between the modernized city centers where the Japanese lived on one hand, and on the other, the old, exotic, noisy and chaotic Chinatown. This contrast was, in effect, celebrated and used as "a 'before and after' advertisement for Manchurian development" by the Japanese travel industry, whose packaged tours continued to attract Japanese customers.[25] Nevertheless, the same image of Manchukuo's capital city raised concerns to Fujimori.

The passage indicates that Fujimori, by the time he arrived at Shinkyō, was very much aware of Manchukuo's stated ideal of creating harmonious relationships among peoples of different backgrounds and of Kendai's mission to actualize that goal. However, his use of the term *manjin* ("Manchurians") sets up a simple dichotomy between the Japanese and any other peoples who were seen as local residents of Manchuria, including Han Chinese, ethnic Manchus, Mongolians, and other ethnic minorities like Hui. By using *manjin* in his discussion of the goal of "ethnic harmony," Fujimori appears to have affirmed—quite inadvertently— the colonial mindset shared by the Japanese military and civilian officials in Manchukuo. The quoted passage nonetheless shows that Fujimori fully and genuinely embraced this idealism. His initial dismay at the segregated society he observed in Manchukuo only strengthened his determination to work hard at Kendai to do his part in making the utopian vision of Manchukuo a reality. In other words, Fujimori became even more committed to the stated purposes of Kendai's proclaimed educational mission.

When Morisaki made his first trip to Manchuria in 1942, three years after Nishimura and Fujimori, Japan was already at war with the Allied Powers in the Pacific and Southeast Asia. During the pre-matriculation orientation program in Tokyo, he received a letter from his father. The letter informed him that his eldest brother, who was stationed in Guangdong, China, for military service, had participated in the invasion of Singapore on February 8. His father ended the short letter with the following message, which Morisaki quoted in his diary: "Even if you leave Japan, you must devote your life to the country, lead Manchukuo, and become renowned for excelling in spiritual development and practical accomplishments. Rouse yourself to make great exertions."[26] In his diary, Morisaki vowed to meet this expectation. This episode shows that Morisaki and his father both recognized that "lead[ing] Manchukuo" would mean "devot[ing] [one's] life to the country," Japan, while viewing Japan and

Manchukuo as distinct entities. Confident in his worldview, Morisaki crossed the Japan Sea with a high sense of mission, as Japanese who would help guide the newly founded state, Manchukuo.

For this young idealist whose passion was shaped by Japan's wartime empire, Kendai's orientation further stimulated his enthusiasm. Unlike Nishimura, who recorded tourist-like excitement, or Fujimori, who found problems in Japan's policy in Manchukuo, Morisaki appears to have been moved by visits to significant battlefield sites commemorating Japan's past battles. In Lushun (Port Arthur) he paid homage at Hakugyosan Shrine, where the ashes of Japanese war dead from the Russo–Japanese War (1904–5) were enshrined. Morisaki vowed that he, as a Japanese male, "will never allow [their] sacrifices to go to waste."[27] He also excitedly noted that he had the opportunity of listening to a Japanese local staff officer's talk on the Battle of Lushun and of participating in military field training at this historically significant site. Morisaki's enthusiasm only increased when he arrived at Kendai and was welcomed by current students and faculty members. He wrote:

> The big brothers of the upper classes welcomed us with smiles and applause. They all looked strong and healthy, with glowing eyes. Their clothes were dirty with sweat and dirt but their faces were suffused with vigor, youthfulness, and energy—seeing them made me happy indeed. Oh, Kendai, I knew you wouldn't betray my expectation. I am grateful. These people surely are worth regarding as my big brothers, seniors, and comrades.[28]

Thus, Morisaki appears to have started his campus life with unbridled enthusiasm and a firm commitment to Japan's imperial project.

Interestingly, the first-day experience of the Kendai campus disappointed another Japanese student, Kaede Motoo (third entering class). On April 10, 1940, Kaede and a group of students coming from Japan arrived at Shinkyō Station. Someone in the group said "So, this is the 'Mongolian wind,'" referring to the yellow sand that blows in from the continent, which stirred Kaede's "boyish imagination."[29] Here, he must have been referring to the image of Manchuria-Mongolia that was created and advertised by the Japanese travel industry. As historian Louise Young shows, the travel industry facilitated a massive production of artworks and travel literature to promote the image of Manchuria as a mixture of the modern and the old by mobilizing Japanese novelists, journalists, and photographers of the time.[30] The "Mongolian wind" and the "boyish imagination" in Kaede's diary entry apparently refer to the exotic image of Manchuria that he had so longed to experience in person.[31] As soon as he arrived on the Kendai campus, however, Kaede was shocked by the gap between the dream-like image of the school he had nurtured and the reality he faced. As the group walked through the broad, empty campus, about two hundred current students welcomed them with applause. To Kaede's eyes, these Kendai students appeared as "a motley crowd" and left a bizarre impression.[32] "Some wore ragged clothes, others were in their work uniforms; they wore rain boots, leather shoes, or Chinese-style shoes made from cloth."[33] Realizing that this was the reality of Kendai students that he had so longed for, Kaede was disenchanted. In Kaede's diary entries one sees no evidence of the ideological fervor that is so evident in Morisaki's diary and was generally typical of newly matriculating students from Japan. Kaede's view of Manchuria appears to have been no different from that of any tourist. What both Kaede's and Morisaki's accounts reveal, however, is something akin to the experience of any study-abroad student—the excitement and shock at encountering a foreign culture.

The Horse Barn Incident, or *Umagoya Jiken*

The "Horse Barn Incident" reveals the depth of some of Kendai students' idealism, as well as their shock at Manchukuo society's actual conditions and glaring disparities. A group of seven Japanese students of the first entering class registered their disapproval of what they perceived as a contradicting practice of Manchukuo's founding principles at Kendai in a dramatic protest action. On September 2, 1938, only four months after the matriculation of the first class, the seven Japanese students boycotted the *juku* life and moved into the university-owned horse barn on campus as a protest. In the following one and a half months, they lived in the small barn while skipping classes except agricultural training. Two factors inspired these students to carry out this protest.

First, they were influenced by their *jukutō*, Fujita Matsuji, Assistant Professor of Agriculture and Agricultural Training. Fujita exhorted his students that only through the sweat and toil at agricultural labor could they hope to become genuine leaders of Manchukuo and contribute to the realization of "ethnic harmony."[34] His message appealed to these Japanese students who were desperate to overcome the gap between their idealistic visions of ethnic equality and what they had heard from their non-Japanese classmates about brutal Japanese aggression in Manchukuo and East Asia.

Moreover, a school field trip to northern Manchuria from August 12 to 20, 1938 had exposed the students to the poverty of local peasants. The shock at observing their poor living conditions ignited the idealism of these seven students, who vowed not to take advantage of the much better living conditions provided at Kendai. Sakuta Yoshio, one of the protesters, recalled that he was concerned that Kendai's overly comfortable environment would only nourish empty idealism and elitism in students. He elaborated on his reasons for participating in the dorm boycott as follows: "In order to become a truly capable leader of Manchukuo and make Manchukuo my final home, I decided to leave the easy life, put myself in the same life condition as that of the peasants in Manchuria, and experience their suffering for myself."[35] One of the initiators of the protest, Ochi Michiyo, later gave the following explanation:

> [The Japanese and non-Japanese students] had formed a kind of cozy relationships. However, I knew we were nowhere near the true "ethnic harmony." Such superficial interactions could never improve the situation. In desperation, I decided to move out of [my *juku*].[36]

Reflected in these protesters' accounts is their egalitarian conception of Pan-Asianism. Observing the poverty that typified the lives of most of the local farming population shocked the protesters to realize that rule by the "kingly way," the Japanese authorities' promise to guide the people by virtue, was not carried forward in reality. Moreover, they were dispirited by the "superficial interactions" among Kendai students. Their solution was to recreate in their own daily lives what they perceived as the lives of peasants in Manchuria. What we also find in their accounts is a strongly felt determination to become citizens of Manchukuo. In Sakuta's quote, he clearly expresses his intention to "make Manchukuo [his] final home." The literal translation of this Japanese metaphorical expression is "to bury one's bones in the land of Manchukuo," meaning that one would remain in Manchukuo until the last moment. Or, put more dramatically, it could mean "to offer one's life for Manchukuo." This is a commonly used expression by Kendai's Japanese students, which reflected the prewar Japanese discourse of Manchuria as the imperial frontier and the Japanese emigrants there as pioneers. However, the problem that these enthusiastic pioneers encountered was that Manchukuo as a state never established a legal definition for its citizenship. In fact, the largest barrier for the government to establish a citizenship law was the Japanese settler community's resistance to the idea of moving citizenship from Japan to Manchukuo.[37] In that sense, Kendai's Japanese students distinguished themselves from the other Japanese residents in their dedication to Manchukuo.

We get a glimpse into other students' reactions to this dramatic event on campus in a transcript of a panel discussion among six Japanese and two Chinese members of the first entering class and Professor Miyagawa Yoshizō, held on September 9, 1942.[38] Kamemura Tetsuya, a Japanese student, shared his and his friends' frustration with the fact that the protest was carried out by an all-Japanese group. By doing so, Kamemura stated, the protesters appeared to have disregarded everyone's effort to live out the ideal of "ethnic harmony." Kamemura further noted that the incident prompted his *mankei juku*-mates to hold serious discussions.[39] The Chinese panelist Liu Xingtan, who was one of the students leading discussions among the Chinese students during the Horse Barn Incident, testified that some of them even felt like giving up on the goal of "ethnic harmony." That was because they felt offended by the fact that the Japanese protesters had not even considered talking to them before proceeding with their plan.[40] The former protester Iwabuchi admitted that they lacked consideration for *mankei* friends' feelings. According to Iwabuchi, his *mankei juku*-mates came over to talk with the protesters. The protesters were strongly moved when their friend Sui said that if they were to continue living in the horse barn those Chinese students would join them in the protest.[41] "Only then did we realize that we had done something wrong," said Iwabuchi.[42]

It appears that the seven students ended their protest without achieving any specific goals when they accepted Fujita's advice and returned to the *juku* one and a half months later. One of the protesters, Mimura Fumio, withdrew from the university on September 30.[43] While Ochi and Sakuta chose to stay on campus and continue searching for a way to realize genuinely harmonious relationships, Mimura left campus in despair. Looking back on his experience, Mimura explained his state of mind at the time:

> Having witnessed Japanese imperialism and oppression of the native *manjin* ["Manchurians"] in the name of "the kingly way"—the reality I had never imagined before matriculating at Kendai—I could not think any better course of action than quitting the University that was part of such exploitation. That was my way of resolving the contradiction.[44]

It appears that Mimura could not view Kendai, Manchukuo's highest seat of learning, as anything other than complicit with Japanese imperialism. To his eyes, studying at Kendai meant being part of this mechanism of oppression he so abhorred.

Mimura's departure appeared to be a memorable event not only for his fellow protesters but also for other students of the first entering class. In addition to his six fellow "Horse Barn" protesters, seventeen students and two *jukutō* demonstrated solidarity by accompanying Mimura either to the school entrance, Shinkyō downtown, or to Shinkyō Station. It is important to note that this group included seven Chinese and three Russian students.[45] This fact indicates that these non-Japanese students at least regarded Mimura as their good friend and, very likely, shared his frustrations.

As Mimura recalled nearly three decades later, the Horse Barn Incident was only "the tip of the iceberg."[46] Moreover, it was the beginning of many Japanese students' struggle to overcome the obstacles they encountered to realizing Kendai's lofty goal of "ethnic harmony." The contradiction between the reality of Manchukuo, student life at Kendai, and students' idealistic visions clearly tormented a number of Japanese students. Their diaries suggest that the more genuinely the students were committed to the institutions' founding principles, the more frustrated they grew over time.

School life at Kendai: Four Japanese students' experiences

As part of the *juku* training, Kendai students were required to keep a diary and occasionally submit it to their *jukutō*, who returned it with a few comments. While most of these diaries have been lost, fortunately a few diaries kept by Japanese students survived. I have selected the diaries of four students: Nagano Tadaomi (first entering class), Fujimori Kōichi (second entering class), Nishimura Jūrō (second entering class), and Morisaki Minato (fourth entering class). Selective entries from Nagano's and Fujimori's diaries were published in *Kenkoku daigaku nenpyō [The chronological timetable of Nation-Building University in Manchuria]* (1981), which was compiled by a Japanese alumnus, Yuji Manzō (second entering class), in an effort to preserve the university's records. Among several students' diary entries compiled in the timetable, I chose the entries from Nagano's and Fujimori's diaries because they appear most comprehensive and expressive of their feelings at the time. Their writings also reveal contrasting trajectories of the formation of their senses of identity. Nishimura published an edited version of his diary in 1991, under the title *Rakugaki: manshū kenkoku daigaku waga gakusei jidai no omoide [Scribbles: recollection of my student life at Nation-Building University in Manchuria]*. Morisaki's published diary, *Isho [The Will]* (1971), is an exception in that it was his personal diary and thus was not read by the *jukutō*. I focus more attention on Nishimura's and Morisaki's diaries because they are the only book-length diaries of Japanese students that cover the entire time period of their student life at Kendai and thus provide rich sources on the changes in these students' perspectives. In this section, I will describe these four students' experiences drawing on materials in their diaries. What one sees is a wide variety of responses and the emotional and intellectual conflicts they experienced as Kendai students. From these documents there emerges a complicated picture of how they perceived Manchukuo and conceptualized Pan-Asianism.

Nagano Tadaomi (first entering class)

In his first year at Kendai, Nagano Tadaomi experienced cultural shock. On May 3, 1938, one day after he matriculated at Kendai as a member of the first entering class, Nagano wrote in his diary: "Some *manjin* must have eaten garlic. I smelt it when I entered our dorm room."[47] To this entry, his *jukutō* Ehara Fushinosuke responded: "If the smell of garlic becomes an issue, we won't be able to fulfill our mission."[48] Thus, Nagano's student life started with this seemingly innocent expression of discomfort with his *mankei* classmates' habits, for which he was chided by his *jukutō*.

Nagano's diary records other examples of his intolerance of cultural differences. On August 10, 1938, his class was taken to the final day of the *sumō* wrestling tournament in Shinkyō. This Japanese traditional martial art had a special significance to the Japanese as a Shinto ritual. The fact that the Japanese authorities had brought this sport to Manchukuo indicates the importance with which it was regarded by the Japanese. Nagano was no exception. However, when he asked his non-Japanese classmates' impressions on that day's *sumō* match, he was disappointed to learn that "only a few found fun in the gallant contest."[49] He further commented in his diary that they "failed to grasp the spirit imbedded in *sumō*. It seems that anything that the Yamato (Japanese) people has created does not easily make inroads into foreign cultures … This is evident when considering the fact that the large crowd at today's *sumō* match did not include any local residents" except those from Kendai.[50] Nagano's response to the fact that the *mankei* were indifferent to what he considered as a highly significant tradition of Japan was to fault them for their lack of cultural understanding, rather than to question his own assumptions.

The following entry, dated October 26, 1938, reveals that Nagano was not alone in failing to show sensitivity towards the feelings of his non-Japanese classmates. On that day, Kendai students received the news that the Japanese Army had taken the City of Hankou in Hubei Province, China. It was one in a series of Japanese military victories in the early stages of the Second Sino–Japanese War (1937–45). Nagano's account shows that he and his Japanese friends made plans to hold a celebration party, but the *jukutō* prevented them. He wrote, "At first

I did not understand why the *jukutō* stopped us. After giving some thought to this incident, however, I now assume that he did so out of consideration for the feelings of the *kanjin* ('Han Chinese')."[51] Noting also that the *jukutō* advised them to hold the celebration after the war between Japan and China was over, he and his friends nevertheless silently celebrated the victory. This episode shows that these Japanese students were emotionally committed to Japan's war in China and that they were not hesitant—at least initially—to demonstrate this to their Chinese classmates, whom Nagano referred to as *kanjin* ("Han Chinese"). Nagano's comments on the *sumō* match and Japan's military victory hint at his strong sense of Japanese pride verging on chauvinism, which he felt at liberty to express at Kendai, the highest learning institution of the ostensibly independent state of Manchukuo. It is nevertheless instructive that at least some of the Japanese faculty members took the ideal of "ethnic harmony" seriously. Nagano was chided by his *jukutō* to be more sensitive to the feelings of his classmates. These experiences led him to ponder the meaning and means to achieve the goal of "ethnic harmony," as seen in the following entry.

On April 7, 1939, the day the students of the second entering class arrived on the Kendai campus, Nagano expounded on his Japan-centered vision of Pan-Asianist education at Kendai:

> At the present moment, Japan is the one that leads East Asia … Moreover, many of Kendai's customs and systems are something that we have already experienced or observed in our home country. Thus, I think that Kendai students must improve themselves with the Japanese help, cooperation, and leadership … What should we do then? … It's not enough to instruct with words. We must show examples through our attitudes. In other words, we must affirm our own identity as Japanese and guide other peoples by example—with the spirit of persevering to the bitter end.[52]

It is interesting to note that Nagano coped with his frustration at the cultural difference he encountered by reaffirming his Japanese identity and commitment to exercising leadership as a responsibility incumbent on him as Japanese. In that sense, his understanding of interpersonal relationships on the Kendai campus was shaped by Japan's colonial relationships with other Asian peoples. Obsessed with his Japanese identity, which he believed to be superior to others, Nagano assumed it was natural that many Kendai customs took Japan as their model. In his mind, strong leadership by Japanese students was the key to success of Kendai's Pan-Asianist education.

Nagano affirmed his belief in Japan's superiority and in the Japanese mission to guide other Asian peoples on June 1, 1939, when he visited a nearby school that trained military officials. Impressed at seeing *manshū-jin* ("Manchurian people") carrying out a Japanese-style military training in a professional manner, Nagano was convinced that "with spiritual training ... even *manshū-jin* could master skills as perfectly as the Japanese do."[53] He continued:

> Moving to the [Asian] continent as Japanese, somehow I found other students' lackadaisical and slovenly attitudes unbearable ... In time, however, I began to overlook the situation, as I was repeatedly chided by my senior [Japanese] and others for having such feelings towards my non-Japanese classmates. But, after seeing the military training today, I realized that ... my present attitude was wrong.[54]

This passage conveys Nagano's assumption concerning relations among the various students enrolled at Kendai and in Manchukuo society at large. Clearly seeing the teacher–pupil relationship between the Japanese and *manshū-jin*, or the people of Manchuria, he appears to have believed that Japanization of other Asian peoples was possible and even desirable. In the last sentence, Nagano criticizes himself—and by implication all the Japanese who had persuaded him to be sensitive to different cultures—for not serving as a model to help others rise to the level of the Japanese. Thus, he decided to act on the principle of the "kingly way," one of the founding principles of Manchukuo, in his daily life at Kendai. When he found many of his non-Japanese classmates were slacking off during morning cleanup, he attributed it to the lack of self-awareness of the Japanese students. He wrote: "Because the superior are not setting the right example, it's inevitable that the inferior ones behave in a similar manner."[55] This, of course, is a quintessentially Confucian concept of exercising leadership by embodying virtue.

As seen previously, Nagano's assumption of Japanese superiority and guidance of the less advanced Asian peoples diverged significantly from Ishiwara Kanji's initial hope that Kendai's diverse students would interact as equals. Rather, Nagano's idea was close to that of the four professors who modeled Kendai on their conception of "Japaneseness" and of the majority of the Japanese faculty, as seen in the previous chapter. Yet, we should not overlook the fact that it was a "harmonious" relationship that Nagano strove to create at Kendai even if premised on a hierarchical relationship between the Japanese and non-Japanese and the "kingly way" concept that the superiors guide inferiors by example. In that sense, his attitude was deeply paternalistic. Whenever he saw lackadaisical non-Japanese students, he blamed himself for not being able to guide them by setting the right example. Furthermore, Nagano grew disappointed at the Kendai administration and faculty, who, in his eyes, were not sufficiently committed to

Pan-Asianist education. On June 4, 1940, he criticized the current curriculum at Kendai as "a weird mixture of (Japanese) higher schools and military training" and essentially "doing the same things as the universities in Japan."[56] We do not know what type of experience Nagano had in the following three years while enrolled at Kendai because his diary for those years is lost. What the available entries show, as seen earlier, is that Nagano strengthened his sense of Japan's unique mission as he interacted with his non-Japanese classmates, to a degree that even went further than the Kendai administration in advancing the Japan-centered approach to Pan-Asianist education.

Fujimori Kōichi (second entering class)

Unlike Nagano, who never delved deeply into the reasons for some non-Japanese students' "lackadaisical and slovenly attitudes," Fujimori Kōichi of the second entering class grew increasingly sensitive to non-Japanese students' sentiments as he interacted with them. At an informal party at his *juku*, which was held soon after Fujimori matriculated at the university in May 1939, he noticed that the non-Japanese students were not only unable to understand what the Japanese students were discussing but also unwilling to share their opinions. At that night, he wrote in his diary:

> It couldn't be helped. It's been only half a month since we entered this school. Even if we ask them to share how they really feel, they wouldn't do so because they don't know what kind of people we are. Just as Yan (a Chinese student) said, they are probably still scared of us. The history of Han Chinese and Manchuria, and all this kind of things make them feel uneasy about sharing their true feelings with us.[57]

Fujimori understood that his friends' reluctance to share their opinions and true feelings derived from the history of contested claims over Manchuria by different countries—most prominently China and Japan. Yet, Fujimori could not help but desire genuine dialogue with these non-Japanese students. He closed this day's diary by writing: "I must master *mango* ('Manchurian language') and learn about the ethnic and cultural differences (of Kendai students) as soon as possible, so that I'll be able to understand their viewpoints."[58] It is interesting to note that Fujimori uses the word *"mango"* to refer to the Mandarin Chinese. *"Mango"* was a commonly used term that reflected Japan's official stance that the residents of Manchuria were all *manjin* ("people of Manchuria") regardless of ethnic diversity.

Longing to develop a true friendship that would transcend ethnic and cultural boundaries, Fujimori sometimes got irritated with his fellow Japanese students who appeared not at all willing to understand non-Japanese students' perspectives. In his diary on June 19, 1940, Fujimori criticized other Japanese students for being "stubborn" and "closed-minded."[59] In addition, Fujimori grew frustrated at Kendai's token commitment to the equality of all students. For example, when student representatives were to be chosen for some activities, the unspoken rule was that not all the representatives should be Japanese, hence the necessity of selecting one student who was a native of Manchuria. Fujimori disliked this type of superficial practice of equality. Because he believed that all Kendai students must be united in spirit, Fujimori did not care if all the representatives were Japanese or *mankei*. All that mattered to him was the ability and personality of those who would represent his group.[60] Thus, Fujimori was striving to live up to the official vision of Manchukuo as a state and to become a citizen of that state. His diary entries show that he prioritized this new identity over the Japanese identity with which he had grown up.

As he interacted further with non-Japanese students, Fujimori came to experience inner conflict between his deep respect for the Japanese Emperor and his sympathy towards his non-Japanese friends' ethnic nationalist sentiments. Despite his increasing distrust of Japan's political leaders as well as Kwantung Army officials, Fujimori remained loyal to the Japanese Emperor, whose virtue, he believed, embraced all Asian peoples. It appears that Fujimori grew skeptical about the genuineness of the principles of the "kingly way" and "ethnic harmony" enunciated in the discourses of Manchukuo leaders, Kendai administration, and other people around him. However, he never questioned his loyalty to the emperor, at least in writing. Nevertheless, there is one significant diary entry, which, by implication, suggests doubt about the righteousness of the ongoing war in China, which was being waged in the emperor's name. On June 19, 1940, Fujimori wrote about his conversation with Yao, a student of Han Chinese descent. After chatting about themselves, their friends, and the *juku* life, the conversation moved to the ongoing China–Japan war. Although Fujimori did not record what Yao said, he apparently sympathized with Yao's reasons for being anti-Japanese. Fujimori wrote: "I would be the first to flock to the banner of Chiang Kai-shek [the leader of the Nationalist government of China], if I were Chinese."[61] He further contemplated the contradiction between the ideal of building a united Asia and the fact that Chinese, Koreans, and other Asian peoples were suffering from the Japanese Army's aggression. Deeply troubled by this matter that night, Fujimori could not sleep until 4 a.m. He wrote in closing:

"I felt like I could even go to join Chiang Kai-shek, if I were with Yao. I wish Yao and I could have a heart-to-heart talk with the [Chinese] youth of the Nationalist Party. I must study harder."[62]

He ended his long diary entry by telling himself to "study harder." This final sentence, which reads like a non sequitur, is indicative of his sense of confusion and dilemma. It can be interpreted as self-reproach for entertaining thoughts that implied disloyalty to the emperor. Even though the entry is not explicit on this point, he must have been aware that "[flocking] to the banner of Chiang Kai-shek" would mean making himself an enemy of the Japanese Emperor. This feeling of guilt perhaps made him resolve that "he must study harder" to still be a loyal subject of the emperor. Thus, the short final sentence reveals the dilemma in Fujimori's mind. It is also important to note that he felt at liberty to express such dilemma in his diary even though his *jukutō* would read it. It points to the remarkable freedom that the Kendai students enjoyed at this institution. In the end, as later diary entries show, Fujimori reaffirmed absolute loyalty to the emperor, whose virtue, he believed, would lead all Asians to live harmoniously. However, one thing is clear: he was no longer uncritically supportive of the political leadership in Manchukuo and Japan. He believed that only through mutual understanding, could Asian peoples realize harmonious relationships as equal members.

Nishimura Jūrō (second entering class)

While Nagano's and Fujimori's inner struggles arose from their relationships with other students, Nishimura Jūrō of the second entering class was more obsessed with his inner self and failing health. In addition to suffering frequent minor illnesses, serious health issues forced him to take leaves from Kendai. Moreover, in June 1941, in his third year at the university, Nishimura learned that his extremely poor eyesight was incurable. His diary shows how he increasingly turned inward to find meaning in his studies and eventually developed his own brand of humanism.

As mentioned earlier, Nishimura delighted in his very first experience of Kendai's agricultural training; however, he soon found out that the university demanded more physical labor than his body could take. One day, the agricultural training lasted for seven hours until 8:30 p.m. Nishimura wrote angrily:

Does [Mr. Fujita] think we possess immortal physical strength? … We need to review today's lessons and prepare for tomorrow's classes. Does he think we can go on like this? … This is intolerable. What's more exasperating is that he never opens his mouth without mentioning the five yen [the monthly allowance for Kendai students allotted from the Manchukuo government expenditure], as if he is giving us that money … It's downright offensive to be treated as traitors to the country when we do understand and appreciate it.[63]

Indeed, he was constantly exhausted and complained of not being able to concentrate on his studies. In addition, his frequent outings to Shinkyō's downtown for movies and drinking were undoubtedly partly responsible for his constant fatigue, which he admitted in his diary. It appears that Nishimura's initial delight at partaking in Manchukuo's nation-building did not deter him from fully enjoying college life—typical of any college freshmen. He wanted to study, and he wanted to enjoy life.

Although he does not explicitly state so, Nishimura appeared to have a detached, if not somewhat alienated, attitude toward the school events that the Kendai administration regarded as highly significant. One example is the omission of any expression of enthusiasm for a special lecture by Tsuji Masanobu, Staff Officer of the Kwantung Army, in commemoration of Navy Anniversary Day on May 27, 1939.[64] The lecture took place at a bridge at Kiryū Park near the Kendai campus. Nishimura reported that according to Tsuji's allegory, "that bridge was the Battleship Yamato, the lake below us was the Korean Strait, and we were all Commander Tōgō."[65] Then, he wrote: "the lecture at the bridge lasted about one hour."[66] Thus, this special event occupies only a few lines in his diary. It seems that Tsuji spoke about one of Japan's most significant and celebrated victories, the Battle of Tsushima of 1905, where Japan won a remarkable victory over the Russian Baltic Fleet. By likening the lecture site to the battle site, Tsuji intended to create the feeling of being on a real battlefield and inspire the students to be like the heroic Commander Tōgō. Nishimura's brief and emotionless entry noticeably lacks even a single reference to a moment of inspiration or surge of patriotic feeling inspired by the lecture but rather ends with a simple, factual statement on its length as if to imply his impatience with being kept standing for so long. Rather than attending these school events, Nishimura preferred reading literature. Indeed, that day's diary entry concludes with the statement that he enjoyed reading Natsume Sōseki's *Kusamakura [Grass Pillow]*.

By 1941, his third year at Kendai, his poor health and the prospect of the expansion of the war led Nishimura to rethink the meaning of his student life. In July 1941, after learning that he could expect no cure for his failing eyesight, he describes himself indulging in "errant enjoyment of youth" by going bar crawling several days in a row.[67] At this time, the prospect of war hit him. Upon hearing about the volatile situation on the Soviet Union–Manchukuo border and the fact that the Kwantung Army troops were on the move, Nishimura regretted his fast-living days.[68] He closely followed the news of intensifying tension between Japan and the United States following Japan's expansion into southern Indochina and the United States' and Great Britain's freezing of Japan's assets in retaliation.[69] He regretted that his fellow Kendai students merely passed their time on campus as if they were oblivious to the ever more serious conditions outside the campus. He lamented: "Is Kankirei [the name of the hill on which Kendai was located] a world of its own, apart from the outside world? [We] do not even read newspapers or listen to news. But, how long does this utopia last?—Not long."[70] Clearly, these words of reproach are cast at not only his fellow Kendai students but also himself.

His unusual circumstances, namely despair over his disability, led Nishimura to become increasingly independent-minded. On August 15, 1941, after attending Vice President Sakuta's lecture, which Nishimura commented favorably, he added a qualification to Sakuta's call for becoming a *tairiku-jin*, or the "person of the continent" (referring to Manchukuo, and Asia more broadly). Nishimura wrote:

> I believe that we should not lose the aesthetic sensibility that is unique to the Japanese ... I want to cherish forever the habits of composing a poem when seeing the sunset or of adorning one's desk with wildflowers when studying. Isn't it a drawback of today's intelligentsia that they live their lives so rationally and mechanically? I regard those who shed tears for literature more worthy of respect than ones who buy into Marxism.[71]

Here we see Nishimura defining the Japaneseness as having a unique sense of beauty, which while not contradicting the ideal of Pan-Asianism, appears to differentiate him from Fujimori's burning desire to empathize with the non-Japanese peoples. Meanwhile, he read a wide variety of literature, both Japanese and foreign, sometimes even skipping class to read favorite books.

Nishimura's diary became more explicit about his feelings after the outbreak of the war between Japan and the US-led Allies and another sick leave that lasted until March 1942. The following entry from April 1942 shows that he had grown skeptical about the current war:

> While riding a horse in the suburb (of Shinkyō), I imagined that my horse transformed into a Pegasus and we flew to the moon and surveyed the earth from there. Compared to the eternal universe, our lifetime is so ephemeral. Still, people continue fighting, saying it's for the sake of survival, or it's for one's ethnic nation. What would one feel if watching all these things on the earth from the universe?[72]

As seen in this passage, he appears to question the very purpose of all wars. At the same time, although he does not specifically state so, he seems to question Japan's current war, which the Japanese government claimed to fight "for the sake of survival" and "for one's ethnic nation."

Nishimura also expressed his discontent with the Japanese education policy in Manchukuo. On December 7, 1942, when he visited a nearby *kokumin gakkō* (elementary school) on a school trip, he was shocked to see that "children, who were too young to be called citizens, were taught that to die (for the country) was the only duty of the Japanese."[73] He angrily continued, "it appears that there continued to be the kind of education that one could find in a concession. The office in charge of education in Manchukuo thinks only of producing Japanese subjects, flatly refusing to provide education that fosters the citizens of Manchukuo."[74] Here we see Nishimura's distress when brought face to face with the contradiction between the stated status of Manchukuo as an independent country and the actual policy that imposed Japanese-style education on its diverse population.

Nishimura eventually embraced humanism. In January 1943, he wrote: "[h]arboring skepticism of Marxism and resentment against Fascism, I see humanism as the most compelling answer today."[75] Broadly defining the essence of humanism as the idea that "to live is to trust human beings,"[76] Nishimura continued, "before the war in Europe broke out ... why couldn't people attain the worldview in which people live in mutual trust and cooperation?"[77] He concluded the day's diary entry as follows: "Perhaps this kind of idea can be accepted only among ourselves, who live on this campus, forgetting about the ethnic and national difference and attempting to transcend the past."[78] This entry is interesting for two reasons. First, why did he refer to "the war in Europe" and not the Pacific War or the war between Japan and China? He was writing this entry in January 1943, when Japan had been at war with the United States and Allied Powers for two years and with China for more than five years. Yet, he referred to the outbreak of war in Europe to blame people who chose war over the path of mutual trust and cooperation. Does Nishimura take for granted and therefore excuse Japan's descent into war? Or, did he simply not want to express opinions that could get him into trouble? In light of his emerging humanism, this entry may also imply that Nishimura simply did not care which countries were to be blamed, because he opposed all wars. Second, the last line of the entry expresses an optimistic and uncritical view of interpersonal relationships on the Kendai campus. He describes the Kendai community as capable of "forgetting about the ethnic and national difference," even though more than ten Chinese students, including his own classmates, had been arrested for their anti-Japanese activities, the news of which Nishimura had received with "severe shock" in November 1941.[79] Then, what did he mean by "forgetting about ethnic and national difference"? There are two other entries in which he used the same phrase. In both cases, he used it to describe his experiences of having fun with his fellow Kendai students after hours on a school trip[80] and at the welcoming party for new students.[81] Apparently, the vision of "ethnic harmony" that he refers to in these entries is a state of sharing good times and laughter together but nothing deeper than that. As this entry reveals, Nishimura's diary tends to avoid disruptive and unpleasant truths such as the complicated and at times conflicted interpersonal relationships on campus that were shaped by Japan's colonial and imperial policy in Asia.

Nishimura experienced a bitter departure from Kendai when he was drafted in November 1943 together with the other Japanese students twenty years of age or over. Surprisingly, his extremely poor eyesight did not disqualify him. His campus life at Kendai was thus cut short, though the university later granted diplomas to the students of Nishimura's class. Curiously, Nishimura's diary does not reveal much about his reactions after he received the news of student conscription in the fall of 1943.[82] Rather than continue writing about his humanism and lament over war or complaining about the conscription, Nishimura kept brief records of each day's occurrences. However, we can easily imagine how depressed he was during this time. Nishimura had made his career goal working in the film production, which he regarded as the most effective means of mass education in Manchukuo where a large number of people were illiterate and uneducated.[83] Japan's intensifying war shattered this dream. Furthermore, the conscription of the Japanese students at Kendai undeniably betrayed this young Japanese who followed the state's lead and made up his mind that he would become a citizen of Manchukuo to work for this new country. Japan's student conscription got Nishimura not in Japan, but in an ostensibly independent state, Manchukuo.

Morisaki Minato (fourth entering class)

As mentioned earlier, Morisaki Minato of the fourth entering class brought with him to Kendai the Pan-Asianist dream of a community infused with harmonious relationships of peoples of different backgrounds. Soon, however, Morisaki became aware of an unbridgeable gap between the *mankei* and the *nikkei* students.[84] He noticed that "the *mankei* classmates, even those who generally seemed to feel kindly towards [him], sometimes were looking at [him] suspiciously, as if to indicate … that they would never be off their guards," which is not surprising, in light of arrests of Chinese students.[85] After this day, Morisaki began complaining about *mankei* students' behavior, such as being too much concerned about "face-saving," banding together against the *nikkei* students and slacking off during agricultural training.[86] On June 13, 1942, he angrily noted that only two *mankei* students came out when his class visited a nearby shrine dedicated to the soldiers who died for the nation-building in Manchukuo.[87] When the whole class bowed before the shrine, those two students made only token bows while chatting with each other. Rather than trying to understand what made them act in this way before a Japanese war shrine, Morisaki posed a rhetorical question in his diary: "Do they ever think about the true essence of the Japan–Manchukuo relationship?"[88] He had an answer in his mind: "there is no place in their minds for 'Manchukuo.'"[89]

The divide between the *mankei* and the *nikkei* in his *juku* intensified and culminated in a big quarrel. It started with the persistent efforts of a Japanese student, Yamada Shun'ichi, to establish a close relationship with a Chinese student, Zhang Yujian. The more Yamada tried, the more Zhang teased him, insulting him jokingly and sometimes kicking him. One day in June 1942, when Zhang threw water over Yamada's back, Yamada's patience snapped, and a tense standoff ensued. Though it did not develop into a physical fight, the tense atmosphere permeated the *juku* in the following days. Then, one night Zhang began speaking to Yamada in a combative tone, first in Japanese, and when Yamada began ignoring him, Zhang continued in Chinese. Other Chinese students joined Zhang and continued talking among themselves in Chinese until late at night. At this time, the few Japanese students who spoke good Chinese were not present at their *juku* room. Not knowing exactly what the Chinese students were saying, and not knowing how to respond in Chinese, Morisaki and other Japanese students hid under their blankets, swallowing their anger.[90]

This incident eventually led to a change in Morisaki's thinking whereby he affirmed that both the *mankei* and the *nikkei* were "citizens of Manchukuo."[91] After a period of frustration and anger at the Chinese *juku*-mates, whom Morisaki referred to as either the *mankei* or "they" sharply contrasted with "we," the *nikkei*, he had a sober moment of realization. "If we go on like this, Japan's policy of cooperation will be a complete failure. The incident (at *juku*) could be repeated at anytime, anywhere."[92] Recognizing that the current challenge at Kendai's integrated *juku* was a miniaturized version of the complicated relationships among the peoples in Manchukuo and Asia at large, Morisaki made up his mind to face this challenge. The question was how he would proceed. He indicated that some Japanese on campus thought that they should strive harder to earn respect so that non-Japanese students would follow their examples—a way of thinking articulated in Nagano's diary. However, Morisaki disliked this idea because he felt that it "appear[ed] as if Japanese are superior to others."[93] He wrote: "we say *mankei* and *nikkei*, but, we are all citizens of Manchukuo, aren't we?"[94] Here, Morisaki's use of the term *kokumin*, or citizens, does not imply the legal status of Kendai students. Rather, it reflects the common consciousness of Japanese Kendai students who moved to Manchukuo determined to devote themselves for the nation-building project of this newly established state, as we saw in the account of one of the "Horse Barn" protesters. Thus, Morisaki began to challenge the clear division between the *mankei* and the *nikkei* that dominated his mind previously.

Meanwhile, his conversation with a close friend, Bak Sam-Jong, a Korean student, further revealed to Morisaki the difficulty of putting the principle of "ethnic harmony" into action. He did not specifically record the content of the conversation with Bak, but the following entry from August 2, 1942 implies that Bak honestly shared his negative experiences of the Japanese Empire as Korean:

> I had a conversation with Bak Sam-Jong. What a dreadful thing ethnic nation is! I never knew that he was thinking and struggling in anguish to this extent. It appears that people all have their own perspectives and suffering. I came to wonder if to prosper eternally means to suffer eternally. For Asia to prosper for eternity there should be eternal suffering.[95]

This last line must have referred to the suffering of Asian people, like Bak, under Japan's colonial rule. For, after his conversation with Bak, Morisaki renewed his resolution to study hard, in order to know "what Japan has done to the comrades in Asia, and what Japan plans to do in the future" as well as the aspirations of Chinese and Russian peoples.[96] Thus, his close interaction with his non-Japanese classmates and his genuine desire for actualizing "ethnic harmony" motivated Morisaki to expand his intellectual horizons. He developed a particular interest in Chinese Communism, which he saw as winning the hearts and minds of more and more Chinese people.

Such study and contemplation about the meaning of "ethnic harmony" brought Morisaki to another realization: his *mankei* classmates were in fact Chinese. Recognizing that "the more patriotic one is, the more sturdily he would see himself as 'Chinese' rather than Manchukuo citizen," Morisaki even came to respect those "Chinese" students who left Kendai to join the anti-Japanese movement.[97] In April 1943, he saw his "*mankei*" classmates—he still used this term interchangeably with "Chinese"—gathering in a recreation room and intently listening to the radio broadcast of Zhou Fohai's talk. The speaker Zhou was an influential Chinese politician of the Japanese-supported collaborationist government in Nanjing under Wang Jingwei. Seeing the intense expressions on his classmates' faces, Morisaki strengthened his belief that those *mankei* classmates were indeed Chinese. That day's diary entry also indicates his disagreement with a Japanese instructor's optimistic view that the merger of Japan and Manchukuo might be possible before too long. Morisaki wrote: "If it [the merger] happens, that will be the very time the land of Manchuria would become a lost territory for China. The [Chinese] residents of Manchukuo would then suffer even bigger torments."[98] He thought that even if Manchukuo were to bridge the gap between Japan and China, it would be impossible to instill Chinese people with patriotism towards Manchukuo that could surpass their love of their mother country, China.

Kendai's summer labor service offered another opportunity for Morisaki to reflect on the ideal of constructing "ethnic harmony." From June 14 to July 28, 1943, about 600 Kendai students were sent to Dongning in Heilongjiang Province to assist various construction projects.[99] There, Morisaki's group of seven or eight students, which included Japanese, Chinese, Koreans, and Russians, had the opportunity of engaging in group discussion with younger Korean students who had also been recruited for labor service. Morisaki described these Korean boys as "passionate, easily agitated, rebellious, at the same time, fearless, and somewhat giving in to despair," then he added he somehow felt "uncomfortable finding such characteristics in [these] Korean people."[100] Morisaki continued:

> Children are recruited for labor service; and boys are severely trained in a Japanese [military] style. While the intellectuals are distressed, discussing the issues of ethnic nation with their armchair theories, without noticing that they are aging at that very moment, harsh and practical training is being forced upon the new generation increasingly imbued with the spirit of the new age. This is all happening while the old intellectuals are discussing worriedly.[101]

This entry clearly reveals Morisaki's criticism of the Japanese policy in Manchukuo. Furthermore, it shows that Morisaki was struck by the sharp gap between his ideal and the reality outside campus. The "intellectuals" here seems to refer to Kendai faculty members, students, and Morisaki himself, whose idealistic thinking was often confined to the small campus of Kendai.

Ironically, the source of further disappointment for Morisaki was a Japanese *jukutō*, Associate Professor Manda Masaru, and a senior student adviser, Mizushima, an upper-class student who was assigned to supervise Morisaki's *juku*.[102] His diary in the summer of 1943 is full of complaints about Manda and Mizushima, who resorted to every means of controlling Morisaki's *juku* members—they would inspect students' personal diaries, verbally abuse them or beat them severely. However, it is not clear why Morisaki's *juku* became the target of such extremely tight control. Because Manda and Mizushima required students to submit not only public but also personal diaries for inspection, we can assume that Morisaki chose not to write certain facts, which probably explains some of the ambiguity in his diary during this time. After one of his closest friends, Nagahama, quit Kendai, Morisaki, too, began to think about leaving the school and volunteering for military service. Interestingly, one of the things that pushed him to choose this path was his remembering the "courage of the *mankei* comrades who had left campus for … Yan'an and Chongqing," the strongholds of Chinese Communists and Nationalists, respectively, to join the anti-Japanese movement.[103] At this point, what appeared more important to Morisaki was the sincerity and purity of intent rather than the purpose of one's act. In other words, the political causes of Morisaki's joining the Japanese military and his friends joining the anti-Japanese movement were diametrically opposite; but, in Morisaki's mind, they had equal value as long as the intent was pure. He wrote on August 11, 1943: "As long as I am resolved to carry it through, it doesn't matter if I remain at Kendai or join the military. The essential thing is whether I am determined to carry out my intention."[104] Morisaki chose the latter option and left Kendai on October 9, 1943, deeply disappointed that his *juku* experience had been destroyed by the Japanese *jukutō* and senior student adviser.[105]

While Morisaki did not directly state his reasons for quitting Kendai, there is a story that has become a kind of legend among Kendai graduates about Morisaki's last days at Kendai. According to the editor of Morisaki's published diary, Izumi Santarō, Morisaki was part of a group of Kendai students who had secretly been sending student delegations to both the CCP headquarters, Yan'an, and the GMD wartime capital, Chongqing, to open Japan–China peace talks. The group had already sent two delegations, but none had returned to campus. The third attempt, which Morisaki had planned to lead, was thwarted by the school administration. When the students' scheme was leaked, the administration sent Morisaki home with a forged doctor's note indicating he had severe heart disease. Upon visiting a doctor in his hometown and discovering that the diagnosis had been faked, Morisaki officially dropped out from Kendai.[106] A Japanese historian, Matsumoto Ken'ichi, casts doubt on this story. Matsumoto speculates that the story of his role in the student peace initiative actually emerged out of Morisaki's close friends' and his father's desires to remember Morisaki in light of "resistance within aggression" by young Japanese.[107] Surely, one can find no other reference to Morisaki's scheme except in Izumi's "Editor's Note." There is no record by the school administration that verifies Morisaki's scheme. Nonetheless, considering the highly political nature of his student activism, it is highly possible that the University deliberately did not keep a record. While the facts are uncertain on Morisaki's fanciful plans of Japan–China peace negotiations, I concur with Matsumoto on the point that one can find in Morisaki's diary signs of "resistance within aggression," as shown earlier. Morisaki's distress over the contradiction between his idealism and the reality of Manchukuo and his burning passion for understanding the sentiments of his non-Japanese classmates were so intense that his close friends, such as Bak Sam-Jong, would fondly remember Morisaki as an initiator of the Japan–China peace negotiation scheme. Assuming planning was actually underway, Chinese students would have taken the lead role in sending delegations to Yan'an and Chongqing. Politically naïve in the extreme, the incident nevertheless demonstrates that Morisaki and his friends were genuinely pursuing the ideal of Pan-Asian cooperation, even if it meant risking their lives. At the same time, it attests to the fact that the Kendai administration did not welcome these students' high idealism and their remarkable energy and courage to act on the Pan-Asianist ideal.

Morisaki's enthusiasm for Pan-Asianism did not dissipate after the failure of the peace initiative or even after his resignation from Kendai. After giving up hope he might further Japan–China reconciliation, which he regarded as the key to the Pan-Asian crusade against the West, Morisaki chose to literally devote his life to this cause through a military action. He voluntarily enlisted in the Japanese Navy's special attack corps. While Morisaki spent time at home before joining the Navy in August 1944, his perception of Pan-Asianism continued to diverge from the Japanese official version that emphasized Japan's supremacy and leadership. On March 22, 1944, Morisaki compared the Meiji Restoration of 1868 and what he saw as the "Shōwa Restoration," the current revolutionary project of creating the Greater East Asia Co-Prosperity Sphere. He wrote:

> Just as the Meiji Restoration brought the equality of all people to Japan, the successful Shōwa Restoration should be followed by the abolishment of feudalistic system based on ethnic nation. Based on the principle of equality among all peoples, the Greater Asia will progress through free and vigorous competitions ... there shall be no discrimination in Asia; Asia will be an equal world for its one billion people. Without such vision and hope, what use would there be to speak about 'eternal peace for the East' or '*hakko ichiu*'?[108]

This entry reveals that Morisaki was not satisfied with the current hierarchical order that the Japanese Empire imposed on Asian peoples. Nor did he see the Japanese as inherently superior to other Asian ethnic nations. Indeed, as Tamanoi shows, Morisaki was increasingly disillusioned with the "vulgar" Japanese.[109] For him, the current war was only a transitional period, which must lead to "an equal world" for Asian peoples. And, he claimed, "Kendai's mission was to foster a new generation of leaders" who would construct that new world.[110]

Morisaki's equalitarian vision of Pan-Asianism and strong commitment to the creation of a better Asia for all Asians did not allow him fully to accept Japan's defeat. On August 16, 1945, he ended his twenty-two years of life by committing ritualistic suicide, hara-kiri, at the beach near the Mie Fleet Air Arm Base where he had been waiting for his mission to take off as a special attack pilot.[111] In a suicide note to his parents, Morisaki wrote: "I fear that if I went on living, I would destroy the peace, go against national policy, and thus cause trouble for my family and relatives."[112] Given the fact that he was genuinely committed to the realization of "an equal world" for all Asian peoples, his choice of death is not so unfathomable. For Morisaki, the tragedy of "Asian peoples" was not at all an abstraction; he had witnessed and heard in person how much the Japanese Empire tormented his Korean friend and how intensely his Chinese classmates were struggling in Manchukuo. Thus, to Morisaki, Japan's defeat signified that all the sufferings of his friends in the name of the Pan-Asianist dream had been futile. The reference in his suicide note to "going against national policy" pointed to Morisaki's anger toward the Japanese leaders who had imposed hardships on him and his friends in the name of Pan-Asianism and betrayed them all.

Four paths to leadership

In the literature on Japan's prewar Pan-Asianism, the studies that focus on the political elites' perspectives represent the dominant perception of Pan-Asianism by the 1930s as Japan-centered. In her macro-level analysis of Japan's wartime ideology, Eri Hotta convincingly calls this strain Meishuron Pan-Asianism, where *meishu*, or leader, refers to Japan.[113] However, when taking a micro-level perspective by looking at the diaries of four Japanese students enrolled at Kendai in the late 1930s and early 1940s, we get a more complicated picture of Japan's Pan-Asianism. As seen in Chapter 2, the Kendai administration and the majority of the faculty embraced Japan's central position within the projected Pan-Asian unity, despite the university's pledge to train a generation of new leaders who would make the goal of "ethnic harmony" a reality. Nevertheless, for at least some students, the life at Kendai prompted the development of thinking that did not necessarily conform to Japan's official ideology of Pan-Asianism.

While at Kendai, Nagano came to embrace Meishuron Pan-Asianism. To overcome ethnic and cultural differences, Nagano tried hard to fulfill the "Japanese" responsibility and mission of leading other peoples in Asia, conforming to the official version of Pan-Asianism that envisioned a hierarchical order with Japan at the top. It did not mean, however, that Nagano abandoned the ideal of harmonious relationships. In effect, he was more committed to it than ever. Thus, Nagano resolved his frustration with non-Japanese students' behavior by confirming his belief in Japanese superiority and by pursuing his "Japanese" mission at Kendai and Manchukuo at large. It is instructive that Nagano, experiencing Pan-Asianist education in his daily life, eventually developed a firmer belief and attitude towards the perceived hierarchical relationship between the Japanese and the others, as shown in his discontent with Kendai's lukewarm commitment to the ideal of "ethnic harmony."

Unlike Nagano, Fujimori and Morisaki came to question Meishuron Pan-Asianism and developed a more egalitarian conception of Pan-Asianism. Fujimori first made efforts to understand non-Japanese students' perspectives, and then confronted the contradiction between his loyalty to the Japanese Emperor and his sympathy towards non-Japanese friends' ethnic nationalist sentiments. His emphasis on equality and the importance of mutual understanding reflected the egalitarian and communal perception of Pan-Asianism. For Morisaki, the impact of the day-to-day interactions with his friends at Kendai was much larger. He came to utterly reject Meishuron Pan-Asianism, which he had previously embraced. Furthermore, as if to protest against Japan's wartime leadership that had caused anguish for himself and his Asian friends, Morisaki dramatically demonstrated the purity of his failed intent to work for eternal peace for all Asians, by closing his young life. Nishimura rarely mentioned his non-Japanese classmates or his view of Pan-Asianism in his published diary. Nor did he seem to undertake a serious and sustained examination of the meaning of "ethnic harmony." Yet, his emerging humanism clearly showed discontent with Japan's policy in Manchukuo and the continuing war.

One remarkable difference between Nishimura's and Morisaki's experiences is the identity they developed while enrolled at Kendai. Moving to Manchukuo in 1939 when not many people anticipated the end of the Japanese Empire, Nishimura intended to settle in Manchukuo and hold important positions in the society as a future graduate of prestigious Kendai. With this plan in mind, he strove to become a Manchukuo citizen himself. Disappointed in what he saw of the school system in Manchukuo, he hoped to contribute to the betterment of education in Manchukuo through film production. In contrast, Morisaki, who was enrolled at Kendai after the outbreak of the war in the Pacific, became preoccupied with the need of resolving the Japan–China conflict, which, in his mind, impeded the ongoing Asian crusade against the West. When he realized that the ethnic nationalisms of his friends were irreconcilable with Japan's vision of Meishuron Pan-Asianism, Morisaki altered his conception of the ideology into an egalitarian version. Moreover, by choosing to remain Japanese in his identity, Morisaki planned to literally use his life as a *kamikaze* pilot to end the war, which he saw as the first step in the construction of a new order on the basis of equality. Despite the difference in their choice of identity, both Nishimura and Morisaki tried to become the kind of Manchukuo or Japanese pioneering leaders who were different from the talent that the Japanese state attempted to foster among its youths.

Hence, the diaries of the four Japanese students show that well into the 1930s and even until the end of Japan's war, Pan-Asianism continued to be perceived and practiced in various ways. Moreover, these texts remind us that in such acts of exploring the meanings of Asia, non-Japanese actors played important roles. Essentially, it was the observations of their non-Japanese classmates' responses to Meishuron Pan-Asianism that drove Nagano, Fujimori, and Morisaki to contemplate the meanings of Asia. In that sense, they strove to construct, reconstruct, and act on their visions of Asia, in response to their Asian peers' perspectives. At Kendai, these young Japanese were growing into a generation of new leaders—in their own ways.

Calling Asia a new home: Korean and Taiwanese students' experiences at Kenkoku University

Approximately eighty Korean and twenty-five Taiwanese students were enrolled at Kendai between 1938 and 1945.[1] Among the total number of roughly 1,400 who attended Kendai during the same period, these students from Japan's formal colonies represented a minority. Nevertheless, they could claim to be part of the majority given that the Japanese Empire recognized Koreans and Taiwanese as Japanese citizens in theory. Indeed, the Kendai administration was inconsistent in its categorization of these students from Japan's formal empire. For instance, on one hand, they were seen as *nikkei* ("of Japanese descent") in the administration's outline of applicants' qualifications. On the other hand, the administration followed the Manchukuo government's practice of applying the student mobilization laws to these students and Japanese students differently. The situation was even more complicated in daily life on campus; the students from Korea were called *nikkei* or *senkei* ("of Korean descent"), and students from Taiwan were seen as *nikkei, taikei* ("of Taiwanese descent"), or *kankei* ("of Han Chinese descent"). In examining the experiences of Korean and Taiwanese students at Kendai, this chapter concentrates on their sense of identity.

Core materials of this chapter mainly come from three different sources. First, former Korean students published an anthology of recollections in 1986. This collection has thirty-one essays all written in Korean. I have access to the Japanese translation that was published in 2004 as *Kankirei—manshū kenkoku daigaku zaikan dōsō bunshū [Kankirei: collection of memoirs written by alumni in Korea]* (hereafter, I call it a Korean collection).[2] Twenty-one essays were translated, and fifteen of them were checked by the authors for accuracy of translation before publication. Unlike the Chinese alumni's collection *Huiyi*, whose authors uniformly write negatively about Kendai with varying degrees, this Korean collection contains both positive and negative memories and feelings

about Kendai. Second, Hong Chun-Sik, a former Korean student of the second
entering class, who also contributed his essay in the aforementioned Korean
collection, published a book-length memoir in Japanese as *Hankyore no sekai:
aa nihon [The world of my countrymen: Ah, Japan]* in 1999.[3] Third, a Taiwanese
alumnus of the first entering class, Li Shuiqing, published a book-length memoir
in 2007.[4] This source is important because it is the only substantial writing
authored by a former Kendai student from Taiwan.

I have to admit that these sources, produced decades after their actual
experiences of Kendai, were shaped by the authors' postwar lives. However,
while memories do not necessarily reflect how they were actually experienced
in the past, these candid recollections can give insights into the complicated
circumstances in which these colonial subjects made decisions to move to
Manchukuo, studied at Kendai, and interacted with other Asian youths. The rich
materials found in these sources reveal a unique pattern that distinguished the
experiences of this group of students from others on the Kendai campus. That is,
the Korean and Taiwanese students were often confronted with hard choices that
were particular to their colonial background. Besides the question of identity, the
Korean students struggled over the divisive political debate among themselves—
the support of Japan's *naisen ittai* policy or Korean nationalist aspiration for
independence. They and the Taiwanese students also had to make a hard choice
of whether to volunteer for armed services when the Japanese government
launched the Student Special Volunteer Soldier System in October 1943 to allow
Korean and Taiwanese students to "voluntarily" enlist in the army. This chapter
attempts to show how they experienced Kendai's Pan-Asianist education while
navigating through those difficult choices.

Assimilation policy and colonial schools
in Japan's formal colonies

Little is known about the boyhood experiences of individual Taiwanese and
Korean students of Kendai. When memoir authors write about their lives
before enrolling at Kendai, they usually focus on their decisions to apply for
the university. Luckily, existing literature on Japan's assimilation policy and
colonial schools provides a glimpse into the kind of lives that they experienced
as children in Taiwan and Korea.

Unlike the British Empire's model of "indirect rule" and "separate
development," the newly emerging Japanese Empire chose assimilation as

a guiding principle in its colonial administration.[5] The Meiji policymakers examined colonial administration models of British, French, and German empires, and found the French assimilation policy to be most suitable to the Asian empire. When Japan acquired its overseas colonies in the late nineteenth century, the Japanese colonial authorities started with partial assimilation that sought to produce literate and efficiently working colonial subjects while simultaneously seeking to maintain the distinction between the colonizers and the colonized.[6] Japan's assimilation policy, called *dōka seisaku*, developed based on two assumptions. One was the theory of *dōbun dōshu* ("same script, same race") between the Japanese and other Asians. The other was the mythical self-image of the Japanese people as *kōmin*, or "imperial people." These two theories together presented the appeal of idealism and justification for Japan's leading role in Asia.[7]

In the implementation of assimilation policy in colonial Taiwan and Korea, schools played an important role. While acknowledging variations, Harry J. Lamley defines assimilation as the process that "entails the transformation of the languages, customs, habits and institutions of a subject people until they become more at one or merge with the nationals of the home country."[8] Schools, from the colonial authorities' perspectives, were to become a useful place to generate these transformations. Thus, in both Taiwan and Korea, education reform was one of the first tasks for the colonial authorities.

Reflecting the Japanese Empire's gradualist attitude to assimilation in general, early Governors-General of Taiwan and Korea established education systems with the idea of segregation and inequality. Both regimes built public schools for the elite class of the local population, separate from elementary schools (*shōgakkō*) for the children of Japanese residents in the colonies. The ultimate objective of the former was to foster literate and cooperative workforces and loyal colonial subjects. The priority of such schooling was Japanese language instruction.

In Taiwan, the fourth Governor-General, Kodama Gentarō, issued the Common School Regulations of 1898 to introduce primary education for the children of Taiwanese gentry and the wealthy merchant class.[9] The six years of schooling at common schools (*kō gakkō*) started at age eight and ended at age fourteen, which was extended to include children of seven to sixteen years old in 1904. While Chinese classics was part of the curriculum in an effort to win the support of Taiwanese upper-class parents, the emphasis was put on the Japanese language and ethics.[10] Later, the Common School Regulations of 1907 and 1912 promoted more practical instruction, seeking to attract more enrolment by the children of the local elites while intending to discourage Taiwanese pupils to rise above the level of primary education.[11] As Patricia E. Tsurumi's influential work concludes, "the common school was definitely meant to assimilate Taiwanese but only at the bottom of the Japanese social order."[12]

Similarly, the education system in Korea under Japanese colonial rule started out with segregated schools. In fact, even before Japan formally annexed Korea in 1910, the Japanese Residency General (*tōkanfu*) had begun building public schools in Korea.[13] Like the system in Taiwan, Japanese-run elementary schools for Korean children were operated separately from elementary schools for Japanese children. The schools, named common schools (*futsū gakkō*), offered four-year primary education for Korean children between the ages of eight and twelve. One year after Japan annexed Korea, the first Governor-General of Korea, Terauchi Masatake, issued the Education Ordinance of 1911, which continued the already installed system of primary education. One significant change was that the instruction of national language (*kokugo*), which was formerly Korean, became Japanese.[14] Higher common schools (*kōtō futsū gakkō*), four years for male and three years for female students, offered practical training for Korean pupils who graduated from common schools. The four-year elementary program of common schools was two years shorter than the elementary schools for Japanese pupils. This means that the Korean students who aspired to continue their education had to gain extra schooling to make up for the lag.[15] Like the Taiwanese counterpart, colonial education in Korea focused on language instruction. As Ronald Toby points out, "during the first years of the colony, the study of Japanese occupied over 37 percent of the curriculum time in boys' common schools" in Korea.[16]

An important change in Japan's colonial education occurred in the wake of WWI. In the context of worldwide anti-colonialism and the rising liberalism in Japan's political circle, Japanese colonial regimes in Taiwan and Korea set to work in earnest to further assimilate colonial subjects. Moreover, a nation-wide anti-Japanese independence movement in Korea, the March First Movement of 1919, was shocking evidence to the colonial authorities in Korea that colonial education thus far had failed to produce loyal subjects. For the activists who took part in the movement included a great many graduates of Japanese-run schools.[17] By contrast, many upper-class Taiwanese, the target patron, had accepted Japan's colonial schools and even demanded the expansion of it to achieve greater equality. In 1922, both Governments-General of Taiwan and Korea introduced integrated schools to the colonies through the Taiwan Education Ordinance of 1922 and the Second Education Ordinance in Korea. Segregation at school was abolished on paper but had only a limited impact. Elementary schools were now open for all children who could speak Japanese. Common schools in Taiwan and Korea—now serving the same age group as elementary schools—remained in operation for those who did not speak Japanese. This restriction by Japanese language ability effectively limited the integration of classrooms. Furthermore, the colonial authorities in Taiwan set official quota, and only 10 percent of the enrolment at formerly all-Japanese elementary schools was available for Taiwanese children.[18] Under this circumstance, even though post-secondary schooling, too, was integrated in 1922, it was so overly competitive that an easier path to higher education for Taiwanese pupils was to attend schools in Japan rather than in Taiwan.[19] The situation was similar in Korea; although common schools now had six years like Japanese elementary schools, one continued to find a great majority of Korean students who attended Japanese-run schools did so at all-Korean schools.[20] Thus, introduction of integrated schools in 1922 in theory departed from the earlier gradualist approach; but, the impact of the change was quite limited.

Japan's assimilation policy took another turn in the late 1930s. The Second Sino–Japanese War (1937–45) and the war with the Allies (1941–45) presented an ever-increasing need of soldiers and laborers. In this new context, the earlier *dōka seisaku* was replaced by *kōminka seisaku* ("imperialization of subject people"). Assimilation was no longer a local concern for Taiwan or Korea; it became part of an empire-wide campaign to foster patriotism and loyalty toward the Japanese imperial leadership.[21] Aiming to mobilize colonial subjects for Japan's war effort, *kōminka seisaku* took a more aggressive and often coercive approach toward assimilation. It entailed reforms to Japanize all aspects of colonial subjects' lives. The Japanese state religion, Shinto, was imposed on people; the use of languages other than Japanese was strictly prohibited at school; and colonial subjects began to be slowly incorporated into the Japanese military.[22] The Japanese-style household registration system was installed in Taiwan and Korea in February 1940; and, though not legally enforceable, Korean people faced great pressure to adopt Japanese-style surnames.[23] The colonial administrations advertised this imperialization campaign to the colonial subjects as their effort to create greater equality between the Japanese and the local population. In Korea, *naisen ittai* ("Japan and Korea as one body") was a repeated slogan.

Imperialization was most notably characterized by the extension of military service to Taiwanese and Korean men. Takashi Fujitani's recent study convincingly explains that the Government-General of Korea as well as the media committed themselves both verbally and in actual deeds to the ideal of creating a multi-ethnic empire in order to fill the manpower shortage under the total war condition. For instance, the Government-General of Korea encouraged inter-racial marriage between Japanese and Koreans, unlike Western colonial regimes. Fujitani also shows that some Koreans, especially those who could benefit from Japan's rule, supported and in some cases even demanded more progressive assimilation.[24]

How did this change in assimilation policy in the late 1930s affect education policy in colonies? Imperialization translated into equal instruction at classrooms in Korea but not equal access to higher education. The Government-General of Korea's Third Education Ordinance of 1938 integrated elementary schools and common schools, naming all schools of primary education "elementary schools" (shōgakkō).[25] Still, integration of classrooms occurred only to a limited extent due to the higher cost of attending certain schools that enrolled largely Japanese pupils. Korean enrolment at predominantly Japanese elementary schools, which cost more, increased from 5.0 percent in 1935 to 10.8 percent in 1940.[26] Aside from this marginal change, a more notable result of the merging of the two school systems was the intensified Japanization that took place at school. National history became Japanese history; the Korean language became an elective; more emphasis was put on Japanese language and ethics; and by 1943, no school offered Korean language courses.[27]

By contrast, the education system in Taiwan did not change much during the 1930s and early 1940s; the system installed by the Taiwan Education Ordinance of 1922 remained intact with some minor changes. There continued to be common schools and elementary schools while post-primary schools were integrated. Patricia E. Tsurumi cites three reasons for the absence of drastic reforms during this period. First, the Government-General was generally satisfied with the achievement of the common school system thus far. In terms of assimilation, officials thought the next target must be Taiwanese adults and children who were not enrolled at common schools. Second, the Government-General faced more pressing issues of defense during the war due to the island's geographical proximity to Southeast Asia. Third, the massive increase of Japanese residents in Taiwan required building more schools for Japanese pupils rather than improving the whole educational system.[28] Interestingly, Tsurumi finds, the result of this lack of interest in education reform in wartime Taiwan resulted in less ultra-nationalistic content in school lessons at Taiwan's colonial schools compared to schools within Japan.[29]

What about the higher education in Taiwan and Korea? Like elementary and secondary education, the basic structure of higher education in the formal empire resembled that of Japan proper. Taihoku Imperial University (1928) was one of the first institutions of higher learning established in Taiwan. Besides, there were Taihoku Medical College, Taichu Agriculture and Forestry College, Tainan Commercial College, Taihoku Commercial College, Tainan Industrial College, and Private Taihoku Girl's College. These institutions of higher education in Taiwan had two purposes. The first was to foster skillful workers who could serve Japan's colonial regime. Indeed, all colleges except Taihoku Imperial University focused heavily on technical training and provided courses for three or four years. Taihoku Imperial University offered a six-year course of study. The second purpose was to conduct research about not only Taiwan but also south China and the South Pacific regions—the regions of interest in Japan's imperial expansion. For this purpose, a number of Japanese scholars were hired. Taihoku Imperial University's ratio of instructors to students was three to five. These schools of higher education continued to be dominated by the Japanese.[30]

Korea had a similar system, with Keijō Imperial University (1924) as the most prestigious institution of higher learning. Compared to Taiwan, there were many more schools of higher education in Korea both public and private. Many of the private colleges were founded by religious organizations but put under the administration of the Government-General of Korea. Like its counterpart in Taiwan, Keijō Imperial University was the only institution that offered six years of higher education. The similarity with Taiwan can also be found in the fact that the Japanese continued to dominate both the faculty and student enrolment at Keijō Imperial University. According to Mark Caprio, 76 percent of the faculty were Japanese in 1938, and 68 percent of students enrolled between 1929 and 1938 were Japanese.[31]

The practice of the *dōka* and *kōminka* policies was less clear in Manchukuo, Japan's informal empire. In principle, Manchukuo was an independent state, with its own government, jurisdiction, and emperor. Although the Japanese used similar slogans for Japan's relationship with Korea and with Manchukuo—*naisen ittai* ("Japan and Korea as one body") and *nichiman ittai* ("Japan and Manchukuo as one body") respectively—the meanings of the two terms differed. The former was the slogan of Japan's assimilation policy, emphasizing the cultural and racial commonalities between the Japanese and the Koreans. By contrast, the latter term pointed to the formation of a strong diplomatic tie between the two states—Japan and Manchukuo—that would become the core of a new order in Asia. Thus, in principle, Manchukuo as an independent state did not adopt Japan's assimilation policy. Nevertheless, in reality, Japanese military and civilian officials dominated the Manchukuo government's important positions, and the state's official language was Japanese, although non-Japanese populations were not drafted as Japanese soldiers, as happened in Korea and Taiwan.[32]

Given that admission to Kendai required Japanese language proficiency, most students who attended Kendai from Taiwan and Korea went through these Japanese-run public schools. Kendai's "Guidelines for Applicants" issued on June 9, 1937, stated that Japanese applicants, including those from Japan's formal colonies, must be twenty years old or younger and have graduated from middle schools.[33] Thus, all students from Taiwan and Korea who attended Kendai must have received primary and secondary education after the education reform of 1922. That means they likely had very limited chances to interact with Japanese children in classrooms, though their teachers were Japanese. It is also expected that those students were keenly aware of the *de facto* segregation at school enforced by the Japanese rulers. At the same time, they went through Japanization education and repeatedly heard the promises of making Taiwanese and Koreans equal to Japanese and of building a multi-ethnic empire for all Asians.

How did such colonial conditions affect their decisions to apply to Kendai? What made them decide to leave their countries and study at the highest educational institution of Manchukuo? What identity did they bring to Manchukuo, and what changes, if any, did they experience? How did they respond to Manchukuo, an informal colony of Japan, which was different from their own home countries? And to Kendai's practice of Pan-Asianism? In what follows, I attempt to answer these questions.

Mixed motives: Career advancement, romanticism, and nationalism

Korean and Taiwanese students chose to attend Kendai of their own will. Their recollection essays suggest that these youths were typically outstanding students who excelled at school and sports. For that reason, many of them were recommended by their middle school teachers to apply for Kendai. Bang Hui (third entering class), a former Korean student who contributed his essay to *Kankirei*, the Korean collection mentioned previously, recalls that he found almost everyone who took Kendai's entrance exam with him in August 1939 wore a badge that marked him as the head of a class. Normally, homeroom teachers appointed a top student to be the head, and one had to be outstanding not only in exam grades but also in sports and character. Knowing that all these heads of class were his rivals at the entrance exam made Bang extremely nervous.[34] Given the important roles played by colonial schools in Japan's assimilation policy in Taiwan and Korea, it is plausible to characterize these "outstanding" students as fully Japanized, at least from the perspectives of their teachers. Applicants from private middle schools in Korea that sought to keep distance from Japanese-style schooling belonged to a minority. Still, the successful candidates from those private schools were proficient in Japanese. More than half of available memoirs authored by these students from colonies indicate that Korean or Taiwanese ethnic nationalist sentiment had no significant or only limited influence on the authors' decisions to apply. Other, fewer, authors testify that their decisions were shaped by their sense of ethnic nationalism.

Those who do not mention Korean nationalism as their primary reason frequently write that they took Kendai's entrance exam without thinking much about it. What this means is that they did not know much about Manchukuo, nor did they think deeply about Kendai's educational objectives before taking exams. For them, decisions to apply to Kendai were related more closely to their available options in career advancement. For the brightest Korean and Taiwanese young men under Japanese colonial rule, popular options of higher education were *gokō* (five higher schools in Japan that served as preparatory institutions for the admission to Imperial Universities) or the preparatory programs of top colonial universities, Keijō Imperial University in Korea or Taihoku Imperial University in Taiwan. These were the paths to the elite within the colonial hierarchy. However, these highly competitive schools admitted only a small number of colonial applicants vis-à-vis Japanese candidates each year. Kendai presented another option. While admission to Kendai was no less competitive than *gokō* and Imperial Universities, this new school in Manchukuo had two great appeals—that tuition, boarding, and other expenses were covered by the Manchukuo state, and its stated commitment to equality among its students of diverse backgrounds.

Most former Korean students who contributed their essays in the Korean collection testify that their school teachers recommended that they would apply to Kendai. As noted previously, this recommendation itself was an honor to the students because teachers nominated only the best students at their schools. When this option was presented to Tae In-Seon (fourth entering class) in 1941, along with the information that Kendai was free of charge and highly competitive, he accepted the advice at once. He had dreamed of attending *gokō* in Japan, but the financial burden seemed too huge to him.[35] Jeong Gi-Su (eighth entering class) was similarly an outstanding student in his middle school. He always aspired to be the top student, and he did achieve this goal, as he graduated from

Zenshū Kita Middle School in February 1945 with the Governor's Award, which was presented to the best student each year. His initial hope was to enter *ichikō*, the best of the *gokō* in Japan, and then attend Tokyo Imperial University. Only because Kendai's entrance exam was held earlier than that of *ichikō*, Jeong took it, regarding it as a prep test. Admission to Kendai apparently was as honorable as being admitted to *ichikō*, as he ended up choosing to attend Kendai instead.[36]

Bang Hui's (third entering class) experience reveals the strong commitment of his middle school in Korea to sending its graduates to Kendai. Like Tae and Jeong, Bang wanted to go to Japan's higher schools or Imperial Universities but decided to take Kendai's entrance exam when recommended by his homeroom teacher. Although he regarded the exam just as a mock test to prepare for other entrance exams as Jeong did, his school exempted him from summer labor service to let him focus on preparing for Kendai's entrance exam. After passing the first written portion of the exam, Bang was exempted from classes and was advised to practice horse riding to prepare for the second part of the exam. Bang later learned that horse riding was not part of Kendai's entrance exam; it was misinformation that his teachers believed to be true. In any case, this was the extent of enthusiasm with which Bang's middle school supported him in gaining entrance to Kendai. When he received Kendai's admission, the school celebrated it as a great honor and even pressured him to accept the admission by saying that his rejection may negatively influence the results of future applicants to Kendai from this middle school. After reluctantly matriculating at Kendai, Bang continued to prepare for transferring to *gokō* during his first year, but decided to stay by the end of that year. It appears that Kendai's *juku* life convinced him of the school's genuine commitment to the principle of "ethnic harmony." In addition, he was quite impressed that Kendai "did not practice thought control."[37]

The experiences of Tae In-Seon, Jeong Gi-Su and Bang Hui seem to have been typical among Kendai students from Korea. All three were outstanding students in middle schools and accepted teachers' recommendations to apply to Kendai. Financial incentives and the honor of gaining admission to a highly competitive school played a large role in these three applicants' decisions to attend Kendai.

In addition to these two common reasons, other students indicate that curiosity about Kendai and Manchukuo motivated them to enroll in Kendai. An Gwang-Ho (first entering class) and Hong Chun-Sik (second entering class) both had the opportunity of listening to a talk by one of the Kendai faculty members, Tsuji Gonsaku, who toured middle schools in Korea to advertise Kendai to prospective students. An and Hong do not provide details of Tsuji's talk in their essays but write that it raised curiosity about the new school in Manchukuo and influenced their decisions. Both authors stress that it was just a curiosity and nothing deeper than that. An writes that he took the entrance exam "without thinking much about it."[38] Hong explains his decision as follows: "I did not know about the lofty ideal of Ishiwara, nor did I have profound understanding of Manchukuo. Falling for Tsuji Gonsaku's big talk, (my decision to enter Kendai) derived from a simple desire of living on a vast land of desert and prairie rather than being confined in the close quarters of Korean peninsula."[39] Hong further states that he had been so busy studying to become the top within the *kōminka* educational system that he "had no spare time and energy to think about other things."[40]

Kim Jae-Jin (fifth entering class) applied to Kendai only because it was the only option available for him due to his family's financial situation. However, he fell in love with Kendai when he found a curious criterion used in the interview exam. His friend Jeong Seong-Taek, who took the exam together with Kim, was a Christian. Knowing this, Kendai's interviewer asked "Christ or Sun Goddess, which do you think is greater?"[41] This was an ill-natured question that forced Jeong to weigh his sincerity in faith against his loyalty to the Japanese Empire, which was represented in this question by the Sun Goddess, the primary deity of Shinto. According to Kim, the conversation continued as Jeong responded, "Of course, Christ is greater."[42] To this, the interviewer asked, "Do you dare to enter this university with such an idea?" "Even if you say so, there is no doubt that Christ is great" was the end of this conversation.[43] Kim recalls that Jeong was disappointed at how his interview exam turned out and was sure that he did not pass. To their surprise, however, Jeong did make it. Kim continues in his essay, "If anyone scoffs at Kendai and says what kind of school it was, let him. Since this interview exam, I have started liking Kendai."[44] For Kim, Jeong, and other students from formal colonies who grew up under the strict surveillance of words and deeds, it must have been a fresh surprise to observe such openness that Kendai seemed to possess. It certainly raised curiosity about this school in their minds. On a side note, Kim also testifies that he, too, like An Gwang-Ho and Hong Chun-Sik, had no idea about Korean nationalism before attending Kendai. Even his father, who had been one of the leading members of the March First Movement of 1919, never told his son about this dramatic nationalist activism of the past.

What does these former students' ignorance of and indifference to Korean nationalism mean? First, it suggests that these top students who attended Japanese public schools in Korea during the 1930s had very few opportunities to learn about the dynamic anti-Japanese ethnic nationalist movement that had sprung up in Korea immediately after WWI. As Takashi Fujitani shows, the Government-General of Korea increased its effort to improve the lives of Korean people and commitment to the claim of equality between Japanese and Koreans under the total war condition that started in 1937.[45] At least among the elite and those who aspired to be the elite including these applicants, *naisen ittai* was not just a pep talk of the colonizer. It certainly meant a real possibility in which they may be able to negotiate and secure better lives.

If so, why were An Gwang-Ho, Hong Chun-Sik and Kim Jae-Jin interested in Kendai? Why were others willing to leave their homeland, Korea, to attend Manchukuo's university? It seems that these young Koreans were certainly aware of the persistent discrimination in Korea. An In-Geon (seventh entering class) recalls that he "shared, without knowing [he] did, the common social impulse of launching into the continent."[46] This is one of the key reasons for his decision to matriculate at Kendai. As he writes, many aspiring youths in Korea were likely to share this romantic view of going to the continent, outside of Japan's formal colony. It is also interesting to note that An In-Geon was under the influence of this romantic view of going to Manchukuo as late as the fall of 1943 when the Japanese Empire was fighting on the defensive. A year later, over seventy students from Korea took the interview exam, out of whom only fifteen gained admission.[47] Taking into consideration that there were many more that did not pass the earlier written portion of the exam, Kendai clearly retained its popularity among Korean students even in the fall of 1944. If these young Koreans knew that the empire would soon collapse, why would they seek a better career opportunity in Manchukuo? It appears that they had no doubt about the continuance of Japanese rule.

Some other contributors to the Korean collection explicitly state that they chose to attend Kendai out of Korean nationalist sentiment. For Gang Yeong-Hun (third entering class) and Jin Won-Jung (third entering class), the fact that a prominent Korean nationalist, Choe Nam-Seon, belonged to the Kendai faculty was a major reason to choose Kendai.[48] I will describe the interactions between Choe and Kendai's Korean students in detail later; here, suffice it to note that some applicants did know about Choe's contribution to the March First Movement and decided to attend Kendai because of their respect for this Korean nationalist hero of the past. Gang also writes that he was impressed by a talk by one of the Kendai faculty members at his interview exam. According to Gang, the Japanese professor first criticized the existing universities in Japan that had been heavily influenced by Western liberalism and failed to provide answers to the current problems that the world was facing. Then, the professor continued, as Gang describes in his essay, "Kenkou University aims to break through this impasse and contribute to the advancement of academia especially in humanities and social sciences."[49] Intrigued by this speech, Gang decided that Kendai would be the place where he could "search for a new avenue for the Korean ethnic nation."[50] Thus, Gang found a match between his sentiment of Korean nationalism and the explicitly anti-Western academic inclination of Kendai.

Other unique aspects of Kendai also attracted some Korean applicants who were conscious of their identity as Korean. The significant presence of non-Japanese students was one of the reasons for Kim Sang-Gyu (fifth entering class) to apply to Kendai.[51] Another appeal was the degree of cultural tolerance that Kendai students seemed to enjoy. When Bak Hui-Seong (sixth entering class) visited the Kendai campus in 1943 to take the interview exam, he was surprised that the current Kendai students from Korea made welcoming speeches in Korean. This was quite shocking to Bak, as his middle school in Korea would expel anyone who was found speaking Korean even outside school facilities. Observing Kendai's Korean students speaking Korean in public, Bak felt as if he "came to another world," and found that the scene "aroused the spirit of ethnic nationalism that had been dormant within [him]."[52] He then decided to attend Kendai, believing that "there was no other place than this school where [he] would want to invest [his] time and energy in youth."[53]

For applicants who strongly identified themselves with Korean nationalism, Manchukuo seemed to have offered an opportunity to somehow make revenge on Japan. Kim Yong-Hui (eighth entering class) writes that although he did not understand the politics of Manchukuo back then, he had a vague idea that going to Manchuria may teach him a method for "reclaiming the Korean rights over the territory since the Goguryeo era."[54] Goguryeo was an ancient Korean kingdom that ruled much of the Korean peninsula and Manchuria. In addition, Kim liked that Koreans in Manchukuo were recognized as *senkei* ("of Korean descent"), one of the five Asian ethnic nations that would make up the "ethnic harmony." This, he thought, was much better than the Japanization policy in Korea.[55] Im Seon-Jun (eighth entering class) was deeply aware that the colonial situation in Korea limited his career path. He found Manchukuo a better place for him to nurture strength and abilities with which to "take vengeance against Japan that had been exploiting the Korean nation under colonial control."[56] Thus, both Kim and Im outspokenly recall dissatisfaction with Japanese rule in Korea and the desire for revenge against Japan as their motives for choosing a school in Manchukuo over *gokō* in Japan or Keijō Imperial University in Korea.

Whether one was primarily concerned with choosing a better career opportunity and honor within the hard reality of colonial rule or being influenced by Korean nationalism, it seems that applicants from Korea regarded Manchukuo and Kendai as better choices. For the former group, it was a realistic choice for better personal career advancement, financial incentives, curiosity about the new school in Manchukuo, or a romantic view of the continent that influenced their decisions. A Taiwanese student, Li Shuiqing (first entering class), had a similar reason when he applied to Kendai in 1937. After graduating from common school and night school, he passed a competitive exam to become a civil official for the Government-General of Taiwan at fifteen, a record-breaking young age. Li, an aspiring young man, was preparing for another exam to step up in his career when he came across Kendai's advertisement for student recruitment. Li immediately decided to apply because he believed that "Taiwanese could not compete fairly with Japanese if they stayed in Taiwan."[57] Like many of the Korean applicants discussed earlier, Li made a realistic choice for a better future within the colonial situation. For the latter group of Korean students that was influenced by their sense of ethnic nationalism, it was the knowledge of political status of Manchukuo as an informal colony and Pan-Asianist commitment found at Kendai that made it appear a better place—at least not worse—than Korea. In either case, these students from Japan's formal colonies chose to leave their countries to attend Kendai, out of awareness—though the degree varies— of the limit of the promised equality between the colonizer and the colonized in their own countries.

Korean students' experiences: Awakening to a Korean identity—but what kind?

Although the timing varied, students from Japan's formal colonies eventually became conscious of their national identities as either Korean or Taiwanese. As discussed in the previous section, many students chose to matriculate at Kendai for practical reasons such as a better career opportunity and financial incentives. For those students, it appears that their experiences at Kendai played a large part in opening their eyes to their ethnic national identities. Former Korean students' memoirs show that their awakening to Korean nationalism was not a simple process shared by all of them. Rather, they were constantly faced with a difficult question—whether to support Korea's national independence or *naisen ittai* ("Japan and Korea as one body"), a colonial policy aiming at greater assimilation of Korea into Japan. While the former option was more popular among the Korean students enrolled at Kendai, there were some who believed that the latter route would be desirable for Korea.

Interactions among Koreans

The Korean students at Kendai utilized the university's lenient policy toward students' freedom of speech to engage in dialogue among themselves, which was difficult in Korea. Kim Jong-Cheol (third entering class) recalls that Korean upper-classmen hosted a welcome party for him and others from Korea immediately after they entered Kendai in April 1940. For Kim, who knew nothing of the real world, as he admits in his memoir, all the talk of Korean spirit and ethnic nationalism at this party brought him a fresh perspective.[58] This practice of the Korean seniors welcoming incoming students from their homeland became a tradition. When Im Seon-Jun (eighth entering class) participated in pre-matriculation orientation on campus in February 1945, some current students from Korea hosted study meetings to discuss Korean independence from Japan.[59]

For Choe Heung-Cheol (sixth entering class), the best memory of his student life at Kendai is that of having banquets among the Korean students on campus. They harvested potatoes from the school's farm, cooked potato salad, brought along their school meals, and enjoyed their "feasts" while conversing in Korean. Naturally, their conversation often moved to the future of Korea. They also sang some Korean songs that were prohibited in Korea at that time.[60] Where were they having these good times? According to Choe, these banquets were held on the Kendai campus, and interestingly, those were not secret events. Choe indicates that they felt at ease in having these banquets on campus because "no one was interested in [their] conversation, nor were there someone covertly monitoring their activities" on the Kendai campus.[61] Even if there were such surveillance, Choe continues, "no one would be able to understand the Korean language."[62] Here, we see a uniquely high degree of freedom that students enjoyed on the Kendai campus. It appears that one of Ishiwara Kanji's proposals—letting students interact freely among themselves in their own languages—was indeed put into practice.

Conversations about a Korean ethnic nation occurred not just among the Korean students on the Kendai campus but also between them and Korean residents in Manchukuo outside campus. For instance, Kim Sang-Gyu (fifth entering class) had a fierce argument with a Korean official who worked at the Manchukuo emperor's advisory council in spring 1945. When Kim visited the politician's official residence, he asked the official's opinion on his urgent question. Kim asked: "Now that Japan's defeat appears imminent, what is your take on the possible clash between the United States and the Soviet Union over our homeland Korea?"[63] The response Kim received was far from satisfactory from his standpoint. Kim recalls the official saying angrily: "How dare you bring up such a subject at this crucial time? ... Think about it! Would a woman who married to a man abandon him when confronted with crisis?"[64] Kim ended the conversation by saying: "It is only you, who has married to Japan."[65] In this conversation, we see two different and opposing views of Korea's future. It is clear that the official believed in the *naisen ittai* principle, likening Korea to a loyal wife who would accompany her husband, Japan, no matter what happens. He used a typical gendered discourse on the colonial relations between the Japanese and colonial subjects. In contrast, Kim held that Korea must seize the moment to secure its national independence once Japan surrenders to the Allies.

The same debate over the future of Korea—whether to support Korean independence or *naisen ittai*—happened among the Korean students enrolled at Kendai. As noted earlier, many of them enthusiastically supported Korea's national independence; however, there were few students who believed *naisen ittai* to be a better choice. Not surprisingly, none of the available memoirs confesses that the author himself supported the *naisen ittai* policy. Doing so would feel inappropriate in the postwar society of the Republic of Korea. Nonetheless, the Korean memoir collection provides some evidence that the Korean students on the Kendai campus were divided in their opinions on Korea's future. For instance, Gang Yeong-Hun (third entering class) writes that by the time he started his second year at Kendai in 1941, he had increasing difficulty in determining where his heart lay. He found that his fellow Korean students approached the issue of Korea's future from three angles—national independence, the principle of *naisen ittai*, and communism.[66] Gang struggled to find his own stance and eventually set his mind on the goal of national independence. Kim Yong-Hui (eighth entering class) recalls that when he arrived at Kendai in 1945, two Korean alumni were working at the University as Probationary Senior Government Officials.[67] One of them told him that "Korea must gain independence, or at least be granted the right of self-rule like India" under British rule.[68] By contrast, Kim continues, the other Korean alumnus who worked at the University insisted that "Korean people would be happier under the principle of *naisen ittai*."[69] These two entries attest to the fact that Korean students, including alumni, were not of one mind about Korea's future.

For those who set their minds on Korean independence, the influence of one of the Korean faculty members, Professor Choe Nam-Seon, was significant. As discussed in Chapter 2, it was Ishiwara's idea that Kendai recruit Choe, a leader of the March First Movement of 1919, to its faculty. I have discussed his perspective on the history of Manchuria in Chapter 2; here, I will focus on Choe's interactions with the Korean students. Removed from a teaching position and granted a title of Honorary Professor at Kendai, Choe did not teach actual courses. His influence on the Korean students was rather through his informal conversations with them. Choe's house near campus came to serve as a gathering place for Kendai's Korean students. Many students recall their fond memories of Choe. I Jong-Hang (first entering class) is one of them. He and his friends often visited Choe on Sundays, "ate foods, had fun, as if being at [their] own homes, and listened to [Choe's] talks."[70]

Gang Yeong-Hun, whose struggle on the issue of ethnic nationalism I have discussed earlier, also had close interactions with Choe. Gang and six other Korean students of the third entering class visited Choe's residence immediately after matriculating at Kendai in 1940. Gang summarizes what Choe told them as follows:

> Nowadays, Japanese people say *naisen ittai, dōso dōkon* ["same ancestor, same origin"], and so on, but those are all sheer nonsense. Our [Korean] people must shape our own fate while riding on the unique strength and culture of our homogeneous race. I know there are some even among us [who are at Kendai] who believe in the principle of *naisen ittai* and are wishing to become Japanese. But, that is like you climb a tree to catch a fish. We must never forget that we are Korean.[71]

In his memoir, Gang notes, this conversation with Choe convinced him that he had made the right decision to choose Kendai over Hiroshima Higher Normal School, from which he had received admission.[72]

Kim Yeong-Rok (second entering class) recalls a similar interaction. When he visited Choe for the first time in 1939, Kim asked this former leader of the March First Movement if he had actually believed that Korea would gain independence through the movement in 1919. Kim describes the ensuing conversation, which he vividly remembers.

> [My] question apparently made [Professor Choe] uncomfortable. But, although he looked pensive, his answer was simple and clear.
> "Yes, I thought so."
> "Do you still believe now that Korea will be able to gain independence?"

I asked this question with great curiosity.

"We live our lives solely for that purpose. Without that hope, how would we keep going?"[73]

Kim writes that the word "we" that Choe used in answering his question made a deep impression on him. Indeed, the word "we" clearly separated the Koreans from the rest, and particularly in this context, the Japanese. For Kim and the Korean youths of his generation who grew up under Japan's assimilation policy, drawing this line between the colonizer and the colonized had been taboo. Even if they could see clear difference and inequality between the two peoples in real life, they were not allowed to express their awareness of that fact. That is why it must have been a great sensation to see a prominent nationalist activist do just that and explicitly identify them as the same kind as him.

On December 8, 1941, when the news of Japan's Pearl Harbor attack brought excitement to the Kendai campus, a group of Korean students spent some time at Choe's house. Hong Chun-Sik (second entering class) and Min Gi-Sik (third entering class) were among them, and both write in their memoirs what they heard from Choe. According to them, Choe explained the huge gap between the national strength of Japan and the United States and the current world situation, and stated that Japan would soon be defeated and Korea would win independence.[74] Hong writes in his memoir that on this day he "awakened to his Korean identity with an electrified feeling thanks to Professor Choe."[75] This indicates that Hong had not thought about the issue of ethnic national identity so intensely for over two years since he matriculated at Kendai. In that sense, Hong's experience of awakening to his Korean identity makes a contrast with that of Gang Yeong-Hun (third entering class), whose prolonged struggle over this issue I have discussed previously. While Hong experienced the moment of awakening relatively late with an "electrified feeling," Gang continued to ponder on the same issue ever since he entered Kendai.

Cross-cultural interactions

Cross cultural interactions on the Kendai campus also influenced the Korean students' sense of ethnic national identity. Some authors of the Korean collection detail their unique experiences of sharing their school and *juku* life with not only Japanese but also other Asian students. The following seven accounts show different responses to the Pan-Asianist experiment of living out the ideal of "ethnic harmony" on the Kendai campus.

A member of the first entering class, An Gwang-Ho, describes in his memoir how he faced challenges in working to realize harmonious relationships during the five years of his campus life. Among many things that influenced his ideas, two events stand out. The first was Vice President Sakuta Sōichi's resignation in June 1942. As introduced in Chapter 2, Sakuta was one of the four Japanese academics who led the planning and founding of Kendai. Although his dictum of the centrality of the Japanese Emperor estranged many of the non-Japanese students, Sakuta was often fondly remembered by Japanese, Korean, and Taiwanese students for his diligent pursuit of learning. A Taiwanese alumnus, Li Shuiqing (first entering class), writes in his memoir that Sakuta's course entitled "*shūshin dōtoku*," or "living a virtuous life based on morality" was one that "all students listened in with utmost enthusiasm."[76] The aforementioned Korean student Gang Yeong-Hun agrees and attributes the uniquely open academic culture of Kendai to Sakuta's scholarship.[77] After a group of Chinese students were arrested for their anti-Japanese activities, and his efforts failed to release them, Sakuta resigned his position to take responsibility for the event. His position was replaced by Suetaka Kamezō, a former lieutenant general and the nineteenth division commander of the Japanese Army. The appointment of Suetaka was arranged by the Kwantung Army and thus indicated the increasing interference of the Kwantung Army with Kendai's administration. An Gwang-Ho writes, "all students from the first to fifth entering classes felt resistance toward the runaway Kwantung Army and uneasiness that the ideal of creating *ōdō rakudo* ('a peaceful land governed by the Kingly Way'), the founding principle of Manchukuo and the University, was vanishing away."[78] This indicates that all those students, including An himself, did embrace the stated ideal of Manchukuo and Kendai in mid-1942, well into Japan's war with the Allies. For, otherwise, he would not worry about the changing situation at the time.

The second event that reveals An's response to Pan-Asianism occurred in March 1943, a few months before his scheduled graduation from Kendai. One day he went out for a drink with his classmates. An writes that the following conversation "turned out to make a significant impact on [his] life."[79] At a bar, the non-Japanese students complained that the wage gap that persisted in Manchukuo betrayed the ideal of creating "ethnic harmony." To this, the Japanese students replied: "Korean students do not have military obligation. It is inevitable that their wages are different [lower] from that of Japanese who dedicate their lives to the nation [through military service]."[80] This response deeply upset An, who thought to himself: "There is nothing that we are incapable of doing ... OK, we will dispel such self-righteousness in our generation."[81]

This sentiment was so strong that An took it into action immediately. In a few weeks, An absconded from Kendai, returned to his home in Seoul, Korea, and enlisted in army training as a volunteer. As his Japanese classmates indicated in the bar conversation, the Japanese government did not extend its compulsory conscription of adult males to colonial subjects until 1944 in Korea and 1945 in Taiwan. However, starting in April 1938, the Army Special Volunteer System Law had allowed Korean males of seventeen or older to serve in the Japanese Army.[82] An chose this path two months before his scheduled graduation from Kendai. In fact, An was so close to completion of his Kendai program that the school administration decided to grant him a diploma. This episode clearly shows that An volunteered for army training in order to challenge the contradiction between the promised ideal of ethnic equality and the existing discrimination. Moreover, it demonstrates that he perceived the goal of "ethnic harmony" to be spontaneous partnership among equal peoples. Hence, An responded to the challenges of realizing "ethnic harmony" by committing himself to the cause rather than discarding the ideal in disappointment. His voluntary enlistment in the army in this context derived from his desire to prove that Koreans were equally capable and dedicated to the ideal of Pan-Asianism. Here, we find a case in which one's seeming support of Pan-Asianism and Japan's war, as demonstrated through voluntary enlistment in the Japanese Army, coexisted with his sense of Korean nationalism.

Like An, Kim Yeong-Rok (second entering class) embraced the dream of "ethnic harmony" and was quite honest in sharing his opinions with his classmates. He recalls one discussion meeting at his *juku* where students discussed the ways to make this goal a reality. According to Kim, someone said that the principle of *naisen ittai* could provide a model for the actual practice of "ethnic harmony" in Manchukuo, virtually proposing the Japanization of all peoples of distinct ethnic and cultural identities residing in Manchukuo. Kim openly opposed this opinion because he thought that *naisen ittai* was "the worst colonial policy" that sought to "annihilate the Korean ethnic nation."[83] In front of both Japanese and non-Japanese *juku*-mates, Kim described Japan's oppressive measures taken in Korea under the policy of *naisen ittai*—the prohibition of Korean language, requirement of paying homage to Shinto shrines, suppression of nationalist activities and so on. Then, Kim recalls, he ended his remark as follows: "If I held the power of life or death, I would kill half of the Japanese living in Korea."[84] Kim admits that his comment created a tense atmosphere, which urged the Mongolian student who was in charge of leading the discussion on that day to end the meeting abruptly.

Kim's outspoken personality drew three Chinese students close to him. Kim notes that he and the three used to converse through writing in the study room in the *juku* building. He does not provide the content of those conversations; but, it is highly likely that they discussed some sensitive matters that they did not want the other students, especially Japanese, to know. For, otherwise, they would have simply talked to each other out loud. One day, the three Chinese students invited Kim for a walk. At a quiet place on campus where no other people could hear them talk, the three asked Kim: "If we want to hold a meeting, should we inform the school administration of it, or should we keep it secret? We want to know what you think."[85] Kim replied: "How would I know what you should do? But, perhaps you can think about it more simply. If (the meeting) is welcomed by the school, let them know. If not, you cannot tell them."[86]

While this appears to be a simple and insignificant conversation, it certainly had some importance to Kim, who writes about it in his memoir. Kim believes that if he had asked for more details, his friends would have shared what they had in their minds. Kim did not ask because he thought the issue at hand must be a significant matter that "he should not get involved."[87] Nonetheless, the fact that the three students initiated this conversation with Kim appears to have made him quite happy. He writes, "unless they felt genuine trust toward [him]" they would not have talked to him in this manner.[88] This is one example of many interactions among non-Japanese students at Kendai. Without clearly stating, they could communicate who the word "we" referred to. In this case, it referred to the Chinese students. Such communication was possible because there were clear groupings on campus based on one's ethnic national identities both in an official level and in students' consciousness. Nonetheless, we should note that such an act of identifying oneself in a group presented a challenge for many students from Korea and Taiwan.

Hong Chun-Sik's (second entering class) experience shows two different types of interactions between the Korean and Chinese-speaking students on the Kendai campus. As mentioned earlier, Hong initially had no particular feeling toward Korean nationalism. He even admits that he behaved like a Japanese at that time. This was not surprising because Hong attended Keijō dai-ichi kōtō hutsū gakkō (Keijō higher regular school No. 1), the top public middle school for Korean children in Keijō, Korea, which served as a model school for *kōminka* education.[89] Hong's Japanese-like words and deeds invited two different reactions from his Chinese classmates at Kendai. He writes: "one person secretly told [him] about the current activities of Korean independence activists in China, while another person disparagingly said: 'You guys used to belong to China's vassal state. Stop behaving like Japanese."[90] The former person's comradely gesture apparently derived from his assumption of a shared resentment against Japan's expansionist policy in Asia. By contrast, the latter's comment intended to separate Koreans from Japanese by bringing up the past tributary relationship between imperial China and the Korean kingdom. Yet, both of these remarks reveal those Chinese students' resentment against Japan, which they assumed was to be shared by Hong, a Korean student. This also shows that ethnic national consciousness, colonialism, and war all shaped Kendai students' interpersonal relations.

In addition to this incident, one conversation with a group of Japanese classmates affected Hong's sense of identity. One day, he happened to be the only non-Japanese when several students were having a conversation. Noticing Hong's presence, one of them identified Hong as Japanese, saying, "Hear me out on this, as you are Japanese too."[91] Hong does not recall the content of the conversation that followed; however, he does remember finding himself in an awkward position. He could feel that the person who called him "Japanese" did so out of goodwill and perhaps the uneasiness about Hong's presence there. Through these two incidents and everyday interactions with his friends who had roots in different corners of East Asia, Hong gained a fuller sense of "the sorrow of the people who have lost their country."[92] Hence, a young Korean who arrived at Kendai in 1939, as one of the top students from a model school of *kōminka* education in Korea, gradually awakened to his Korean identity through interactions with his classmates at Kendai.

By contrast, when Bak Hui-Seong (sixth entering class) became a Kendai student in 1944, he already had a strong sense of Korean nationalism. He attended the required pre-matriculation orientation trip from Tokyo to Shinkyō with about ninety other prospective students of Japanese and Korean origins. During the trip, the incoming students had the opportunity of attending a banquet with the Japanese Korean Army's commander-in-chief, Itagaki Seiichirō. In the presence of this military dignitary, the students were asked to share their resolutions as prospective Kendai students. When it became his turn, Bak first talked about a Korean marathon runner who became a world champion and enthusiastically discussed how competent the Korean people are. Suddenly finding that his excited remark was not appropriate, Bak concluded his comment by stating that he was determined to "repay [his] deep debt of gratitude to the emperor by bringing forth such world-class Korean national characteristics at Kendai and working toward the realization of the founding principles of Manchukuo."[93] This entry shows that Bak knew the model answer expected of a colonized citizen at the time, which was a consequence of Japan's *kōminka* education in Korea.

On the other hand, some, although not many, Korean students continued to feel at ease in expressing their opposition to the incomplete practice of "ethnic harmony" at Kendai. The so-called separate meal incident of March 1944 shows one such example, as described by Kim Sang-Gyu (fifth entering class). The incident involved a violation of Kendai's proud tradition of absolute equality at meal serving. The Manchukuo government had a discriminatory grain ration system that prohibited the *mankei* residents from eating white rice. In order to keep control of the volatile economy of the newly established state, the government regulated production, export, import, and distribution of key items including steal, coal, and grain.[94] The ration system, which prioritized export of white rice to Japan, allowed a ration of white rice only to Japanese residents and the upper-class *mankei*; the Korean residents were given a mixture of white rice and millet; the *mankei* received sorghum, other coarse grains, and wheat, and the white Russians were allotted wheat. This ethnicity-based grain ration system was infamous in Manchukuo society, and especially embittered the *mankei* residents.[95] Kendai students of the first entering class collectively rejected this discriminatory practice and subverted the government's regulations. They collected rationed grains from all students, and mixed them all together so that all students ate the same food. In doing so, Kendai students upheld the principle of absolute equality in meal serving as part of their practice of the Pan-Asianist vision of "ethnic harmony" in clear defiance of the government policy.

When this proud tradition of Kendai was violated on March 9, 1944, Kim Sang-Gyu could not help but speak up against what he saw as contradicting the principle of "ethnic harmony." According to Kim, in the morning of that day, many Kendai students were shocked to find a sudden change in meal serving. Japanese and Koreans, who were recognized as Japan's imperial subjects, were served bowls of steamed white rice, while other students received sorghum gruel.[96] Although Kim does not provide the background of this incident, his Korean friend Kim Jae-Jin (fifth entering class) explains in his memoir that this unequal meal serving occurred because some Japanese students who had been drafted for military service insisted that they would eat white rice before leaving campus. Kim Jae-Jin writes: "I will never forget the courage of Kim Sang-Gyu, who protested in front of everyone, asking 'is this the spirit of ethnic harmony?'"[97] It is important to note that Kim Sang-Gyu remonstrated against this change in the meal system even though he, as Korean and thus a Japanese imperial subject in theory, received a bowl of white rice like the privileged group. In other words, what he was served did not matter to Kim. He raised his voice because equality was integral to the principle of "ethnic harmony" in Kim's understanding. Thus, we find evidence of an egalitarian perception of Pan-Asianism, embraced by a Korean youth as late as spring 1944. Moreover, he was willing to express it openly in public on the Kendai campus.

For Kim Yong-Hui (eighth entering class), who entered Kendai in 1945, encountering some of the "eccentric" Japanese students and faculty was quite confusing.[98] One day, his Japanese *juku*-mate Yamamoto Masao and a few other Japanese students called Kim out to the school yard "to have a heart-to-heart talk."[99] They asked Kim: "Do Koreans think it better to pursue *naisen ittai* as it's currently implemented? Or, do they hope to gain independence?"[100] This question startled Kim as he could not know whether it came from their genuine curiosity or from their scheme to trick him into disclosing some inappropriate ideas. He only answered that he "never thought about this issue and needs some time to think more."[101] In the end, Kim never spoke with them on this topic because apparently he could not trust these Japanese classmates. What appears like an overly cautious reaction by Kim should be placed in the context of tight control of speech in Korea under Japanese rule, which he had experienced all his life before moving to Kendai. One would be imprisoned for months or even a year for being caught expressing criticisms of Japan's policy in Korea.[102] Kendai's institutional commitment to freedom of speech makes a sharp contrast to the outside world; and there is no surprise in Kim's skepticism in this context. In retrospect, however, he writes in his memoir: "when I think of it now, there were some Japanese [at Kendai] with outstanding characters," which appears to imply the possibility of those Japanese classmates being such good-hearted ones.[103] He goes on to describe another such "outstanding" Japanese, a professor, who appears to be Fujita Matsuji, Professor of Agriculture.[104] Kim recalls that when this "eccentric" teacher mentioned the emperor during farm work at school, students stood stiffly at attention as normally required by other instructors. To Kim's surprise, this instructor told them: "Hey, the emperor is a human being too! You don't need to react that way."[105] This is a remarkable deviation from the Japanese official deification of the emperor, which provided grounding for the legitimacy of imperial rule. The fact that in his memoir Kim groups the Japanese classmates who asked him about *naisen ittai* together with this instructor indicates that he now thinks that his Japanese classmates' question came from their genuine curiosity. He describes these Japanese as "outstanding" and "eccentric" in the sense that they exhibited an unusually high level of curiosity and openness towards the colonized subjects and that their words and deeds diverged from the official line of thought.

Another member of the eighth entering class, Jeong Gi-Su, mentions in his memoir another such "eccentric" Japanese student, Horie Hiromasa of the sixth entering class. Jeong came to know Horie through a Korean student, Yu Chi-Jeong (sixth entering class). Yu and Horie were in charge of the management of the school cafeteria, and they and Jeong spent a lot of time together working there and going downtown to buy foods. Jeong writes of Horie as follows: "Even though Horie was Japanese, he became a firm supporter of Korean independence just as we [Koreans] were."[106] This brief comment reveals that some Korean students felt at liberty to share their opinions about colonial politics with certain Japanese classmates. It also shows an example of Japanese students developing political views that diverged significantly from Japan's official line through their close interactions with their non-Japanese classmates.

Voluntary enlistment in the army, 1943

Living among the diverse student body of Kendai, the Korean students had ample opportunities of contemplating their ethnic national identity. As seen previously, many Korean students recall various moments that prompted them to think about the complex position they found themselves in as Japanese imperial subjects coming from Korea. The student mobilization that occurred in the fall of 1943 was one such crucial event that pressed them to think hard about their identity.

The drafting of students was a massive empire-wide campaign to fill the ever-increasing wartime need of manpower. Previously, students enrolled in universities, higher schools, and vocational schools were exempt from military duties until the age of twenty-six. The Japanese government lifted this deferment in October 1943, starting to draft Japanese students of age twenty and over, except for students majoring in sciences and those who were being trained to become school teachers. The state conscripted Japanese students and celebrated ostentatiously with the catchword "departure of students for the front" (*gakuto shutsujin*). Due to legal issues, this new policy could not be applied to Korean and Taiwanese students. Nonetheless, the Japanese government implemented the Student Special Volunteer Soldier System in October 1943 that enabled Korean and Taiwanese males in higher education over the age of twenty to volunteer for the army.[107] Following the announcement, both the Government-Generals of Korea and Taiwan made a great effort to encourage eligible young men to volunteer to serve the army. As Brandon Palmer illustrates in the case of Korea, colonial authorities first gained the cooperation of the Korean elites "through financial and social inducements," and when the initial responses did not meet their expectation, the authorities "resorted to coercion to control and mobilize the Korean masses."[108] The early applications and enthusiastic responses largely came from the sons of elite Koreans. Nonetheless, in early November, two weeks into the application period, only around 15 percent (124 of 1,000) of eligible Korean students or recent graduates residing in Korea volunteered to join the army. Among the eligible Koreans residing in Japan, the rate was even lower; approximately 4 percent, or 90 out of 2,300 submitted applications.[109] Thus, colonial authorities began to use coercion. Mass media, school administrations, professors, teachers, pro-Japanese local leaders and even students' former middle-school teachers were mobilized to persuade eligible Korean students to "volunteer" for the army. Even police officers were dispatched to search for escapees and exert further pressure to submit applications.[110] By 1944, when general conscription began in Korea, 4,385, or 70 percent of all eligible Korean men had enlisted in the army as volunteer student soldiers,[111] joining 19,664 other Korean men who served the Japanese armed forces through regular volunteer soldier systems.[112] While similar statistics regarding the Student Special Volunteer Soldier System in Taiwan are not available, regular and student volunteer soldier systems enlisted a total of 16,500 Taiwanese as soldiers before general conscription began in March 1945.[113]

The student mobilization of 1943 affected the Korean students enrolled at Kendai in a slightly different manner than it did in Korea. As discussed in Chapter 3, the Manchukuo state did not have a law that defined Manchukuo citizenship. Korean residents in Manchukuo were registered both under the Korean Household Registration and Manchukuo's *minseki* ("people's register"). This generated uncertainty as to whether the Japanese government's announcement of the Student Special Volunteer Soldier System applied to Koreans residing in Manchukuo. The confusion about Manchukuo's political sovereignty could be found in the responses of Kendai's Korean students to the news of the Student Special Volunteer Soldier System. After the Kendai administration delivered the news in early October 1943, the Korean students engaged in serious discussion over whether to volunteer for the army. In his memoir, Kim Yeong-Rok (second entering class) explains how he and other Korean students felt pressure to volunteer:

Because Manchukuo was an independent state, the authorities could not immediately act on the new regulation [the Student Special Volunteer Soldier System] like they did in Japan and Korea. It initially appeared impossible to force voluntary enlistment on Koreans in Manchukuo. Soon, however, [the Manchukuo state] began to have a stance of accepting volunteers if any. Then, it started to solicit volunteers. It was a matter of time before the authorities in Manchukuo would force their way through as it happened in Korea and Japan.[114]

Kim's classmate, Hong Chun-Sik, also recalls a shared concern among the Korean students at that time. He writes: "Everyone knew by then that Japan would collapse and Korea would gain independence."[115] Therefore, Hong continues, "any Korean detested the idea of dying in this losing battle and thus not being able to savor the day of independence."[116] Unable to find a solution, the Korean students sought out the advice of Professor Choe Nam-Seon, who was quite busy at the time.

As mentioned previously, Choe had been a great resource and inspiration for many of the Korean students enrolled at Kendai. In fact, as a leading Korean historian of that time, Choe was also called upon to lead a group of other prominent Koreans to tour around university campuses in Japan to encourage Korean students to submit applications for the Student Special Volunteer Soldier System. To highlight the benefit of looking into the subjective experiences of Kendai's Korean students, I shall digress here to discuss Choe's encounter with a group of Korean students in Japan in a more public setting. The delegation was arranged by *chōsen shōgakukai*, a GGK-sponsored organization that supervised and controlled the Korean students in Japan. Choe, along with another famed Korean literary figure, Yi Kwang-su, led the delegation of ten other pro-Japanese Korean men, which was informally dubbed "the mission of glory." Starting on November 8, the delegation's oratorical tour covered university campuses in Tokyo, Kyoto, Osaka, and Hiroshima, and urged hundreds of—and perhaps more than one thousand—Korean students to voluntarily take up arms as Japanese.[117] Choe and Yi, who had once led the March First Independence Movement of 1919, argued in 1943 that serving Japan's armed forces would be an honor for Korean people, as they had much to learn from Japan. They also identified Western imperialism as a shared threat for Asians—a typical Pan-Asianist argument in support of the Japanese-led struggle against the West. It is easy to dismiss these Korean men of letters as "collaborators" of Japanese imperialism, working to obliterate Korean identity.[118] Indeed, the Japanese authorities must have recognized the words of such well-respected Koreans as effective tools to draw many reluctant Korean youths into enlistment. Certainly,

Choe and Yi must have been aware of this fact, too. Nonetheless, in the context of long-standing colonial rule that had cultivated close ties between the colonial authorities and the Korean elite, there is no surprise that one carefully conceals any signs of disconformity in such a public setting.

As expected, Choe's private conversation with Kendai's Korean students in the fall of 1943 gives a different impression of this man than a mere "collaborator" of imperialism. Hong Chun-Sik (second entering class) and Gang Yeong-Hun (third entering class) report in their memoirs what they heard from Choe. The fact that their descriptions are almost identical adds credibility to their recollections of Choe's words. According to Gang, Choe told his students that "military power and technologies" would be of the utmost importance once Korea became independent.[119] Gang continues to quote Choe: "Now that the Japanese Empire … is trying to use us Koreans, we must see this as an opportunity and take advantage of it to nurture our people's military power."[120] Likewise, Hong recalls Choe saying that "if you serve the [Japanese] military and gain knowledge, you'll later serve our country well."[121] If we reduce his words into the main message—that they should voluntarily enlist in the army—Choe was essentially providing these Kendai students with the same advice that he would offer in a more public setting in Japan. However, in this private conversation, Choe cited an ethnic nationalist reason for encouraging his Korean students to volunteer, rather than expounding on the official line of Pan-Asianism. Gang's and Hong's accounts reveal that Choe's advice derived from his patriotism towards Korea. He assured Kendai's Korean students that serving the Japanese armed forces would eventually benefit Korea once it gained independence. In this sense, Korean students' compliance with the Student Special Volunteer Soldier System could derive from their Korean nationalist aspiration for self-government and for the future of Korea.

After talking with Choe, Hong writes, the students finally decided that "all would volunteer for the army" and informed the Kendai administration of this decision.[122] On that night, the University hosted a special banquet for these students. One gets a different picture from Kim Yeong-Rok's recollection. According to Kim, while Kendai's Korean students were debating whether to volunteer for the army, a group of students asked the Korean students of the second entering class, who were the oldest Korean students enrolled at Kendai at that time, to make a decision for all younger students. When the students of the second entering class got together to discuss the matter, Kim proposed that they draw a lot, and half of the Korean students volunteer and the rest remain on campus to work for Manchukuo. He explains the rationale behind it in his memoir. The mission of Kendai's Korean students was, in Kim's understanding, "to work for the three million Korean residents in Manchukuo."[123] In order to ensure that at least some of them would be able to fulfill that mission, he believed, others must volunteer for the army in a show of cooperation. Kim thus suggested drawing a lot to make the selection of volunteers. He thought drawing a lot would make the selection fair for everyone. His classmates rejected this proposal. Still unable to find a solution, the group decided to leave the decision up to each student and their parents. Thus Kim went home to Korea to consult his parents. During his stay there, the university sent him a telegram to summon him to campus. When he returned to Kendai, Kim writes, the school administration "had already ordered all of its Korean students (who were eligible) to volunteer for the army."[124] This last statement contradicts with the aforementioned Hong Chun-Sik's account about the spontaneity of the Korean students' enlistment.

While there is no existing official record that clarifies this important point about Kendai's Korean students' enlistment, other evidence support Hong's version of the story. First, on November 12, 1943, a Japanese student, Yamashita Kōichi (fifth entering class), wrote in his diary that he learned about Korean students' decisions to volunteer. "I am deeply impressed to learn that all *senkei* students, without exception, are going to volunteer [for the army]. It's a prodigious feat, indeed."[125] Not surprisingly, Yamashita's diary does not indicate the nationalistic motive behind Korean students' decision. Nonetheless, it does show that the Kendai community perceived its Korean students' decision as voluntary and celebrated it. Second, Hong Chun-Sik indicates that of all the schools in Manchukuo, Korea, and Japan, Kendai was the only one in which all of its Korean students responded to the call for voluntary enlistment.[126] This fact itself does not directly answer the question of whether Kendai's Korean students voluntarily served the army. What is more indicative is Hong's explanation of why Kendai's Korean students were more responsive to the call compared to Korean students enrolled in other schools. He writes: "Having lived in Manchukuo and closely interacted with people of different ethnicities, we (Kendai's Korean students) knew too well the sorrow of belonging to a lesser ethnic nation. Thus, we could not help getting on the same boat."[127] Indeed, the Korean students were having an intense debate over whether to volunteer for the army. As we saw in Kim Yeong-Rok's account, the younger students even asked their seniors to determine a solution for *all* Korean students enrolled at Kendai. They seem to have wished to make a group decision rather than making it a problem for each individual. In this context, Hong's explanation cited earlier makes sense. It is unlikely that they volunteered willingly; nonetheless, it was their decision to respond to the call.

Then, why does Kim Yeong-Rok remember being ordered by the school administration to volunteer? I suspect that Kim's brief trip to his home at that time left him out from the final decision making of his fellow Korean students on campus. The application period for the Student Special Volunteer Soldier System was from October 25 to November 20, 1943. Hence, Kendai's Korean students made their final decision somewhere during this one-month period. Meanwhile, on October 21, the Kendai administration announced that those students who would join the army were not allowed to return home unless there was an extraordinary reason.[128] Kim's visit to his parents, thus, was an exception. Most—if not all—of his fellow Korean students remained on campus, engaging in further debate and making their collective decision to enlist in the army. Thus, it is likely that Kim, who was absent in the final decision-making process, mistook the decision of enlistment to be one forced on students by the university.

Despite the contradiction on the question of spontaneity, these three accounts by Hong Chun-Sik, Gang Yeong-Hun, and Kim Yeong-Rok reveal two intense emotions likely shared by Kendai's Korean students. One is the sense of hopelessness regarding their situation as colonial subjects residing in Manchukuo; there seems to have been no possibility of ignoring the pressure to "volunteer" for the army. The other is the strong desire to work for the Korean people. For Kim, this desire was so powerful that it convinced him to leave his own fate and that of his friends to a simple lottery. Likewise, Hong and Gang claim that it was precisely this same patriotic aspiration that pushed them to "volunteer" for the army.

Thus, the student mobilization of October 1943 provoked one last moment of deep self-reflection about identity before these Kendai students left campus. Whether they had believed in *naisen ittai* or independence, this occasion confirmed that they were different from Japanese, despite the official claim of the unity of the two peoples. The empire treated Japanese and Korean students differently, leaving the latter a choice, at least in theory. Moreover, the Korean students themselves felt about serving the army quite differently compared to their Japanese classmates. Hong Chun-Sik writes in his memoir that he and his Korean friends "envied [their] Japanese classmates who excitedly set their minds on serving their homeland."[129] In contrast to the Japanese students whose Japanese citizenship now required military service, the Korean students had to struggle to find reasons and meanings to enlist because of the choice given to them. Their campus life in Manchukuo continued to press them to contemplate the meaning of Korean nationalism. Furthermore, this challenge continued even after the end of the war. After returning to Korea, some chose the north and others the south as their new home. Even now, the Korean memoir collection only contains entries authored by those residing in South Korea. The whereabouts of many of those who chose to live in North Korea are not known.

A Taiwanese student's experience: Pursuing two dreams at the same time: to realize a Pan-Asianist Utopia in Manchukuo and to bring honor to a Taiwanese ethnic nation

Just as Taiwanese residents belonged to a tiny minority in Manchukuo, only a few Taiwanese students were enrolled at Kendai in each class. Li Shuiqing was one of the three Taiwanese students of the first entering class that matriculated at Kendai in 1938. His pre-university life in Taiwan characterizes Li as a highly aspiring and competent young man. After completing six years of primary education at the Japanese-run common school in Taiwan, he passed the competitive entrance exam of the commercial school.[130] To his disappointment, Li's parents could not afford the expensive school fee, and he chose to attend a night school instead. This bitter experience was somewhat typical of young, capable men of colonial Taiwan. Even though they went through assimilationist Japanization education and repeatedly heard the colonial officials' promises of making the Taiwanese equal to the Japanese, opportunities of post-primary education and employment were quite limited for them in Taiwan. Li did not give up, however. As introduced earlier in this chapter, he passed a competitive exam to become a civil official for the Government-General of Taiwan at the age of fifteen. Being an aspiring man, Li was not satisfied at that level of work. He moved to Tokyo and began preparing for the higher civil service exam. This exam was to select the best and brightest to serve the empire as high-ranking government officials. Because Taiwanese were recognized as Japanese citizens, Li was eligible to take this highly competitive exam. While he was studying hard for this exam, Li came to know about Kendai, a high seat of learning in Manchukuo that aimed to train government officials. As mentioned previously, Li chose to apply to Kendai because he felt it was a better career path than staying in Taiwan. He refers to the inequality and discrimination found in colonial Taiwan, and writes in his memoir that "the situation did not seem to improve in the future."[131] Thus, by matriculating at Kendai, Li seemed to have made a rational choice with his mind set on a goal of climbing up the ladder of social hierarchy within the empire.

What is interesting about his experience is that by the time he graduated from Kendai, Li was no longer interested in becoming an elite-track official. Instead, he desired to work in a remote rural village in Manchukuo, pursuing a Pan-Asianist dream of creating *ōdō rakudo* ("a peaceful land governed by the Kingly Way"). Li's memoir helps explain how this transformation occurred while he was enrolled at Kendai.

Moving from Taiwan to Manchukuo and suddenly becoming a "foreign" national, Li started to think deeply about who he really was. Li writes:

> In Taiwan, I needed to think only of my personal matters. The situation was completely different [at Kendai]; when thinking about myself, I had to consider my own origins, that is, my fellow Taiwanese and, even more broadly, the Han Chinese people. No one regarded me as one individual but rather saw me as a person from Taiwan or of Han ethnicity.[132]

Li suddenly found himself representing a Taiwanese ethnic nation whenever Kendai students and faculty engaged in discussion about lofty goals of creating "ethnic harmony." This was a fresh surprise for Li because, as he admits, he had been caught up with his personal achievements while in Taiwan. The difference between the political systems of Taiwan and Manchukuo also helps explain Li's response. In Taiwan, despite the *de facto* discrimination, Taiwanese were officially regarded as Japanese subjects. The colonial regime did not encourage Taiwanese to uphold their own distinct culture. On the contrary, the Manchukuo state's founding principles stipulate the harmonious coexistence of peoples of distinct ethnic and cultural identities. Kendai was to become the testing ground for the realization of such harmonious relationships. Naturally, the campus community expected Li to represent the Taiwanese ethnic nation.

Li's awakened sense of Taiwanese identity brought him close to other Taiwanese residents in Manchukuo. He often visited those Taiwanese who worked for Manchukuo's government agencies or nearby universities. For instance, Li was one of the participants at the evening study meetings hosted by Wu Jinchuan of the Central Bank of Manchukuo. Because Wu's residence was five kilometers away from Kendai, Li had to obtain his *jukutō*'s permission to take leave and miss end-of-the-day meetings at *juku*. It is interesting to note that Li had no problem getting approval for these outings.[133] Besides, he frequented the homes of other Taiwanese who lived in Shinkyō City. Li fondly recalls one such meeting with Guo Songgen, Professor at Medical University of Shinkyō.[134] Guo told Li and his friend that for Taiwanese as a small ethnic nation to be recognized in the world, they must foster as many top class talents as possible in every field. Li shared this belief. He writes:

> For our fellow Taiwanese who reside in Taiwan under the Japanese rule, it is impossible to come to the front regardless of their abilities. But, if we find opportunities outside of Taiwan, we can prove ourselves by fully exerting our potentials ... Although we are all Japanese by law, we strongly identify ourselves with the Han ethnicity.[135]

Hence, close interactions with other Taiwanese residents in Manchukuo reinforced Li's sense of Taiwanese identity as well as the sense that he belonged to a broader ethnic group of Han Chinese. He found a new meaning to his hard work at school—to make his mark in the world as a representative of the Han people from Taiwan.

Li's response to Kendai's curriculum was very positive. As a member of the first entering class, he spent most of his school life when Sakuta Sōichi was leading the Kendai administration. As indicated by a number of students, Kendai's Pan-Asianist education was in its prime under Sakuta's leadership. Particularly, the administration put a great amount of effort into *juku* education. Li characterizes Kendai's *juku* as a place where teachers (*jukutō*) and students learned together by engaging in honest dialogue. Students spontaneously organized a number of study groups and invited faculty members as speakers. Those meetings were normally held in the evening, but professors and *jukutō* willingly gave their time. The essence of what he learned at *juku* was, Li writes, that one must "pursue the primary purpose of life ... without seeking personal fame and gain."[136] By the late 1930s and early 1940s when Li was enrolled at Kendai, Japan's education emphasized *kōminka*, or imperialization, not only in Japan but also in Taiwan and Korea. Intending to foster loyalty to Japan's imperial leadership, schools across the empire clearly defined the "primary purpose of life" for all subjects—it was, of course, to work for the empire. In Li's perception, Kendai's *juku* education was directly opposite to this trend. The university openly encouraged its students to define the "primary purpose of life" on their own.

From Li's perspective, Kendai students were doing just that. One example that he cites is the creation of the equal meal system that I have discussed earlier. Many former students of Kendai—both Japanese and non-Japanese—mention this tradition as a notable characteristic of the Kendai community. As a member of the first entering class that initiated this school tradition, Li explains how he and other students thought about it.

At that time, we thought it all natural that we ate the same meal because we shared all other aspects of life [in *juku*] … it was nothing special for us, not a subject worthy of mention. Besides, we were undertaking the same farm work and labor that ordinary peasants would do. How could we not eat the same meal that those peasants were having? If we could not eat the foods produced locally, how could we go out to the corners [of Manchukuo] to serve the country?[137]

This passage reveals that the student body regarded equality as essential to their lived experiment of "ethnic harmony." Equally notable is Li's emphasis on the spontaneity in the creation of the equal meal system. In Li's summation, the students of the first entering class of Kendai were genuinely committed to the vision of harmonious relationships on the basis of equality, and they were determined to serve Manchukuo.

During the course of his study at Kendai, Li developed close relationships with some of the Japanese faculty members and others who supported Ishiwara Kanji's vision of an East Asian League. As discussed in Chapter 2, Ishiwara advocated the creation of a Pan-Asian political alliance to counter the threat coming from the West. Associate Professor Tagawa Hiroaki was one of the Japanese faculty members with whom Li established genuine trust. During the summer break of 1941, Li and two of his classmates visited Tagawa in Chengdu, a southwestern prefecture of Manchukuo. During their stay, Tagawa asked Li to read the manuscript of his article for feedback. Tagawa took Li to a café that was beyond the reach of the Japanese military so that they could freely exchange opinions. While not remembering details, Li recalls the main point of the article was to call for the creation of a new order in East Asia. In their long discussion, Li made remarks on two points. First, Li told his teacher that his article failed to understand that Chinese communists' Eight Route Army was fighting against the Japanese "not just for communism but also for the survival of the ethnic nation."[138] Second, Li frankly pointed out the gap between the Japanese authorities' words and deeds and told Tagawa that discussing lofty ideals in the article was not timely. This second remark appeared to have derived from his observation of the harsh living condition of peasants in Chengdu under Japanese rule. Drawing from a story of Mongolian conquest of China in the thirteenth century, he shared a passage: "if one does not follow the way of morality, how could he discuss the Mandate of Heaven?"[139] It is remarkable that Li could feel at liberty to share with his Japanese teacher such direct criticisms of Japan's rule. He also notes that Tagawa, while seeming a little disappointed, sympathized with the passage that Li shared. This episode shows an example of one characteristic of Kendai, which Li terms "*shitei kyūgaku* ('mentor and disciple learning together')."[140]

By the time the arrest of a number of Kendai's Chinese students shook the campus in 1941 and 1942, Li had developed a clear understanding of what "ethnic harmony" meant for Kendai students. Among Li's eight Chinese *juku*-mates, three were taken by the military police. When the remaining students talked about this incident, Li told them: "this isn't a personal problem of those who were arrested. It's a problem that we together have to solve ... Because so much injustice exists in the society outside [Kendai], we must make even greater efforts to make our ideal [of 'ethnic harmony'] a reality."[141] Li's *juku*-mates agreed with him, he notes. Li believed that creating "ethnic harmony" required two steps. First, "one must recognize his own ethnic national identity."[142] Then, "one must be able to put himself in the shoes of others."[143] Through this process, there emerged a mutual understanding, Li believed, that is called the "true harmony of peoples of different ethnicities."[144] In that sense, it appears that this Pan-Asianist ideal was not far from reality, at least from Li's perspective. For, he states, the arrest of Chinese students led to "deeper friendship among the students," which implies that the students were able to share their feelings about the incident and reach some understanding, regardless of their different backgrounds.[145]

At the same time, Li recognized that Kendai students were increasingly disappointed at the world surrounding them. He believed that Ishiwara's vision of creating an East Asian League through cooperation among Japan, China, and Manchukuo had given hope to the students who were committed to Pan-Asianism. By the early 1940s, however, the drawn-out Sino–Japanese War and the Kwantung Army's increasing interference with the Kendai administration swayed their determination. The situation worsened when Sakuta resigned from the position of Vice President, to be replaced by Suetaka Kamezō, a military man. Li describes the suffering that he believed was shared by Kendai students around that time as follows: "Even though the students of different ethnicities felt deep friendship and understanding, they could not share the same goal. All they could do was to work for their own goals despite the fact that none of them could see a rosy future ahead of them."[146]

While some students, especially non-Japanese, lost hope in the Pan-Asianist ideal that Kendai and Manchukuo were to represent, Li personally continued to set his mind on working for it. The following episode shows both Li's disillusionment with the new Vice President Suetaka and Li's determination to work for the nation-building of Manchukuo. In November 1942, Suetaka invited all students of the first entering class, two at a time, to his residence to stay with him for one day. Through this one-day live-in guidance, Suetaka hoped to personally train the students who were scheduled to graduate from Kendai the following year. When Li and his Japanese classmate Ōsawa Chōtarō were having dinner with Suetaka, he asked about the two students' career plans after graduation. Assuming that Li wanted to return to Taiwan, Suetaka said that if Li would like, he "could write a recommendation letter to the military commander" in Taiwan.[147] Li replied without a moment's pause: "I do not wish to return [to Taiwan]. Taiwan does not need us because there are many talents. By contrast, here [in Manchukuo] many more works must be done, and there is not enough manpower."[148] Clearly, Suetaka's suggestion came from his goodwill. However, it disappointed Li because he thought Suetaka "failed to understand the primary purpose of Kendai's foundation," which was to foster a generation of leaders who would make Manchukuo a Pan-Asian utopia.[149] A similar recommendation was made for Li and his Taiwanese classmate by another Kendai professor, shortly after they graduated from Kendai. At that time, too, they rejected the offer for the same reason.[150]

Indeed, Li planned to stay in Manchukuo and work for the development of rural villages. As early as the winter of 1940, he had already set his mind on this plan. When he had a chance to talk with Tsuji Masanobu, Ishiwara Kanji's right-hand man who had contributed to the founding of Kendai, Li described his career plan to Tsuji as follows. He hoped to work at one of the youth training centers built in every prefecture of Manchukuo. "[T]ogether with peasants there," Li wished to "raise the level of education and industry so that [Manchukuo's] rural villages could catch up with those in Taiwan and Japan as quickly as possible."[151] As we have seen, this plan is remarkably different from the kind of career path that Li had envisioned before moving to Manchukuo. After spending two years on the Kendai campus, Li was no longer interested in climbing up the social ladder to join the elite. Rather, he wished to enter the lower section of society, working to realize the lofty ideal of "ethnic harmony" in Manchukuo. Furthermore, Li even suggested to Tsuji that all Kendai graduates should work at the youth training centers to cover all 167 locations throughout Manchukuo.[152] Thus, by the fall of 1942, when Suetaka offered him a helping hand that could open a way for Li to get into the elite group of the colonial hierarchy in Taiwan, this option no longer interested him.

Nonetheless, Li took up a position at the Ministry of Foreign Affairs under Manchukuo's State Council after completing the ten-month training course at Daidō Gakuin, which was required of all Kendai graduates. This change of mind did not indicate the weakness of Li's will to work for Manchukuo's rural peasants. On the contrary, the story behind this change of course reveals Li's dedication to the ideal of Pan-Asianism. From late May to early June, 1943, right before

Kendai held its first graduation ceremony, former Vice President Sakuta Sōichi visited the university to deliver special lectures. At that time, Sakuta summoned Li to have a secret talk. According to Li, Sakuta told him that a Kendai faculty member, Professor Nakayama Masaru, and the aforementioned Tsuji Masanobu were currently in Nanjing, China. Then, Sakuta asked if Li would like to join them after graduating from Kendai. Although Sakuta did not specify what tasks Nakayama and Tsuji were undertaking, Li could immediately understand that they were working to find a way to achieve China–Japan peace.[153] For, Nakayama, Tsuji, and, to a certain extent, Sakuta all supported Ishiwara Kanji's vision of an East Asian League. Li responded to Sakuta that he wanted to go to Nanjing. Li explains in his memoir that he could "sacrifice anything for the withdrawal of Japanese troops from the continent and for complete peace" between China and Japan.[154] He regretted that he would not be able to dedicate his life to the rural development of Manchukuo as he had planned; however, he could count on his "classmates who would be working [at the youth training centers] in all prefectures along the Great Wall."[155] What this story exposes is that Li was strongly committed to the type of Pan-Asianism that Ishiwara advocated—the idea that cooperation among Japan, China, and Manchukuo was the key to creating an East Asian League and that the development of Manchukuo would provide a model for the new order.

Unfortunately, the effort of Nakayama and Tsuji in Nanjing was not leading to any positive result. Li spent half a year doing office work at the Ministry of Foreign Affairs in Shinkyō and waited for his turn to move to Nanjing. That chance never came. By mid-1944, Li grew frustrated, feeling that he alone was not doing any meaningful work when most of his Japanese classmates had been drafted and his non-Japanese friends were engaging in the rural development of Manchukuo. After consulting a few of Kendai's Japanese faculty members who believed in the vision of an East Asian League, Li left his job and applied for a position at youth training centers. When he was notified of an opening at Gannan Prefecture in Qiqihaer City, Li was reluctant to take up that position because the place was already "abundant in agricultural crops," and he "wanted to go to a peripheral region that was full of challenges."[156]

In February 1945, Li finally landed the job of his dreams: manager of the youth training center at Weichang Prefecture in Rehe Province. Located on the southwestern frontier of Manchukuo, the region was important in defending against Chinese communist forces. Weichang was a designated cultivation area for opium poppies, yielding 75 percent of all opium produced in Manchukuo.[157] The residents, who were mostly Han Chinese, were largely uneducated and illiterate. Li could find opium addicts throughout the prefecture. The youth center, which was administered under the Concordia Association (kyōwa kai), was to provide these rural young men with basic education and training so that they would become leading members of the Manchukuo Imperial Army or the Labor Service Corps in that region. In his memoir, Li admits that such a youth training program was part of the Japanese effort of mobilizing youth for the war. The center's program, which typically ran for a few months, was vital for successful implementation of Manchukuo's Labor Service Act of 1942 that required all men between the ages of twenty-one and twenty-three who were not serving the military to fulfill labor service for twelve months.[158] At the same time, however, Li writes that he believed in the potential of its long-term impact—"bringing education to the mass and encouraging the local people to unite ... so that they would be able to create a modern state."[159]

As a manager and an instructor at the youth training center, Li modeled himself after the Kendai faculty members whom he continued to respect. For instance, just as Kendai's *jukutō* did, Li lived in the dormitories together with his students.[160] Even though he received rationed foods that were of higher quality compared to those allotted to his students, he ate the same meals as his students. When he realized that the rationed foods were not enough, Li and his students transformed a tract of unused land into a vegetable garden and grew potatoes and other vegetables that could be served as additional dishes. This project, too, Li states, was modeled after Kendai's agricultural training. Li's students thus cultivated vegetables as part of their training to nurture physical strength and the spirit of self-reliance.[161]

Li was as committed to his students' education and wellbeing as his own mentors at Kendai. He made an exception to admit a particularly underprepared young man, Jiang Huai, on the condition that Jiang would master basic reading and writing skills through Li's one-on-one tutoring for one hour each night after everyone went to sleep. At the end of the training program, Jiang was selected, as one of the most capable trainees, to form a Youth Action Group (*seinen kōdō tai*), an elite group that engaged in various tasks such as propaganda and information gathering.[162] Li also dedicated his time and effort to the rehabilitation of his trainees who were addicted to opium. Until they overcame addiction, Li would not let them return home.[163]

Thus, a young man from Taiwan, who had once aspired to work his way up to the elite, found himself busy working together with Manchukuo's rural youths. He was not just fulfilling his duties; he was taking great initiatives at work, which he believed would lead to the educational and industrial development of this remote region. When looking at the surface, the Kendai administration and the Manchukuo government could cite Li's experience to boast about the university's success in fostering such a dedicated young leader in support of Manchukuo's ideological construct. His case was particularly remarkable because Li was not from Japan but from Taiwan, Japan's colony. But, when looking into the subjective experience of this young Taiwanese student, we realize that his dedication to the Pan-Asianist dream in Manchukuo was shaped by his nationalist aspiration to make a mark to assert Taiwanese citizenship within the increasingly hierarchical and oppressive Japanese Empire. In other words, Li came out of the University being a staunch Pan-Asianist and a Taiwanese nationalist.

Li's endeavor toward Manchukuo's nation-building was suddenly terminated when Japan capitulated and Manchukuo collapsed in August 1945. Although Soviet troops crossed the Manchukuo border on August 9, the news did not reach Li in the rural village. It was as late as August 15 that Li heard a rumor of a massive Soviet invasion and of its conquest of Harbin, an important city 170 miles north of Shinkyō. On the following day, Li visited the Concordia Association's prefectural headquarters and met the Japanese General Manager whom Li recalls as Yokose. Yokose did not share with Li the important news about Japan's surrender. Instead, he ordered Li to have the Youth Action Group destroy the Weichang Airport and public roads to obstruct the Soviet troops' advance. Even though Li still did not know of Japan's capitulation at the time, he felt that the situation was much worse than he had imagined. After returning to the training center and receiving Yokose's order to meet him at the headquarters once again, Li and one of his subordinates who had helped Li manage the training center decided to hide themselves from the Japanese supervisors. Thus, Li's work for the dream of an East Asian League abruptly fell apart, leaving him feeling bitter toward his Japanese supervisor, who betrayed him at the crucial moment. What followed was an eight-month journey that finally brought him home to Taiwan in April 1946. He remembers this trip as an arduous one in which he had to hide himself from not only Japanese but also Soviet troops and Chinese communists.

Conclusion

In terms of Japan's policy and official pronouncements, Pan-Asianism found different expressions in different parts of the empire: Korea and Taiwan, on one hand, and Manchukuo, on the other. In the former, the colonial authorities implemented assimilation policy, claiming to make the local population the same as the Japanese. By contrast, the Manchukuo government sought to create a unity among peoples of distinct ethnic and cultural identities under the slogan of "ethnic harmony." Thus, within the Japanese Empire, one finds different models of Pan-Asianism expressed in official terms.

This difference seems to have shaped the experiences of Kendai's Korean and Taiwanese students in three ways. First, the difference within the empire presented them with options of staying in their home countries or moving to a new place. They had the privilege of choosing between these options because they had been top students at their middle schools. As seen in this chapter, reasons for deciding to enroll at Kendai differed among individual students. For many of them, Kendai's prestige, generous financial aids, and the promise of secure employment after graduation presented practical appeals. For others, the vision of "ethnic harmony" upheld by Kendai aroused curiosity. Whichever it was, they made a conscious choice on their own volition when moving to Manchukuo to attend Kendai.

Second, the differing expressions of Pan-Asianism in formal colonies and Manchukuo complicated their sense of identity. In formal colonies, they grew up being told that they were Japan's imperial citizens while simultaneously being discriminated against in the colonial school system. After moving to Manchukuo, although they were officially "Japanese," the Manchukuo society and especially the Kendai community often regarded them as representing the Korean or Taiwanese ethnic nation. Again, they had a choice of how they wished to identify themselves. Indeed, the former Korean students' memoirs reveal that their opinions were divided between the *naisen ittai* principle and the aspiration for Korean national independence.

Third, Manchukuo's stated promise to encourage harmonious co-existence of diverse peoples created room for idealists to act on the egalitarian version of Pan-Asianism. The idealistic part of Kendai such as the equal meal system and some open-minded Japanese faculty members and classmates appeared quite foreign to the students from formal colonies. Essays written by Kendai's former Korean and Taiwanese students show that such commitment to equality was welcomed by many of these students. Some authors even express enthusiastic support for Pan-Asianism, which is absent in the Chinese alumni's recollections, as we will observe in the next chapter. Li Shuiqing's experience is a prime example of genuine support for Pan-Asianism expressed by Kendai's non-Japanese students. As seen in this chapter, Li truly embraced the Pan-Asianist dream of creating an East Asian League.

At the same time, these students' experiences show that Kendai's and Manchukuo's iterations of "ethnic harmony" never fully convinced them that Japan's colonial relationship with Korea and Taiwan did not matter in Manchukuo, an ostensibly independent state. Despite the stated ideals, segregation and discrimination prevailed in Manchukuo society, especially outside the Kendai campus. In addition, the opportunities of close interactions within the diverse student body and beyond the campus influenced them to identify more strongly with their own ethnic nations. When Korean students finally decided to volunteer for military service, they did so for the sake of the Korean people and not for the Japanese Empire. Even Li, who had become a strong supporter of Ishiwara's vision of an East Asian League, kept in his mind that he was representing the Taiwanese and that his personal achievements would bring honor to Taiwan. In that sense, these students pursued their own dreams while participating in Kendai's experiment of Pan-Asianist education.

Learning to become "Chinese" at a Japanese school: Chinese students' experiences at Kenkoku University

Today in the People's Republic of China (PRC), Kenkoku University is officially known as *Weiman jianguo daxue*, Bogus Manchukuo Nation-Building University. While a number of Kendai's Japanese alumni have published full length memoirs, and the Japan-based alumni association and class organizations have published collections of short essays by their members reminiscing about their school days, very few writings by Chinese alumni appeared until the late 1990s. For this reason, earlier works on Kendai had a limited amount of written materials about former Chinese students' experiences. The two foundational academic works by Eriko Miyazawa and Fumiaki Shishida nonetheless provide invaluable information based on their interviews with Chinese alumni.[1]

In 1997, six decades after the founding of the university, fifty-eight Chinese alumni published the first anthology of recollections to appear in print in the PRC, *Huiyi weiman jianguo daxue* [*Remembering Bogus Manchukuo Nation-Building University*] (hereafter *Huiyi*). This collection, although produced under undeniable political constraints, makes an invaluable contribution to the research archive.[2] This chapter attempts to recover the experiences of Kendai's former Chinese students by mining these source materials.[3]

While historical memory is an issue in all retrospective literature, the recollections written by Kendai's former Chinese students and published in the PRC present the particular problem of how to read narratives produced under severe political constraints. After Japan's defeat in WWII in 1945 and the dissolution of Kendai and Manchukuo, former Chinese students were thrown into chaotic political struggle during the Chinese Civil War (1946–49). After the communist victory and the establishment of the PRC, they faced varying degrees of political persecution as *hanjian* ("national traitor"), due to Kendai's close association with Japanese imperialism in China. Nevertheless, the improvement in relations between Japan and the PRC beginning in the 1980s created an opening. In 1995, seventeen former Chinese students of Kendai established an editorial committee, sponsored by the Changchun City Government's Chinese People's Political Consultative Committee, to solicit and publish recollections of the Chinese Kendai alumni. Changchun City used to be the capital of Manchukuo, Shinkyō, and many former Chinese students lived in the city in the 1990s.[4] In the preface of the *Huiyi* collection, the editors state that the project commenced in commemoration of the "fiftieth anniversary of the end of the Anti-Fascist War and China's Anti-Japanese War of Resistance."[5] Recognizing that Kendai itself was the "product of and historical evidence of Japanese political and cultural invasion in China," the editors claim that recording their experiences of Kendai "will benefit patriotic education of youths today and in the future."[6] As seen in the language used, the editors of the *Huiyi* collection were conscious of the political baggage of having been students at Kendai.

A recent encounter between a Japanese journalist Hideyuki Miura and Chinese alumni Yang Zengzhi (first entering class) and Gu Xueqian (seventh entering class) illuminates the severe political constraints Kendai's former students still face in the PRC. Miura visited them in Dalian and Changchun in 2010 to conduct interviews. His meeting with Yang at a café at Dalian Hotel was cut short by a man who claimed to be Yang's son, when Yang began sharing his experience of the communist military blockade of Changchun (1948).[7] No further meeting could be arranged. All three letters Miura sent to Yang since then never reached him.[8] Moreover, Miura's scheduled meeting with the other alumnus, Gu Xueqian, Professor of Japanese Literature at Northeast Normal University, was abruptly cancelled a few hours before the promised time. A staff member of the university called Miura to inform that the Education Ministry had cancelled the meeting. In despair, Miura called Gu, and the two had a brief conversation on the phone that they both knew was being tapped by the PRC authorities. Gu told Miura how much he had looked forward to the meeting and how saddened he was to learn that the authorities still considered him suspicious. In fact, as a son of Manchukuo's high-ranking governmental official and as a former Kendai student himself, Gu had endured decades of political persecution until 1979 when the CCP exonerated all of his past "offenses." Gu went on to become PRC's leading scholar on Japanese literature. Still, in 2010, Gu could do nothing but cry on one side of the phone when the communist government obstructed his meeting with a Japanese journalist.[9]

Given the degree of constraints that the authors faced, there is no surprise that the *Huiyi* anthology presents a uniformly negative view on Kendai. It is perhaps tempting to dismiss such a politically charged narrative as a history in the service of the CCP. However, even after allowing for the ideological and political limits of the production, the *Huiyi* essays show how the Chinese students' experiences diverged from Kendai's official goal of instilling Pan-Asianism as the dominant political consciousness and forging a community of supporters of the ideology. Moreover, the close reading of *Huiyi* reveals a subtle variation in the Chinese students' experiences of Kendai. Following analysis of the *Huiyi* essays, the last section of this chapter will focus on two short memoirs authored by former Chinese students and printed in *Hakki [Eight flags]*, an anthology of reminiscences published in Japan in 1985.[10] Authored by two of the few former Chinese students who responded to the request of the Japanese alumni group to contribute to their volume, these essays in *Hakki* present a different perspective from those in *Huiyi*. By reading these two essays in comparison with the *Huiyi* entries, the last section will attempt to add further nuances to our understanding of the Chinese students' experiences at Kendai.

Going to the colonizers' school: Motives for applying to Kendai and their arrivals on campus

Between 1938 and 1945, about 520 Chinese students attended Kendai.[11] Except for a few who were from China proper, all of them came from various provinces throughout Manchukuo and the Kwantung Leased Territory.[12] Almost all of them graduated from National Higher School (*kokumin kōtō gakkō*), which taught pupils of thirteen to seventeen years of age who were non-Japanese residents of Manchukuo.[13] It is important to keep in mind that they attended Kendai of their own volition. These young Chinese students chose to apply to the school, passed highly competitive entrance exams, and received hearty congratulations from their families and friends when they gained admission to Kendai. Historian Eriko Miyazawa highlights the impoverished family background of some of the former Chinese students. Indeed, many of the essays published in *Huiyi* concur with that view. Nonetheless, it is also important to note that some were from well-to-do families of the Chinese migrant settlers in the Manchurian region.[14] What drove these Chinese teenagers to apply to a university that was established by Japan, a country that was at war with China?

First, Kendai's generous scholarship attracted students from poor families. Tuition and living expenses were paid in full by the Manchukuo government. Of twenty other institutions of higher education in Manchukuo as of 1939, twelve national universities and a normal university offered full tuition scholarships to all enrolled students.[15] However, Kendai's former Chinese students stress the particular generosity of Kendai's scholarship. In addition to all necessities such as "uniforms, caps …, a pair of leather shoes and sneakers …, gloves, a lunch box, a water bottle, a school bag, [and] school supplies," students received monthly allowances of five yen.[16] Medical fees were waived, too.[17] Second, Kendai's six years' course of study, longer than the three- to four-year programs at other colleges in Manchukuo, held out the promise of a more complete education. Indeed, Kendai and Shinkyō University of Law and Politics were the only general universities; all other national universities in Manchukuo provided technical education.[18] Third, Kendai offered a secure career path to its graduates. After a three-month period of training at the Daidō Gakuin, Manchukuo's government clerk training institution, all graduates were promised positions in state or local governments or in the Kyōwakai (Concordia Association), a state-sponsored civil organization dedicated to the principle of creating "ethnic harmony." The guaranteed government-sector jobs must have been particularly appealing to the young Chinese residents of Manchukuo considering the fact that important white-collar jobs tended to be dominated by Japanese residents. Finally, as I will show in this chapter, Kendai's reputed commitment to the ideal of "ethnic harmony" seemed to have had a measure of appeal to Chinese applicants.

The competitiveness of Kendai's entrance exams, rather than deterring applicants, was an added incentive. Many of the *Huiyi* entries mention it. The entrance examination consisted of written exams on math, geography, history, composition, and Japanese language proficiency; a physical exam; and interviews.[19] The interviews were conducted in both Chinese and Japanese to test applicants' skills in Japanese, which was Kendai's language of instruction. The exams were especially competitive in the early years. Yan Tingqiao (first entering class) recalls that he "was among the four who passed the exam out of two hundred applicants from Harbin Daiichi Middle School."[20]

Even though *Huiyi* authors often note the competitiveness of Kendai, they rarely elaborate on their desire to enter the university. If they write about their motives for applying to Kendai, they do so only in passing and stress that they became disappointed immediately after the school started. Pei Rong (fifth entering class) begins his memoir by mentioning his "burning desire for learning" that led him to Kendai but was extinguished as soon as he arrived on campus.[21]

Zhang Wensheng (seventh entering class) states that he chose to attend Kendai because it provided everything for free, but was immediately disheartened by the skimpy portions served at meals. By 1944 when Zhang matriculated, Kendai was also subject to restrictive food rationing.[22]

Yue Yishi (first entering class), whose motives for attending Kendai were similar to Zhang Wensheng's, writes at length about his subsequent disillusionment. First, he was shocked when the university provided students with a rifle along with school supplies. Yue's intention in noting this shock is to highlight his naïve expectation of leading a life of learning, which was betrayed by the militaristic curriculum of Kendai. Second, the haughty attitudes of his Japanese classmates angered him. He recalls his feeling at the time: "both the sky and the earth (of Manchukuo) belong to China. How come the Japanese behave so arrogantly?!"[23] He writes that he did not interact with the Japanese students but hung out only with a few Chinese classmates. Third, rather than experiencing *juku*, Kendai's integrated student residences, as a gesture toward the principle of "ethnic harmony," he criticizes it as a tool to "keep the Chinese students under surveillance."[24] Finally, Yue claims that the language barrier further alienated him from Kendai education. He complains that much of the instruction was given in Japanese, which significantly impeded his studies, because he "had no interest in learning" the language.[25] Considering the fact that all non-Japanese students had to pass highly competitive entrance exams including Japanese language proficiency, Yue's testimony raises a number of questions, including his desire to show that he was not a cultural traitor of China.[26]

As shown in these three *Huiyi* essays, the Chinese anthology is awash with episodes of authors' instant disillusionment with school life at Kendai; however, one can find some evidence of positive first impressions the university made on them. For example, Yu Jiaqi (first entering class) stresses that Kendai's entrance exams were not only competitive but also administered with strict fairness. As evidence, he states that even the son of Kendai's President Zhang Jinghui failed the exams.[27] Other authors agree that Kendai's entrance exams were known to be free from favoritism and class bias, which attracted some Chinese applicants. In addition, some authors mention their first meal on campus. All students were served a bowl of rice mixed with sorghum as a staple diet, which is one example of Kendai's practice of egalitarianism, as discussed in previous chapters. The practice of absolute equality in meal servings starkly distinguished Kendai from the formal and informal patterns of Japanese privilege that were ubiquitous outside the university. This was so pleasantly surprising that even the contributors to *Huiyi*, who tend to be critical about Japanese imperialism and Kendai, mention it favorably.

Kendai education and *Juku* life

For many Chinese students, the heavily ideological education and the *juku* life
that was filled with Japanese rituals were the sources of further disappointment
with Kendai. To begin with, many took notice of the imbalance in the faculty's
ethnic identities, which appeared inconsistent with the institution's stated
promise of the equal treatment of peoples of different ethnic and cultural
backgrounds. Although Kendai administrators planned to invite prominent
scholars and even revolutionary activists from around the world to join the
faculty, their effort met with mixed success, as previously discussed.[28] In the end,
all but a small minority of the faculty were Japanese. Gao Ke (eighth entering
class) writes that "Japanese professors constituted 90 %" of the Kendai faculty.[29]
According to the list of the courses that Yu Jiaqi (first entering class) took,
non-Japanese faculty members typically taught relatively "dry" subjects such
as mathematics, bookkeeping, and languages, while Japanese professors taught
the more ideological courses.[30] As Gao's and Yu's accounts indicate, Japanese
instructors continued to dominate the Kendai faculty throughout its short
history from 1938 to 1945. In addition, *Huiyi* essays point out rightly that the
majority of the Japanese faculty advocated Japan-centered political views such
as *kōdō* ("imperial way") and *hakkō ichiu*, which means "the entire world under
a single roof," a metaphor for Japan's imperial expansion in Asia and beyond. In
the words of Yan Defan (first entering class), many of the Japanese professors
were not independent thinkers and true intellectuals but "scholars in the service
of Imperial Japan."[31] As we saw in Chapter 2, there is a good deal of truth to what
may appear to be a blanket statement.

While criticisms against the Japanese professors were common, one can also
find quite a few instances of *Huiyi* authors denouncing those they regarded as
traitors among non-Japanese faculty members. "*Doufu zongli* ('Prime Minister
Bean Curd')" and "*doufu jiang* ('bean curd cooker')" were the epithets of ridicule
that the Chinese students secretly applied to Kendai's President Zhang Jinghui.
Zhang, a Chinese politician and the Prime Minister of Manchukuo, who also
held the position of Kendai's President, was so obsequious to the Japanese
authorities as to appear emasculated. His perceived personality of being weak
and frail matched the texture of bean curd; and in fact, he once had been a bean
curd manufacturer, thus providing grounds for the perfect epithets. Within
Kendai's administrative structure, too, Zhang Jinghui was president in name
only; all administrative authority was exercised by the Japanese Vice President
Sakuta Sōichi, who was succeeded by Suetaka Kamezō in 1942.[32] Another non-

Japanese faculty member who became a target of *Huyi* authors' criticisms is a Mongolian professor, Gao Qiyuan. He disheartened the Chinese students because he spoke disparagingly of *baihua*, the Chinese vernacular prose style that was the hallmark of Chinese Nationalist writers.[33]

Not surprisingly, most criticisms of the instruction they received are targeted at the Japanese faculty and the courses they taught. For instance, Liu Shize (fifth entering class) condemns the course devoted to expounding the theory of "ethnic harmony." He recalls that the instruction was in fact all about "the superiority of the Yamato [Japanese] ethnic nation" and was intended "to erase ethnic nationalist consciousness of non-Japanese students, assimilate them, and consolidate the rule by the Japanese."[34] To Liu, such a hierarchical and Japan-centered vision of harmonious coexistence never made sense; on the contrary, he took it to mean the hypocrisy of Japan's Pan-Asianism. Liu does not identify the professor by name, and there is a formulaic ring to his criticisms. Nevertheless, Liu's characterization of this particular instructor's Pan-Asianist conception is in general agreement with what we observed in the Japanese faculty's scholarly publications. Despite subtle disagreement on the crucial questions of Japan's proper relationship to other countries of Asia, the Japanese faculty members generally emphasized the centrality of Japan in the new order.

Though few in number, some of the essays in *Huiyi* speak positively about certain Japanese instructors. After criticizing Sakuta Sōichi's course on Manchukuo's history at length, Pei Rong (fifth entering class) briefly mentions two Japanese teachers whom he liked. "Some Japanese instructors had a sense of righteousness. Professor Itō who taught Japanese language and Professor Takahashi who taught history were among them. In class, they at times spoke with sincerity that we Chinese students welcomed."[35] Without elaborating on the content of these instructors' "sincere" sentiments, Pei quickly brings the thought to an end by noting that "of course, these teachers had to face Japanese authorities' investigation and rebuke."[36] Clearly, the author's emphasis is on the undesirable consequence that the "sincere" teachers had to face, rather than what they said in class. By separating his favorite Japanese instructors from the Japanese authorities, Pei seems to imply that those "sincere" Japanese were also the victims of Japanese imperialism. Again, one finds a *Huiyi* author carefully expressing his liking of his former Japanese teachers in a politically correct logic often utilized by top CCP officials.[37]

Besides classes, the ideological aspects of the life-based education at *juku* were another source of Chinese students' grievances. The Kendai administration proudly regarded its *juku* system as the most explicit expression of the university's commitment to the ideal of "ethnic harmony." Sharing a large bedroom, eating the same meals, and waking up and going to bed at the same time, *juku*-mates were supposed to receive character-building discipline through inter-cultural interactions. Considering the fact that the reality of people's life outside of the Kendai campus was rife with discrimination and far from "ethnic harmony," not even ethnic integration, the *juku* system must have surprised the Chinese students at first. One author of *Huiyi* even expresses his positive feelings, emphasizing the equality in all students' living conditions.[38]

Nevertheless, the students soon discovered that daily life in *juku* was filled with Japanese rituals and customs. As described in Chapter 2, all students were forced to participate in daily flag-hoisting ceremonies of both Manchukuo's and Japan's flags. They also had to bow facing east to show respect for the Japanese Emperor, and the recitation of an ancient Japanese poem was required before breakfast. In addition, at the meeting convened in the *juku* at the close of school days, all students had to sit on the floor in Japanese *seiza* style, the proper seating posture in Japan, which non-Japanese students found painful. Under these conditions, even if Liu Shize's (fifth entering class) protestation of "spiritual enslavement" has a ring of ideological correctness, we can infer that many of the non-Japanese students felt this way at the time.[39]

At the same time that a number of *Huiyi* authors criticize practices associated with Japanese imperialism, they insist that *juku*'s use of rituals and *jukutō* ("*juku* headmasters") never succeeded in controlling their minds. They uniformly insist that they merely went through the motions. When the Chinese students paid reverence while performing obligatory Shinto rites, they did so only to avoid the *jukutō*'s rebuke.[40] When the *jukutō* was absent, some students appeared to skip out. For instance, Pei Rong reports failing to bow when he passed by a mausoleum dedicated to Japanese soldiers who died in the fighting that followed the Manchurian Incident of 1931. He writes: "Why bow to those devils that had massacred Chinese people and were killed because of that? It did not make sense to us."[41] Indeed, when requiring students to pay reverence to Manchukuo's martyrs enshrined at this mausoleum, the Kendai administration did not take into account that those "Manchukuo's martyrs" were in fact Japan's army of invasion of Chinese territory. Unfortunately for Pei, *jukutō* Terada was hiding behind the mausoleum and caught and scolded Pei. That Pei provides the detail of being caught adds credibility to this story.

Liu Diqian (sixth entering class) describes how his *jukutō*'s behavior defied the *juku*'s stated commitment to the principle of "ethnic harmony." The Chinese students were not the only students to resist. Liu reports that his close friend

Batbayar from Mongolia once told him about an exchange with *jukutō* Arata. Arata first said that the Qing Dynasty, whose royal family were Manchus, and the Japanese had historically treated the Mongolians well, and asked Batbayar if he was having trouble at Kendai because Mongolians were a minority on campus. Finally, Arata told him: "if the Chinese students treat you badly, tell me. I will support you."[42] Here, we need to recall the ethnic politics of the region. In 1912, the Republic of China came into being in the wave of anti-Manchu Han Chinese nationalism. Then, in 1932, the Japanese Kwantung Army orchestrated the foundation of Manchukuo in China's northeast, claiming to help the marginalized Manchus and Mongolians achieve independence from Chinese rule. Arata's comment clearly came from an awareness of this ethnic politics. We do not know if Arata was pretending to be concerned about Batbayar's situation or genuinely cared. In any case, Batbayar must have doubted Arata's intentions, as he shared this incident with his Chinese friend, Liu. In his entry in *Huiyi*, Liu cites this story as evidence that Arata attempted "to create rifts among students of different ethnicities," contrary to the principle of "ethnic harmony."[43] From Liu's perspective, the *juku* education's real goal was "to train Japanese as colonists and make slaves out of the '*mankei*' students."[44] Yu Jiaqi (first entering class) is more sarcastic; he writes that the *juku* training actually aimed "to teach [non-Japanese students] the contradiction of the principle of 'ethnic harmony' through experiences."[45] Here, Yu's use of the word "contradiction" refers to the unequal power relationship of the ruler and the ruled, and the implication is that the ruled must learn to conform.

Becoming "Chinese": Anti-Japanese activities on campus

The *Huiyi* anthology shows that despite its stated adherence to the principle of "ethnic harmony," Kendai's regime failed to win the hearts and minds of its Chinese students. Among the Chinese students who were enrolled at government-run colleges in Manchukuo, Kendai students actually constituted the largest number of "political criminals" or "thought criminals" arrested by the Kwantung military police for their anti-Japanese and anti-Manchukuo activities.[46] The Kwantung military police originated in the Russo–Japanese War (1904–5), when the military police was dispatched to accompany Japanese troops. When Japan acquired the Kwantung Leased Territories and the South Manchurian Railway zones from Russia in 1905, the military police began to function not only as military police but also as civil police in the region. Eventually, by the

1930s, its primary function became the liquidation of dissidents, which meant purging anti-Japanese activists in the context of Manchukuo politics. Together with the Manchukuo police, the Kwantung military police arrested at least 2,000 activists involved in underground Chinese communist groups and anti-Japanese patriotic associations between 1935 and 1945. These arrests were followed by torture, execution, and sentencing of life term or long-term imprisonment.[47]

Chinese Kendai students' anti-Japanese activities, which often took the form of secret reading of progressive books, is the most frequently discussed subject in the memoirs compiled in *Huiyi*. While we should not be surprised that Chinese alumni's memoirs exhibit this strong anti-Japanese sentiment, the detailed accounts that they provide make their stories credible and add valuable insights to our understanding of Kendai. The authors discuss their activities as evidence of their patriotism towards China. The essays in *Huiyi* collectively suggest that their experiences at Kendai made them awaken to their Chinese identity—a narrative that we also find in many of the former Korean and Taiwanese students' recollections. In addition to ethnic and national identity, the Chinese authors claim that they were also learning to choose between political ideologies: Nationalist or Communist. It is important to note here that the rivalry between the Chinese Nationalist Party (GMD) and the Chinese Communist Party (CCP) was deepening throughout the war, even though the two had officially established a United Front to fight against their common enemy, Japanese invading forces, in 1936. Keeping in mind that the *Huiyi* authors had a strong interest in affirming their patriotism in leftist terms, this section will describe the development of anti-Japanese activities on campus. For this purpose, Gao Ke's (eighth entering class) article in the *Huiyi* collection is illuminating because he writes about the anti-Japanese activities on campus based on not only his own experience but also interviews with more than ten former Chinese students.

Their resistance stemmed from a shared sense of disillusionment and loss of purpose among the Chinese students of the first entering class as seen in the case of Yue Yishi (first entering class). After losing his passion for learning at Kendai and deciding not to socialize with his "haughty" Japanese classmates, Yue and his close Chinese friends found some progressive books at a secondhand bookstore in town. Finding new joy in reading books by Lenin, Marx, and Japanese Marxist Kawakami Hajime, they secretly began circulating them among Chinese classmates. He and his friends often took walks after dinner to talk about books and current events.[48] In this way, the Chinese students of the first three classes spontaneously formed small reading groups. Until 1942, they encountered few obstacles because Kendai, under Vice President Sakuta Sōichi's leadership, encouraged its students to read a wide variety of books, including leftist works, in order to learn how to criticize them. The Chinese students seized this opening to read many "progressive" books.

Meanwhile, their secret anti-Japanese activities on campus began to branch out in 1940. First, a few Chinese students established a connection with an off-campus secret society member, Zhang Fusan, without knowing, or so they claim, that he belonged to the Nationalist organization. Acting on the agent's suggestion, the students launched an on-campus secret society, *jianda tongzhi hui* (Kendai Comrade Group), in April 1940. Later, in June 1941, they reorganized it as the *jianda ganshi hui* (Kendai Executive Group) to accommodate the expanding membership. The nineteen leaders also decided to publish a semiannual bulletin, the *Qianshao* (Outpost), which unfortunately has not survived to the present.[49] In addition, during the school trip to Japan in November and December 1940, some Chinese students secretly met with Chinese study-abroad students in Tokyo and were inspired to join anti-Japanese activities in Manchukuo.[50] Some Chinese students left school for Chongqing to join the GMD or for Yan'an to join the CCP.

These activities led to the arrest of a number of Chinese Kendai students. On March 2, 1942, Japanese military police came to the school and arrested thirteen students in the presence of *jukutō* Arata Shinji. Around the same time, two more students were arrested in their hometowns. Including the two students who had been arrested since November 1941 and an additional seven students who were caught in December 1943, Shinkyō Prison housed altogether twenty-four Kendai students as "political criminals."[51] The sentences given to them were severe, including life imprisonment for two students and five- to fifteen-year imprisonment for the others.[52] Although some of them were released before completing their terms, while incarcerated, they had to endure the horrible conditions of life in the prison, frequent beating by the guards, and torture. Two Kendai students died in prison. Wang Yongzhong (second entering class) became insane after being tortured and died two days after he was severely beaten by a guard. Chai Chunran (first entering class) died in prison because the guards denied him medical treatment despite his high fever.[53]

This harsh treatment is not surprising; the Japanese military police during WWII were known for their brutality toward prisoners. What is interesting, however, is how the Kendai administration responded to this incident. Before turning to the response of the academic head of the university, Vice President Sakuta, a brief mention of a reaction of some of the former planning members is helpful. Upon receiving the news in Shanghai, a Japanese army official, Mishina

Takayuki, who had sat on the Kendai planning committee, shared it with his colleague, Tsuji Masanobu, also a key member of the committee. Mishina recalls that they saw the incident as "a remarkable proof that the University is doing its job well."[54] They felt strongly that Vice President Sakuta, who informed them of the news in a letter, "should feel proud rather than feeling responsible for it."[55] Mishina and Tsuji immediately arranged to send Sakuta a congratulatory message by wire, and the two raised a toast.[56] The reader might be surprised at their excitement and positive reaction to the arrest of Kendai's Chinese students for engaging in anti-Japanese and anti-Manchukuo activities. To understand their response, we must recall that Kendai's curriculum stressed the importance of a link between one's learning and actions. The institution's anti-elitist inclination was also found in daily reminders—in lecture halls, *juku* discussions, students' diary entries, and so on—that they should become leaders who truly understand and share the struggles of the people. The faculty and students understood that they were expected to bring changes to the current practice of "ethnic harmony" in Manchukuo society. They were to recognize the problems in society and address them to make Pan-Asianist ideals a reality. In that sense, Mishina and Tsuji, sharing the perspective that the current Manchukuo society was far from the founding principles, could easily empathize with the arrested students' indignation. Thus, these Japanese members of the institutional planning committee chose to acknowledge the arrested Chinese students' courage to take actions on their beliefs, even risking their careers and lives.

Meanwhile, on the Kendai campus, the top Japanese administrator, Sakuta, was busy responding to the incident. He first demanded the release of those students, but to no avail. Then, he turned his energy to the task of showing support and taking care of those arrested students. According to Liu Diqian (sixth entering class), Sakuta visited his students and told them: "You did not commit a crime because you were morally corrupt. Rather, your willingness to sacrifice your lives for the sake of your ethnic nation brought you here to this prison … I do not blame you but just hope that you will feel confident and proud."[57] This is telling evidence of the expansive understanding of Pan-Asianism expressed by Kendai's top leader. Sakuta praised the students for "sacrifi[cing] [their] lives for the sake of [their] ethnic nation," by which he meant China. Even in 1942, after the outbreak of war in the Pacific, we see that Kendai's highest Japanese administrator demonstrated a surprising level of commitment to the ideal of Pan-Asianism as a voluntary community. His praise of these Chinese students' sense of ethnic nationalism seems to resonate with Ishiwara Kanji's vision of an East Asian League, in which each ethnic nation spontaneously joins its hand while preserving its sovereignty. In other words, cooperation is not something that can be imposed on someone by force. The fact that Liu quotes Sakuta in his account subverts the official line of thinking in the PRC that Kendai was nothing more than a vehicle of Japanese imperialism. Indeed, Liu does not directly praise Sakura, very likely because this might make him appear too sympathetic to an important Japanese official and expose him to accusations of being pro-Japanese.

These sympathetic words by Sakuta are not mentioned in Zhao Hong's (second entering class) account of the incident. As one of the arrested students, all Zhao writes is that Sakuta visited them and "forced them to listen to his lecture."[58] Although Zhao does not elaborate on the content of Sakuta's "lecture," his word choice in this short line gives the impression that Kendai's Japanese leader was acting coercively and even reprimanding the students. This may well be how Zhao actually remembered Sakuta's address to the students, which would be consistent with the CCP's official history of Manchukuo that regards all Japanese officials as agents of Japanese imperialism. The weight of evidence, however, suggests the contrary. Although Zhao does not mention it in his essay, some Kendai students, including their Japanese classmates, also visited them in prison in a show of solidarity. One also finds that some former Korean and Taiwanese students wrote in their memoirs about the incident and Sakuta's actions. For those authors, this was one of the touching moments that convinced many of the Kendai students of Sakuta's sincere commitment to Pan-Asianism and the genuine friendship of some of the Japanese students. Sakuta was dearly missed by most of the students when he resigned his position in June 1942 to take responsibility for the arrest of Chinese students.

Other Japanese faculty members frequently visited their students in prison, too. One of them was Takigawa Yūken, *jukutō* and Assistant Professor, whose seven students were arrested in December 1943. Takigawa recalls an immense sense of relief when all of his seven students were released on September 30, 1944, after nine months of harsh life behind bars. On that night, Takigawa invited them over to his home and threw a small party. It appears that this Japanese *jukutō* was quite sympathetic to his students' sense of ethnic nationalism. As for the reason for his growing sympathy, Takigawa cites one memorable interaction with his student. About one year prior to the arrest of seven of his students, Takigawa had the opportunity of talking the night away with a Chinese student, Hu Bingyuan (fourth entering class). The heart-to-heart dialogue took place shortly before Hu absconded from Kendai to join the GMD forces in Chongqing, China. Takigawa writes in his memoir that listening to Hu that night made him realize that "any ethnic nation intrinsically aspires to obtain self-government."[59]

We also find an important fact about some of the arrested students from a Taiwanese alumnus Li Shuiqing's memoir. According to Li, one of the top students of the first entering class whom we encountered in Chapter 4, three of the arrested students had been actively involved in the production of Kendai's school song in 1940, about one year before their arrest. Reflecting the ideal of "ethnic harmony," the Kendai student body created lyrics in two different languages: Japanese and Chinese. It was one of the arrested students, Sun Baozhen (first entering class), who composed the Chinese lyrics for this school song.[60] The Taiwanese alumnus explains that initially these Chinese students were genuinely committed to the ideal of Pan-Asianism, but by 1941, they became alienated by Japan's continuing expansionist policy in Asia.[61] Understandably, none of the Chinese memoirs mention the fact of these students' earlier commitment to the strain of Pan-Asianism identified with Kendai; rather, they represent the arrested students as Chinese patriotic heroes and strong resisters of Japanese imperialism.

After Sakuta left Kendai in June 1942, the new Japanese Vice President, Suetaka Kamezō, tightened his hold on students' activities. Liu Shize (fifth entering class) recalls that with Suetaka in charge his *jukutō* intensified efforts to suppress the Chinese students' anti-Japanese activities. The *jukutō* would inspect students' possessions to confiscate progressive books and carry out "midnight surprise attacks" on students' rooms in an effort to discourage Chinese students from holding secret meetings.[62] When one Chinese student openly expressed his resistance by leaving a lecture about the inevitable victory of Japan's "sacred war" in the Pacific, spoke about the Allies' triumphs in the Pacific theater, and even urinated in front of the *kenkoku* (nation-building) shrine, the *jukutō* put this student under house-arrest in a dorm room for a month. When he showed no sign of regret, he was expelled.[63] Liu states: "this savage act of *jukutō* willfully insulting and persecuting Chinese students was not an isolated incident. Consequently, it ignited stronger anti-Japanese sentiment and patriotism toward China among the Chinese students."[64]

Gao Ke (eighth entering class) agrees and argues that Kendai's oppressive measures led to the radicalization of the Chinese students, who increasingly allied with the CCP over the GMD as their activities' inspiration.[65] They collected study materials by stealing Soviet journals from Kendai faculty's research building, finding the Japanese translation of Chinese communists' articles in Japanese journals, translating them into Chinese, and circulating them secretly among themselves.[66] Meanwhile, upper class Chinese students recruited newly entering Chinese students, especially those from their hometowns, by holding secret lectures, passing along study materials, and teaching them how to sing revolutionary songs. Thus, Gao argues, the leftist-inspired anti-Japanese secret activities became a tradition on campus and prepared Kendai's Chinese students to sacrifice themselves for the revolution once Japan capitulated and the civil war erupted between the GMD and the CCP. As we have seen before, the formulaic CCP rhetoric with which Gao concludes is laid over the well-documented fact of GMD-inspired resistance activities by some, if not the majority, of Kendai's Chinese students.

While many authors of the *Huiyi* collection emphasize the unity among Chinese students in carrying out their anti-Japanese activities, they do so differently. Pei Rong (fifth entering class), Zhang Wensheng (seventh entering class), and Gu Xueqian (seventh entering class) recall their fond memories of time spent with their upper class Chinese students, *laodage*, or older brothers, whom they credit with awakening their ethnic nationalism as Chinese.[67] Even after graduating in June 1944, the several graduates of the second entering class visited the underclassmen to hold secret lectures.[68] Moreover, we learn from Wang Yeping (eighth entering class) that some non-Chinese students shared anti-Japanese sentiment as well. Kim Yong-Hui (Korean), Ba Tu (Mongolian) and Tu Nanshan (Taiwanese) often joined Chinese students' secret meetings at the storehouse.[69] While Gao highlights the role that the secret campus organization played in these activities, Zhang claims that it was an "organization without a formal structure."[70] To him, it was never clear who the organization's leaders were and who among Kendai students were actually members. By so stating, Zhang seems to underline the spontaneity of the anti-Japanese activities at Kendai and to imply that students came and went at will. On the other hand, it may have been that the organization's leaders concealed their identity for fear of arrest.

One commonality evident in the entries in the *Huiyi* anthology is the authors' insistence on their own leftist affiliations. Although some of the contributors mention that there were Chinese students at Kendai who were influenced by GMD ideas, understandably, none states that he himself was on the side of the Nationalist government.[71] First, Liu Shize (fifth entering class) cites the high enrollment of Chinese students in Russian language courses as evidence of their progressive political thought, where "progressive" was shorthand for Marxism.[72] Second, in explaining what he learned from the secret reading of progressive books, Pei Rong (fifth entering class) offers his understanding of the foundations of a harmonious society, which clearly challenges the traditional Confucian hierarchical vision of social harmony preached by Japanese professors.

People should be equal, and the age of Great Harmony should come. Only when the poor, who constitute the majority of the population, rise up, can there be equality and the world can gradually move to the direction of the Great Harmony.[73]

Pei thus suggests class struggle as the path toward the achievement of the ideal of the Great Harmony, a formulation that represents a blending of Confucian and Marxist theories. Then he adds, "from this type of superficial understanding, I gradually built up the correct philosophy and worldview, which guided me to the path of revolution."[74] While there is an obvious CCP cast to this last sentence, it is easy to surmise that the alienation that some of the Chinese students experienced at Kendai and in outside society made them receptive to the basic equalitarian tenets of Marxism.

Another conscious effort to characterize Kendai's Chinese students as left-leaning can be found in some of the *Huiyi* authors' choice to attribute the arrests of their classmates to a broader episode known as the December Thirtieth Incident. It refers to Kwantung military police's wholesale arrest of communist secret societies in Manchukuo in December 1941. Around the same time, the military police also rounded up GMD-led anti-Manchukuo secret organizations. Even though these were two separate incidents, the closeness in the timing of those arrests has generated some confusion. As a result, the name "December Thirtieth Incident" has been used for all of the arrests that occurred in late 1941, giving the impression that all those who were arrested around that time were affiliated with the CCP. In the context of the PRC's long history of persecution of rightists, *Huiyi* authors' choice to associate the arrest of Kendai's Chinese students with the December Thirtieth Incident is understandable. However, this link is questionable. Recent research shows that among Kendai's Chinese students more were involved with the GMD-led off-campus organizations than with the ones led by Communists. Moreover, they were under the influence of Luo Dayu's ideas. He was a leader of a GMD-led secret society in Manchukuo, and after Japan's capitulation in 1945, went on to serve the GMD during the Chinese Civil War and then in Taiwan after 1949. Historian Hideki Okada states that the Kendai students under the influence of Luo believed that their actual struggle to drive off Japan from Manchuria would begin only when Japan would be significantly weakened in the war against the United States, allowing the Republic of China to take a stronger stance against Japan.[75] Thus, recent research questions the link between the wholesale arrest of Kendai's Chinese students and the December Thirtieth Incident, as well as the general left-leaning inclination of Chinese students on the Kendai campus. One of the essays in

Huiyi suggests—perhaps inadvertently—that this may have been the case. Yan Tingqiao (first entering class) states that only after graduating from Kendai in 1943 did he learn about the Communist Eight Route Army, its guerrilla activities against the Japanese, and Mao Zedong's theory of New Democracy.[76] Unless Yan's experience was atypical, his admission implies either that Kendai's Chinese students' anti-Japanese activities did not have much communication with off-campus Communist organizations or that he was out of the loop of the campus anti-Japanese activities. It seems likely that Kendai students whose daily lives were somewhat isolated from society at large were not in fact aware of the extent of the GMD–CCP divide. It is important to recall in this regard that the GMD and the CCP formally entered into a United Front for the War of Resistance against Japan in 1936, and both championed the cause of patriotic resistance against Japanese aggression. Undoubtedly, many Chinese students were exploring their political options while enrolled in Kendai, but the strong leftist inclination that fills the pages of the *Huiyi* anthology is questionable.

Escape and launching revolution: The end of Kendai student life for Chinese students

By 1945, Japan's military situation was desperate, and it affected Kendai to the extent that the university could not follow its regular curriculum. Once the Japanese government ended the deferment of conscription of students in higher education in October 1943, Japanese students at Kendai were not exempted. Except for a few students who were physically unfit, all Japanese students twenty years of age and over left school to bear arms. Japanese faculty members were drafted as well. As seen in Chapter 4, Korean students "volunteered" to join the army, too. The university cancelled almost all academic classes and only offered military training.[77] In addition, the remaining students were mobilized for labor service. In April 1945, a group of about 100 mostly Chinese students of the fourth and fifth entering classes were dispatched to the airplane factory at Gongzhuling, Jilin Province, located 60 kilometers northeast of the Kendai campus. Under these circumstances, many Chinese students fled from the Kendai campus and the factory at Gongzhuling before the end of the war. A number of the entries in *Huiyi* describe their last days as Kendai students in detail and portray their actions as heroic acts of patriotism.

Liu Chengren (fourth entering class) had been conscripted to work at the factory at Gongzhuling since April 1945. When seventy to eighty Chinese high school students joined Kendai students at the factory, he and his Kendai classmate were assigned to train the younger students. Liu explains in his essay that he made use of this opportunity to fill them with Chinese patriotism and encourage them to slack off at work. On August 14th, one day before the end of the war, the *jukutō* who had been supervising the student factory workers announced Vice President Suetaka's order that the group must return to the Kendai campus immediately. On the way back, at noon on the following day, the group heard the Japanese Emperor's announcement of Japan's surrender over the radio. Liu recalls this moment as follows:

> the *jukutō* said: " … all we should do now is to follow Vice President Suetaka's order and return school immediately. What do you think?" The Chinese students scowled at him. After a moment of silence, he said: "why don't we say this then. Those who're willing to return school with me, step forward now!" All Japanese students did so but not a single Chinese student, which forced the *jukuō* to dismiss the group on the spot. The Japanese students and *jukutō* gathered together and glared at Chinese students with baleful looks. Because the Japanese still were in charge, the Chinese students could not do more than shout after them, "Good riddance! Hit the road!"[78]

The Chinese students of the seventh and eighth entering classes who were still on campus were faced with a similar situation. On August 12, in response to the Soviet Union's invasion of Manchukuo that began on August 9, Vice President Suetaka gathered all the remaining students together and announced that they would form two units: a fighting unit of Japanese and a labor unit of non-Japanese students. Then, Suetaka asked the non-Japanese students who wished to join the fighting unit to step forward. Song Shaoying (eighth entering class) and Wang Yeping (eighth entering class) both recall Suetaka's rage-filled eyes fixed on the Chinese students when none responded. The contributors to *Huiyi* all insist that no one volunteered. In fact, we know from other sources that one Korean student did volunteer; however, the entries in *Huiyi* omit this detail, insisting that "not a single person stepped forward!"[79] According to Wang, this was proof of the complete failure of "the foolish scheme to train Chinese youths to become Japanese slaves."[80] In the afternoon, the labor unit set out for Gongzhuling on foot. Curiously, not a single author mentions the tearful parting between them and the remaining Japanese students on campus, which the latter discuss in memoirs. The anti-Japanese sentiment and friendship toward their Japanese classmates may have coexisted in Chinese students' minds. However, the fact that nationalistic antagonism was emphasized over the personal bond reminds us of the conscious choices the authors were making in constructing their narratives.

Although Xue Wen's (seventh entering class) account is one exception that reveals a good-natured interaction at parting, he stresses the unexpectedness of the event. Xue recounts his group's unpredictably amicable parting of the ways with their *jukutō*, Satō Hisakichi and Nakajima Saburō, during their trip to Gongzhuling. Xue was assigned to be a student leader of the labor unit consisting of about 160 Chinese students. While en route, Xue claims, he and his friends made a secret plan to desert. The plan was that when the group reached a remote place, they would set upon and kill the two "*guizi*" ("devils" referring to the *jukutō*) and run off.[81] Before they could execute the plan, however, many students absconded under cover of darkness and only twenty-three remained by the next morning. They changed their plan, deciding first to demand disbanding the group before resorting to violence. To their surprise, the *jukutō* not only agreed but also offered to issue a certificate authorizing them to return home. They had a last meal together, and distributed what funds remained equally. Then, the two teachers shook hands with each student and bid farewell. Even after this amicable parting, Xue recalls, the Chinese students lost no time heading off, fearing that the *jukutō* might report them to the police, which did not happen.[82]

What are we to make of Xue's account? Did he and his classmates really plot to kill the two *jukutō*? One cannot help but notice the ring of fanciful heroism layered upon his memory of what is actually the most significant revelation. What we see is how differently various Japanese staff at Kendai reacted when they realized the war was finally drawing to an end. Further, given the political constraints under which Xue writes this story, we can surmise that the unexpectedly amicable parting of the ways of the Chinese students and the two *jukutō* left a deep impression on him. Finally, one sees that Xue felt at liberty to feature in his piece an incident that reveals that the Japanese instructors at Kendai were not all fanatic advocates of Japanese imperialism.

Song Shaoying (eighth entering class) and Wang Yeping (eighth entering class) were among those who absconded from the group on the way to Gongzhuling. They ran away because, in Song's words, "no one wanted to go to the factory and make the weapons that would be used to kill our own people."[83] Song stresses that their escape was not an act of passive resistance or cowardice but rather "a courageous and heroic act" toward revolution.[84] Likewise, Wang relates his desertion to a decision to take a stand against the Japanese and join the revolutionary army. He writes that he had been waiting for the Soviet Union's invasion because that would offer an opportunity for the Chinese to launch the offensive against the Japanese invaders in Northeast China that they had been planning.[85]

The imprisoned students also experienced a dramatic moment of liberation at the end of the war. According to Zhao Hong (second entering class), one of the arrested students, the police headquarters decided to execute all political prisoners on August 14. At Shinkyō Prison, Guard Murakawa took more than seventy prisoners outside, including Zhao and other incarcerated Kendai students. They were handcuffed and told to walk to another prison. In fact, Zhao believes, the plan was to take them to another spot and shoot them all. Luckily, the group came across a contingent of Chinese cadets who had revolted against their Japanese officers. They beat Murakawa to death and released the prisoners.[86]

The challenge of reading former Chinese students' memoirs: The *Huiyi* and *Hakki* accounts contrasted

As seen earlier in this chapter, the *Huiyi* entries, though produced under heavy political constraints and read critically, provide considerable insight into the resistance of Chinese students to the Japan-centered conception of Pan-Asianism implemented in Kendai's educational curriculum and aspects of the *juku* education. However, reading two essays authored by former Chinese students and published in *Hakki* for Japanese readers provides a different insight into Chinese students' experiences at Kendai. One of the *Hakki* essays, "The Days I Spent at Nation-Building University," authored by Zhang Tailu (eighth entering class) and published in Japanese in 1985, was later revised and published in Chinese in the *Huiyi* collection in 1997. While the bulk of its essay remained the same, the Chinese version had a different title, "Student Life under Colonial Rule," and was published under a different name, Zhang Yimen.[87] As this section will show, the additions and omissions that Zhang made to his original essay offer an interesting insight into his conscious effort in constructing his narratives for different audiences. The other contributor to the Japanese collection, Han Weiping (eighth entering class), did not write for the Chinese anthology, but his essay in *Hakki* provides a unique insight worth comparing with the *Huiyi* entries. The most visible difference between the Japanese and Chinese sources lies in their descriptions of motives for attending Kendai and the experiences after the closing of Kendai. In this section, I will show how the *Hakki* accounts differ from that of *Huiyi*.

Unlike the *Huiyi* accounts, the contributors to *Hakki* discuss their motives for applying to Kendai at length. Han Weiping decided to apply to Kendai because he wanted to pursue study at college rather than becoming a soldier. His decision was supported by his friend who had studied abroad at Waseda University in Tokyo and by his older brother who was serving in the Manchukuo Army as a sergeant.[88] Han's friend and brother both had received Japanese education and were working as government and military clerks in Manchukuo. Their success apparently convinced Han that attending Manchukuo's highest learning institution would put him on a secure career path. We should note that Han made this decision in mid-1944, when Japan was suffering a series of devastating military losses in Saipan, the Philippines and Guam. While some of the accounts published in *Huiyi* report that Chinese Kendai students were anticipating the war's end, despite Japanese censorial control over news, and were preparing to join the CCP-led revolution, Han's story shows no sign of his and his family's awareness of the imminent end of the war and the collapse of Manchukuo.[89] Otherwise, Han would not have chosen to apply for Kendai in April 1945, five months before Japan surrendered to the Allies.

Han's entry raises another important question—how much weight it had in Chinese students' choice of Kendai that the institution was a training ground for Manchukuo's government officials. Despite the explicit statement of that fact in the university's educational objective and its advertisement to prospective students, the *Huiyi* authors omit the knowledge that Kendai trained future government officials. The omission of this fact in the Chinese anthology is understandable because no reasonable author would expect his Chinese readers to learn that he had once set his mind to work for the Manchukuo government.[90] However, a desire to find government-sector jobs, which is implied by the *Hakki* author Han, actually reflects Chinese people's historical understanding of glory and fame associated with serving the government. Although terminated in 1905, China's century-old Civil Service Examination System had created a cultural memory of young aspiring men exerting all their energy on studies to pass the exam and become government officials. In light of such tradition, it was natural for Chinese people in Manchukuo to regard passing Kendai's competitive entrance exam as a contemporary equivalent of passing the Civil Service Exam.

Another Chinese contributor to *Hakki*, Zhang Tailu, writes that Kendai's generous scholarship was a powerful incentive. Zhang writes that "for [him], a son of an underprivileged family, Kendai was perfect because all expenses were covered by state funds."[91] While this claim can also be found in a number of the *Huiyi* essays, Zhang's subsequent mention of his earlier affinity with the Japanese separates his essay from those in the *Huiyi* anthology. Zhang notes that his middle school in Liaoning Province was unique in that although it had separate classes for Chinese and Japanese students, they all sat in the same classroom for certain subjects. Zhang claims that this experience made Kendai a natural choice, hinting at a favorable—at least not horrible—experience of studying together with Japanese pupils in middle school.[92] Not surprisingly, when writing for the Chinese anthology *Huiyi*, Zhang skipped over this crucial fact—his affinity with the Japanese in middle school—presenting the financial reason as the only factor that shaped his choice of Kendai.

In *Hakki*, both Han Weiping and Zhang Tailu write at length about how much they wanted to gain admission to Kendai. Once his mind was set, Han reports, he began putting extra efforts into his study of Japanese. To pass the physical exam, he jogged every morning and did calisthenics. He worried about his family's police record, for his father had been arrested by Manchukuo police for what the author calls "thought crimes," and died in prison in 1942. In the context of Manchukuo politics, the term refers to the crimes of acting on subversive beliefs, including anti-Japanese sentiment and leftist ideas. Interestingly, this family tragedy did not turn him against Japan, and neither did his father's political crimes disqualify him in the eyes of Kendai's Japanese administrators. Han further reports that he was so elated when he received the letter of acceptance that he quickly recovered from typhoid fever, which he had contracted after taking the entrance exams.[93] The other *Hakki* author, Zhang, also stresses how hard he had studied in preparation for Kendai's entrance exams. He sought out advice from the Chinese students from his hometown who were enrolled at Kendai at that time. One piece of advice he received was that "as long as [he] thoroughly reads newspapers [he] would pass the interviews."[94] Being aware of the Japanese audience of his memoir, Zhang does not elaborate on the meaning of this advice. However, it is obvious that Chinese applicants were expected to parrot the mainstream perspective on current news as narrated in the Japanese press, and that he himself was willing to do so in order to be admitted to Kendai.

Zhang's brief mention of his Japanese-language interview exam gives a different impression in *Hakki* and *Huiyi*. He writes that one of the questions asked was about a recent US bombing of a Japanese factory in his hometown Anzan (currently Anshan City in Liaoning Province). The examiner asked: "Did that American bombing scare you?" to which Zhang replied "no, it didn't." In *Hakki*, Zhang follows up on this story by stating that "even today, I get nervous when recalling that moment in the interview exam."[95] In *Huiyi*, however, Zhang omits this last line and replaces it with his internal monologue at the exam. After responding to the question in the negative, Zhang writes, he thought to himself: "Americans bombed the Japanese factory. Why should I get scared of it?"[96] Thus, the two accounts by Zhang offer different pictures. On one hand, the *Hakki* version shows a nervous young student sweating through an interview exam. On the other hand, the *Huiyi* essay depicts a Chinese man trying to gain admission to a Japanese university by hiding his resentment against Japanese rule of his country. In any case, Zhang was admitted to Kendai. As expected, his delight at the news is recorded only in *Hakki*. To his Japanese audience, Zhang shares his joy at having finally arrived at "*akogare no* Kankirei," the Kankirei of my dream.[97] "Kankirei" is the name of the hill on which the Kendai campus was located.

The comparison of the entries penned by the former Chinese students in *Huiyi* and *Hakki* should not surprise us. Writing at the request of their former Japanese classmates, Han Weiping and Zhang Tailu show no hesitation in expressing their strong desires to become Kendai students but appear reluctant to discuss their disappointment at the reality of their campus life. By contrast, the contributors to *Huiyi* tend to emphasize how disappointed they were with the Japan-centered Pan-Asianism they encountered after they arrived on campus. Indeed, the majority of *Huiyi* accounts skip over the period in which the authors excitedly applied to the university, which may well be because they do not wish to portray themselves as Japanese sympathizers or collaborators to their Chinese readers. When read together, however, the recollections published in *Huiyi* and *Hakki* convey the appeal that Kendai had for Chinese students.

Another difference between *Huiyi* and *Hakki* is evident in their accounts of the chaotic period following the closing of Kendai in August 1945. As discussed earlier, the contributors to *Huiyi* portray their absconding from the Kendai campus as an act of patriotism toward China. By contrast, writing about his departure in his entry in *Hakki*, Han Weiping reports the same event matter-of-factly. He writes he left the Kendai campus on August 10, 1945, one day after the Soviet Union invaded Manchukuo. Conscious of his Japanese readers, Han merely mentions that he and his friend left campus "to go home."[98]

Following the war's end, which also brought an end to both Kendai and Manchukuo, Chinese students who had attended Kendai were caught up in the complicated politics of China's civil war between the Nationalists and Communists. The comparison of the accounts in *Huiyi* and *Hakki* on this topic illuminates the complex reality that they faced as former Kendai students in the late 1940s. While severely criticizing Kendai for offering an education that aimed at the enslavement of non-Japanese students, many contributors to *Huiyi* claim that their experiences at the university taught them an important lesson: patriotism toward China. Through on-campus anti-Japanese activities that mainly took the form of secret meetings and discussion of progressive books, they portray themselves and by implication all of the Chinese students who were enrolled at Kendai as preparing themselves for the political struggle that followed Japan's capitulation in August 1945. They also insist that most, if not all, of them were on the side of the Communist Party. For instance, Wang Yeping (eighth entering class) states that his days at Kendai motivated him "to leave the dark and rotten domain ruled by the Nationalist government (of GMD) and enter the bright and progressive liberated district (under the CCP control) to join the revolution."[99] Wang may well have joined the CCP after Japan's defeat; however, the specific rhetoric he employs sounds suspiciously politically correct.

Although many of the *Huiyi* accounts emphasize the leftist leaning of the Chinese Kendai students' post-Kendai activities, there is reason to believe the actual situation was more complicated. Here we first turn to the entry in *Huiyi* of Gao Ke (eighth entering class), whose account is based on his interviews with former Chinese Kendai students as well as his own experience. According to Gao Ke, eight students from the first to fourth entering classes established *dongbei qingnian tongmeng* (Northeast Youth League) on August 23, 1945. He describes the league as a "supra-partisan, spontaneous gathering" that "supported Nationalist–Communist cooperation and unity for nation-building."[100] Among the eight leaders, two leaned toward the GMD and six the CCP. Their disagreement led to a split, and the pro-CCP members established *xin qingnian tongmeng* (New Youth League) in Shinkyō City, now renamed Changchun City, in October 1945 under the CCP's guidance.[101]

We do not know whether the three to one ratio in the division of political allegiances within the leadership was reflective of the entire student membership. Nevertheless, Gao, perhaps inadvertently, provides evidence that not all "patriotic" Chinese students at Kendai were committed leftists. Without further explaining what happened to the students who joined the GMD, Gao goes on to describe the communists' activities. Many former Kendai students went on to attend colleges and share the leftist study materials that they had collected while at Kendai with their fellow students. They also resisted discriminatory treatment by the GMD in Changchun City, Jilin Province, together with the former students of other Manchukuo schools. For instance, they demonstrated against Changchun University's decision to require special exams for former Manchukuo students in August 1946, which led to the so-called *jiqiang dianming* (taking attendance by machine guns) incident of September 18, in which the Nationalist Army fired at student demonstrators. In the end, the students pressured the university to abolish the special exams and made the GMD promise not to repeat such violence again.[102] Meanwhile, many students left Changchun University to join the CCP, while some stayed, disguising themselves as Nationalists and contributed to the communist revolution through espionage.[103]

We get a fuller account of the political affiliations of Kendai's former Chinese students in an essay contributed by Han Weiping (eighth entering class) to *Hakki*. Writing for a Japanese audience, and thus removed from Chinese government oversight, Han reveals more information about former Kendai students' connections with the GMD. According to Han, in March 1946, some former Kendai students participated in an anti-communist demonstration that was organized by the GMD. About 300 college students from Changchun, Shenyang, Harbin, and Jinzhou traveled to Beijing and demonstrated with slogans such as "expel the red imperialists from our country" and "we will not tolerate the second 'September 18' [Manchurian Incident] by [communist] Army."[104] The author notes that he and his friends joined this activity because they thought that uniting the country and bringing stability would allow them to pursue learning. Han also states that "strong enthusiasm and determination for nation-building united the former Kendai students" who participated in the event.[105] After returning home, they attended colleges in the Nationalist-controlled region in the Northeast, where he reports they secretly studied Mao Zedong's works. Han writes that he bade farewell to three of his friends, including one former Kendai student, who left Shenyang to join the communist revolution. Han stayed for reasons that he does not explain.[106]

Two other sources supply further information on Kendai's former Chinese students' post-1945 engagement with the GMD. First, we turn to Professor Miyagawa Yoshizō's recollection of his encounter with his former Chinese students shortly after the war's end. Miyagawa was hiding from the Soviet troops in a former government building on Tōan Street (currently Yueyang Jie) in Shinkyō City. One night, his colleague Professor Egashira Kōji woke him up and took him to a large building in a district where Chinese people lived. There, the two former Kendai professors met a group of their former Chinese students. The group was anticipating an imminent conquest of Manchuria by GMD armies and was preparing to join the party to work for the reconstruction of the region. Miyagawa reports that the students asked him and Egashira to offer advice as they drafted the general plan for their new nation-building project. Happily, the two teachers spent the rest of the night engaging in discussion with their former students. Miyagawa notes that one of the leaders of this group was Yang Zengzhi (first entering class), who had been arrested as a political criminal in 1941.[107]

Another notable source on Kendai's Chinese students' post-1945 involvement with the GMD is a memoir of a Taiwanese alumnus, Li Shuiqing (first entering class), whom we encountered in Chapter 4. The last section of Li's memoir concerns the eight months between the war's end and his return home to Taiwan in April 1946. In it, Li records his interactions with and news about several of his Chinese friends from the Kendai years, mostly on the GMD side. Fu Zhendong (second entering class) and Cui Wanxian (first entering class) were both working for GMD-affiliated media, writing and editing essays, while Kang Xiangchun (fourth entering class) shared with Li his confidence that the GMD forces, with more advanced military technology, would surely take back the region from the communist forces.[108] Li also reports tragic news of his friend Ye Xiangtong (first entering class). When visiting Ye's home, Li heard from his brother that Ye had recently been killed by communist forces because of his involvement in anti-communist activities in a mining community in Chaoyang.[109] Thus, the Taiwanese alumnus's memoir provides further evidence of former Chinese students' affiliations with the GMD following the war's end.

The contrast between the narrative present in the *Huiyi* collection and other sources on Kendai's former Chinese students' political views and affiliations reminds us that we must approach politically charged topics with considerable caution. In the chaotic political struggle in Northeast China during the latter half of the 1940s, former Kendai students' patriotism was tested. As revealed in Han Weiping's and Gao Ke's accounts, not every Kendai student chose the CCP as an expression of their patriotism. Some aspired to national unification, while others chose to join the GMD. Nevertheless, the pages of the Chinese anthology are filled with indications that Kendai's Chinese students were leaning toward communism. Even the *Hakki* entries do not speak in detail about political activities by Kendai students that were not leftist in character, especially if the authors themselves were involved.

These tendencies are not so surprising when the historical memories in question are so politically charged and the authors of the memoirs are sensitive to contemporaneous political contexts. Especially in the context of the Chinese Civil War (1946–49), which ended with the CCP's victory, and the subsequent violent persecutions of rightists in the PRC, one would expect the Chinese authors to highlight their active participation in the communist revolution. And, as we have seen, none of the authors clearly admits to formal ties with the GMD. However, Japanese alumni who have kept in contact with their Chinese classmates report that some former Chinese Kendai students faced persecution during and after the communist revolution because they were regarded as affiliated with the GMD. For instance, Tsutsui Ryūta (seventh entering class), a Japanese contributor to *Hakki*, mentions the experience of Zhang Jinduan (seventh entering class), who had visited Tsutsui in Japan in the 1980s. Following Japan's capitulation, the Soviet Union Army confiscated Zhang's family property and his family scattered. During the Cultural Revolution, he was sent to a compulsory labor camp in a rural village for eleven years because his family was considered anti-revolutionary.[110]

All of Kendai's former Chinese students must have strongly felt the need to defend themselves from political persecution, for anyone who was closely associated with Japanese imperialism was deemed a national traitor. The authorized interpretation of Chinese students' experiences at Kendai is found in *Riben qinhua jiaoyu quanshi* [*General history of Japanese colonial education*] published by People's Education Press in 2005. The entry on Kendai concludes that the university ultimately aimed to enslave Chinese students through education. This "official" history considers the former Chinese students of Kendai to be either victims or collaborators of Japanese imperialism.[111] As we have seen, the reality was more complex.

The political nature of historical memory poses a challenge to our understanding of former Chinese students' experiences at Kendai. Nevertheless, a close examination of the *Huiyi* essays, especially when read against the *Hakki* memoirs written for a Japanese audience, reveals not only commonalities but also differences in former Chinese students' experiences and perspectives about Kendai. The common experience was that they *chose* to attend Kendai and arrived on campus with hope and aspirations. For some students it was the joy of learning, for others the incentives of free education and the prestige of passing highly competitive exams, and for still others, as we saw in *Hakki*, it was the author's earlier affinity with the Japanese people. The uniformly negative portrayal of Kendai's curriculum in the *Huiyi* anthology maintains that the Chinese students became disappointed at the Japan-centered ideology that dictated the curriculum and the haughty attitudes of many of the Japanese teachers and students. The *Huiyi* essays further claim that the campus life— especially the aspects of the institution that disappointed them—had the opposite effect to Japan's imperialist scheme of enslaving Chinese youths. In other words, the authors insist that they became true patriots of China while attending Kendai. This chapter has challenged the universality of this editorial line of the *Huiyi* anthology by careful readings of its essays and other sources. In the next chapter, as we examine Kendai's student-organized *juku* publications, we will find that the Chinese students indeed held truly diverse views just as other groups in the campus community did.

Building a utopia together: *Juku* publications as a window into Kenkoku University's institutional practice of Pan-Asianism

The central concern of this book has been Pan-Asianism as theorized and practiced at Kenkoku University in Japanese-occupied Manchuria. While the chapters thus far have separately examined the institution and faculty, and students of different ethnic national identities, Chapter 6 aims to bring those campus community members, particularly the students, more closely together. Here, we must recall the educational objective of the institution. The Imperial Ordinance on Kenkoku University, issued on August 5, 1937, under the name of Puyi, the Emperor of Manchukuo, stipulates that "Kenkoku University aims to nurture a generation of talented young men who embody the essence of (Manchukuo's) founding principles, master the depth of learning that informs their actions, and become pioneering leaders who will construct a world of high moral."[1]

In the context of Manchukuo politics, it was clear that "the essence of (Manchukuo's) founding principles" referred to the state's stated promise of creating a Pan-Asian utopia based on the ideals of "ethnic harmony" and rule by the "kingly way." Still, these were ambiguous conceptions that were open to a wide variety of interpretation. At the ethnically integrated student residences, *juku*, Kendai students grappled with the difficult question in everyday life, in one-on-one conversations, discussion meetings, casual conversations at the bar and in solitude. By 1940, Kendai students created yet another medium of open discussion: student-run *juku* periodicals. Starting in the spring of 1940, the beginning of Kendai's third year, the students published at least four different periodicals with varying frequency. This chapter analyzes those student-run publications.

Published during the three academic years from 1940 to 1943, these periodicals recorded Kendai's institutional practice of Pan-Asianism and students' discourses on the ideology in the most eventful period for the university. In 1940, one of the *juku* of the third entering class published their own *juku* periodicals titled *Reimei [Dawn]*. Copies of its five issues have survived to this day. Ranging from twelve to thirty-eight pages, the hand-written issues of *Reimei* contain a number of essays, short novels and poems authored by the members of the fourteenth *juku*.[2] Also available in the archive is one issue of a similar, hand-written periodical, *Kanki [Joy]*, published in June 1940 by a group of second entering class students.[3] Unlike *Reimei* and *Kanki*, two other *juku* periodicals were typed and professionally published. *Kenkoku: kenkoku daigaku juku zasshi [Nation-Building: Kenkoku University Juku Journal]* published three volumes in August 1940, August 1941, and April 1943, and each volume had 145 to 229 pages and 25 to 40 entries.[4] *Kenkoku* did not publish a volume in 1942, probably because the students were busy launching a new periodical, *Kenkoku daigaku juku geppō [Kenkoku University Juku Monthly]*.[5] *Juku Monthly*, in spite of its name, published seven issues irregularly between June 1942 and November 1943. Each issue was about eight pages long and contained about fifteen entries, except for the last issue that ran seventy-three pages. This last issue of *Juku Monthly*, which was the final issue of any student-run periodical available in the archive, was published as a special issue before the majority of upper-class *nikkei*—Japanese, Korean, and Taiwanese—students left the campus to join the armed forces.[6]

Although no existing research on Kendai has analyzed these materials, these four student-run periodicals provide a perfect window into the university's institutional experience of Pan-Asianism.[7] As mentioned previously, the three academic years from 1940 to 1943 were eventful both on campus and in the world at large. During this period, Kendai's student enrolment steadily grew to its peak at about 900 in the spring of 1943 when the university housed all six classes on campus for the first time. Meanwhile, the mass arrest of Kendai's Chinese students, perhaps one of the most dramatic events for the campus community, occurred in 1941 and 1942, followed by a personnel change of the university's top academic administrator. Outside the campus, this three-year period observed the ongoing war between Japan and China, the start of Japan's war against the US-led Allies in December 1941 and the escalation of the war that led to student enlistment in the fall of 1943. On the pages of the *juku* publications, the students responded to these events directly and indirectly; and, their responses show a surprising level of variety. All four periodicals had student editors. *Reimei* and *Kanki*, the smaller journals, each had a Japanese student editor, while *Kenkoku* and *Juku Monthly* had editorial boards consisting of Japanese and Chinese students.[8] All four periodicals were bilingual in Japanese and Chinese and published entries authored by students of all ethnic identities.[9] Editors frequently note that they received a lot more works than pages allowed. For instance, *Juku Monthly*'s first issue received over sixty works when the limited space permitted only fifteen of them to be published.[10] Faculty members made a small number of contributions when invited by editors; but, these periodicals were truly a medium of discussion created by and for the students. One even finds instances in which authors make reference to ideas expressed in previous issues. Hence, reading these materials provides invaluable insights into the lively interchanges of ideas among Kendai students in the eventful periods of the early 1940s.

The two sections that follow focus on Kendai students' discourses on Pan-Asianism that are found in two types of published writings. First, the *juku* periodicals published a number of academic research essays in which student authors attempted to answer the call to create a new culture and society for Manchukuo. After the outbreak of the Japan–US war, this academic inquiry among the students enlarged its scope from Manchukuo to a Greater East Asia Co-Prosperity Sphere. Second, the central theme that persistently shaped the *juku* periodicals was "ethnic harmony." What exactly is it? How can it be achieved? Tackling these tough questions in their everyday life at *juku*, student authors often wrote about these questions on a more personal level. The fundamental question that they faced was whether Pan-Asianism and ethnic nationalisms should and can coexist.

Academic inquiries into a new culture for Manchukuo and Greater East Asia

The *juku* periodicals provide evidence that Kendai students were fully aware of the high expectation placed upon them. As future governmental officials of Manchukuo, Kendai students were to pursue learning that would inform them of the current situation of the country as well as creating a new culture for the multi-ethnic state of Manchukuo, which would be the model for East Asia. The academic research reports, essays, and literary works published in the *juku* periodicals reveal Kendai students' candid criticisms of the current status of Manchukuo society and Japanese rule as well as a variety of approaches to the new culture and society that they hoped to create.

Students' criticisms of Japan's policy in Manchukuo came from their direct observations of the society surrounding the Kendai campus. Writing under a penname, a Japanese student of the third entering class points out three defects in the Japanese government officials and entrepreneurs living in Manchukuo. First, he writes: "Among the Japanese residing in Manchukuo, quite many desire to return home in Japan after succeeding in career ... being homesick, they find every reason to visit home in Japan, such as paying homage to ancestral graves and attending family events."[11] Contrasting such tendency with that of white Christian missionaries in Asia and Chinese peasants in Manchukuo who tended to settle down in their new homes for a longer period or for the rest of their life, the author laments the half-hearted attitude of his compatriots. Second, he finds it unpleasant that the Japanese people tend to form their own small community and refuse to intermingle with peoples of other ethnicities. Third, the author points out pretentiousness typical of the Japanese as a detriment to Japan's policy in Manchukuo. He states: "if you are putting on airs ... by claiming to serve all and work for the country, you will be morally inferior even to the individualistic white people."[12] Such is a direct criticism of Japan's policy in Manchukuo coming from a Japanese student who was disappointed at the gap between Japan's official rhetoric and practice. In his understanding, Japan's policy in Manchukuo, if it continued as it was, could even compare unfavorably with Western colonial exploitation in Asia.

Similarly, a Chinese student of the third entering class presents his criticism of Japanese rule in Manchukuo through a short novel written in Chinese and published in *Kenkoku*'s volume 2 in 1941. Entitled "Father and Son" and written under a pen name, the story tells of young Chinese man Weijian's years of futile efforts to become Manchukuo's government official. The grueling preparation required of Weijian and the seriousness that his entire family and village community show in encouraging him along the way reminds the readers of the traditional Chinese perception of glory associated with passing the Civil Service Exam and becoming a government official in imperial China. The only difference is that Weijian had to master the Japanese language, instead of Confucian texts, pass competitive entrance exams of a Japanese-run middle school, and excel at studies while enrolled. Upon graduation, Weijian was unofficially given a temporary position of an entry-level government clerk. Even though the contract was not yet finalized, the news spread in his small village community, which threw a big party for Weijian and his proud father. Then bad news came; the position had actually been filled by a Korean man. Weijian's point of contact, a Chinese official, explained: "As you know, these days, the Japanese vice prefectural governor has more say than our prefectural governor … I've certainly done my utmost to work things out for you. I am truly sorry [that I couldn't help you]."[13] Needless to say, "*our* prefectural governor" in this quote refers to a Chinese governor. The power relationship between the *mankei* official and his *nikkei* vice official described in this story was reflective of the convention found in many organizations in Manchukuo. An example that was familiar to the author was Kendai's administration. Even though the university had a Chinese President, Zhang Jinghui, a Japanese Vice President, Sakuta Sōichi, exercised actual administrative leadership. It is evident that the author uses the fictional story of Weijian to condemn the persisting reality of Japanese hegemony in Manchukuo society. This was a matter of high interest to the *mankei* students at Kendai, who would become government officials after obtaining a diploma.

While the two works discussed in this section point out the problems of Japan's rule in Manchukuo, another entry by Chinese student Yang Liufeng (pen name; second entering class) exposes the author's knowledge of—and likely his own engagement with—underground anti-Japanese activities in Manchukuo society. It takes the form of the author, Yang, a university student, writing a letter in Chinese to his friend M, who lives in his hometown. The story does not name the author's school; and thus, it could be read either as a fiction or an actual letter that the author, a Kendai student, has written to his friend. The letter concerns their female friend Naxia, who was killed by their "enemies" half a year previously, and the shared resolve between Yang and M to take revenge for her death.[14] Though lacking an explanation, details of the story make it clear that Naxia was killed by the Japanese authorities due to her association with an anti-Japanese underground organization. In his letter, Yang regrets that despite Naxia's and M's repeated encouragement during his stay at home in the previous summer break, he was not able to make up his mind to join them in the cause at that time. Yang ends his letter by reiterating his determination to carry on the legacy of Naxia. He addresses M: "it's been already half a year since Naxia died, but I read her writings, diary, and essays every night … and her words 'the moment has come!' continue to refrain in my heart."[15] Even though it remains unclear whether the letter was for real or fictional, in either case, this entry informs the readers that such life-and-death struggles between anti-Japanese activists and the Japanese authorities were unfolding in the vicinity of Kendai campus life.

It is remarkable that these Japanese and Chinese students were willing to publish their sharp criticisms of Japan's rule in Manchukuo in 1940 and 1941.

Publishing one's work under a pen name was quite common in the East Asian literary world, and some Kendai student writers followed that convention. However, given the contents of their works, the three authors previously discussed in this section certainly made a reasonable choice to use pen names to shield them from possible repercussions. Yet, they also made a conscious choice of delivering these works to the student editors, who likely knew their identities, which indicates the level of trust that existed among the students.

Besides critiquing Japanese policy in Manchukuo, students' academic inquiries also encompassed their resolve to create a new culture for the country. Two essays in *Kenkoku*'s volume 1 (1940), authored by members of the first entering class, concern Manchukuo literature. Terada Kazuo, a Japanese student raised in Manchuria, critiques the emerging literary genre of Manchurian *haiku* poems. *Haiku* takes a form of a three-line poem with each line containing five, seven, and five syllables. It originated in Japan in the seventeenth century and continued to be popular among the Japanese. The use of cultural references to the Japanese aesthetic sense of seasonal changes and nature presented a challenge when contemporary Japanese poets began to develop a genre of Manchurian *haiku*. One problem Terada points out is that some existing works of Manchurian *haiku* stick to the Japanese aesthetic sense of beauty and thus fail to represent the beauty of Manchuria. Conversely, if Manchurian *haiku* poems utilize cultural references specific to the region, many connoisseurs of *haiku* dismiss them because they "can only see Manchuria through their Japanese eyes."[16] Terada argues that "the pursuit of Manchurian beauty begins only when one recognizes and appreciates the bleak and monotonous landscape of the region and its harsh natural environment including the yellow sand and the coldness of winter at the temperature as low as 40 degrees Celsius below zero."[17] Similarly, a Chinese student, Shan Jingxiang, criticizes the *nikkei* novelists in Manchukuo by stating that their works "cannot be fundamentally separated from the works of the Japanese novelists."[18] In order to create Manchukuo literature that reflects the ideal of "ethnic harmony," he argues, "the lives and customs of the Chinese people [in the region] must inform the foundation of Manchukuo literature, to which the elements of Japanese and other peoples' cultures add colors."[19] Shan's claim of the central role that Chinese culture plays in this formula makes sense demographically—the Han Chinese continued to make up the majority of the Manchukuo population. Politically, however, Shan is making a bold claim in Japanese-occupied Manchuria. In the end, Shan presents a Pan-Asianist conclusion on the subject. He asserts that the mission of Manchukuo literature is "to facilitate interchanges among Japan, Manchukuo and China, and foster cooperation among the three countries to advance the Eastern culture."[20] Hence, in their conceptions of new Manchukuo literature, Terada and Shan both reject the supremacy of Japan. Shan goes further to place China at the center of the new multi-ethnic culture of Manchukuo.

The academic works published in the *juku* periodicals reveal that Kendai students had a high level of interest in China. Largely—but not exclusively— authored by Chinese students, these Sinological works identify certain problems in the field and suggest solutions from different angles. For instance, a Chinese student Yu Ziwo (pen name; second entering class) problematizes the tendency among the existing Sinological works to view China through Western evolutionary theory.[21] Yu asserts: "The Chinese society today is not necessarily in a certain phase of the Western evolutionary theory. It is just one society that exists in its current form."[22] In his understanding, China faced two challenges. Externally, the Western powers disrupted China by bringing in "the shackles of liberalism"; and internally, "the triad of government officials, landlords, and capitalists" further damaged society because they showed no concern for the ordinary people.[23] Interestingly, Yu does not indicate the ongoing China–Japan war that obviously took a huge toll on people's lives in China. By identifying the Western incursions and the failure of Chinese elites to respond to them as the sole problems faced by the current Chinese society, and by omitting Japan's war in China from the picture, Yu seems to conform to the Japanese Pan-Asianist rhetoric on the China war that it is Japan's attempt to liberate the Chinese people from the current unfortunate situation.

While Yu's omission of the China–Japan war may indicate his conformity to Pan-Asianism by implication, Kang Fengjun directly addresses the war and expresses his support of the ideology. Kang, a Chinese student of the first entering class, urges his readers to look at the current war "in a broader history of humankind and the natural progression of the universe."[24] By taking such a broad perspective, Kang argues, one can see the current war as an opportunity to create a new order and culture. In other words, he seems to encourage the Chinese readers to put aside their nationalistic sentiment about the ongoing war, which he admits is "unbearable."[25] Hence, Kang's take on the China–Japan war is in perfect accord with the Japanese official line of thinking. That is probably why this Chinese student felt at ease to publish this rather lengthy essay under his real name. Evidence of Chinese students' support of Japan's war in China is interesting; but, what is more important is that Kang goes further to advocate that the new culture to be generated through the war should be based on an egalitarian conception of Pan-Asianism. Kang writes: "[t]he new culture must be created not by advancing the culture of just one ethnic nation or by obliterating the cultures of others, but by having each ethnic nation contribute to the creation of it."[26] This should be read as Kang's challenge against Japan's policy in East Asia. For, having lived together with students from Taiwan and Korea, Kang must have been aware of Japan's assimilation policy in the empire. Thus, Kang demonstrates his support for Japan's war with China, with the condition that the war would generate an inclusive new culture for a multi-ethnic empire in the future.

Kendai's young aspiring Sinologists also took an interest in the ongoing Chinese intellectual movement to reform the language. This broader initiative originated in the New Culture Movement of the 1910s and 1920s in which Chinese intellectuals—mostly those who returned from study abroad in Europe, the United States, and Japan—sought to create a new culture for China in place of the Confucian tradition. On the topic of Chinese language reform, one of the Sinological research pieces in the *juku* periodicals is worth noting. Yan Tingchao (first entering class) first observes how some of the early human languages like the Sumerian initially developed as hieroglyphics and then transformed into phonograms.[27] In this context of linguistic development, Yan sees that the ongoing movement to reform the Chinese language follows this pattern. Recognizing that the Chinese characters currently used in China and Manchukuo had not yet entered into the stage of phonograms, Yan suggests creating "a new East Asian alphabets," by simplifying Chinese characters, using *katakana*, a syllabary used in the Japanese writing system, as a model.[28] Yan's proposal is interesting because it comes with his inexplicit rejection of Japanese as a new common language for Manchukuo and Greater East Asia. By the time Yan wrote this essay in 1943, Japan had imposed the Japanese language on its colonial subjects in Taiwan and Korea for decades. Yan's Korean classmates' works in the *juku* periodicals, written in highly sophisticated Japanese, were the unmistakable proof. Even Kendai designated Japanese as the language of instruction, while demonstrating a remarkable level of cultural tolerance by allowing students to converse in the language of their choice outside of class. In this context, Yan's proposal could be read as a bold act of protesting against the ethnocentric, top-down approach of Japan's rule in East Asia.

Besides using the Chinese culture to propose an alternative future for Manchukuo and broader East Asia, Kendai's young scholars were also interested in the question of how to work with the Han Chinese who constituted the large majority of the Manchukuo population. One example of such an inquiry is found in the essay authored by a Korean student, Yi Zhong-Hang, and published under his Japanese name, Tokuyama Shōkō (first entering class).[29] The well-researched essay examines the legal regime of the Liao Dynasty (907–1125) of the Khitan people, who once ruled a multi-ethnic empire that encompassed present-day Manchuria, Mongolia, parts of Russia, and northeastern Korea. Tokuyama shows Khitans' failed attempts to efficiently incorporate the large Han Chinese population into the empire while protecting the Khitan and other peoples' cultures from the strong Sinicization effects of Chinese culture. For instance, the Liao state initially established two different penal codes. The Khitans and other tribes were placed under the simple penal code of the Khitans, while the Chinese continued to be ruled under the Chinese code. The Khitan laws were simpler and involved much harsher punishments for offenses compared to the Chinese laws. In time, though, the Liao state altered the Khitan penal code to soften punishments and eventually adopted the more complex but logical and sophisticated system of the Chinese for the entire state.[30] Tokuyama concludes that despite this and other similar attempts to preserve their own culture, by the time the Jurchen people rose to power in the region in the early twelfth century, the Khitans had lost their military might and combative spirit, "having been softened and acculturated to the Chinese culture."[31] Tokuyama hopes that Kendai students, as future leaders of Manchukuo, could draw some lessons from the Khitan people's experience.

As shown in these examples, the *juku* periodicals prove a high level of interest about China among Kendai students. Sinological research pieces appear in every issue published from 1940 to 1943 and were authored mostly by the Chinese but also by Korean and Japanese students. In the final issue of the student-run periodical *Juku Monthly* no. 7, a Japanese student of the fourth entering class contributed a short message of farewell shortly before departing the campus to enlist in the army.[32] The author encourages the *nikkei* underclassmen to make extra efforts to master the Chinese language and visit the Chinese district whenever they have the chance to go out downtown. He writes: "To know about others is the first step to love and respect them."[33] The author urges the *mankei* students to explore more deeply into their own cultural roots. Finally, the author shares his hope that Kendai will build a reputation of "excellence in Sinology," which he believes is essential in the ongoing Pan-Asianist endeavor to achieve "ethnic harmony" in Manchukuo, end the war in China and construct a new order in East Asia.[34] This sustained interest in and commitment to Sinology was one of the unique characteristics of Kendai. Although a number of Japanese scholars at universities throughout the empire researched China, Kendai was the only Japanese-run institution of higher education where Chinese students could freely pursue Sinology with academic rigor.[35] While the Chinese anthology of memoirs *Huiyi* does not explicitly acknowledge this fact, there is no doubt this aspect of Kendai's intellectual culture had a certain appeal for the Chinese students.

Why did so many Kendai students take an interest in China? The *juku* periodicals reveal that one of the reasons for Kendai students' passion for Sinology was the persisting influence of Ishiwara Kanji's conception of an East Asian League. As discussed in Chapter 2, Ishiwara, the initiator of the foundation of Kendai, envisioned a Pan-Asian partnership among Japan, Manchukuo, and China, as a vital means of defending East Asia from Western imperialism. Ishiwara's vision for Kendai was based on this idea of a Japan–Manchukuo–China confederation, and his proposal of an ethnically integrated *juku* system and insistence on ethnic equality as a basic principle for the university certainly reflected the most idealistic aspects of his Pan-Asianism. Nonetheless, as we recall, Ishiwara was not able to engage directly with the institutional planning of the school, and that the planning committee and the school administration took the institution in a different direction. Ishiwara openly expressed his indignation with the status of Kendai in 1942, as the institution diverged from his original expectation.[36] It does not mean, however, that his idea of an East Asian League ceased to influence the campus community. Some of the key faculty members, including some *jukutō*, had been recruited by Ishiwara and shared his vision. Associate Professor Ehara Fushinosuke was one of them. After living on campus with students as *jukutō* for one year, he left Kendai when a few other faculty members left the university due to disagreement over the direction of the institution.[37] Ehara kept in touch with his former students even after leaving his position. As shown in a transcript of a panel discussion by a group of eight students of the first entering class and Professor Miyagawa Yoshizō, Ehara and two other *jukutō* had nurtured strong bonds with their students and had a strong influence over them.[38] The student editors of *Kenkoku*'s volume 1 included recent letters they received from Ehara and another *jukutō* who had also recently left Kendai. In his letter, Ehara introduces Ishiwara's most recent publication regarding the East Asian League and strongly recommends it to the students, stating that "it is an essay that every Kendai students must read."[39]

With or without Ehara's letter, Kendai students were already well versed in the conception of an East Asian League. For instance, in the same volume of *Kenkoku*, a Chinese student of the first entering class, Guan Naifeng, contributed a long essay reflecting on the current challenge Asia faced.[40] After reviewing European colonial rule in South and Southeast Asia, and the Middle East, as well as the pressure of the USSR's expansion felt in its bordering areas such as Siberia and Central Asia, Guan offers what appears to be excessive praise for Japan and its colonies for achieving a high level of culture. In his review, Manchukuo receives a brief but rosy outlook. As for China, Guan has a host of things that he laments—from its incompetent leaders, semi-colonial situation, failing economy, down to the spread of communism.[41] However, the most lamentable, in Guan's eyes, is the current war between China and Japan. He writes that "Japanese and Chinese are killing each other in cold blood while the Westerners are watching from the ramparts, as if to enjoy … an entertainment show."[42] Following these observations, Guan presents his main argument that the war should be terminated immediately and "Japan, Manchukuo, and China must develop a genuine partnership."[43] Here, we see clear evidence of the continuing influence of the East Asian League idea. To achieve this goal, Guan urges Japan to "cast aside any desire for conquest" and China to "abandon vengeful thoughts."[44]

Of course, Kendai students knew too well that it is easier said than done. For the Japanese students, in particular, Guan's advice meant that they must convince their Chinese friends of their genuine commitment to the Pan-Asianist conception of an East Asian League. We find such an effort in Imamura Yasuji's report of his group field trip to the Northern China region that was under Japanese occupation at that time.[45] Imamura, a Japanese student of the first entering class, reports that the Chinese people in the region seemed uninterested in politics, which he interprets as their lack of trust and faith in the pro-Japanese regime that administered the region under a group of Chinese politicians. Imamura then argues that "Japan must not engage in conquest or economic control of China. Unlike Western countries that have exploited the Chinese for their own gain, Japan must work together with the Chinese and guide them towards shared prosperity."[46] In these lines, Imamura is acknowledging and responding to the perspective of the anti-Japanese camp that Japan's current war in China was essentially the same as Western imperialist aggression. Then, he moves on to write about his encounter with the Japanese civil and military officials in the region and shares his admiration for their strong dedication to the reconstruction of China. His conclusion of the report reads: "Asia will become one in a true sense only when each country and particularly Japan truly manifests its moral virtues. Japan's moral virtues are being tested in our country Manchukuo. Thus, the advancement of Manchukuo can determine the future of China and Greater East Asia."[47] In this report, Imamura seems to be speaking to the two audiences by using the typical East Asian League formula that connects Japan, Manchukuo, and China. First, he reminds his fellow Japanese students of their important responsibility of manifesting moral virtues in their actions. Second, he hopes to assure his non-Japanese and especially Chinese friends that Kendai's Japanese students are not conquerors but can become their committed partners.

Like Guan and Imamura, other Chinese and Japanese student authors expressed their support for the concept of an East Asian League through the *juku* periodicals. One does not find evidence of the ideology's direct influence on students of other ethnicities, except for a Russian student of the first entering class, Seredkin. In his essay, written in proficient Japanese, this Russian student insists that white Russian residents in Manchukuo share the dream of an East Asian League.[48] He writes: "Even though we white Russians look different from the peoples of East Asia, we have been living under the protection of Japan and Manchukuo for over twenty years and thus share the same fate."[49] The Russians, he asserts, are particularly grateful that Manchukuo has offered a place for them to freely practice their religion, unlike the communist government of the Soviet Union. Their first-hand experience of the brutality of communism has made the Russian residents in Manchukuo strongly committed to Manchukuo's endeavor to construct a highly moral world. In addition to the task of building a utopia in Manchukuo, Seredkin argues, white Russian youths bear additional responsibilities of "expelling the Comintern from Russia, creating a new society in Russia, and thereby contributing to the construction of a new order in Greater East Asia."[50] Thus, Seredkin seeks to emphasize that these Russian residents' anti-communist and anti-Comintern agendas are compatible with Manchukuo's Pan-Asianist endeavor. Writing this essay in 1943, however, this bright Russian student at Kendai must have been aware of the Soviet–Japanese Neutrality Pact that was signed in April 1941. Even though wartime Japan and Manchukuo continued to take an anti-communist stance, this political pact with the USSR makes one wonder how Seredkin's argument would be received. As if to further stress the compatibility between his agenda and Pan-Asianism, Seredkin briefly discusses Russia's past uneasy relationship with Britain and the United States and claims that the Russians and Asians share the same enemies: Anglo-Americans.

One finds a similar effort at establishing the link between one's political agenda and Pan-Asianism in a Mongolian student's essay. Mengheboyan (second entering class) first reviews the current political division of the Mongolian people.[51] According to Mengheboyan, Inner Mongolia had been working with the Japanese and observing recent development of their culture—the western part constituted five provinces of Manchukuo, while the eastern part of Inner Mongolia had established the Mongol United Autonomous Government in 1939 and had worked together with Japan. As for Outer Mongolia, Mengheboyan laments that living conditions were inferior under communist rule.[52] Then, he asserts that "we the Mongolian people of Manchukuo should partake in the construction of a new order in East Asia under the Japanese guidance ... save our compatriots from white evils' rule ... and achieve a unified, independent Mongolia."[53] While this may sounds like a nationalist aspiration, Mengheboyan assures the reader that his Mongolian nationalist goal can concur with the Pan-Asianist ideal of Manchukuo. To do so, he reminds readers that Manchukuo's founding principle of "ethnic harmony" can be achieved through each ethnic nation's efforts to advance their own culture, so that they can contribute to the construction of the world of high moral.[54] At the same time, Mengheboyan does acknowledge that "the advanced nation of Japan is in the position of leading this Pan-Asian cooperation."[55] Then, as a partner, he demands certain qualities in the Japanese who would work with him for the development of Mongolia. He writes: "We do not want to import highbrows who are addicted to elitist education. We want to work with someone who wholeheartedly commit themselves to the tasks of guiding the peoples of Manchuria and achieving the rule by the 'kingly way.' We want someone who can turn completely into the native peasants and serve the people."[56] What is clearly articulated in these lines is Mengheboyan's vexation with the current Japanese politicians in Manchukuo. For, he ends his essay by expressing his hope that Kendai would foster the true Japanese leaders that he desires.

Once war broke out between Japan and the US-led Allies in December 1941, it was natural for Kendai students to express their responses in the *juku* periodicals. As one can expect, all of those essays showed enthusiastic support, but with some variation. In early December 1941, Japan's attack on Pearl Harbor, Hawaii, was not the only news that enlivened the Japanese Empire. Emperor Hirohito's imperial subjects throughout the empire were flooded with news of Japan's victories in Southeast Asia and the Pacific. The Japanese Navy sank British Royal Navy battleships off the coast of Malaya; the Japanese invading forces defeated the British forces in Hong Kong within eighteen days; and Japan was making steady progress in the Philippines, overwhelming MacArthur's US Army Forces in the Far East. These remarkable military successes in the early phase of the war buoyed up many Kendai students, especially the Japanese students, who penned their thoughts about the war in essays, poems, and *tanka* poems.

The essays written by two Japanese students, Bandō Yūtarō and Arashida Masuo (both second entering class), convey two typical messages. Bandō expresses his deep sense of responsibility as a youth living in the significant turning point in world history and his joy at having this honor.[57] He shares these emotions in the hope of encouraging his fellow Kendai students to join him in heeding the call. He states: "We students should never see ourselves as reserve troops ... As citizens we bear responsibility for today, and as youths, we take tomorrow on ourselves."[58] Meanwhile, Arashida's response to the war is shaped by the concept of an East Asian League. Writing his essay in the spring of 1942 when Japan was still on the offensive, Arashida is overjoyed not because of Japan's military successes but because of the prospect of the China–Japan War ending soon.[59] He admits that Japan has not been able to gain understanding and support in China because of the war, which he regards as "the most lamentable thing in the history."[60] It is obvious that he is referring to the contradiction between Japanese pronouncements of Pan-Asianism and the fact that Japan and China had been at merciless war since 1937. Now that Japan had launched its direct offensive against the real enemies of Asia, Anglo-Americans, Arashida believed that he "no longer needs to dwell in the depressing meditation." His heart is filled with joy as if he is "looking up at the cloudless sky."[61] Then, he warns his readers not to get carried away by the victorious news from the Pacific and Southeast Asia, because they have an urgent task before their eyes: bringing an end to the China–Japan War quickly. Hence, Arashida's response to Japan's war against the United States reveals the influence of the concept of an East Asian League, whose tenets included the importance of reconciliation between China and Japan.

One finds similar enthusiastic support for the war in an essay published under a Japanese name, Hiranuma Kōgen.[62] Printed right next to an essay authored by a Japanese professor, Mori Shinzō, Hiranuma's essay on the significance of the Japan–US war does not compare unfavorably with Mori's work in its sophisticated writing style and level of support for Japan's policy. What is important to note is that Hiranuma was a first entering class student from Korea, whose original name was Yun Gyeong-Hyeon. He expounds on the significance of the war by reviewing the history of East–West relations in the last two centuries. Following the conventional view, Hiranuma treats the Opium War of the mid-nineteenth century as a starting point of Western incursions in East Asia, against which Pan-Asianism emerged as a popular philosophy. In his narrative, Japan's annexation of Korea, his country, was not a case of colonization, but one manifestation of emerging Pan-Asianism. Meanwhile, Hiranuma continues, "the East accepted the West into its region," probably referring to Japan's interwar rapprochement with the Western powers and the amity that emerged between the Nationalist government of China and the United States following the revolution of 1911.[63] Nevertheless, Western imperialism continued to torment the peoples of the East, which prompted "the leader of East Asia, Japan, to act on the vision of the [Greater East Asia] Co-Prosperity Sphere."[64] Placing the outbreak of the war between Japan and the Allies in this historical context, Hiranuma argues that the war embodies "East Asia's self-assertion" to a world that has been dominated by the West and its sacred endeavor to create a world history that is not synonymous with Western history but inclusive of all cultures.[65] Thus, Hiranuma, a Kendai student from Korea, presents an understanding of the Greater East Asia War in perfect accord with the Japanese official discourse.

Living in the ethnically diverse *juku* of Kendai, the students also had opportunities to be exposed to different perspectives on the war. For instance, a Mongolian student of the first entering class called readers' attention to the importance of Mongolia while the majority of students were caught up in the ongoing war in the Pacific.[66] The author argues that Mongolia is important for two main reasons. First, the vast territory bordering Manchukuo, the USSR, China, and others could be an excellent natural buffer zone. Second, the Mongolians are the strongest people when it comes to defending and further developing this important buffer, as they are accustomed to the climate of this region. In that sense, he asserts, "Mongolia should never be forgotten in the current endeavor to construct the Greater East Asia Co-Prosperity Sphere."[67] Furthermore, the author believes that while Southeast Asia makes significant contributions through its resources, Manchukuo and Mongolia make equally important contributions through the construction of a new culture. Nonetheless, Japan has failed to manage the resources within the Co-Prosperity Sphere so that the southern resources could facilitate efficient development of the northern region.[68] This Mongolian student urges his fellow Kendai students to understand that the construction of the Co-Prosperity Sphere depends on strong protection in the north and that a strong buffer could be maintained only through active cooperation of the people living there: Mongolians.[69]

On the pages of the *juku* periodicals, one also finds a disagreement between two authors regarding the significance of the Japan–US war. In *Juku Monthly's* second issue, a Chinese student of the fourth entering class, Liu Di, defines three objectives of the war.[70] First, the war is a direct attack against the British and American powers to eradicate their influence from East Asia. Second, the war should "indirectly help bring a quick end to the China Incident," by which he refers to the war between China and Japan.[71] Liu regards the final objective of the war as the revival of East Asia and the construction of the Co-Prosperity

Sphere. Liu's Chinese essay concludes with his main argument as follows: "We must unite the powers of East Asia and the oppressed peoples of this region and fully achieve ethnic harmony on an equal basis, only then can we bring changes to the world."[72] In the subsequent issue of *Juku Monthly*, a Japanese student of the third entering class, Hayashi Shintarō, presents what appears to be a direct response to Liu's argument.[73] Hayashi rejects the idea that ethnic harmony connotes a partnership of equal members, an idea that Liu emphasizes in his essay. Hayashi argues that ethnic harmony should be seen as an embodiment of the Shinto conception of *hakkō ichiu*, where various peoples around the globe all live under the same roof, or the protection of the Japanese Emperor, "by fulfilling their proper roles."[74] Moreover, Hayashi seems to take aim at Liu's formulation in which an egalitarian partnership of Asian peoples is essential for bringing changes to the world. In Hayashi's understanding, ethnic harmony itself is the goal and should not be seen as a means to prepare for and execute the war. He further complains that those who have such "shallow" and "vulgar" understanding of ethnic harmony grumble about unequal treatment of different ethnic nations within the empire.[75] In this instance of sharp disagreement about the definition of ethnic harmony and its relationship with the ongoing war, we find the two students freely articulating their versions of Pan-Asianism. Hayashi's hierarchical and ethnocentric approach to the ideology stand in direct opposition to Liu's conception of an egalitarian community of the oppressed peoples of Asia.

Among the works published in the *juku* periodicals that are academic in nature, Liu's and Hayashi's essays that appeared in two consecutive issues of *Juku Monthly* present the sharpest disagreement among student authors. However, if we turn to other types of entries that concern Kendai students' daily lives and inner thoughts, we see a wider variety of ideas and competing articulations of Pan-Asianism. The following section concentrates on the entries of the *juku* periodicals that reveal Kendai students' experience of living out the ideal of ethnic harmony in their everyday life.

Ethnic harmony in everyday life

On the very first page of *Kenkoku's* first volume, the student editorial board—consisting of two Japanese students and one Chinese—notes as follows: "We hate to repeat the old saying that a philosophy is born out of everyday life; but, this volume undeniably represents the real life of ours. In that sense, we can learn a lot [about ourselves] by critically analyzing this periodical."[76] One of the editors, Yuge, also indicates in the "Editorial Note" at the end of the volume that the *juku* periodicals, as the embodiment of students' intellectual passion, should serve as a forum of heated discussions in which he hopes to see "sparks fly."[77] Indeed, the *juku* periodicals offer a glimpse into Kendai students' efforts to critically examine themselves both as individuals and as a student body; and, they disagree with each other. One of the central themes that emerges in such inquiry is the ideal of ethnic harmony. While this theme also appears in their academic works as examined in the previous section, a lot more works approach it on a more personal level. What does ethnic harmony mean in the context of their everyday life at Kendai? How can they achieve it? This section uses the *juku* periodicals to demonstrate Kendai students' lively discussions on these questions in print.

In the first three issues of *Juku Monthly*, student authors present two competing conceptions of ethnic harmony and how to achieve this goal. Published on June 15, 1942, a couple of months after the university welcomed its fifth entering class, the first issue of *Juku Monthly* included Japanese student Matsumoto Hiroshi's message to the new students.[78] Representing the senior classmen, Matsumoto (second entering class) offers his advice on how to approach the *juku* training. Rather than trying to become the same or be the best of all, he states, Kendai students must "aspire to be the best of themselves."[79] In other words, Matsumoto regards the ideal of ethnic harmony at Kendai as a unity of diverse members who all strive to bring out their best and unique potentials. In the following issue of *Juku Monthly*, another Japanese student of the second entering class, Arashida Masuo, further elaborates on this articulation of Pan-Asian unity. In what appears to be his response to the arrest of his Chinese classmates, Arashida states: "We all live in Manchukuo and are determined to work for the sacred endeavor of creating this utopia. But, at the same time, we are Japanese and Chinese."[80] Remaining optimistic about the potential of building a true partnership that surpasses difference in ethnicity, Arashida defines ethnic harmony as "the comradery of brothers full of passion and love of their country and of their ethnic nations."[81] Here, he seems to refer to Manchukuo by the words "their country," which is distinguished from "their ethnic nations." In this formulation, his Chinese classmates who were arrested for their involvement in anti-Japanese activities were worthy of admiration for their dedication to "*their* ethnic nations"; unfortunately though, those students did not share the love of "their country," Manchukuo.[82] This view was not unique to Arashida and Matsumoto but was common among many authors who contributed to the *juku* periodicals.

For instance, a Chinese student of the third entering class, Liu Peiquan, asserts that "only after awakening to our own sense of ethnic nationalism can we work together to construct ethnic harmony."[83]

As if to respond to the vision of unity in diversity just discussed, a Chinese student of the third entering class presents a very different conception of ethnic harmony in the subsequent issue of *Juku Monthly*.[84] The author, writing under the pen name of Er'yu, uses two chemistry terms to explain his perspective on Pan-Asian unity. The first term is *huahe*, which means a chemical compound made from multiple different elements whose original properties are altered to make a new material. The other term, *hunhe*, in contrast, refers to a composite of multiple different parts whose original properties remain intact. This Chinese author advocates that *huahe* rather than *hunhe* must be the model for Pan-Asianism.[85] That is to say, he perceives the ongoing Pan-Asianist endeavor to be an effort to create an entirely new culture and identity rather than a mere combination of diverse cultures. At first glance, his emphasis on the uniformity in the outcome bears a resemblance to what the Chinese anthology *Huiyi* claims Kendai attempted to do: Japanization of all students. We recall, for instance, that Liu Shize (fifth entering class), one of the authors writing for the PRC audience in 1997, accused Kendai of attempting "to erase ethnic nationalist consciousness of non-Japanese students, assimilate them, and consolidate the rule by the Japanese."[86] However, we must realize that Er'yu's use of *huahe* as a model contains another important message. That is, he promotes a vision of Pan-Asian unity in which all the member ethnic nations, including the Japanese, equally go through changes in the process of creating an entirely new identity. Given the fact that the Kendai administration imposed a lot of Japanese beliefs and customs on its students, this Chinese essay could be interpreted as the author's challenge against the Japan-centered approach. The subtle but significant disagreement about ethnic harmony that emerged in the three consecutive issues of *Juku Monthly* published in 1942 and 1943 shows that Kendai students' passion and interest to define that ideal continued well into Japan's war against the Allies. And, they disagreed.

On the question of how to achieve ethnic harmony in the *juku* halls, Kendai students' writings seem to identify empathy, self-criticism, and honest, open discussions as their answers. The importance of having empathy towards others was frequently discussed by the Japanese students. For instance, Japanese student Sano Kōichirō (third entering class) writes about the difficulty that he experienced in trying to correct his friends' behavior.[87] He found that his attempt to use logic to explain and persuade his friend had failed miserably, which led him to realize that his friend had his own standpoint that he could explain using a different logic. Furthermore, the more Sano tried, the more his effort incited antagonism in his friend, who perceived that Sano was trying to subjugate him. Based on this experience, Sano stresses the importance of empathizing with others because it can connect individuals in ways that judgment and criticism cannot.[88]

This was not how another Japanese student, Kamemura Tetsuya (first entering class), approached the challenge of forging understanding among Kendai students. On the pages of *Kenkoku*, Kamemura urges his fellow Kendai students "not to shy away from criticism"– both the acts of criticizing others and receiving criticisms.[89] As the next generation of leaders in Manchukuo, they should constantly engage in critical reflections of their actions. For these reflections to produce positive outcomes, Kamemura asserts, "[we] must stand on an equal footing" when criticizing each other, and "those criticisms themselves should be scrutinized as well."[90] Thus, Kamemura envisions the ideal relationship among Kendai students to be equal partners who boost each other up through constructive criticisms.

A number of student authors emphasized honesty among themselves and open discussions as vital means of achieving ethnic harmony. At the time of writing his essay in September 1942, Japanese student Aizawa Hiroshi (third entering class) was tired of toying with theories and merely talking about idealism. He uses strong words to criticize the current situation on campus. "Comradery and ethnic harmony—these words still feel empty because they are nothing more than words ... We cannot achieve them merely by getting along with each other or making compromise [among different perspectives]."[91] Aizawa continues that "ethnic harmony is a game played in earnest by peoples of different ethnicities."[92] He desires to engage in honest discussions with clashing opinions. In the same essay, Aizawa models honesty and openness by sharing his inner struggle regarding religious faith in Shinto *kami*, or deities. He writes: "Some people insist on not believing in any religion even though they cannot live without it. Others proclaim faith in religion even though they actually do not believe in it. And, looks like I belong to both of these categories."[93] This honest confession of struggle over his own religious faith in Shinto was not unique to Aizawa. The *juku* periodicals contain similar revelations of not being able to wholeheartedly believe in Shinto.[94] While the main audience of these periodicals was the Kendai students themselves, there is evidence that the staff and faculty members also had access to them. Yet, Aizawa and other students felt at ease to openly discuss their disbelief in Shinto well into Japan's war against the Allies.

One also finds supporters of Japan-centered Pan-Asianism presenting their points of view in all honesty. A Japanese student of the third entering class, Ōtsuka Munemoto, for instance, is keenly aware of some of his non-Japanese friends' aversion to Japan's ethnocentric approach. He writes: "We are deeply aware that it is insensitive to expound on the superiority of Japan's *kokutai* ('national polity') to non-Japanese peoples. We also know through our day-to-day experience that doing so would alienate the hearts of the non-Japanese."[95] This awareness and sensitivity to the non-Japanese peoples' feelings were particularly strong for Kendai students and set them apart from most of the faculty, not to mention Pan-Asianist theorists who did not have the opportunities of interacting with non-Japanese peoples. Those scholars could espouse Japan-centered Pan-Asianism without facing any direct consequences—other than perhaps a boost to their credentials in the eyes of the Japanese state. In contrast, Kendai students like Ōtsuka had to take the risk of souring his relationship with some of his friends on campus. Still, Ōtsuka chose to publish his essay on *Kenkoku* in 1943 because he believed that "the true friendship lies in telling the truth to my friends" and that "the new order we construct in Asia would undeniably be centered on Tokyo."[96] Thus, Ōtsuka took upon himself the very challenging task of explaining why his fellow Kendai students should embrace Japan's supremacy over the ongoing Pan-Asianist endeavor.

Ōtsuka's argument itself is nothing new to his audience. Kendai students have heard from their Japanese professors a number of times that Japan's policy and theories such as "*hakkō ichiu*" do not infringe upon their respective ethnic nationalist aspirations. What set his essay apart from his teachers' scholarly commentaries is that Ōtsuka pays close attention to the non-Japanese peoples' perspectives and blames Japan and the Japanese for making their friends in Asia skeptical about Japan's intention. One example that he discusses is the Japanese government's imposition of the so-called Twenty-One Demands on the Nationalist government of China in 1915. This set of demands that sought to expand Japan's interest in Manchuria and political and economic control over China, Ōtsuka argues, not only ignited strong anti-Japanese sentiment among Chinese youths but also has continued to help Chiang Kai-shek as his government mobilizes the Chinese people in the China–Japan war.[97] Ōtsuka urges his Japanese classmates to awaken to their Japanese identity as the leaders of the Pan-Asianist community. To him, that means "the stronger [their] Japanese identity is, the more respectful [they] become for other peoples' ethnic nationalist aspirations."[98] This last statement by Ōtsuka could easily be dismissed as an abstract argument if this was to appear in Japanese scholars' publications elsewhere rather than as a Kendai student's assertion. For, by publishing in the *juku* periodicals, Kendai students, including Ōtsuka, were engaged in cross-ethnic dialogue, with a surprising level of honesty and openness. Ōtsuka, in writing this essay, must have been aware of his non-Japanese friends' points of view and was probably responding to their previously published opinions, such as the very revealing essay written by a Korean student and published in *Kenkoku*'s first volume.

In this essay, a Korean student of the first entering class, writing under the pen name Seikei, outspokenly shares his two-layered sense of isolation at Kendai.[99] He shares his story not out of his indignation but because of his desire to offer constructive criticisms of the Kendai community. The author's choice of using a pen name in itself embodies his struggle over his own identity and speaks to one layer of his sense of isolation. The author knew that his family back in Korea would soon adopt a Japanese-style name for the entire family including himself. Seikei admits that his old self back in middle school days in Korea would have wholeheartedly celebrated the occasion, since he grew up as an enthusiastic supporter of the empire, believing that he was a Japanese imperial subject. However, ever since matriculating at Kendai, Seikei had grown embittered by the clear division between the rulers and the ruled. In his essay, the author writes about a crucial experience that shattered his Japanese identity. Shortly after matriculating at Kendai in 1938, all the students of his class were gathered in one room to take a required physical exam. When a staff member entered the room and ordered the Japanese students to line up, he followed the instruction. Nonetheless, while the other students were called into the exam room one by one in alphabetical order, Seikei's name was skipped. He asked the staff member why his name was not called, which led to a conversation he would never forget.

"What is your name?"

"My name is Sin."

"Sin? Where are you from?"

"I am from Korea."

"I am currently calling in just the Japanese. The rest of you will have your turns in the afternoon. Listen to my instruction carefully."[100]

When the staff member made the last remark while quickly turning away from Seikei, he was dumbfounded. Although he wanted to say "I am Japanese, too," he could not utter a word because Seikei became conscious of his classmates' icy stare that was fixed upon him. Unable to stop the tears coursing down his cheeks, he rushed out of the room.[101] This incident "completely shattered

[him] and compelled [him] to make a fresh start in life."[102] Surprisingly, this bitter experience of rejection by the Japanese did not lead him to abandon his Pan-Asianist dreams. Seikei, now fully aware of his distinct identity as Korean, remained committed to the ideal of constructing a multi-ethnic utopia in Manchukuo and East Asia. In that sense, he continued to support the educational missions of Kendai, even though he felt alienated from many of the Japanese members of its community.

Unfortunately, the second layer of isolation that Seikei felt on the Kendai campus stemmed from his genuine support of Pan-Asianism. Once he felt estranged from his Japanese classmates, he sought to connect with his Korean friends. However, among the several Korean students who matriculated at Kendai in 1938, Seikei could not find anyone who shared his political views. Here, we must recall the political division among Kendai's Korean students, discussed in Chapter 4. The reminiscent literature produced by the Korean alumni reveals that most Korean students strengthened their sense of Korean identity while enrolled at the university and yet their political views remained divided between support for Japan's *naisen ittai* policy on one hand and the aspiration for Korean independence on the other. Clearly, Seikei alone belonged to the former among the students of the first entering class, though he would eventually find some Korean students who shared his views in younger classes.[103] Seikei writes: "[People] denounce and reject ethnic nationalism while at the same time admire ethnic nationalists. I, who had placed trust in Japan, found myself in complete isolation because of that."[104] These lines capture the author's experience of making a transition from a model student at an assimilationist middle school in Korea to a confused and lonely student at Kendai in Manchukuo. In Korea, he grew up supporting Japan's Pan-Asianist endeavor as Japanese, rejecting his Korean identity. At Kendai, however, he was denied membership of Japanese identity due to what appears to be the lack of sensitivity at the institutional level or sheer discrimination. Seikei was also despised by his Korean friends as "spiritless."[105] Furthermore, as we have observed on the pages of the *juku* periodicals, there was a persisting discourse among Kendai students that the Pan-Asianist partnership should be formed by those who are awakened to their ethnic national identity. In other words, one's support of Pan-Asianism should come from one's deep love and dedication to one's own ethnic nation. Seikei eventually chose to embrace this idealistic version of Pan-Asianism, thanks to a Chinese classmate with whom he was able to develop a deep bond.

The deep friendship between Seikei and the Chinese student originated in their shared sense of isolation, struggle with the contradiction between their ideal and reality, and their genuine support of Pan-Asianim. Seikei writes about his past conversations with the Chinese classmate, who was taking medical leave at the time of his writing the essay. The Chinese student told the author:

> Many things make the *mankei* students unmotivated and skeptical [about Kendai]. To name a few, there are strict obedience that is required in any trainings on campus, the language barrier in classroom instruction, and the lack of consideration for our struggle [with those cultural and linguistic barriers]. For instance, [some instructors] yell at us when we do not understand their instructions or lag behind because of that, or, they would ignore us. They prioritize the *mankei* students who are fluent in the Japanese. After all, even though the Japanese show respect to individual *mankei* persons, they continue to feel contempt for the *mankei* people as a whole.[106]

These words of his Chinese friend, Seikei indicates, saved him from the depth of isolation and despair, because he was finally able to empathize with another individual at Kendai. He further asserts that since the understanding that bound them together grew based on their shared experience of "all sorts of disdain and scorn" by the rulers, this feeling cannot be easily understood by the rulers who "have become too familiar with their privileged position."[107] What is remarkable is that Seikei and his Chinese friend did not abandon their Pan-Asianist dreams but rather discovered their own unique mission within the endeavor to construct a multi-ethnic utopia. Seikei ends his essay by reminding himself of the mission that he and his friend once identified together: "We must save our fellow countrymen from the world of skepticism. Simultaneously, we must address a poignant warning to the people who sit in their comfortable, privileged position and thus continue to fail to perceive the true reality of the world."[108] Indeed, this sense of mission was what motivated Seikei to publish this essay. From the perspective of a Korean student who is truly dedicated to the Pan-Asianist ideal, he presents candid criticisms of Kendai and its Japanese members. Seikei feels entitled to do so because he and those Japanese members of the community share their belief in the educational objective of Kendai: fostering a new generation of leaders who would actualize the principle of ethnic harmony. At the same time, Seikei takes upon himself the challenge of persuading his fellow Korean students to join him in the Pan-Asianist endeavor, which he believes was compatible with his Korean ethnic nationalism. Thus, this essay by a Korean student presents a clear challenge to a dichotomous perception of the non-Japanese in Manchukuo as either collaborators or resisters of Japanese imperialism.

While the level of honesty found in many of the entries surprises us, some student authors used caution in expressing their opinions. As we have observed thus far, this tendency was found most frequently among the Chinese students. The essay authored by Zhang Ximing (first entering class) is one such example. Zhang's main message is rather simple: he criticizes some of his *juku*-mates who have developed the attitude of "just drifting along through school days without working towards high ambitions."[109] Although Zhang recognizes that one has many reasons to give up on high ambitions when faced with contradictions that exist in the current society, he still urges his fellow Kendai students not to give up on ideals. If they do, he asserts, such "easy-goers" would "eventually make themselves slaves of the current society."[110] Despite the simplicity of his message, his use of ambiguous words leaves his intention open to different interpretations. For instance, when he writes "we must transform the society of our own" or "at least, we should not add further contradiction and chaos to the society," which "society" is Zhang referring to?[111] Which people is it that Zhang identifies as "we"? Throughout his essay, he never makes clear reference to any country, ethnic nation or culture. As a result, his essay could be read as a passionate call for action to address the mounting problems of Manchukuo society. In this case, he addresses this message to his fellow Kendai students. Or, it could also be read as encouragement for his Chinese compatriots to rise up and work for their own society of China, which, from the perspective of anti-Japanese and anti-Manchukuo resisters, encompasses Manchuria. Given his peculiar and thorough avoidance of clear reference to any specific country or ethnic nation, we cannot rule out the second interpretation.

The "easy-goers" that Zhang criticizes in his essay were by no means a minority among Kendai students. By the spring of 1943, when the university housed all six classes on campus for the first time, the presence of such students along with other problems prompted some concerned students to initiate a *juku* reform. In writing about the initiatives on the first page of *Juku Monthly*'s fourth issue, one of the student leaders, Kobayashi Gunji (first entering class), described one aspect of the present challenge as follows: "Some students are uninterested in anything, avoid confrontation, and just play their cards while waiting to get their diplomas … These 'easy-goers' … damage the morale of the entire *juku*, depriving others of cheerfulness and passion."[112] The viewpoints of those "easy-goers" were not well represented in the *juku* periodicals because they did not find much interest in publishing their opinions. Besides those students who were indifferent to the idealistic aspects of Kendai's education, quite a few students were unable to commit themselves fully to the *juku* training due to illnesses. In addition to physical ailments that required students to take medical leave from school, some students had to leave campus for a certain period of time or for good due to depression. While there is no official record on such statistics, a transcript of a roundtable discussion among eight students of the first entering class and a professor, dating from September 1942, notes that the spring of 1940 saw the largest number of medical leave cases for that class. Of the 130 students who were enrolled, 55 took a leave of absence. This uniquely high number of absences was, according to the panel, due to the general disillusionment that many of the first entering class students experienced by their third year—over the contradiction between their ideals and the reality of Manchukuo and the university.[113] Though this was an extreme case, there indeed were quite a few students who had to take medical leave. Like the "easy-goers," most of these students with physical and mental challenges missed the opportunities of publishing their views on the *juku* periodicals. Nevertheless, a couple of entries provide a glimpse into these students' perspectives.

Kanki, a hand-written periodical published by the second entering class, includes a letter from a Japanese student who withdrew from Kendai. Aki Takeo, from the solitude of his home village, writes his "last letter" to his friend on campus and shares his past and present thoughts.[114] For instance, he shares his continuous struggle with faith. He writes: "What is the real happiness? Perhaps I am supposed to find it in the faith in [Shinto] *kami*. But, I do not want that type of facile *kami* in my life. Yet, I have no idea where my philosophy [of not believing in *kami*] would take me."[115] His religious view was not the only reason for Aki's feeling of not fitting in. He openly shares in the letter how he used to feel while still on campus: "You guys seem to think that yours is the only correct way of life. But, I don't need to follow that path. Who knows, I may choose a path that you guys have never imagined."[116] That is how Aki chose to quit Kendai. However, now that he is on his own and deep into a lonely life of endless contemplation, Aki seems to have lost a purpose for his life. Claiming that any interaction with other people causes intolerable torment, Aki writes that this is going to be the final letter from him. Other than this letter that was published on *Kanki*, no other record about this student exists.

While Aki's letter reveals the agony of not fitting in to the close-knit community, another entry shows a perspective of a student who remained uninterested in and indifferent to all the passionate discussions about their mission, ethnic harmony, and the like. A Japanese student of the third entering class published excerpts of his diary in *Reimei*, using a pen name, Mōja.[117] One of his diary entries starts with the line "how monotonous and boring my days are!"[118] Writing this entry on

Monday, the author cannot wait until the next Sunday when he can escape from campus life and go out to the city's downtown. In another day's entry, the author vents his frustration: "People say simply working hard on everything is not the desired attitude of Kendai students. And yet, folks here never act frivolously. But, I say, I have my way of doing things."[119] Perhaps this entry is one rare case of the so-called easy-goer expressing his honest feeling. Together with Aki's letter, this entry reveals the pushback from students who felt out of place amongst their peers who passionately engaged in idealistic discussions about ethnic harmony and the future of Manchukuo and East Asia.

Can Pan-Asianism and ethnic nationalisms coexist?

This chapter has examined Kendai's *juku* periodicals as an intellectual space that Kendai students created, maintained and cherished. Keeping it bilingual and encompassing different and even competing articulations of Pan-Asianism, the student-run periodicals epitomized Kendai's institutional commitment to cultural tolerance and ethnic equality among students. Being a popular mode of media on campus, these periodicals even facilitated exchanges of opinions in print on hot topics such as the outbreak of the Japan–US war and the desired model of ethnic harmony on campus. Due to the demise of these periodicals in the fall of 1943, they published the works of only the first through fourth entering class students. The empire-wide student enlistment policy deprived the Kendai campus of a number of students, institutional functionalities, and students' enthusiasm for the *juku* periodicals. Nonetheless, other records show that this type of honest and open discussions among students did not completely vanish in the last couple years of the university. For instance, Minaguchi Haruki, a Japanese student of the seventh entering class, writes in his memoir about his conversation with a Chinese classmate, Zhang Jingyun, that occurred in the spring of 1945. When Minaguchi asked for Zhang's impressions of a Japanese professor's lecture they had just attended, the Chinese student commented that "what the Japanese believe to be their sincere effort [in Asia] is not necessarily seen as such by the Chinese."[120] Zhang also indicated without hesitation that he respects Chiang Kai-shek, the leader of the Chinese Nationalist government, as his inspiration.[121] Here, we find a legacy of open discussions that was nurtured through the *juku* periodicals.

On the forum of discussion that they created on the pages of the *juku* periodicals, did Kendai students find a consensus on the questions of ethnic harmony? Politically, we find a strong and persisting influence of Ishiwara Kanji's concept of an East Asian League among not only the Japanese but also the Chinese students, and at least one Russian student, as seen in this chapter.[122] Besides the concept's clear focus on the Japan–Manchukuo–China relationship, the attention given to China emboldened Kendai's Chinese students to delve deep into their cultural roots and share that knowledge and their perspectives with their classmates. In that sense, in addition to the secret anti-Japanese study groups that the Chinese anthology *Huiyi* highlights, Kendai's Chinese students had another avenue of pursuing rigorous studies of their own roots and presenting the outcomes: the *juku* periodicals. Another striking pattern we find in Kendai students' printed forum of discussion is that some of the non-Japanese students perceived a match between their political agendas that were often specific to their ethnic nations and the Pan-Asianist endeavor of creating "a world of high moral" in Manchuria. Some of them even embraced Japan's leading position. What is important to highlight is that those students were not submissive or obsequious collaborators. Believing in ethnic equality among Kendai students as future leaders of Manchukuo, they voiced their candid criticisms of Japan's policy in Manchukuo and East Asia. Kendai's *juku* periodicals demonstrate that the students acted on Pan-Asianism through such honest exchanges of ideas as equal partners. Beyond the influence of the East Asian League and the political commitment to Pan-Asianism expressed by a number of students, however, disagreements persisted as to the type of new culture that Kendai students hoped to create for Manchukuo and East Asia.

Consensus was even harder to form when it came to ethnic harmony in the context of their own day-to-day life in Kendai's *juku*. Even with empathy, self-criticism and open discussions—the three means that periodical entries often promoted—the students could not find satisfying answers for everyone. Nevertheless, though nowhere near a consensus, a dominant discourse emerged to celebrate the model of unity in diversity. More specifically, this idealistic conception posited that dedication to one's own ethnic nation was not only compatible with Pan-Asianism but also an essential attribute of a true comrade in ethnic harmony. Examining this conception on a personal level—in their own relationships with *juku*-mates—Kendai students' inquiries on ethnic harmony boiled down to the question of whether Pan-Asianism and ethnic nationalisms could really coexist. While the dominant discourse answered in the affirmative in full idealism, many students, including those idealists themselves, continued to face the reality that challenged their optimism. Many could not make peace with the contradiction of pursuing Pan-Asianist dreams with equal partners when those members' ethnic nations were fighting a brutal war against each other or one was exploiting the other in colonial domination. One's concern about the future of his ethnic nation may drive him to become Pan-Asianist; but, his concern about the present situation of his ethnic nation often strengthened his ethnic nationalism in opposition to Japan. Facing this inherent contradiction in wartime Pan-Asianism, some students sank into despair, while others took the "easy-going" attitude, staying indifferent to the difficult question of the ideal of ethnic harmony. Still, as a student body, Kendai students did not give up on the potential of reaching an understanding as comrades. That is why they kept the print forum of discussion going and thriving with clashing opinions until the fall of 1943.

Epilogue

As described by the students themselves in their diaries and memoirs, for Kendai students the end of the war in August 1945 was the beginning of an entirely new life regardless of their country of origin. Kendai students, whose future career had been promised by the Manchukuo state, had to fashion new lives for themselves under radically altered circumstances. After going back to their "homes," which often required a long and arduous journey and even cost some of them their lives, Kendai alumni established new lives that were even more diverse than those they had left behind several years earlier when they had matriculated at Kendai. How did their experiences at Kendai affect their post-1945 lives, when, to varying degrees in every country including Japan, the wartime concept of a Pan-Asianist empire was widely denounced, discredited or disavowed? The sources available provide only partial answers to these questions.[1] Nevertheless, where individual lives can be documented, one sees widely divergent and in some cases unexpected legacies.

Even before war's end, Kendai as an educational institution had been severely impacted by the war. In the fall of 1943 when conscription of students began, with the exception of the physically unfit, all Japanese students twenty years of age and over left the school to bear arms. In the following year, the draft age was lowered to nineteen. The Japanese graduates of the first three classes who were employed in Manchukuo were also drafted. On August 11, 1945, two days after the Soviet Union's Red Army crossed the border into Manchukuo, all the non-Japanese students were dispatched as forced laborers to a munitions factory in Gongzhuling.[2] On August 12, the remaining Japanese students of more than eighteen years of age were called to arms in the so-called *nekosogi dōin*, "root-and-branch mobilization." This left approximately seventy Japanese students and an unknown number of Japanese faculty members to defend the Kendai campus from the invading Red Army and the "rebel" forces of mostly Chinese soldiers who had deserted from the Manchukuo Imperial Army.[3] The fighting around the Kendai campus continued even after the official closing of the war on August 15. Yamada Shōji, a Japanese student of the eighth entering class, recalls engaging in exchange of fire with an armed group of Chinese-speaking men who attacked the school facilities late in the evening of August 15.[4] Such conditions continued until sometime between August 18 and 20.

Kendai officially declared its closing on August 23, 1945, and a difficult journey back to Japan began for the Japanese students and instructors.[5] The younger students who remained on campus to the end took refuge in Kendai's Japanese faculty members' residences while waiting to be repatriated. Because the Soviet Union's occupation army prohibited people from gathering in large groups, each faculty's family took a few students into their homes. Some older Japanese students who had been demobilized and returned to the Kendai campus found lodgings together in Shinkyō—now renamed Changchun. Although the administration distributed the school's remaining financial resources to faculty, staff, and students, the sums of money did not feed them long. Some former students worked as wage laborers in order to feed themselves, while the entrepreneurial-minded others sold personal assets of their host instructors' families on their behalf. Meanwhile, some Japanese faculty members and students were captured by the Red Army and sent to Siberia for forced labor. Among them was Associate Professor of Philosophy Koito Natsujirō, who died from the harsh working conditions of the Soviet camps.[6] The exact number of those who were sent to Siberia is unknown. Historian Eriko Miyazawa conducted research on the whereabouts of Japanese students of the first entering class and found information on thirty-five out of seventy-five students who had initially matriculated at Kendai. Of these thirty-five graduates, eleven were held as prisoners in Siberia for two to four years before returning to Japan. Undoubtedly, some others died in Soviet camps while awaiting repatriation. As Miyazawa speculates, in all likelihood the situation was similar for the Japanese Kendai students of other classes. In addition, some Japanese students who had been drafted into the Japanese military found themselves stranded in various parts of the empire when the war ended. They all headed back to Japan as *hikiagesha*, or repatriates.

What about the non-Japanese students? Memoirs written by Japanese faculty and students indicate that some of the former Russian students served in the Soviet occupation army immediately following war's end, often as Japanese translators. As described in Chapter 5, the Chinese students were thrown into the political struggle between Chinese Communists and Nationalists. Available sources suggest that more former Chinese Kendai students allied themselves with the Nationalists at the end of the war than indicated in the Chinese anthology *Huiyi*. Korean and Taiwanese students were left on their own. They headed back to their home countries, often in groups, determined to work for their countries' new future. Interestingly, when a group of Korean students were about to leave Shinkyō, they asked Tanaka Kazuo, a Japanese alumnus of the first entering class, if he would join them. Tanaka and his family had lived in Jeollabuk-do, Korea. Although Tanaka did not join the group, assuming his family would soon be repatriated to Japan, the fact that the Korean students reached out to Tanaka, a son of Japanese colonial settlers, testifies to bonds of friendship among at least some Kendai students, which transcended ethnic nationality.[7]

During the chaotic time following the Soviet Union's invasion of Manchuria, a number of Japanese instructors and students had their opportunities to hear the real feelings of some of the non-Japanese students. Assistant Professor Nishimoto Sōsuke, who had also served as *jukutō*, wrote in 1967 that his last interactions with some non-Japanese students were something to be remembered for the rest of his life.[8] A Chinese student came to see Nishimoto around Kendai's closing day. Nishimoto identifies this student as "G," who had been one of his students at *juku* and had been arrested by the military police in the spring of 1945 for his involvement with anti-Japanese activities. Nishimoto remembers that after apologizing for betraying the teachers' good will, "G" addressed him as follows: "Even if faculty members were well meaning, and no matter how great the ideal of an East Asian League was in theory, it was obvious to us that Manchukuo was nothing more than a puppet state and a creature of Japanese imperialism."[9] Meanwhile, a Korean student visited Nishimoto's residence to bid farewell. At that time, he confessed that with few exceptions, the Korean students at Kendai had been secretly involved in national independence movements, which somewhat corresponds to the testimony found in the collection of Korean alumni's memoirs. Then he stated: "Cooperation between Korea and Japan is only possible when Korea achieves liberation from Japanese imperial rule. I will return to Korea to work for my homeland's independence and reconstruction."[10] Thus, Japan's defeat and the closing of Kendai exposed the Japanese teacher to the most direct expressions of honest feelings of his former students.

Nishimoto also had a surprising encounter with Stavitski, a Russian student of the fifth entering class.[11] Nishimoto was taken prisoner by the military police of the Soviet occupation army together with more than ten Japanese students and Professor of Philosophy Mori Shinzō. When Nishimoto found that the Red Army officer who interrogated him at prison was his former student Stavitski, Nishimoto was so astounded he "lost his head."[12] Whatever Stavitski's ideological convictions may have been at this time, Nishimoto concluded that Kendai's anti-communist instruction failed to take root in this Russian student. Undaunted by the role reversal, Nishimoto demanded the release of his Japanese students and the elderly Professor Mori. While there is no concrete evidence, Nishimoto believes that it was Stavitski who worked behind the scene to secure the release of these Kendai students and Professor Mori a few days later. In the end, Nishimoto was the only one in this group who was actually sent to Siberia.[13]

A Japanese student of the eighth entering class, Yamada Shōji, received direct help from one of Kendai's former Chinese students. Before he managed to return to Japan, Yamada worked as a live-in servant at a bread factory owned by the father of a former Chinese student Li Wanchun of the third entering class in the northeastern part of Shinkyō City. In effect, Li and his family protected Yamada from being captured by the Chinese Communist Army. The Li family even offered Yamada the opportunity to marry their daughter and inherit the family business. When they learned that Yamada wanted to return to Japan, they arranged for his safe trip back.[14] This episode was not a rare case for the Japanese students who managed to return home safely; a number of Kendai alumni reported cases of Japanese students receiving protection and assistance from their former Chinese classmates.[15] These testimonies again call into question the Chinese anthology *Huiyi*'s one-sided emphasis on the hostility between them and the Japanese students and faculty.

While the evidence is far from being comprehensive, these stories suggest that although many non-Japanese students, and especially the Chinese students, opposed Japanese imperialism, they drew a distinction between their former classmates and instructors and the wartime Japanese state. Thus, their hostility towards Japanese imperialism did not prevent many Chinese former students from helping their Japanese friends who appeared sincerely devoted to the ideal of equality and "ethnic harmony." Ironically, the collapse of Manchukuo and closing down of Kendai produced individual interactions of this kind that attest to the existence of personal friendships nurtured at Kendai. At the time when the institution was falling apart, Ishiwara Kanji's hope for honest exchange of ideas among Kendai students and faculty materialized most dramatically.

Perhaps because of these strong bonds among students and faculty and their intense experiences of Kendai's grand experiment of Pan-Asianist education, Kendai's alumni maintained contact despite the turbulent situations of post-1945 East Asian societies. Initially, these contacts were made and maintained within each country. As for the Chinese alumni, historian Miyazawa reports that as many as 120 of them attended Dongbei University (Northeastern University), which was established by the Nationalist government of China in Shenyang City, Liaoning Province, in 1946. As noted in Chapter 5, both Gao Ke and Han Weiping testify that Kendai alumni were working closely together at Dongbei University to achieve Nationalist–Communist reconciliation. By the fall of 1948, however, the region fell under Communist control, and many of these Kendai alumni had to go through "thought reform" under the CCP.[16] Moreover, many of them faced political persecution during the Cultural Revolution (1966–76), being imprisoned and subjected to forced labor.

For the Japanese alumni, the prolonged process of repatriation and social and economic dislocations of the immediate postwar period made it difficult to reestablish contact with fellow alumni. Nonetheless, some alumni started to create rosters as soon as they settled down in their postwar lives. The earliest list was compiled by a group of alumni residing in the Kyūshū region in July 1946 and contained contact information for seventy-one former Kendai students. In 1947, the alumni who lived in the Greater Tokyo Area and the members of the eighth entering class created their own rosters.[17]

Meanwhile, Kendai alumni and former faculty members experienced political persecution during the Allied occupation of Japan. In January 1947, the Supreme Commander for the Allied Powers (SCAP) banned those who had attended or worked for Kendai from holding public office.[18] This was part of SCAP's policy of purging Japanese society of militaristic and ultra-nationalistic elements. At the same time, the Japanese government allowed Kendai's former students of the fourth through eighth entering classes—the students who had not graduated Kendai due to war mobilization and the closing of the school—to transfer to public universities in Japan if they passed the required exam.[19] To arrange the transfer of credits, the Foreign Ministry of Japan designated Professor Mori Kyōzō as representative of Kenkoku University's alumni and the issuer of various forms. Thus an unofficial alumni association was created in December 1950.[20]

It was on May 2, 1954 that the Kenkoku University Alumni Association in Japan was officially founded.[21] Commemorating the sixteenth anniversary of Kendai's opening, eighty-nine members—sixty-seven former students and twenty-two former faculty members—gathered in Tokyo and selected former Vice President Sakuta Sōichi as the first president of the alumni association.[22] Well advanced in age and suffering from ill health, Sakuta's nomination was nevertheless significant for its symbolism. By selecting Sakuta, as we have seen, the alumni signaled their desire to remember Kendai as it was in its early years under Sakuta's administration rather than its subsequent years under Suetaka's administration.[23] The association continued to meet annually until 2010, when the fifty-seventh general meeting declared it to be the final meeting due to the advanced age of its constituents. Over the years, participation in the annual reunions actually increased as more alumni began to bring their families, and as the association started to invite the alumni and their families from overseas. In 1988, 239 people attended the thirty-fifth meeting, which commemorated the fiftieth anniversary of Kendai's opening.[24] Even the last reunion held in Tokyo in 2010 had about 120 participants, including an alumnus from South Korea.

Aiming to promote continuing friendship among former Kendai students, the alumni association in Japan continued to expand its rosters, adding not only Japanese but also non-Japanese alumni. The latest list compiled in 2003 includes names of 1,408 former students and 400 faculty members. These names are categorized under the faculty and staff and each entering class; and under each category, they are divided into three groups: those who are alive, those known to be deceased, and those whose status is unknown. Astoundingly, the alumni association in Japan obtained information on 1,213 or 86 percent of all former students (including those known to be deceased) and 191 or 48 percent of all former faculty members (including the news of their death). As of 2003, the association was in contact with 691 former students who were still alive.[25]

The alumni rosters compiled in 1955 and 2003 and other sources provide an overview of Kendai alumni's post-1945 occupations. Table 1 shows the occupations of 268 former Chinese students who were alive and stayed in contact with the alumni association in Japan as of 2003. The list contains former Mongolian students who resided in Inner Mongolia, an autonomous region of the PRC in 2003.[26] Given that these alumni were in their mid-70s to late 80s at that time, many of the reported occupations must have been the posts they had held before retirement. Not surprisingly, many alumni made professional use of their Japanese language skills, most commonly as Japanese language instructors, researchers, and businessmen. Several of the Chinese graduates achieved prominence in their fields and played a role in the normalization of relations between the PRC and Japan. Nie Zhanglin of the fourth entering class was among the first several Chinese journalists dispatched to Japan in 1964 after the signing of the Sino–Japanese Journalist Exchange Agreement, which secured a line of communication before the normalization of the two countries' diplomatic relations in 1972.[27] Chen Kang, a member of the fifth entering class, was a politician who played an important role in China–Japan relations, which I will discuss later. Strikingly, more than 100 members were employed

Table 1 Occupations of alumni residing in the PRC in 2003 (of 268 who were alive and stayed in contact)

Occupation	Number
Faculty or researchers at universities or other research institutes	84
Public sector	73
Teachers in secondary education	25
Lawyers	3
Medicine	3
Military	3
Family-owned business	2
Press	1
Occupation unreported	74
Total	268

Source: *Kenkoku daigaku dōsōkai meibo [Kenkoku University Alumni Association Roster]* (Tokyo: Kenkoku daigaku dōsōkai, 2003).

as educators: university professors, researchers, and secondary school teachers. According to historian Miyazawa, this was because in post-1949 PRC society, teachers had fewer chances of being asked about their revolutionary pasts or lack thereof, compared to people in other occupations.[28] It is also significant that after education, employment in state enterprises ranked second, which suggests that being a Kendai graduate was not an obstacle to public sector employment. In addition, a significant number of Kendai alumni listed two names on the 2003 alumni roster, which may indicate that they had sought to hide their past affiliation with Kendai by changing their names.[29]

Table 2 shows the occupations held by former Korean students before their retirement. While the Korean students in South Korea established their own alumni association and published two collections of their memoirs in 1986 and 1988, very little is known about the whereabouts of those who settled in North Korea, which is not surprising in light of prohibitions of both the North and South Korean governments on people-to-people communication between the two countries. The latest roster published in 2003 does not include any contact of those believed to be living in North Korea. Table 2 shows that the alumni residing in South Korea have been quite successful in their careers. During the Korean War (1950–53), some Kendai alumni in South Korea achieved high positions in the Republic of Korea military. Min Gi-Sik, a member of the third

Table 2 Occupations of alumni residing in the Republic of Korea in 2003 (of 27 who were alive and stayed in contact)

Occupation	Number
Company or bank employees (including company executives)	9
Faculty or researchers at universities or other research institutes	6
Teachers in secondary education	3
Politicians	3
Accountant	1
Public sector	1
Occupation unreported	4
Total	27

Source: *Kenkoku daigaku dōsōkai meibo [Kenkoku University Alumni Association Roster]* (Tokyo: Kenkoku daigaku dōsōkai, 2003).

entering class, was involved in the creation of the ROK Army, fought in the war as a divisional commander and later served as the Chief of Staff of the Army from 1963 to 1965.[30] Like the Chinese alumni, quite a few Kendai alumni became high level actors in Japan–Korea relations. Bang Hui of the third entering class visited Japan a number of times as a diplomat in the late 1970s and 1980.[31] Another member of the third entering class, Gang Yeong-Hun, is perhaps the most notable Korean alumnus. After serving as the Ambassador to the United Kingdom and the Vatican City State, Gang became Prime Minister (1988–90). He was the first ROK head of state to visit North Korea. When Japanese Emperor Hirohito passed away in 1989, Gang attended the funeral ceremony as a representative of South Korea. After the two years of his career as prime minister, Gang served as president of the Korean Red Cross.[32]

Compared to the relatively plentiful data on Chinese and Korean alumni, information on the post-1945 experiences of the Taiwanese and Russian alumni—two of the smallest non-Japanese student populations in the Kendai student body—is limited. The 2003 alumni roster lists twenty-seven Taiwanese and thirty-one Russian alumni's whereabouts, including ten Taiwanese and eleven Russians who were alive as of 2003. According to interviews with three Taiwanese alumni conducted by Miyazawa, Kendai's former Taiwanese students encountered considerable hardship after 1945. Initially, the Chinese Nationalist government that controlled Taiwan did not allow Kendai alumni to transfer to universities in Taiwan. Only after extended negotiations were they given permission to take transfer exams. Nevertheless, many of them fell victim to the so-called White Terror, political suppression of intellectuals deemed by the Nationalist government as ideologically suspect, either because of leftist affiliation or past experience of collaboration with Japan, and were imprisoned for some time.[33] As of 2003, the reported occupations of Taiwanese alumni are seen in Table 3.

Miyazawa states that the Russian alumni had the toughest time after 1945 due to their affiliation with Kendai. According to the speech that Cheusov (first entering class) delivered at the alumni association's annual meeting convened in Japan in 1988, Cheusov and two other members of the first entering class, Petrov (second entering class), and Baus and Epov of the fourth entering class survived eleven years of imprisonment and forced labor.[34] Miyazawa reports that a few former Russian students eventually used their Japanese language skills to work for Russo–Japanese relations. For instance, Vtorusin of the second entering class served as the Director-General of the Khabarovsk Office of the Soviet Union–Japan Friendship Association. Tolkachov of the third entering class had opportunities of traveling to Japan as an interpreter.[35]

What about the Japanese alumni? The 2003 alumni roster includes information on the whereabouts of 646 former Japanese students, including the 375 who were alive as of 2003. Presumably because most were retired at the time of the survey, the list does not include the occupation of many of the association members. Although less complete, the 1955 roster of 516 alumni provides a more complete picture of career patterns.[36] In 1955, most alumni were between twenty-eight and thirty-five years of age. As seen in Table 4, one remarkable fact is that no fewer than thirty-four alumni worked in journalism at Japan's

Table 3 Occupations of alumni residing in the Republic of China (Taiwan) in 2003 (of 10 who were alive and stayed in contact)

Occupation	Number
Company employees (including company executives)	4
Teacher in secondary education	1
Accountant	1
Occupation unreported	4
Total	10

Source: *Kenkoku daigaku dōsōkai meibo [Kenkoku University Alumni Association Roster]* (Tokyo: Kenkoku daigaku dōsōkai, 2003).

Table 4 Occupations of alumni residing in Japan in 1955 (of 516 who were alive and stayed in contact)

Occupation	Number
Company employees	145
Public sector	92
Banks	36
Press	34
Family-owned business/Farming	30
Teachers in secondary education	28
Attending or teaching at universities	18
Self-defense Force	8
Accountants	3
Lawyers	2
Diplomat	1
Actor	1
Occupation unreported	118
Total	516

Source: *Kenkoku daigaku dōsōkai meibo [Kenkoku University Alumni Association Roster]* (Tokyo: Kenkoku daigaku dōsōkai, 1955).

major newspapers, including *Mainichi, Asahi, Yomiuri, Chunichi* and *Nikkei*. As discussed later, these members played important roles in leading the activities of the alumni association in Japan.

Some of the Japanese Kendai alumni journalists who lived in the Greater Tokyo Area initiated study meetings for Kendai alumni in May 1970. Kaede Motoo of the third entering class, an economics correspondent for *Chunichi*, and Maekawa Mitsuo of the fifth entering class, a political correspondent for *Nikkei*, took the lead. Since then, the meetings were held every month and provided them with a space for exchanging ideas and enjoying meals together. These meetings were named *nisuikai*, which means "meetings held on the second Wednesdays," and marked the 375th meeting in January 2007. The alumni association's record shows that for each meeting they invited a speaker, most of whom were members of the alumni association, and on average twenty-three people attended. The topics of the invited lectures ranged widely, from international economy, energy policy, and China–Japan relations, to more personal subjects such as personal recollections of certain Kendai faculty members, the experiences of *juku* life at Kendai, and reports about recent travels to Taiwan, Korea, or China to meet with former classmates.[37] Occasionally, the *nisuikai* invited non-Japanese alumni as speakers. The first such meeting was held on August 9, 1972, with Kim Sang-Gyu, a Korean member of the fifth entering class, whose talk was titled "Current Issues on the Korean Peninsula."[38] The *nisuikai* meeting with one of the largest turnouts was held on February 2, 1980, when Chen Kang, a former Chinese student and currently the PRC Consul-General in Sapporo, was the speaker.[39] In addition to the Tokyo *nisuikai*, Kendai alumni in the Kansai region, northern Kyūshū, and Hokkaidō organized similar meetings.

I had the opportunity of attending the Osaka *nihuikai* on June 16, 2010 and again on July 13, 2011. The meetings—more correctly called banquets—were held at a Japanese-style bar in the middle of a very busy district of Osaka. The round of drinking of the former Kendai students, who were now in their 80s and 90s, began at 4:00 p.m. at a quiet and empty bar before other customers had arrived. Unlike the *nisuikai* held in Tokyo, which were more formal affairs, the Osaka events were casual and informal. After some exchanging greetings and raising beer glasses in a toast, the party began. At the 2010 meeting, six members from the first, fifth, sixth, and eighth entering classes attended, and in 2011, five members from the first, fourth, fifth, sixth, and eighth entering classes and one friend who graduated from a military school in Manchukuo. Upon learning of my interest in Kendai, they happily reminisced about their student days and campus life. One thing they emphasized was the diversity of experiences among the former students. Mr. Nakamura Masazō of the first entering class discussed how each *juku* had its own color. Mr. Shiokawa Shigeya of the sixth entering class urged me to look at the student experiences of Kendai not just through the sources created by the Japanese alumni but also through the ones authored by the non-Japanese students. Indeed, he kindly gave me valuable documents, including the memoir of the Taiwanese alumnus Li Shuiqing, discussed in Chapter 4. Mr. Ochi Michiyo of the first entering class gave me the collected essays published by the Korean alumni also examined in Chapter 4.[40]

What I witnessed at these *nisuikai* meetings is an astonishingly long-lasting bond among Kendai alumni. Equally remarkable is the fact that the friendship among Kendai's former students transcends national boundaries and continues to flourish. Both the alumni association and individual alumni in Japan have worked ceaselessly to reestablish contact with former Kendai students living in countries other than Japan.[41] Contacts occurred at first among individual alumni living in Japan, Taiwan, and Korea. The alumni association's record shows that while unable to come himself, Taiwanese alumnus of the first entering class Li Shuiqing sent a relative to attend the first general meeting of the Kendai alumni association in 1954.[42] In 1973, Li traveled to Japan to attend the reunion of the first entering class.[43]

The earliest contact between the Japanese and Korean alumni occurred in the 1950s, even before the normalization of state-to-state relations. A Japanese member of the second entering class, Matsumoto Hirokazu, resided in Seoul during the Korean War (1950–53), working as a correspondent for a leading Japanese daily newspaper, *The Mainichi*. During his stay, Matsumoto frequently shared meals with four of his classmates: Hong Chun-Sik, Dong Wan, Kim Yeong-Rok, and Choe Jae-Bang.[44] In addition, as many of the alumni living in South Korea began to travel to the United States for study and on business, the Japanese alumni hosted small gatherings whenever their classmates' flights stopped over in Tokyo.[45] In 1965, Ichikawa Emon, a Japanese member of the second entering class, was dispatched to Seoul as the Counselor of the Japanese Embassy to prepare for the normalization of the two countries' diplomatic relations. Ichikawa was not only able to reestablish contact with many former Korean students but also received crucial assistance.[46] After 1965, small groups of Japanese and Korean alumni continued to visit each other, as in a gathering of the fifth entering class in Seoul in 1989.[47] Meanwhile, the Korean alumni in South Korea established their own alumni association and stayed in close contact.[48]

Despite numerous personal and informal meetings among the alumni in Japan and Korea, it was only in 2004 that a large-scale reunion event was co-hosted by the alumni associations of the two countries. Why did it take so long? Kuwahara Akito, a Japanese member of the fourth entering class and one of the Japanese alumni who led the post-1945 international networking, writes that there were some concerned voices within the alumni association in Japan about "the conflicting views of history in [postwar] Japan and South Korea."[49] While he does not provide further details, he is clearly referring to the long-lasting conflict between the two countries over Japan's responsibility for its thirty-five-year-long colonial rule over Korea.[50] In the early 2000s while the alumni association in Japan was preparing for its fourth trip to the PRC discussed later, the Korean association proposed to jointly hold a reunion meeting for the Japanese and Korean alumni. The event took place in Seoul on May 19, 2004 as the group of more than thirty Japanese alumni, many in their 80s, made a two-day stopover in Seoul on their way to China.[51] Overwhelmed by the enthusiastic welcome they received from the sixteen Korean alumni who greeted them and their families, the Japanese participants instantly knew that feelings of unbridled friendship among Kendai's Korean and Japanese alumni were unaffected by the large issues of Japan's past colonial rule in Korea. Kuwahara later wrote of his strong urge "to apologize for having allowed the contentious understanding of history to delay the Japan–Korea alumni meeting for so long."[52]

As in the case of the Japanese and Korean alumni, early contact between Japanese and Chinese Kendai alumni occurred before the normalization of diplomatic relations. However, it took much longer for the alumni association in Japan to find out the whereabouts of the Chinese alumni. In 1964, Chen Kang of the fifth entering class was dispatched to Tokyo as the Secretary-General of the PRC's trade liaison office that initiated, promoted, and regulated the semi-private trade between the two countries. During the three years of Chen's stay, Japanese alumni Hayashi Rintarō (third entering class), Kaede Motoo (third entering class), and Sugimoto Hajime (fifth entering class) frequently visited Chen at his office. They made these visits even though doing so caused Japanese public security police officers to inquire as to their relationships with Chen and the purpose of their meetings. Chen returned to Japan as the Secretary at the PRC Embassy in Tokyo and subsequently as the first PRC Consul-General in Sapporo, Hokkaidō, in 1980, and continued to play important roles in reconnecting the alumni in Japan and the PRC.[53]

These early contacts between the Japanese and Chinese alumni eventually enabled the alumni association in Japan to organize its first trip in 1980 to Changchun City where Kendai had been located. A few of the Kendai buildings remained and were used by Jilin University of Science and Technology. The initiator of this trip was Kuwahara Akito. On the Chinese side, five alumni, including Wu Dongmin, a member of the second entering class serving as a high-ranking official of the CCP at that time, were involved in the planning. Although the PRC had opened its doors to foreign tourists, the government imposed strict regulations regarding the number of tourists, destinations, and activities. For instance, the trip could not be made under the name of the Kendai Alumni Association. For the purposes of the visit, the Japanese alumni called themselves the Kankirei-kai ("Kankirei group")—named after the site of the Kendai campus—and had to include in its itinerary a visit to the Vice Mayor of Changchun City to discuss China–Japan collaboration on investment. To gain approval, the official purpose of the trip became the promotion of friendship between the two countries. Of course, the participants' primary interest was to reunite with their classmates after more than three to four decades of silence. Altogether, ninety Japanese alumni and their families traveled to Changchun and several other cities and were able to meet with 108 former classmates living in China.[54] After returning from the trip, one of the Japanese participants,

Bandō Yūtarō of the first entering class, wrote a newspaper article as the alumni association's secretary. In it, he reported that "both the hosts and their guests exchanged tearful gazes."[55] Such emotional encounters occurred throughout the trip. For instance, even though the train the Japanese alumni took to Changchun had only a fifteen-minute stopover at the Shenyang train station, and despite the fact that the train arrived late in the night, a group of Chinese alumni were waiting at the platform just to exchange a few words and shake hands with their former classmates. There were also three Mongolian alumni, who traveled all the way from Inner Mongolia to see them.[56]

The alumni in Japan and China kept in close contact and held three more reunions in 1992, 1997, and 2004. All three meetings took the same form as the first one in 1980; a number of the Japanese alumni and their families traveled to Changchun and other cities to meet with the Chinese alumni. The event in 1992 had the largest turnout: 154 Japanese participants, including alumni families, and 209 Chinese alumni and their families.[57] Even in 1997, when all Kendai alumni were in their 70s and 80s, fifty-eight members traveled from Japan to meet with 102 Chinese alumni and their families.[58] On the last trip from Japan in 2004, about thirty members flew to China and met with fifty-eight Chinese alumni.[59]

In the meantime, some Chinese and Japanese alumni joined forces to found a new university, Changchun University, on the former site of Kendai, which was achieved by amalgamating several existing small colleges into a multi-disciplinary university. In the fall of 1985, Chen Kang, who was then serving as the Vice President of the Sino–Japanese Friendship Association, met with four Japanese alumni to request assistance for the project. The list of Kendai alumni involved in the project shows that by the 1980s a number of Chinese and Japanese alumni had risen to high positions in their respective countries. On the Chinese side, Gao Di (eighth entering class) was serving as the General Secretary of the CCP in Jilin Province, Wu Dongmin (second entering class) was the Director of the CCP's Organizing Committee, Chen Xin (seventh entering class) was the Vice Director of the Board of Education in Jilin Province, and Chen Kang had been leading this project.[60] The four Japanese alumni whom Chen Kang initially contacted were Hayashi Rintarō (third entering class), who had been a high official in the Ministry of International Trade and Industry, Bandō Yūtarō (first entering class), the Vice President of the leading typographical printing company in Japan, Nakagawa Kei'ichirō (first entering class), Honorary Professor at Tokyo University, and Dodo Kazu, Honorary Professor at Kōbe University.[61] Among the names Chen Kang initially proposed for the new university was *jianshe daxue*, which would literally translate as "Creation University," using the same initial Chinese character as in *jianguo daxue*, "Kenkoku University." In the end, erring on the side of caution, at the suggestion of Nakagawa they adopted the more conventional name of Changchun University.[62]

As to be expected, relations between Kendai's Chinese and Japanese alumni were not without moments of tension and misunderstanding. When Chen Kang asked his Japanese friends for guidance in planning Changchun University, his primary purpose apparently was to obtain financial support from the alumni association in Japan. During the discussion that took place in Changchun in 1986, it became clear to the Japanese alumni that the Chinese members expected to obtain considerably greater financial support from Japan than the alumni association was capable of delivering. Dodo Kazu, who was present at the discussion, later recorded his feelings of frustration that "the Chinese side could not understand" that as a "non-profit private organization without recourse to public funding," Kendai's alumni association in Japan "could contribute only a limited sum."[63] On the following day, Dodo appears to have been offended when the Chinese members took the group to see an exhibit on the history of the Japanese invasion in the Northeast.[64] Dodo writes that he felt as if the Chinese members' "purpose in calling on [them] to reflect on the past deeds of Japan was to negotiate a larger financial contribution" from the Japanese alumni association.[65] Nevertheless, despite some uncomfortable moments experienced by the Japanese alumni who travelled to Changchun, Bandō Yūtarō subsequently persuaded the Japan alumni association to allocate part of the group's resource to the founding of Changchun University. In addition, he personally solicited donations of 1 million yen from the alumni living in Japan.[66] In 1987, the university opened on the site of Kendai.[67]

The network of relations rooted in mutual friendship continues. Based on anecdotal evidence, quite a few Japanese alumni have served as guarantors of the children and grandchildren of their former Chinese classmates who pursued their education in Japan. Until 1996, it was required that all foreign nationals other than tourists residing in Japan designate a Japanese citizen as their guarantor. Even after this requirement was removed, having a guarantor was necessary for various purposes such as renting an apartment, enrolling in schools, and applying for scholarships. After the alumni association's second trip to the PRC in 1992, the Japanese association expanded these multi-generational exchanges. The first social gathering of the Japanese Kendai alumni and the children and grandchildren of the Chinese Kendai alumni residing in Japan was held in Tokyo on December 5, 1993. Hayashida Takashi (third entering class), the president of the alumni association in Japan, explained that the Japanese alumni association members intended to provide guidance and encouragement to the children of their former classmates, "who as parents must be worried about their children studying or working abroad."[68] The gatherings have been held annually ever since, attended by over 100 participants each time. A significant number of the Chinese alumni's children and grandchildren have received financial aid from the Japanese alumni association.[69]

As seen in this chapter, all through the difficult years of the immediate aftermath of the dissolution of Manchukuo, and even during the period when their respective countries had not yet reopened official diplomatic relations, many Kendai alumni sought out their former classmates at home and abroad. The Japanese alumni association was the earliest to take root, but contact with alumni associations in Korea and China followed in due time as former Kendai students reclaimed the friendship that they had nurtured through the *juku* life at Kendai. Except for a few who were directly involved in international relations, like Chen Kang and Ichikawa Emon, Kendai alumni's postwar interactions occurred on a much more personal basis than Ishiwara Kanji's idea of an East Asian League. Ethnic nationalism and colonialism are antithetical the world over; even the victorious Allied powers soon lost their Asian empires. In hindsight, Kendai as an institution of Japan's colonial education met its inevitable end. So did Ishiwara's vision of spontaneous political alliance among East Asian ethnic nations, and the four professors' conception of Japanese-led Pan-Asian unity. However, by providing a space for the faculty and students of diverse backgrounds to express divergent interpretations of the Pan-Asianist ideal and to critique each other's conception and practice of the theory, Kendai created a repository of uniquely diverse articulations of Pan-Asianism in the midst of war and colonialism. The strong bond among Kendai's former students that has survived the dissolution of the institution is the outcome of their sustained efforts at building an understanding through honest exchange of ideas about Pan-Asianism as equal partners.

Notes

Chapter 1

1   The "kingly way (ōdō or 王道)," also translated as the "Way of Right," is a Confucian concept of an ideal way of governing a country by virtue. Its opposite is the "Way of Might (hadō or 覇道)" or "despotic way," which means ruling by authority and force. Manchukuo's adherence to the "kingly way," meant to propose an alternative to the Western ruling style characterized as the "despotic way." Further discussion can be found in the section "Manchuria and Manchukuo."

2   See the section "Manchuria and Manchukuo" for a discussion about English translation of the term *minzoku*.

3   Shin'ichi Yamamuro, *Manchuria under Japanese Dominion: Encounters with Asia*, trans. Joshua A. Fogel (Philadelphia: University of Pennsylvania Press, 2006), 10.

4   The Japanese Army stationed its forces in Korea from 1904 to 1945.

5   Mark R. Peattie, *Ishiwara Kanji and Japan's Confrontation with the West* (Princeton, NJ: Princeton University Press, 1975), 110–14.

6   My summary of this state-building operation of the Kwantung Army is based on Yamamuro's book.

7   Yamamuro, *Manchuria under Japanese Dominion*, 97–8.

8   "Proclamation on the Establishment of the Manchoukuo [*sic*]," 1 March 1932.

9   For a comprehensive study of Tachibana Shiraki and his contribution to the development of Manchukuo's ideological construct, see Lincoln Li, *The China Factor in Modern Japanese Thought: The Case of Tachibana Shiraki, 1881–1945* (New York: State University of New York Press, 1996).

10 Takeshi Komagome, "Manshūkoku ni okeru jukyō no shisō: daidō, ōdō, kōdō," (*Shiso* 841, July 1994), 61. English translation is quoted in Roger H. Brown, "Visions of a Virtuous Manifest Destiny: Yasuoka Masahiro and Japan's Kingly Way," in *Pan-Asianism in Modern Japanese History: Colonialism, Regionalism and Borders*, ed. Sven Saaler and J. Victor Koschmann (London and New York: Routledge, 2007), 133–50.

11 Brown, 133–4. A Chinese philosopher, Mengzi (372–289 BC), is believed to be the creator of the terms "ōdō" and "hadō."

12 Li, 36–7.

13 Ibid., 93.

14 "Manshūkoku kenkoku sengen [State-founding proclamation of Manchukuo]," in *Gendai shi shiryō, 11: Zoku Manshū jihen [Materials on contemporary history,*

volume 11: The Manchurian Incident, continued], ed. Kobayashi Tatsuo, Shimada Toshihiko and Inaba Masao (Tokyo: Misuzu shobo, 1965), 524. The English translation is cited in Yamamuro, *Manchuria under Japanese Dominion*, 88.

15　The question of which groups constituted "five peoples" remains ambiguous; but, it often referred to the five groups listed above, even though there were other "non-Asian" minorities such as the Russians and the Poles. The concept emphasized the unity of the five major Asian ethnic nations based on the Pan-Asianist founding principle of Manchukuo.

16　Louise Young, *Japan's Total Empire: Manchuria and the Culture of Wartime Imperialism* (Berkeley: University of California Press, 1998), 287.

17　"Manshūkoku kenkoku sengen," in Yamamuro, *Manchuria under Japanese Dominion*, 89.

18　Susumu Tsukase, *Manshūkoku: "minzoku kyōwa" no jitsuzō [Manchukuo: The Reality of "Ethnic Harmony"]* (Tokyo: Yoshikawa Hirobumi kan, 1998), 96–8.

19　Yamamuro, *Manchuria under Japanese Dominion*, 116–17.

20　Ibid., 118–19.

21　Kevin M. Doak, "Building National Identity through Ethnicity: Ethnology in Wartime Japan and After," *Journal of Japanese Studies* 27, no. 1 (2001), 1–39, 4. See also: Kevin M. Doak, *A History of Nationalism in Modern Japan: Placing the People* (Leiden: Brill, 2007).

22　Research that focused on political and economic relationships in the Japanese Empire has revealed exploitative aspects of Japanese policies and presence in Manchuria and Manchukuo. *The Japanese Informal Empire in China, 1895–1937*, ed. Peter Duus, Ramon H. Myers, and Mark R. Peattie (Princeton, NJ: Princeton University Press, 1989) includes articles by Ramon H. Myers, Nakagane Katsuji, and Alvin D. Coox that particularly focus on Manchuria and Manchukuo. Yoshihisa Tak Matsusaka, *The Making of Japanese Manchuria, 1904–1932* (Cambridge, MA: Harvard University Asia Center, 2001) is an expansive examination of Japan's exploitative motives behind its development project in Manchuria from defence, political and economic perspectives. Yamamuro, *Manchuria under Japanese Dominion*, originally published in Japanese in 1993, provides a political history of the region. He shows that the collaboration between Japanese and non-Japanese political figures brought benefits only to the former.

23　Prasenjit Duara, *Sovereignty and Authenticity: Manchukuo and the East Asian Modern* (Lanham, MD: Rowman & Littlefield Publishers, 2003).

24　*Crossed Histories: Manchuria in the Age of Empire*, ed. Mariko Asano Tamanoi (Honolulu: Association for Asian Studies and University of Hawaii Press, 2005).

25　Young; Emer O'Dwyer, *Significant Soil: Settler Colonialism and Japan's Urban Empire in Manchuria* (Cambridge, MA: Harvard University Press, 2015).

26　Rana Mitter, *The Manchurian Myth: Nationalism, Resistance, and Collaboration in Modern China* (Berkeley: University of California Press, 2000); Hyun Ok Park,

Two Dreams in One Bed: Empire, Social Life, and the Origins of the North Korean Revolution in Manchuria (Durham, NC: Duke University Press, 2005); Norman Smith, *Resisting Manchukuo: Chinese Women Writers and the Japanese Occupation* (Vancouver: UBC Press, 2007). In the field of colonial Korea, too, recent research has taken a revisionist approach to the relationships between the colonizer and the colonized. For example, see Jun Uchida, "Brokers of Empire: Japanese and Korean Business Elites in Colonial Korea," in *Settler Colonialism in the Twentieth Century: Projects, Practices, Legacies*, ed. Caroline Elkins and Susan Pederson (New York: Routledge, 2005), 153–70; and *Colonial Modernity in Korea*, ed. Gi-Wook Chin and Michael Robinson (Cambridge, MA: Harvard University Asia Center, 1999). Takashi Fujitani has tackled the same theme with a more expansive and comparative approach. Takashi Fujitani, *Race for Empire: Koreans as Japanese and Japanese as Americans during World War II* (Berkeley: University of California Press, 2011).

27 Another work that has broken away from the framework of Japanese imperialism is Dan Shao, *Remote Homeland, Recovered Borderland: Manchus, Manchukuo, and Manchuria, 1907–1985* (Honolulu: University of Hawai'i Press, 2011).

28 Despite Kendai's paramount significance in the state of Manchukuo, there has been no book-length research on it written in English. While some books on Manchuria and East Asia have briefly mentioned this institution, and while there have been a few shorter works on some aspects of the university, this book provides the first comprehensive study of this unique Japanese colonial educational institution. There have been two foundational monographs on Kendai written in Japanese. Eriko Miyazawa, *Kenkoku daigaku to minzoku kyōwa [Nation-Building University and the ideal of ethnic harmony]* (Tokyo: Kazama shobo, 1997); Fumiaki Shishida, *Budō no kyōikuryoku: manshūkoku kenkoku daigaku ni okeru budō kyōiku [The educational value of Japanese budō (martial arts): The budō training at Kenkoku University in Manchukuo]* (Tokyo: Nihon Tosho Senta, 2005). This book draws on existing Japanese scholarship while mining new primary sources and developing an original argument focusing on the institutional practice of Pan-Asianism.

29 In her study of French Algeria, Andrea Smith describes the French principle of creating an "Algerian melting pot" out of French and other European settlers and Muslim Algerians. Based on former settlers' interviews, she highlights the limits of this idealism. Andrea Smith, *Colonial Memory in Postcolonial Europe: Maltese Settlers in Algeria and France* (Bloomington: Indiana University Press, 2006).

30 One example is the Asian Solidarity Society that was established in Tokyo in 1907 under the leadership of a Chinese revolutionary activist, Zhang Ji. This group consisted of the Marxist-driven radical students of Japan, China, the Philippines, Vietnam, and India, and facilitated intellectual interchanges with a common goal of uniting Asia and protecting it from Western imperialism. For more on this, see Rebecca E. Karl, "Creating Asia: China in the World at the Beginning of the

Twentieth Century," *The American Historical Review* 103, no. 4 (October 1998), 1096–118; and Zensaku Takeuchi, "Meiji makki ni okeru chūnichi kakumei undō no kōryū [Late Meiji interactions between Chinese and Japanese revolutionary movements]," *Chugoku-kenkyu* 5 (September 1948), 74–95.

31 One example of such Asian nationalists was Subhas Chandra Bose, a leader of the Indian independence movement against British colonial rule.

32 Peattie, *Ishiwara Kanji and Japan's Confrontation with the West.* Ishiwara Kanji is an important figure in this book, as he proposed and initiated the founding of Kendai, which Peattie does not mention in his book. My primary sources show a sign that Ishiwara in the late 1930s possessed a more egalitarian perception of Pan-Asianism at least in terms of his vision for an ideal education to actualize the goal of "ethnic harmony." Chapter 2 will analyze his conception of Pan-Asianism as reflected in his vision for Kendai.

33 Joshua A. Fogel, *Politics and Sinology: The Case of Naitō Kōnan, 1866–1934* (Cambridge, MA: Harvard University Press, 1984).

34 Joshua A. Fogel, *Nakae Ushikichi in China: The Mourning of Spirit* (Cambridge, MA: Harvard University Press, 1989).

35 Stefan Tanaka has taken a broader approach to the study of Japanese Sinology and demonstrated the shift in Japanese attitudes toward China from cultural admiration to condemnation as well as a paternalistic sense of mission to save it. See Stefan Tanaka, *Japan's Orient: Rendering Pasts into History* (Berkeley: University of California Press, 1993).

36 Li. *The China Factor in Modern Japanese Thought.*

37 A pioneering scholar in this endeavor in the broader field of the history of US relations with East Asia is Akira Iriye. For instance, in an effort to describe how ideas developed, changed, and influenced the foreign policies of the United States, Japan and China, Iriye did not limit his sources to policy documents but explores discourses that reflected the perspectives of a larger public. See Akira Iriye, *Across the Pacific: An Inner History of American–East Asian Relations,* rev. ed. (Chicago, IL: Imprint Publications, Inc., 1967, 1992). For more discussion of Iriye's advocacy of adding culture to international history, see Akira Iriye, "Culture and International History," in *Explaining the History of American Foreign Relations,* 2nd ed., ed. Michael J. Hogan and Thomas G. Paterson (Cambridge: Cambridge University Press, 2004), 241–56.

38 John W. Dower, *War without Mercy: Race and Power in the Pacific War* (New York: Pantheon Books, 1986).

39 Ibid., Chapter 10.

40 Gerald Horne, *Race War! White Supremacy and the Japanese Attack on the British Empire* (New York, London: New York University Press, 2004).

41 This idea that Japan was a liberator of Asians, or the colored peoples, gained popularity among anti-colonial nationalists throughout Asia after Japan's triumph

over Russia in 1905. One example of the emerging Pan-Asian contacts across nations around this time was the establishment of the Asian Solidarity Society in Tokyo in 1907, which Rebecca E. Karl introduces in her article. Aiming to foster the principle of mutual assistance for national independence movements, this organization consisted of members from India, China, Japan, Korea, Indochina, Siam, the Philippines, Burma, and Malay. Upholding an egalitarian version of Pan-Asianism (as opposed to the nationalist version), the society welcomed any Asians if they were anti-imperialist and were willing to fight against oppression.

42 For more on Japan's policy in Southeast Asia and the role of Pan-Asianism, see: Joyce Lebra-Chapman, *Japanese-trained Armies in Southeast Asia: Independence and Volunteer Forces in World War II* (New York: Columbia University Press, 1977); and *Southeast Asia under Japanese Occupation*, ed. Alfred W. McCoy (New Haven, CT: Yale University Southeast Asia Studies, *c.*1980).

Lebra-Chapman introduces the volunteer armies called *giyūgun* in Malaya, Sumatra, Indochina, Borneo, and the Philippines. The *Peta*, or the "Defenders of the Homeland," was one example of such army among the Indonesians formed in 1943 and trained under the Japanese. The Japanese also promised or even granted independence as a way to advance Pan-Asian alliance against the Allies. In 1943, the Japanese proclaimed the independence of Burma and the Philippines, setting up Japanese-sponsored autonomous states like Manchukuo, in order to represent the formation of the Greater East Asia Co-Prosperity Sphere. Furthermore, the Greater East Asia Ministry hosted the Greater East Asia Conference in the same year, with participation of nationalists such as Subhas Chandra Bose, Ba Maw, Wang Jingwei, and Tōjō Hideki (p. 12). As Lebra-Chapman points out, however, this policy of granting Japan-sponsored independence must have had different levels of appeal to the Burmese and the Filipinos. For, unlike the former, the latter had the words of the American promise of return and guidance for independence. Filipino collaboration with the Japanese often meant "the desire to gain or retain political power" than loyalty to the Japanese (p. 144).

43 Eri Hotta, *Pan-Asianism and Japan's War 1931–1945* (New York: Palgrave Macmillan, 2007).

44 Ibid., 226.

45 Ibid., 45.

46 Cemil Aydin, *The Politics of Anti-Westernism in Asia: Visions of World Order in Pan-Islamic and Pan-Asian Thought* (New York: Columbia University Press, 2007).

47 Masafumi Yonetani, *Ajia/nihon: shikō no furonteia [Asia/Japan: frontier of philosophy]* (Tokyo: Iwanami shoten, 2006).

48 *Pan-Asianism in Modern Japanese History: Colonialism, Regionalism and Borders*, ed. Sven Saaler and J. Victor Koschmann (New York: Routledge, 2007).

49 Sven Matthiessen, *Japanese Pan-Asianism and the Philippines from the Late 19th Century to the End of World War II* (Leiden: Brill, 2016).

50 Manzō Yuji, *Kenkoku daigaku nenpyō [The chronological timetable of Nation-Building University in Manchuria]* (Tokyo: Kenkoku Daigaku Dōsōkai, 1981). Although it does not reflect non-Japanese students' perspectives of the institution, it certainly offers a good sense of events regarding Kendai.

51 I analyze Kendai faculty members' scholarly articles that reveal their perceptions of Pan-Asianism. *Kenkoku daigaku kenkyūin geppō [Kenkoku University Research Institute monthly journal]* published the university faculty's scholarly articles in various fields. Between 1940 and 1945, forty-five volumes were published, and each volume contained a few articles. I have access to thirty-two volumes of this journal.

52 In analyzing former Kendai students' memoirs, I regard them as both historical records and constructed historical memories, as seen in Mariko Asano Tamanoi's and Lori Watt's studies. Mariko Asano Tamanoi, *Memory Maps: The State and Manchuria in Postwar Japan* (Honolulu: University of Hawai'i Press, 2009); Lori Watt, *When Empire Comes Home: Repatriation and Reintegration in Postwar Japan* (Cambridge, MA: Harvard University Press, 2009).

53 *Kankirei—manshū kenkoku daigaku zaikan dōsō bunshū [Kankirei: collection of memoirs written by alumni in Korea]*, trans. Eun-Suk Kim and Yoshikazu Kusano (Kenkoku University Alumni Association, 2004).

54 Chun-Sik Hong, *Hankyore no sekai: aa nihon [The world of my countrymen: Ah, Japan]* (Ansan, 1999).

55 Shuiqing Li, *Dongbei banian huigulu [Memory about the eight years that I lived in Dongbei]*, trans. Kenzō Takazawa (Tokyo: Kenkoku Daigaku dōsōkai, 2007).

56 *Huiyi weiman jianguo daxue [Remembering Bogus Manchukuo Nation-Building University]* (Changchun: Changchun City Government's Chinese People's Political Consultative Committee, Historical Record Committee, 1997).

57 *Kenkoku: kenkoku daigaku juku zasshi [Nation-building: Kenkoku University juku journal]* 1 (August 20, 1940), 2 (August 20, 1941), and 3 (April 20, 1943).

58 *Kenkoku daigaku juku geppō [Kenkoku University Juku Monthly]* no. 1 to 7 (1942–43).

59 *Reimei: Kenkoku daigaku dai jūyon juku juku zasshi [Dawn: Kenkoku University the 14th juku periodical]*, no. 1 to 5 (1940); and *Kanki [Joy]* (June 1940).

60 Hideyuki Miura, "Minzoku kyōwa no yume, jisedai e: Manshū Kenkoku Daigaku saigo no dōsōkai [Passing down the dream of 'ethnic harmony' to the next generation: the final reunion meeting of Manchukuo Kenkoku University]," in *Asahi Shinbun [Asahi Newspaper]*, 9 June 2010.

Chapter 2

1   The Marco Polo Bridge Incident is sometimes represented as a deliberate escalation of hostilities by the Japanese Army in China. In fact, both the Japanese and Guomindang (GMD) local commanders tried to defuse tensions and reach a

settlement, which seemed successful by July 11. Despite the sense of relief felt by the Japanese Prime Minister Konoe Fumimaro, his cabinet, and the army chief of staff in Tokyo, Chiang Kai-shek, the head of the GMD, reversed his previous acquiescent attitude toward Japan and refused to accept the settlement negotiated by local commanders. For a full description of the event, see James L. McClain, *Japan: A Modern History* (New York: W.W. Norton & Company, 2002), 442–7; and Jonathan D. Spence, *The Search for Modern China* (New York: W.W. Norton & Company, 1999), 419–22.

2 Kiyohiko Tsutsui, "Sōsō no koro [The pioneering days]," in *Kendaishi shiryō 2 [Sources on the history of Kendai]* (Tokyo: Kenkoku University Alumni Association, 1967), 17–19, 17; Yuji, 41.

3 "Kenkoku Daigaku rei [Law on Kenkoku University]" (August 5, 1937) in Yuji, 51–2, 51.

4 Peattie, *Ishiwara Kanji and Japan's Confrontation with the West*, Chapter VIII "Against the Tide: Ishiwara and the China War."

5 As the following section shows, Ishiwara left Manchukuo in August 1932 after playing a significant role in the foundation of the state. Subsequently, his military career was mainly associated with the Japanese Army in Tokyo. Although he was appointed Vice Chief of Staff of the Kwantung Army in September 1937, by then, the basic principles and structure of Kendai had been already determined by the planning committee.

6 Hiroyuki Abe, "Ishiwara Kanji no shōgai [The life of Ishiwara Kanji]," in *Ishiwara Kanji to Manshū teikoku [Ishiwara Kanji and the empire of Manchukuo]*, ed. Rekishi dokuhon Henshūbu (Tokyo: Shin jinbutsu ōraisha, 2010), 45–109.

7 For more on the popularity of Pan-Asianism in the wake of the Russo–Japanese War, see Hotta, Chapter 2; and Horne, *Race War!*, Chapter 2.

8 Peattie, *Ishiwara Kanji and Japan's Confrontation with the West*, 27–9.

9 Ibid., 100.

10 Ibid., 169; Duara, 73–9; Young, Chapter 6.

11 Peattie, *Ishiwara Kanji and Japan's Confrontation with the West*, 175. These plans never materialized, as they met opposition from Kwantung Army officials and also because Ishiwara was soon to leave Manchukuo for a new assignment in Japan.

12 Kanji Ishiwara, "Manshū kenkoku to shina jihen [The establishment of Manchukuo and the Shina incident]" (1940), in *Ishiwara Kanji senshū 6*, ed. Yoshiichirō Tamai (Kanagawa: Tamairaba, 1993), 161–94, 166.

13 Ibid., 166.

14 Ibid., 166.

15 Ibid., 166.

16 This group was known as "the two *ki*'s and the three *suke*'s" that consisted of Hoshino Naoki (Director-General for Administrative Affairs), Tōjō Hideki (Commander of the Military Police of the Kwantung Army and Chief of Staff of the

Kwantung Army), Kishi Nobusuke (Vice-Minister of Industry and Vice-Director of the Office of Administrative Affairs), Ayukawa Yoshisuke (President of Manchurian Heavy Industry), and Matsuoka Yōsuke (President of the South Manchurian Railway Company). For details, see Yamamuro, *Manchuria under Japanese Dominion*, 178.

17 Ibid., 179.

18 Peattie's biography does not mention Ishiwara's involvement in the planning of Kenkoku University. Nor did other Japanese works on Ishiwara take note of it. Even the ten-volume collection of Ishiwara's writings, *Ishiwara Kanji Senshū*, does not contain any single document related to the planning of Kendai, though his mention of the school appears in a few entries.

19 Kanji Ishiwara, *Kokubō seijiron [Political theory of national defense]* (1942), in *Ishiwara Kanji senshū 5*, ed. Yoshiichirō Tamai (Kanagawa: Tamairaba, 1993), 9–173, 90, 91.

20 Manshūkokushi hensan kankō kai [Society for compiling and publishing Manchukuo history], *Manshūkokushi sōron [General history of Manchukuo]* in Yuji, 8, lists fourteen members as of February 1937. *Kendaishi shiryō 1* (Tokyo: Kenkoku University Alumni Association, 1966) in Yuji, 12, lists seven members— three army officials and four academics—as of late May 1937. *Shashinshū Kenkoku Daigaku [Photograph Collection: Kenkoku University]* (Tokyo: Kenkoku University Alumni Association, 1986), 3, lists twelve members including three *mankei*, as of July 1937. *Shashinshū*, on page 1, however, lists twenty-five members excluding the three *mankei* to be "people who were involved in the planning." Historian Eriko Miyazawa lists twenty-four members. Miyazawa, 63.

21 Kiyohiko Tsutsui, *Hoki [supplemental memos for the Chronology]* in Yuji, 41; *Shashinshū Kenkoku Daigaku*, 3. The latter source seems to draw information from the former. Both sources list three *mankei* members within the six committee members on site (*Manshū gawa sōritsu iin*). The other three members were Japanese persons who lived in Manchukuo and were involved in the planning of Kendai.

22 We see similarly ambiguous use of other terms like *manshū-jin* (people of Manchuria) and *mango* (Manchurian language), which actually referred to the Chinese language. When these terms are used with ambivalence, I will use the original Japanese words followed by simple English translations in parentheses. For more discussion of ethnic categorization in Japanese-occupied Manchuria, see Mariko Asano Tamanoi, "Knowledge, Power, and Racial Classifications: The 'Japanese' in 'Manchuria,'" *Journal of Asian Studies* 59, no. 2 (May 2000), 248–76.

23 Before being appointed as Prime Minister, Zhang Jinghui was one of the warlords who had collaborated with the Kwantung Army in an attempt at severing Manchuria and Mongolia from China proper and establishing an independent state. About the Kwantung Army's appointment of Zhang as Prime Minister,

historian Shin'ichi Yamamuro cites the Japanese official at the State Council, Kamio Kazuharu, as stating: "The Guandong (Kwantung) Army probably appreciated the fact that he understands no Japanese, cannot read Chinese texts, and seems to have no say in governmental matters." Yamamuro, *Manchuria under Japanese Dominion*, 170. It is telling that Kendai appointed this person as its President.

24 The exact day on which the name was changed from Asia University to Kenkoku University is not known. However, sources show that as early as March 1937, one month after the planning committee was formally established, the core planning members used the latter name. For instance, one of the committee members, Katakura Tadashi, used the name Kenkoku University in his diary on March 26, 1937. Tadashi Katakura in *Kendaishi shiryō 1* in Yuji, 9.

25 Takayuki Mishina, "Ishiwara shōgun no Kendai ni kansuru rinen to kōsō [General Ishiwara's idea and vision of Kendai]," in *Manshūkokushi sōron* in Yuji, 18–19.

26 Ibid., 18.

27 Ibid., 18.

28 Mishina in *Kendaishi shiryō 2*, 6; Mishina in Yuji, 17.

29 Mishina in Yuji, 18.

30 Mishina in *Kendaishi shiryō 2*, 5; Mishina in Yuji, 16–17.

31 Tsutsui, *Hoki* in Yuji, 19–20, 19.

32 Mishina, "Ishiwara shōgun no Kendai ni kansuru rinen to koso," in Yuji, 18.

33 Mishina in *Kendaishi shiryō 2*, 6; Mishina in Yuji, 17.

34 Ishiwara Kanji, *Kokubō seiji ron [Political theory of national defense]* (1942) in Yuji, 118.

35 Mishina in *Kendaishi shiryō 2*, 6; Mishina in Yuji, 17.

36 Miyazawa, 34–5.

37 Tsutsui in *Kendaishi shiryō 1*, 5; Tsutsui in Yuji, 7.

38 Miyazawa, 59.

39 My summary of the Institute for the Study of the National Spirit and Culture (ISNSC) is based on Eriko Miyazawa's description of it. Miyazawa, 57–9.

40 According to Miyazawa, the leftist movement became prevalent on Japanese university campuses from the end of WWI, and the rightist movement since the beginning of the Shōwa era (1926).

41 Kiyoshi Hiraizumi in *Kendaishi shiryō 1*, 5; Hiraizumi in Yuji, 13.

42 Ibid., 13–14.

43 Miyazawa, 59–60.

44 Tsutsui, *Hoki* in Yuji, 18–19.

45 *Manshūkokushi sōron* in Yuji, 18–19.

46 Kida Kiyoshi was the personnel division manager at the Management and Coordination Agency. Nemoto Ryūtarō was the personnel division assistant officer at the Management and Coordination Agency. Tsuji Masanobu was the Kwantung Army Captain.

47 Miyazawa, 84. It is not clear who conducted the survey.

48 *Kendaishi shiryō 1*, 12; Yuji, 15; Miyazawa, 84.

49 Miyazawa, 88. *Hakkō ichiu* (八紘一宇).

50 Ibid., 88.

51 *Kendaishi shiryō 1*, 4–5; Yuji, 15.

52 Miyazawa, 191.

53 *Kendaishi shiryō 2*, 10.

54 Five yen back then is the equivalent of \$20.00 to \$50.00. The currency in
    Manchukuo had the same value as that of Japan. For the purpose of comparison, a
    Japanese official who worked for the Ministry of Commerce and Industry in Tokyo
    earned a monthly salary of 200–300 yen in 1938. Cited in Yamamuro, *Manchuria
    under Japanese Dominion*, 170.

55 Miyazawa, 182.

56 The Japanese school system during the war was different from the current system.
    Until 1944, after six years of elementary school, the middle school for males was
    five years long.

57 "Kenkoku daigaku yoka daiikki seito senbatsu yōkō an [the resolution of guidelines
    for admission of applicants for first entering class of the preparatory course at
    Nation-Building University]" (June 9, 1937) in Yuji, 26–7. Regarding educational
    background, the admission committee made exceptions for those who did not
    graduate middle schools but whose academic abilities were acknowledged as
    satisfactory by the Japanese or Manchukuo governments.

58 Perhaps, the planning committee simply assumed all Japanese applicants would be
    unmarried based on their knowledge of the competitiveness of Japanese middle
    schools. Students enrolled at middle schools at that time were extremely busy
    studying and preparing for the entrance exams of higher schools and other schools.

59 Kida in *Kendaishi shiryō 2*, 10; Kida in Yuji, 59–60.

60 Ibid.

61 Other physical training courses included *sumō* wrestling, *kyūdō*, *jūkendō*, and *kidō*.
    For more on Kendai's physical education through martial arts, see Shishida.

62 Miyazawa, 118.

63 The number of students in each major are based on Kōichi Fujimori and
    Shōjirō Suzuki, *Kenkoku daigaku nenpyō yōran* [*The chronological timetable of
    Nation-Building University in Manchuria*] (Tokyo: Kenkoku University Alumni
    Association, 2007), 44, 54, and 60.

64 "Chikō gōitsu (知行合一)" is an academic theory by a Chinese Confucian thinker,
    Wang Yangming, from the Ming Dynasty.

65 "Kenkoku Daigaku sōsetsu yōkō [Guidelines for the Establishment of Nation-
    Building University]" (August 5, 1937) in Yuji, 52.

66 The numbers of graduates and their post-graduation job postings are based on
    Fujimori and Suzuki, *Kenkoku daigaku nenpyō yōran*, 48, 54, 56 and 60.

67 Mishina in *Kendaishi shiryō 2*, 6; Mishina in Yuji, 17.

68 The second-entering class student Nishimura Jūrō frequently refers to a recreation room in *juku* building in his diary. Jūrō Nishimura, *Rakugaki: manshū kenkoku daigaku waga gakusei jidai no omoide [Scribbles: recollection of my student life at Nation-Building University in Manchuria]* (Kobe-shi: Tosho Shuppan Marōdosha, 1991).

69 Miyazawa, 199.

70 Ibid., 199.

71 According to historian Shin'ichi Yamamuro, Gu Cixiang was a graduate of Tokyo Higher Normal School. Yamamuro, *Manchuria under Japanese Dominion*, 172.

72 Ryūtarō Nemoto in *Kendaishi shiryō 1*, 8; Nemoto in Yuji, 62.

73 Ibid.

74 Both the May Fourth Movement in China and the March First Movement in Korea were major anti-Japanese, national independence movements.

75 Nemoto in *Kendaishi shiryō 1*, 8; Nemoto in Yuji, 63.

76 Ibid. Their appointment to serve the Kendai faculty was also reported in *Tokyo Asahi Newspaper*. "Kenkoku daigaku ni pekin kara ryōhakase [Two professors join Nationa Building University]," *Tokyo Asahi Shinbun [Tokyo Asahi Newspaper]* (April 15, 1937), 3.

77 Fushinosuke Ehara, "Minzoku no kunō: sōsetsuki no Kenkoku Daigaku wo megutte 3 [Hardships of race: the founding period of Nation-Building University 3]" (1989) in Miyazawa, 98–9.

78 Nemoto in *Kendaishi shiryō 2*, 8; Nemoto in Yuji, 63.

79 Miyazawa, 99–101. The numbers of faculty are drawn from "Kenkoku Daigaku yōran [Directory of Kenkoku University]" (Shinkyō: Kenkoku daigaku kenkyūin, 1941). According to *Kenkoku daigaku dōsōkai meibo [Kenkoku University Alumni Association Roster]* published in 1955, the total number of Kendai faculty members between 1937 and 1945, including the planning period, is 295. Approximately forty-five are non-Japanese scholars. In this same period, approximately 1,400 students were enrolled at Kendai. The ratio of faculty member to students was 1 to 4.7. These sources do not explain this improbably large ratio of the faculty. A member of the first entering class from Taiwan, Li Shuiqing, testifies that there were more faculty members than students during his first year at Kendai (Shuiqing Li, 31). In *Kenkoku daigaku dōsōkai meibo [Kenkoku University Alumni Association Roster]* published in 2003, the number of faculty further increases to 400. This number seems to include not only faculty in residence but also affiliated scholars and other staff members. The number of faculty in residence is not known. The incredibly large ratio, however, was not particularly unusual if we compare it with other colonial universities in the Japanese Empire. As mentioned in Chapter 4, the ratio at Taihoku Imperial University in Taiwan was 3 to 5. Many scholars were hired not so much for the purpose of education but more for the purpose of research and information-gathering in service of the empire.

80 Sōichi Sakuta in *Kendaishi 4* in Yuji, 64.

81 The urge to keep any colonial undertakings in the hands of the colonialists was not uncommon in empires worldwide. For instance, Fanny Colonna shows that the fear of losing privileges and of the breakdown of colonial hierarchy played out in the restriction of Arab Algerians from higher education in French Algeria. Fanny Colonna, "Educating Conformity in French Colonial Algeria," trans. Barbara Harshav, in *Tensions of Empire: Colonial Cultures in a Bourgeois World*, ed. Frederick Cooper and Ann Laura Stoler (Berkeley: University of California Press, 1997), 346–70.

82 Mishina, "Mishina memo," in *Kendaishi shiryō 2*, 13–16, 14; Yuji, 39–40. The content of Ishiwara–Sakuta dialogue is unknown. According to Mishina, Sakuta only commented that "[u]nlike many other militarists, Ishiwara is a man of philosophy and conviction," which implied that Sakuta was unable to reach agreement with Ishiwara.

83 Yuji, 61–2.

84 Shuiqing Li, 16.

85 Ibid., 16.

86 Ibid., 16.

87 Ibid., 16.

88 Ibid., 16.

89 Ibid., 16.

90 Ibid., 16.

91 Ibid., 16.

92 Shōji Yamada, *Kōbō no arashi: manshū kenkoku daigaku hōkai no shuki [The rise and fall in storm: memoir about the dissolution of Nation-Building University in Manchuria]* (Tokyo: Kanki shuppan, 1980), 103–4.

93 Kanji Ishiwara, "Kantō-gun shireikan no manshūkoku naimen shidō tekkai ni tsuite [Proposal to stop Kwantung Army commander's intervention in Manchukuo]," in *Ishiwara Kanji shiryō*, ed. Jun Tsunoda in Yuji, 113–14, 114.

94 Despite Ishiwara's proposal to merge Kendai with Daidō Gakuin, the two institutions clearly differed in objectives and characters. Daidō Gakuin, founded in 1932 and administered under the State Council, concentrated on practical training for current government clerks and candidates eligible for such positions. Its program was much shorter than that of universities.

95 Ibid., 113.

96 For details of Ishiwara's conflicting relationship with military bureaucrats, see Peattie, *Ishiwara Kanji and Japan's Confrontation with the West*, Chapter IX.

97 Ishiwara, *Kokubō seijiron* (1942), in *Ishiwara Kanji senshū 5*, ed. Yoshiichirō Tamai, 91; Yuji, 116.

98 Kiyohiko Tsutsui provided this information to Yuji for the compilation of *Kenkoku Daigaku nenpyō*. In Yuji, 19–20, Tsutsui does not discuss the details of the arguments between Sakuta and Kakei.

99   Ehara Fushinosuke resigned from his faculty position in September 1939. Later, in July 1943, he returned to the Kendai faculty. Ishinaka Kōji resigned his *jukutō* position on the same day as Ehara did but remained on the faculty until July 1940 when he left Kendai, only to return to his position in the following year. Fujita Matsuji left Kendai in March 1940 and returned two years later. Unfortunately, the exact reasons and details of their discontent with the administration were not recorded. "Zadankai: gonenkan no juku seikatsu [Panel discussion: the *juku* life in the past five years]," *Kenkoku: kenkoku daigaku juku zasshi [Nation-building: Kenkoku University juku journal]* 3 (April 15, 1943), 70–85; Suzuki, 91, 92, and 97.

100 *Kenkoku daigaku kenkyūin rei [Imperial ordinance on the Kenkoku University Research Institute]* September 1, 1938 in Yuji, 119–20.

101 Ibid., 120.

102 Ibid., 120.

103 *Kenkoku daigaku kenkyūin sōsetsu shuisho [Summary of the plan to establish Kenkoku University Research Institute]* June 20, 1937 in Yuji, 36–8, 36.

104 These numbers are from *Kenkoku daigaku dōsōkai meibo [Kenkoku University Alumni Association Roster]* published in 1955.

105 Katsumi Mori, *Daitōa kyōeiken no rekishisei [Historicity of the Great East Asia Co-Prosperity Sphere]*, 9th ed. (Shinkyō: Manshū teikoku kyōwakai, 1942), 64.

106 Shigejirō Matsuyama, *Daitōa kensetsu no sekaishi teki haikei [The background of the establishment of the Great East Asia in the context of world history]*, 4th ed. (Shinkyō: Manshū teikoku kyōwakai, 1942), 50.

107 Ibid., 51.

108 Mori, 72.

109 Matsuyama, 31–2.

110 Ibid., 43.

111 Mori, 50–1.

112 Sei'ichi Nakano, "Manshūkoku minzoku seisaku eno shoyōsei [Requests for ethnic policies in Manchukuo]," *Kenkyū kihō* 1 (1941), 36.

113 Kazuhito Ono, "Manshū kenkoku to nippon: nippon no taiman kōdō ni kansuru jakkan no rekishiteki kaiko [Nation-building in Manchukuo and Japan: some historical reflections on Japan's attitudes toward Manchuria]," *Kenkyū kihō* 3 (1942), 161.

114 Ibid., 175.

115 Ibid., 161.

116 Ibid., 176 and 177.

117 Nakano, 34.

118 Ibid., 43.

119 Tōjūrō, Murai, *Daitōa kyōeiken no kōiki hōchitsujo [Broad law and order in the Great East Asia Co-Prosperity Sphere]*, 10th ed. (Shinkyo: Manshūkoku kyōwakai, 1942), 14.

120   Ibid., 16.

121   Ibid., 24 and 16.

122   Ibid., 25.

123   Sōchi Sakuta, *Manshū kenkoku no genri oyobi hongi [The principles and the core meanings of the founding of Manchukuo]*, ed. Tōjūrō Murai (Shinkyō: Manshū tomiyama bo, 1944), 84.

124   Ibid., 83–4.

125   Shin'ichirō Nishi, "Kenkoku seishin to ōdō [the nation-building spirit and the Kingly Way]," *Kenkyū kihō* 3 (1942), 57–87, 86.

126   Ibid., 86.

127   Choe Nam-Seon was a prolific scholar who published numerous works on the history of Korea and Asia from 1925. In this section, I will focus on his publications through the Kenkoku University Research Institute.

128   Songwu Li, "Duri de jingguo yu ganxiang [the report and impressions on my trip to Japan]," in *Kenkoku daigaku kenkyūin geppō [Kenkoku University Research Institute monthly journal] (KURIMJ)* 8 (April 1941), 6.

129   For more on this unique mode of communication, see D. R. Howland, *Borders of Chinese Civilization: Geography and History at Empire's End* (Durham, NC: Duke University Press, 1996), 43–4. As an example of such communication, Howland introduces Ōkōchi Teruna, a Japanese former lord of Takasaki-han who lived in Tokyo. Ōkōchi hosted gatherings of Chinese and Japanese scholars between 1875 and 1881. Although those scholars did not speak each other's language, they used brushes and papers to share their poetry and exchange their knowledge and opinions about current issues and so on. This mode of communication was called "brushtalking."

130   *KURIMJ* 26 (February 1943), 4.

131   Songwu Li, "Manzhou wenhua sixiang shi [Cultural and intellectual history of Manchuria]," *KURIMJ* 36 (December 1943), 17–33, 19.

132   Ibid., 19.

133   Ibid., 19.

134   Ibid., 29.

135   Ibid., 29.

136   Ibid., 27.

137   Historian Eriko Miyazawa explains that the Kendai administration allowed Bao and Su to return to China sometime before 1941 while keeping their affiliations with the university. This was because some members of the administration sympathized with these Chinese scholars who lived away from their original homes in Beijing. Miyazawa, 99.

138   *KURIMJ* 8 (April 1941), 7; *KURIMJ* 19 (May 1942), 8.

139   See a recent textbook on Korean History, for example. Kyung Moon Hwang, *A History of Korea* (New York: Palgrave Macmillan, 2017). Also, Chizuko Allen,

who presents a more nuanced interpretation of Choe's scholarship, also provides a helpful discussion on the postwar academic assessment of Choe's scholarship in Korea. Chizuko T. Allen, "Northeast Asia Centered around Korea: Ch'oe Namson's View of History," *The Journal of Asian Studies* 49, no. 4 (1990), 787–806.

140 Nam-Seon Choe, *Tōhō kominzoku no shinsei kan'nen ni tsuite [Regarding the ancient eastern peoples' conception of divinity]* (Shinkyō: Kenkoku daigaku kenkyūin, 1939), 4–5.

141 Ibid., 22.

142 Choe published his theory of the "Purham" cultural zone in his article "Purham bunka ron [theory of Purham culture]" in 1925. According to a Korean historian, Ji Myeong-Gwan, this original theory represented Choe's attempt to demonstrate the commonality in the ancient religious customs of Korea and Japan. For more on this, see Myeong-Gwan Ji, "Sin Chae-Ho shigaku to Choe Nam-Seon shigaku [Sin Chae-Ho's views of history and Choe Nam-Seon's views of history]," *Annals of the Institute for Comparative Studies of Culture, Tokyo Woman's Christian University* 48 (1987), 135–60.

143 Ibid., 21.

144 Ibid., 21.

145 Ibid., 21.

146 While Korean societies have viewed Goguryeo as a Korean kingdom, the PRC holds that it was part of the larger Chinese empire.

147 Nam-Seon Choe, "Sui no kami [the god of *sui*]," *KURIMJ* 9 (May 1941), 3.

148 *KURIMJ* 6 (February 1941), 2.

149 Won-Jung Jin, "Kaiko to sekkei [Recollection and construction]," in *Kankirei— manshū kenkoku daigaku zaikan dōsō bunshū [Kankirei: collection of memoirs written by alumni in Korea]*, trans. Eun-Suk Kim and Yoshikazu Kusano (Kenkoku University Alumni Association, 2004), 108–11, 108–9.

150 Hong, *Hankyore no sekai*, 33.

Chapter 3

1 Samuel Hideo Yamashita, *Leaves from an Autumn of Emergencies: Selections from the Wartime Diaries of Ordinary Japanese* (Honolulu: The University of Hawai'i Press, 2005), 35.

2 In this sense, Kendai's Japanese students' diaries show a stark contrast with the diaries of *tokkōtai* pilots (Special Attack Forces, also known as *kamikaze*) presented in Emiko Ohnuki-Tierney's two books. Given the extremely strict censorship imposed on those young soldiers whose mission was to dive their planes into enemy ships, Ohnuki-Tierney focuses on the private diaries that miraculously

survived. Her treatment of their "public" writings such as wills and letters to families assumes that those documents were produced with authors' awareness of their public nature. Not surprisingly, Ohnuki-Tierney finds a huge gap between *tokkōtai* pilots' "public" and "private" writings. As shown later in the chapter, some of the Japanese Kendai students felt at much greater liberty to express their opinions in "public" diaries. It attests to the surprising level of freedom both Kendai's faculty and students enjoyed on campus. Emiko Ohnuki-Tierney, *Kamikazu, Cherry Blossoms, and Nationalisms: The Militarization of Aesthetics in Japanese History* (Chicago, IL: The University of Chicago Press, 2002); and Emiko Ohnuki-Tierney, *Kamikaze Diaries: Reflections of Japanese Student Soldiers* (Chicago, IL: The University of Chicago Press, 2006).

3   Exceptions were granted to certain applicants who did not attend middle school but could demonstrate comparable or even higher abilities.

4   Henry DeWitt Smith, *Japan's First Student Radicals* (Cambridge, MA: Harvard University Press, 1972), 1–4.

5   Young, 314.

6   Ibid., 259.

7   Ibid., 259–68.

8   Nishimura, 15. This surprisingly low acceptance rate was only partially exaggerated. *Tokyo Asahi Newspaper* reports that for the first entering class, there were over 7,000 applications from which Kendai admitted 150. In this case, the acceptance rate would be 2.14 percent. "Kendai gakusei shinkyō chaku [Kendai students arrive in Shinkyō]," in *Tokyo Asahi Shinbun [Tokyo Asahi Newspaper]*, April 26, 1938.

9   As mentioned earlier, *kōtō gakkō* (higher schools) served as college preparatory schools. Unlike the current high schools in Japan, pre-war *kōtō gakkō* were highly competitive and regarded as guaranteeing admission to Japan's Imperial Universities whose graduates became the elite class. *Kōtō senmon gakkō* (higher vocational schools) were the institutions of higher education that concentrated on professional training. See Donald Roden, *Schooldays in Imperial Japan: A Study in the Culture of a Student Elite* (Berkeley: University of California Press, 1980); and DeWitt Smith.

10 Minato Morisaki, *Isho [The Will]* (Tokyo: Tosho shuppansha, 1971), 20.

11 Ibid., 20. The "will" Morisaki mentions here continued to have considerable significance to him. As discussed later in this chapter, Morisaki increasingly concentrated on the purity of intent rather than the actions and outcomes as he struggled to make sense of the contradiction between his Pan-Asianist ideal and his growing sympathy towards his Korean and Chinese classmates' sense of ethnic nationalism.

12 Anthropologist Mariko Asano Tamanoi has written two essays in 2000 and 2005 in which she analyzed a diary written by a Japanese student of Kendai, Morisaki Minato. Tamanoi examines Morisaki's personal diary from 1940 to 1945 and successfully shows the change in this young man's perception of Pan-Asianism. In her 2000 piece, she compares Morisaki's view of relationships among Asian

peoples residing in Manchukuo with that of Japanese officials and of Japanese farmer settlers, thus expanding the category "Japanese in Manchuria," which has too often been represented either as the victimizers or victims. Tamanoi concludes that Morisaki's evolving perception of Pan-Asianism diverged substantially from Japan's official ideology, which justified Japanese leadership. By showing this case as an example, Tamanoi questions the dominance of this official version of Pan-Asianism in wartime Japan. Nevertheless, while Tamanoi usefully expands the category "Japanese in Manchuria," there remains the question of how representative Morisaki was of Kendai students. In this chapter, I will use not only Morisaki Minato's diary but also the writings of other Japanese students to show a wide variety of experiences and relationships that they developed with Pan-Asianism. Tamanoi, "Knowledge, Power, and Racial Classifications," 248–76; Tamanoi, "Pan-Asianism in the Diary of Morisaki Minato," 184–206.

13 Morisaki, 25.

14 Ibid.

15 One exception, with regard to the location of the pre-matriculation training, were the students who matriculated at Kendai in 1945. The orientation for this group was held on the Kendai campus. Yuji, 517.

16 Morisaki, 37.

17 Louise Young cites Japan Tourist Bureau's (JTB) statistics on the Japanese hotel patrons in twelve major cities in Manchukuo. From 1934 to 1939, the total number increased nearly ten-fold, from 304,012 to 2,964,296. Young, 264.

18 Nishimura, 25.

19 Ibid., 26.

20 Ibid., 26.

21 Ibid., 27.

22 Ibid., 28–9.

23 Kōichi Fujimori, *Jukusei nisshi [Daily log of a juku student]* in Yuji, 147.

24 Ibid.

25 Young, 268.

26 Morisaki, 35.

27 Ibid., 40.

28 Ibid., 42.

29 Motoo Kaede in *Kenkoku daigaku sanki sei kaishi [Bulletin of the third entering class of Nation-Building University]* 15, in Yuji, 215–16, 215.

30 Young, 266–8.

31 Young also notes that during the 1930s the travel industry and the Japanese government promoted travel to the continent—Korea and Manchukuo—especially among school children. Of the 14,141 Japanese who traveled to Manchuria in 1939 through JTB-organized tours, 9,854, or 70 percent, were students, mostly on their graduation trips from secondary schools. Young, 265.

32　Ibid.

33　Ibid.

34　Hiroshi Kawada, *Manshū Kenkoku Daigaku monogatari: jidai o hikiukeyōto shita wakamonotachi [A story of Nation-Building University in Manchuria: the youth who sought to shoulder the time]* (Tokyo: Hara Shobo, 2002), 180; Yamada, 105. Fujita's first name might be pronounced as "Shōji".

35　Yoshio Sakuta, quoted in Yamada, 106.

36　"Zadankai: gonenkan no juku seikatsu [Panel discussion: the *juku* life in the past five years]," *Kenkoku* 3 (April 15, 1943), 70–85, 75.

37　Historian Shin'ichi Yamamuro convincingly argues this point based on his examination of multiple drafts of a citizenship law. See Shin'ichi Yamamuro, *Kimera:Manshūkoku no shōzō [Chimera: The Portrait of a Landscape]* (Tokyo: Chuko shinsho, 1993), 298.

38　"Zadankai," 70–85.

39　Ibid., 73.

40　Ibid., 74.

41　Ibid., 73. Iwabuchi does not provide the first name of his friend, Sui.

42　Ibid., 73.

43　Yuji, 124.

44　Fumio Mimura, in *Kendaishi 3* in Yuji, 124–9.

45　Ibid., 128.

46　Ibid., 126.

47　Tadaomi Nagano, *Jukusei nisshi [Daily log of a juku student]* in Yuji, 97.

48　Ibid. A comment by Fushinosuke Ehara attached to Nagano's diary.

49　Ibid., 109.

50　Ibid., 109.

51　Ibid., 131.

52　Ibid., 144.

53　Ibid., 155.

54　Ibid.

55　Ibid., 157.

56　Ibid., 157–8.

57　Fujimori in Yuji, 149.

58　Ibid., 150.

59　Ibid., 242.

60　Ibid., 191.

61　Ibid., 242.

62　Ibid., 242.

63　Nishimura, 51–2.

64　Nishimura only indicates Tsuji's last name in his diary, but it is clear that he refers to Tsuji Masanobu.

65 Ibid., 48.

66 Ibid.

67 Ibid., 154.

68 Ibid., 154–5.

69 Japanese troops had stationed in northern Indochina since September 1940. In July 1941, after acquiring the consent of French colonial authority in Indochina, Japanese troops moved into southern Indochina.

70 Ibid., 157.

71 Ibid., 162–3.

72 Ibid., 200–1.

73 Ibid., 256.

74 Ibid., 256–7.

75 Ibid., 268.

76 Ibid.

77 Ibid., 269.

78 Ibid.

79 Ibid., 174. I will discuss in more detail the arrest of Kendai's Chinese students for their involvement in anti-Japanese activities in Chapter 5.

80 Ibid., 168.

81 Ibid., 198.

82 Ibid., 318.

83 Ibid., 177.

84 The Kendai administration often used these categories. The *mankei* ("of Manchurian descent") generally referred to those who spoke Chinese language. The *nikkei* ("of Japanese descent") included students of Korean and Taiwanese origins. However, the daily uses of these terms by Kendai faculty and students varied significantly. For instance, some Korean students were often identified as the *senkei* ("of Korean descent") but were grouped together with the Japanese for certain purposes. Mariko Asano Tamanoi discusses in detail the ambiguous use of these classifications of peoples on the Kendai campus and Manchukuo in general. See Tamanoi, "Knowledge, Power, and Racial Classifications"; Tamanoi, "Pan-Asianism in the Diary of Morisaki Minato," 188–90.

85 Ibid., 54.

86 Ibid., 54–7.

87 This shrine is named *Kenkoku chūrei byō* ("Mausoleum dedicated to those who died for the nation-building") and was located in the southern end of downtown Shinkyō. It was Manchukuo's equivalent of the Yasukuni Shrine in Tokyo, where the spirits of the war dead of the Japanese Empire were enshrined as gods.

88 Ibid., 56.

89 Ibid.

90 Ibid., 57–9.

91 Ibid., 61.

92 Ibid.

93 Ibid.

94 Ibid.

95 Ibid., 68.

96 Ibid., 69.

97 Ibid., 71.

98 Ibid., 81.

99 Yuji, 426, 429.

100 Morisaki, 89.

101 Ibid., 89.

102 Morisaki provides only the family names of these two persons. The Kendai faculty roster has one individual with the name Manda: Manda Masaru. Suzuki, 83.

103 Ibid., 97.

104 Ibid., 96.

105 Ibid., 122.

106 Santarō Izumi, "Editor's Note," in Morisaki, 236–42, 237.

107 Ken'ichi Matsumoto, *Shōwa ni shisu—Morisaki Minato to Ozawa Kaisaku [Dying in the Showa era: Morisaki Minato and Ozawa Kaisaku]* (Tokyo: Shinchō-sha, 1988), 78.

108 Morisaki, 204. As mentioned in Chapter 2, the concept of *hakkō ichiu* was a term used by the Japanese government to justify its territorial expansion.

109 Tamanoi, "Knowledge, Power, and Racial Classifications," 263; Tamanoi, "Pan-Asianism in the Diary of Morisaki Minato," 196.

110 Morisaki, 205.

111 Morisaki himself dated his will August 16. However, the actual suicide took place in the early morning of August 17, according to the official report prepared by the Mie Fleet Air Arm.

112 Ibid., 228.

113 For detailed discussion on this literature, see Introduction.

Chapter 4

1 The exact numbers of Korean and Taiwanese students are unknown. The approximate numbers given here are based on *Kenkoku daigaku yōran* (1941), Report memo by Masao Miyazaki (1994) and Miyazawa.

2 *Kankirei—manshū kenkoku daigaku zaikan dōsō bunshū.*

3 Hong, *Hankyore no sekai.*

4 Shuiqing Li.

5   Lewis H. Gann, "Western and Japanese Colonialism: Some Preliminary Comparisons," in *The Japanese Colonial Empire, 1895–1945*, ed. Ramon H. Myers and Mark R. Peattie (Princeton, NJ: Princeton University Press, 1984), 497–525, 516.

6   For more on Japanese learning of European models of assimilation, see Mark E. Caprio, *Japanese Assimilation Policies in Colonial Korea, 1910–1945* (Seattle: University of Washington Press, 2009), Chapter 1 "Western Assimilation Practices."

7   Mark R. Peattie, "Japanese Attitude toward Colonialism, 1895–1945," in *The Japanese Colonial Empire, 1895–1945*, ed. Ramon H. Myers and Mark R. Peattie (Princeton, NJ: Princeton University Press, 1984), 80–127; Peter Duus, *The Abacus and the Sword: The Japanese Penetration of Korea, 1895–1910* (Berkeley: University of California Press, c.1995). Peter Duu's examination of Japan's early colonial policy in Korea finds a tendency to distinguish Japanese colonialism from that of the West. Unlike Western colonial empires that tended to conquer and rule the people whose race was different from that of their own, the Japanese could not ignore the similarities between the Koreans and themselves. Under this circumstance, the Japanese developed the "common race" theory based on the physical, cultural, historical, and linguistic similarities. Duus identifies two implications of this theory. One is that Japan's relationship with Korea differed from Western colonialism. Indeed, the Japanese rarely used the term "colony" to describe Korea; terms like "new territory" or "extension of the map" were used instead (p. 422). Another implication that Duus finds in the "common race" theory is that the Koreans were capable of assimilation through Japanese guidance. Thus, Duus argues, the "common race" theory advanced the belief that "the Japanese annexation of Korea was natural, rational, and perhaps inevitable" because of the commonalities between the two races (p. 423).

8   Harry J. Lamley, "Assimilation Efforts in Colonial Taiwan: The Fate of the 1914 Movement," *Monumenta Serica*, 29 (1970–71), 496–520, 496.

9   Appeared in discussion as early as 1895 when Japan acquired Taiwan—historically called Formosa since the sixteenth century—as its first overseas colony. However, the early colonial administrations were reluctant to implement it in actual practice. Until the fourth Governor-General, Kodama Gentarō, assumed leadership in colonial Taiwan, the regime's priority had been to stabilize the situation rather than to upset the local population. Lamley, 500.

10 Patricia E. Tsurumi, *Japanese Colonial Education in Taiwan, 1895–1945* (Cambridge, MA: Harvard University Press, 1977), 18–20.

11 Ibid., 50.

12 Ibid., 145.

13 As explained in the Introduction, Korea first became Japan's protectorate after Japan pressured Korea to sign the Japan–Korea Treaty of 1905. Prior to this event, Japan

defeated Russia in the Russo–Japanese War (1904–5) and made Russia recognize Japan's special interest over Korea in the Portsmouth Treaty of 1905.

14 Nobuko Furukawa, "Shokuminchi kindai shakai ni okeru shotō kyōiku kōzō: chōsen ni okeru higimusei to gakkō 'fukyū' mondai [Primary education system in the modern colonial society: voluntary enrolment and the problem of the popularization of schools in Korea]," in *Teikoku to gakkō [Empires and Schools]*, ed. Takeshi Komagome and Nobuya Hashimoto (Kyoto: Shōwadō, 2007), 129–64, 131–8.

15 Caprio, 93, 98.

16 Ronald Toby, "Education in Korea under the Japanese: Attitudes and Manifestations," *Occasional Papers on Korea*, no. 1 (April 1974), 55–64, 59.

17 Patricia E. Tsurumi, "Colonial Education in Korea and Taiwan," in *The Japanese Colonial Empire, 1895–1945*, ed. Ramon H. Myers, Mark R. Peattie, and Ching-chih Chen (Princeton, NJ: Princeton University Press, 1984), 275–311, 302.

18 Tsurumi, *Japanese Colonial Education in Taiwan*, 111.

19 Ibid., 126.

20 Caprio, 130–2. The GGK did establish schools for Japanese–Korean coeducation; however, the higher tuition made those schools an option only to the Korean children of wealthy families. Mark E. Caprio argues that such attitudes of the Japanese colonial authorities stemmed from the assumption of Korean inferiority to the Japanese.

21 Lamley, 518.

22 Leo T. S. Ching clearly differentiates *kōminka seisaku* from *dōka seisaku*. According to Ching, *dōka* remains a vague colonial project, whereas *kōminka* imposed a series of Japanese obligations, responsibilities, and customs on the colonized. For more on the difference between the two, see Leo T. S. Ching, *Becoming "Japanese": Colonial Taiwan and the Politics of Identity Formation* (Berkeley: University of California Press, 2001), Chapter 3.

23 The Government-General of Korea launched the so-called *sōshi kaimei* ("establishing household surnames and changing names") campaign on February 11, 1940. While the conventional knowledge has emphasized the forcible aspect of its campaign to change one's surnames in the Japanese fashion, recent works by Kim Yŏng-dal and Mizuno Naoki have revealed the complicated story of *sōshi kaimei*. They explain that while the creation of household surnames was enforced by law, changing names in the Japanese fashion was voluntary, though local authorities often put great pressure on Korean people to "volunteer" for this option. See Fujitani, 336–7; Naoki Mizuno, *Sōshi kaimei: nihon no chosen shihai no nakade [Sōshi kaimei in Korea under Japanese rule]* (Tokyo: Iwanami shinsho, 2008); and Motokazu Matsutani, "A New Perspective on the 'Name-Changing Policy' in Korea," in *Gender and Law in the Japanese Imperium*, ed. Susan L. Burns and Barbara J. Brooks (Honolulu: University of Hawaii Press, 2014),

240–66. As for Taiwan, on February 11, 1940, the Government-General of Taiwan commenced a name-changing campaign as part of the *kōminka* movement. The revised Household Registration Regulations allowed Taiwanese households to apply to change their surnames in the Japanese fashion. The option of changing names was presented only to qualified households. The applicants must undergo layers of investigations to prove that the core adult members of the household spoke Japanese in daily life and that they were committed to Japanizing their lifestyle. Initially, not many Taiwanese responded to this campaign. In the year 1940, the Government-General issued 1,357 name-change licenses island-wide. When the license-issuing power was moved to local governments in the following year, the number significantly increased, which may have been a result of local governments actively promoting name changes under pressure. While the total number of name-change licenses is not known, as of December 1943, 17,526 households (126,211 individuals) changed their surnames into Japanese ones. See Wan-yao Chou, "The *Kōminka* Movement: Taiwan under Wartime Japan, 1937–1945" (Ph.D. diss., Yale University, 1991), 113–29.

24 Fujitani.

25 Even at this point, primary education in Korea was not compulsory. The GGK promised to make it so within ten years. In 1944, the GGK shortened this period, announcing that it would start compulsory primary education in 1946. Caprio, 155.

26 Caprio, 155. The author also notes that the GGK stopped recording statistics by nationalities after the early 1940s, which makes it difficult to know whether the situation improved.

27 Ibid., 153.

28 Tsurumi, *Japanese Colonial Education in Taiwan*, 131–2.

29 Tsurumi analyzes Japanese readers and other textbooks used in Taiwan and compared them with those used in Japan. For more details, see Tsurumi, *Japanese Colonial Education in Taiwan*, Chapter 6.

30 Wen-Hsing Wu, Shun-Fen Chen, and Chen-Tsou Wu, "The Development of Higher Education in Taiwan," *Higher Education* 18, no. 1 "From Dependency to Autonomy: The Development of Asian Universities" (1989), 117–36; Tsurumi, *Japanese Colonial Education in Taiwan*, 122–4.

31 Caprio, 200.

32 Formal conscription began in 1943 in Korea and 1945 in Taiwan, although these soldiers were never sent to the battlefield before the war ended. Before formal conscription started, the Japanese Military recruited volunteer soldiers in these colonies.

33 "Kenkoku daigaku yoka daiikki seito senbatsu yōkō an," in Yuji, 26–7. It appears that "Japanese" includes those who reside in Japan, Manchukuo and Japan's formal colonies such as Korea and Taiwan. Regarding the educational background, the admission committee made exceptions for those who did not graduate middle

schools but whose academic abilities were acknowledged as satisfactory by the Japanese or Manchukuo governments.

34 Hui Bang, "Kenkoku daigaku to gaikōkan [Nation-Building University and my career as a diplomat]," in *Kankirei—manshū kenkoku daigaku zaikan dōsō bunshū*, 34–9, 34.

35 In-Seon Tae, "Kenkoku daigaku to watashi [Nation-Building University and myself]," in *Kankirei—manshū kenkoku daigaku zaikan dōsō bunshū*, 50–6, 50–1.

36 Gi-Su Jeong, "Kankirei no yume [The dream about the Kankirei]," in *Kankirei—manshū kenkoku daigaku zaikan dōsō bunshū*, 93–100, 94.

37 Bang, 35.

38 Gwang-Ho An, "Manchū kenkoku daigaku [Nation-Building University]," in *Kankirei—manshū kenkoku daigaku zaikan dōsō bunshū*, 1–5, 1.

39 Hong, *Hankyore no sekai*, 27.

40 Ibid., 27.

41 Jae-Jin Kim, "Tsuioku no Kendai [Kendai in memory]," in *Kankirei—manshū kenkoku daigaku zaikan dōsō bunshū*, 60–2, 60.

42 Ibid., 60.

43 Ibid., 60.

44 Ibid., 60.

45 Fujitani, 39.

46 In-Geon An, "Kendaisei wa sabishiku nai [Kendai students know no loneliness]," in *Kankirei—manshū kenkoku daigaku zaikan dōsō bunshū*, 77–82, 77.

47 Seon-Jun Im, "Manshū Kendai nyūgaku no michi [My experience before matriculating at Kendai in Manchuria]," in *Kankirei—manshū kenkoku daigaku zaikan dōsō bunshū*, 90–2, 91.

48 Yeong-Hun Gang, "Kioku ni nokoru onshi rokudō sensei no ohanashi [Memorable talk of my former teacher Rokudō]," in *Kankirei—manshū kenkoku daigaku zaikan dōsō bunshū*, 40–43, 40; Won-Jung Jin, "Kaiko to sekkei," 108–11, 108.

49 Gang, 40.

50 Ibid., 40.

51 Kim Sang-Gyu, "Ninen han no kaisō [Recollection of the two and a half year]," in *Kankirei—manshū kenkoku daigaku zaikan dōsō bunshū*, 57–9, 57.

52 Hui-Seong Bak, "Kendai seikatsu no kaiko [Recollection of my student life at Kendai]," in *Kankirei—manshū kenkoku daigaku zaikan dōsō bunshū*, 63–70, 63.

53 Ibid.

54 Yong-Hui Kim, "Kenkoku daigaku seikatsu no kaiko [Recollection of my student life at Nation-Building University]," in *Kankirei—manshū kenkoku daigaku zaikan dōsō bunshū*, 86–9, 86.

55 Ibid., 86–7.

56 Seon-Jun Im, 90.

57 Shuiqing Li, 8.

58 Jong-Cheol Kim, "Kankirei jidai no dansō [My scattered memories about the time I spent at Kenkirei]," in *Kankirei—manshū kenkoku daigaku zaikan dōsō bunshū*, 30–3, 30.

59 Seon-Jun Im, 92.

60 Heung-Cheol Choe, "Kendai no seikatsu wo kangaeru [Regarding the life at Kendai]," in *Kankirei—manshū kenkoku daigaku zaikan dōsō bunshū*, 71–6, 74.

61 Ibid., 74.

62 Ibid., 74.

63 Sang-Gyu Kim, 58–9.

64 Ibid., 59.

65 Ibid., 59.

66 Yeong-Hun Gang, 41.

67 Kim's memoir does not provide names of these two alumni, but according to *Kenkoku daigaku nenpyō yōran*, they should have been Choe Hui-Beom (Japanese name: Yamamoto Yoshio) and Gwon Hyeok-So (Japanese name: Yoshida Tomimitsu). Fujimori and Suzuki, *Kenkoku daigaku nenpyō yōran*, 48. In his memoir, Kim indicates that those two Korean alumni were working at the university as associate professors. However, according to *Kenkoku daigaku nenpyō yōran*, they, together with nine other recent Kendai graduates, were appointed probationary senior government officials and were assigned to Kendai on October 16, 1943. It appears that these alumni were called back to their alma mater to train current students. Details of their duties at the university are not known, but as members of Kendai's founding class, they were expected to play active roles in school affairs. For instance, of the eleven alumni, Gwon Hyok-So and seven others were appointed *jukutō*'s assistants and had constant interactions with students. Yuji, 469. *Seihu kōhō* (Shinkyō), October 20, 1943, in *Weimanzhouguo zhengfu gongbao* 104 (Shenyang: Liaoshen shushe, 1990), 465–80.

68 Yong-Hui Kim, 87.

69 Ibid., 87.

70 Jong-Hang I, "Itsu-ga no mizu wa imammo nagarete irudaro! [The water must still be flowing in the Yitong River!]," in *Kankirei—manshū kenkoku daigaku zaikan dōsō bunshū*, 6–11, 6.

71 Yeong-Hun Gang, 40.

72 Ibid., 40–1.

73 Yeong-Rok Kim, "Kamakiri no yume [The dream about Kenkirei]," in *Kankirei—manshū kenkoku daigaku zaikan dōsō bunshū*, 12–25, 13.

74 Chun-Sik Hong, "Seishun hōkō ki [The record of my youthful days]," in *Kankirei—manshū kenkoku daigaku zaikan dōsō bunshū*, 26–9, 28; Gi-Sik Min, "Kenkoku daigaku to shikikan [Nation-Building University and my career as Commander]," in *Kankirei—manshū kenkoku daigaku zaikan dōsō bunshū*, 44–9, 45.

75 Hong, "Seishun hōkō ki," 28.

76 Shuiqing Li, 14.

77 Yeong-Hun Gang, "Kenkoku daigaku no gakufū ni tsuiteno ichi kōsatsu [Discussion of the academic culture of Kenkoku University]," in *Kankirei—manshū kenkoku daigaku zaikan dōsō bunshū*, 112–15.

78 Gwang-Ho An, "Byōbō sanzen ri [In the remote past, at a great distance]," in *Kankirei—manshū kenkoku daigaku zaikan dōsō bunshū*, 101–7, 101.

79 Ibid., 102.

80 Ibid., 102.

81 Ibid., 102.

82 In fact, by 1943, a total of 16,830 Korean volunteers had served not only the Korean Army but also the Kwantung Army and North China Army. Fujitani, 44.

83 Yeong-Rok Kim, 14.

84 Ibid., 15.

85 Ibid., 15.

86 Ibid., 15.

87 Ibid., 15.

88 Ibid., 15.

89 Hong, *Hankyore no sekai*, 14.

90 Ibid., 28.

91 Ibid., 28.

92 Ibid., 28–9.

93 Hui-Seong Bak, 64.

94 *Manshū kokushi: sōron [History of Manchukuo: general discussion]*, ed. Manshū kokushi Hensan Kankōkai (Tokyo: Manmō dōhō engokai, 1970), 736.

95 Ibid., 740–1.

96 Kim Sang-Gyu, 57–8. Following this logic, the Taiwanese students should have been served white rice as they were Japan's imperial subjects, too. However, Kim Sang-Gyu only mentions the Japanese and Korean students. It is not clear what meal Taiwanese students were served on this day.

97 Jae-Jin Kim, 61.

98 Yong-Hui Kim, 87.

99 Ibid., 87.

100 Ibid., 87.

101 Ibid., 87.

102 Historian Mizuno Naoki introduces a number of cases in which Korean people were imprisoned for expressing their criticisms of Japanese policy in Korea such as *sōshi kaimei* even in private conversations. Mizuno, 116–23.

103 Ibid., 87.

104 Ibid., 87.

105 Ibid., 87.

106   Gi-Su Jeong, 97.

107   In Korea and Taiwan, Japan's formal colonies, serving the Japanese military meant both obligation and right. Despite the fact that the wartime Japanese state recognized Koreans and Taiwanese as the imperial subjects (*kōmin*), conscription of young men from these colonies started only in 1944 for Korea and 1945 for Taiwan. These colonial "Japanese" were only slowly incorporated into the Japanese military forces. In April 1938 Korean males seventeen years and older were granted the right to volunteer for the army, followed by the same change in Taiwan in April 1942. In August 1943, the navy began to take Korean and Taiwanese volunteers of sixteen years old and older. For a detailed explanation of the process of incorporation of colonial subjects into the Japanese military, see Fujitani, *Race for Empire*, "Chapter One. Right to Kill, Right to Make Live: Koreans as Japanese," 35–77; Dokusan Kan, *Chōsenjin gakuto shutsujin—mou hitotsu no wadatsumi no koe* (Tokyo: Iwanami shoten, 1997), 4–5; and Brandon Palmer, *Fighting for the Enemy: Koreans in Japan's War, 1937–1945* (Seattle: University of Washington Press, 2013), Chapters 2 and 3.

108   Palmer, 17.

109   Kan, 71.

110   For details on how each of these groups played roles in exerting pressure on eligible but unwilling students, see Kan, Chapters 6–9.

111   Kan, 370.

112   Palmer 43.

113   Chou, 201.

114   Yeong-Rok Kim, 24.

115   Hong, *Hankyore no sekai*, 35.

116   Ibid., 35.

117   For detailed discussion of the "mission of glory," see Kan, Chapter 9.

118   Hwang, 156–7, 161–4.

119   Yeong-Hun Gang, 42.

120   Ibid., 42.

121   Hong, *Hankyore no sekai*, 35.

122   Ibid., 36.

123   Yeong-Rok Kim, 24.

124   Ibid., 25.

125   Kōichi Yamashita, *Jukusei nisshi [student diary at juku]* in Yuji, 485.

126   Hong is not entirely accurate, as Dokusan Kan indicates that there were two other schools in Korea whose eligible Korean students submitted applications for the Student Special Volunteer Soldier System without exception. Kan uses abbreviated names for those two schools: Hōsen and Kōshō. It is likely that he refers to Keijō College of Law and Keijō Higher School of Commerce. Kan, 155.

127 Hong, *Hankyore no sekai*, 36.

128 Yuji, 453.

129 Hong, *Hankyore no seka*, 36.

130 For the so-called entrance exam hell of the Japanese education system, see Liling Zheng, *Yakudōsuru seishun: nihon tōchika Taiwan no gakusei seikatsu [Vibrant youths: student life in Taiwan under Japanese rule]*, trans. Naoe Kawamoto (Osaka: Sōgensha, 2017), 28–41.

131 Ibid., 8. Historian Liling Zheng indicates that working in the governmental sector in Manchukuo was indeed one of the popular career paths for Taiwanese students enrolled at Taihoku Imperial University. Liling Zheng, "Senjiki taihoku teikoku daigaku no 'gakusei seikatsu chōsa' ['Investigation on student life' conducted at Taihoku Imperial University during wartime]," *Empire and the Higher Education in East Asia* 42 (2013): 173–93, 188.

132 Ibid., 21.

133 Ibid., 17–18.

134 *Taiwan lishi renwu xiaozhuan: ming qing ji rijushiqi [Brief biography of historical figures in Taiwan: Ming, Qing, through the era of Japanese occupation]*, ed. Ziwen Zhang, Guo Qizhuan, and Lin Weizhou (Taipei: Guojia tushuguan, 2006), 478.

135 Ibid., 18.

136 Ibid., 11.

137 Ibid., 11–12.

138 Ibid., 34.

139 Ibid., 34.

140 Ibid., 11.

141 Ibid., 36.

142 Ibid., 36.

143 Ibid., 36–7.

144 Ibid., 37.

145 Ibid., 37.

146 Ibid., 45.

147 Ibid., 45.

148 Ibid., 45.

149 Ibid., 45.

150 Ibid., 52. At that time, the recommendation was made by Kendai's honorary professor and one of the "four professors" who led the planning of Kendai, Hiraizumi Kiyoshi. For more on Hiraizumi, see Chapter 2.

151 Ibid., 29–30.

152 Ibid., 28–9.

153 Nanjing, the capital of the Republic of China until 1937, was now the headquarters of Wang Jingwei's regime, which was supported by the Japanese Empire.

154 Shuiqing Li, 46.

155 Ibid., 46.

156 Ibid., 51.

157 Ibid., 58.

158 The Labor Service Act was implemented on May 27, 1942. Later, the Manchukuo government extended the age limit to thirty, and increased the duration of service to three years. For more on Manchukuo's Labor Service Corps, see Min Zheng "Rōmu shin taisei [The new labor system]," in *Nicchū kyōdō kenkyū: Manshūkoku towa nandattanoka [Collaborative research by Japan and China: what was Manchukuo?]*, ed. Shokuminchi bunka Gakkai (Tokyo: shōgakkan, 2008), 140–50, 142–3.

159 Shuiqing Li, 55.

160 Ibid., 58, 67.

161 Ibid., 58–9.

162 Ibid., 57, 59. For more information on the Youth Action Group, see *Manshū kokushi kakuron [History of Manchukuo: itemized discussion]*, ed. Manshū kokushi Hensan Kankōkai (Tokyo: Manmō dōhō engokai, 1970), 130–2.

163 Ibid., 67.

Chapter 5

1 Eriko Miyazawa, publishing her book in 1997, did not have access to the *Huiyi* collection that was also published in 1997. Fumiaki Shishida's 2005 book incorporates more sources about non-Japanese students. These two works on Kendai offer helpful insights into the Chinese students' experience by relying on oral history and correspondences. More recently, a Japanese journalist, Hideyuki Miura, published a book on Kendai alumni's postwar experiences based on interviews with alumni residing in six countries. Hideyuki Miura, *Goshoku no niji: manshū kenkoku daigaku sotugyōsei tachi no sengo [Five-color rainbow: postwar experiences of Manchukuo Kenkoku University alumni]* (Shūeisha: Tokyo, 2015).

2 In addition to the Chinese anthology *Huiyi*, there is another essay that was written and published in Chinese in the PRC: Diqian Liu, "Wo suo liaojie de weiman jianguo daxue [What I know about Bogus Manchukuo Kenkoku University]," (1985), republished in Chunxi Shuikou, *"Jianguo daxue" de huanying [The illusion at "Kenkoku University"]*, trans. Bingyue Dong (Beijing: Kunlun chubanshe, 2004), 146–95. This essay is similar to the *Huiyi* memoirs in the sense that it was written by a former Chinese student and published in Chinese as part of a Chinese city government's publication. I will use this essay to supplement my analysis of Chinese-language memoirs.

3 As discussed in Chapter 2, the term "Chinese" is not entirely accurate because the Chinese-speaking students enrolled at Kendai consisted of not only ethnic

Han Chinese but also ethnic minorities such as Manchu and Hui and sometimes
Mongolians. However, it is difficult to distinguish Manchu and Hui from Han
Chinese. It appears that the school administration and Japanese faculty and
students did not differentiate these Chinese-speaking students by their ethnicities.
In this chapter, I will use the term "Chinese" to refer to those Chinese-speaking
students.

4   The alumni association in Japan stayed in contact with fifty-four former Chinese
    students living in Changchun City as of 2003. *Kenkoku daigaku dōsōkai meibo
    [Kenkoku University Alumni Association Roster]* (Tokyo: Kenkoku University
    Alumni Association, 2003). Hereafter I call this source the 2003 alumni roster.

5   "Qianyan [Preface]," in *Huiyi weiman jianguo daxue [Remembering Bogus
    Manchukuo Nation-Building University]* (Changchun: Changchun City
    Government's Chinese People's Political Consultative Committee, Historical Record
    Committee, 1997).

6   Ibid.

7   In an effort to weaken the Nationalist defending forces in Changchun City, the
    CCP's People's Liberation Army blockaded the city for months, from the early
    autumn of 1947 to October 1948, starving as many as 200,000 civilians. Although
    it certainly helped the CCP take over Manchuria, the massive civilian casualties left
    a dark mark on the history of the communist revolution. For this reason, public
    discussions of the communist blockade of Changchun have been strictly censored
    by the PRC government. For more on the siege of Changchun, see Diana Lary,
    China's Civil War: A Social History, 1945–1949 (Cambridge: Cambridge University
    Press, 2015), 122–6.

8   Miura, *Goshoku no niji,* 122–41.

9   Ibid., 151–6, 167–72.

10 *Hakki [Eight flags]* (Kendai seventh and eighth classes' bulletin no. 8), ed. Yoshihisa
    Ueda et al., 1985.

11 Shize Liu, "weiman jianguo daxue jishu [The summary of Bogus Manchukuo
    Nation-Building University]," in *Huiyi,* 28–41, 28. He includes Mongolians,
    Manchu, and Hui in this number.

12 "Kenkoku Daigaku yōran."

13 Ibid. This is based on the education system of Manchukuo after 1938.

14 Due to their wealthy backgrounds, some of Kendai's Chinese alumni became the
    targets of political persecution under the CCP after 1945.

15 Shishida, 87–8.

16 Liu Diqian, "Wo suo liaojie de weiman jianguo daxue [What I know about Bogus
    Manchukuo Nation-Building University]" (1985), republished in Chunxi Shuikou,
    "jianguo daxue" de huanying [The Illusion at "Nation-Building University"], 146–95,
    trans. Bigyue Dong (Beijing: Kunlun chubanshe, 2004), 155. For the value of this
    five yen allowance, see Chapter 2, note 54.

17 Miyazawa, 191 and 182; Liu Diqian, 155.

18 Shishida, 88.

19 *Manshūkoku kenkoku daigaku seito boshū kōkoku [Official announcement of student recruitment for Kenkoku University in Manchukuo]* (August 10, 1937), in Yuji, *Kenkoku daigaku nenpyō*, 56–9.

20 Tingqiao Yan, "Weiman jianguo daxue shimou zhaiji [A general note on Bogus Manchukuo Nation-Building University]," in *Huiyi*, 21–7, 23.

21 Rong Pei, "Dushu yu fan dushu de huodong [The activities of reading books and the suppression of them]," in *Huiyi*, 243–8, 243.

22 Wensheng Zhang, "Jianda xianxiang [Kendai phenomenon]," in *Huiyi*, 264–7, 264.

23 Yishi Yue, "Wo likai jianda dao Chongqing [I left Kendai to go to Chongqing]," in *Huiyi*, 117–19, 118.

24 Ibid.

25 Yishi Yue, 118.

26 As noted in Chapter 2, Kendai admitted students who had graduated from middle schools. Thus, the majority of Chinese students enrolled at Kendai had gone through middle school education in Manchukuo. Given the strong emphasis placed upon the Japanese language training of non-Japanese speakers at middle schools in Manchukuo, it is reasonable to expect a high level of Japanese proficiency among the Chinese students. For instance, one finds in the oral history of a former Chinese resident of Manchukuo that the Chinese graduates of the elementary schools in Manchukuo could function as "third-rate interpreters." Yongsheng Wang, "Doreika kyōiku no kōnō wo hikuku hyōka surubeki dewanai [The effects of enslavement education should not be taken lightly]," trans. Ken'ichi Takenaka, in Hongshen Qi, *"Manshū" ōraru hisutorī: "doreika kyōiku" ni kōshite [Oral history of "Manchuria": resistance against the "education of enslavement"]* (Tokyo: Kōseisha, 2004), 501–14, 502.

27 Jiaqi Yu, "Weiman jianguo daxue ji qi pouxi [Analysis of Bogus Manchukuo Nation-Building University]," in *Huiyi*, 1–20, 19.

28 For more on Kendai administration's effort to recruit non-Japanese scholars for the faculty see Chapter 2.

29 Ke Gao, "Weiman jianda fanman kangri huodong ji qi fazhan [The activities of anti-Manchukuo and anti-Japanese aggression and their development at Bogus Manchukuo Kendai]," in *Huiyi*, 86–116, 95.

30 Jiaqi Yu, 12–13.

31 Defan Yan, "Weiman jianda renwu sumiao [Sketch of people at Bogus Manchukuo Kendai]," in *Huiyi*, 56–62, 58.

32 Cheng Chang, "Guanyu Zhang Jinghui he Weigao Guicang [About Zhang Jinghui and Suetaka Kamezō]," in *Huiyi*, 52–5, 52; Rong Pei, 244.

33 Diqian Liu, 171.

34 Shize Liu, 35.

35 Rong Pei, 245.

36 Ibid.

37 One prime example is Premier Zhou Enlai, who in 1971 stated that the people of Japan are the victims of Japanese militarism.

38 Tingqiao Yan, 23.

39 Shize Liu, 31.

40 Ibid., 41.

41 Rong Pei, 248.

42 Diqian Liu, 183.

43 Ibid., 183.

44 Ibid., 171. As discussed in Chapter 2, the term "*mankei*" was used confusingly. It generally referred to Chinese, Manchu, Mongolian, Hui, and Russian who resided in Manchukuo. In some cases, the term was used as a synonym of "Chinese."

45 Jiaqi Yu, 4.

46 Diqian Liu, 150.

47 For more on the Kwantung military police's purge of political dissidents, see Maojie Li, "Chian kikan [The organizations for the public order]," 70–3, and "Chian no jittai [The reality of the maintenance of the public order]," 73–82 in *Nicchū kyōdō kenkyū: "Manshūkoku" towa nandatta noka [The Chinese-Japanese collaborative research: what was "Manchukuo"?]*, ed. Shokuminchi bunka Gakkai (Tokyo: Shokuminchi bunka gakkai, 2008).

48 Yishi Yue, 118–19. In fact, Kendai's library held those leading Marxists' books, but they could not be lent out. Some *Huiyi* authors indicate that some Chinese students even stole those library books to expand their secret archive.

49 Ke Gao, 93.

50 Tingqiao Yan, 24–5.

51 The number of the arrested students is based on three sources: Hong Zhao, "Wo de kongsu: 1954 nian shenpan riben zhanfan shi de kongsu shu [My accusation: my letter of appeal to the Japanese war crime tribunal in 1954]," in *Huiyi*, 154–63. (Originally published in 1989 as part of another Chinese publication vol. 8 of *Riben diguo zhuyi qinhua dangan ziliao xuanbian dibaquan: dongbei lici dacanan [The selected archival records about Japanese imperial encroachment in China: the tragedy in the Northeast]* (Beijing: Zhonghua shuju, 1989).); Miyazawa, 228 and 269; and Ke Gao, 93–4.

52 Miyazawa, 228; and Ke Gao, 94.

53 Hong Zhao, 156.

54 Mishina in *Kendaishi shiryō 2*, quoted in Yuji, 320.

55 Ibid, 320.

56 Ibid, 320.

57 Diqian Liu, 150.

58 Hong Zhao, 162.

59 Yūken Takigawa in Yuji, 468.

60 The lyrics of the school song were published in the first volume of *Kenkoku*, a
    student-organized *juku* journal, in June 1940. *Kenkoku: kenkoku daigaku juku
    zasshi [Nation-building: Kenkoku University juku journal]*, vol. 1 (Hōten, 1940).

61 Shuiqing Li, 41–2.

62 Shize Liu, 36–7.

63 Ibid., 38.

64 Ibid., 39.

65 Ke Gao, 95.

66 Ke Gao, 88 and 96. The fifth entering class student who stole Soviet journals was
    severely scolded by *jukutō* and quit the school. The Japanese journals that they used
    were *Tōa* and *Tōa Junkan*. In terms of direct action, some fourth entering class
    students distributed anti-Japanese fliers on the streets of Manchukuo's capital city,
    Shinkyō (Xingjing), and at some schools, which Gao claims had a big impact (Ke
    Gao, 101).

67 Rong Pei, 243; Wensheng Zhang, 265; and Xueqian Gu, "Shenghuo zai minzu
    maodun zhi zhong [Living under the paradox of 'harmony among various peoples
    residing in Manchukuo']," in *Huiyi*, 268–73, 270.

68 Ke Gao, 106.

69 Yeping Wang, "Chongpo laolong ren niao fei [Quickly breaking the prison, birds
    flew away]," in *Huiyi*, 77–85, 78–9.

70 Wensheng Zhang, 267.

71 Between 1927 and 1937, the Republic of China under the GMD (Nationalist Party)
    had its government in Nanjing. Shortly before Japanese troops conquered the city
    in December 1937, which triggered the event commonly known as the Nanjing
    Massacre or Rape of Nanking, the GMD leaders fled to Chongqing and established
    their new headquarters there. Meanwhile, Chinese politician Wang Jingwei
    established a new regime in Nanjing in March 1940, sponsored by Japan. Because
    of his collaboration with the Japanese and his career in the Nanjing regime that
    proclaimed Pan-Asianism as one of its founding principles, Wang was and still is
    recognized in the PRC as a national traitor.

72 Shize Liu, 33.

73 Rong Pei, 246.

74 Ibid.

75 For more on this new interpretation, see Hideki Okada, "Jūni ten san zero jiken
    to kenkoku daigakusei [The December thirtieth incident and Nation-Building
    University students]," *hōsho gekkan* 179 (August 2000), 33–5.

76 Tingqiao Yan, 26.

77 Yamada, 150.

78 Chengren Liu, "Lingming qian de kanzheng [Struggle before the dawn]," in *Huiyi*,
    63–6.

79 Yeping Wang, 81. Japanese historian Eriko Miyazawa, former Japanese students and Liu Diqian, the author of another Chinese publication, all note that a student from Korea volunteered to join the fighting unit.

80 Yeping Wang, 81.

81 Wen Xue, "Ji 'ba yi wu' qianhou de ririyeye [Note about the days around 'August 15']," in *Huiyi*, 67–72, 69.

82 Ibid., 69–71.

83 Shaoying Song, "Qianye da taowang [The great escape in the night before]," in *Huiyi*, 73–6, 74.

84 Ibid., 76.

85 Yeping Wang, 84.

86 Hong Zhao, 156.

87 A number of Kendai's former Chinese students changed their names at some points after 1945. For Zhang, Tailu was his original name, and Yimin was the name he used as of 1997.

88 Weiping Han, "Shūsen zengo no ashioto [The footsteps around the war's end]," trans. Yoshihisa Ueda, in *Hakki*, 21–5, 21.

89 One contributor to *Huiyi* who hints at the awareness of the war's imminent end is Wang Yeping. As I discussed earlier, he was anticipating and waiting for the Soviet Union's entry to WWII against Japan.

90 In fact, regarding any individuals who worked for Manchukuo as national traitors was a long-standing official stance of both the Nationalist Government and the Communist Party from 1932. Shortly after the foundation of Manchukuo in March 1932, both parties announced their non-recognition policies against Manchukuo. Furthermore, the Nationalist Government publicized its intent to punish any collaborators for the act of treachery against China. See Yamamuro, *Kimera*, 213–14.

91 Tailu Zhang, "Kenkoku daigaku de mananda hibi [The days I spent at Nation-Building University]," trans. Yoshihisa Ueda, in *Hakki*, 43–6, 44.

92 Ibid.

93 Weiping Han, 22.

94 Tailu Zhang, 45.

95 Ibid., 44.

96 Yimen Zhang, "Zai zhimin tongzhixiade xuexi shenghuo [Student Life under Colonial Rule]," in *Huiyi*, 282–8, 283.

97 Tailu Zhang, 45.

98 Weiping Han, 23.

99 Yeping Wang, 85.

100 Ke Gao, 108.

101 This new organization was committed to the youth education in Northeast China and published its journals *Qingnian Xinbao, Xin Shaonianbao,* and *Buyecheng.* Ke Gao, 108–9.

102 Ibid., 111.

103 Ibid., 112.

104 Weiping Han, 23–4.

105 Ibid., 24.

106 Ibid., 25.

107 Yoshizō Miyagawa in *Kendaishi shiryō 2* quoted in Yuji, 321.

108 Shuiqing Li, 84–5.

109 Ibid., 83.

110 Ryūta Tsutsui, "Tōhatsu nagakeredo gankō mijikashi [Wearing her hair long, while fixing her eyes near]," in *Hakki*, 46–9, 48.

111 *Riben qinhua jiaoyu quanshi [General history of Japanese colonial education]*, ed. Enrong Song, Zixia Yu, and Bihong Cao et al. (Beijing: renmin jiaoyu chubanshe, 2005).

Chapter 6

1 "Kenkoku Daigaku rei," 51–2, 51.

2 *Reimei*, no. 1 to 5 (1940).

3 *Kanki [Joy]* (June 1940).

4 *Kenkoku: kenkoku daigaku juku zasshi [Nation-building: Kenkoku University juku journal]* 1 (August 20, 1940), 2 (August 20, 1941), and 3 (April 20, 1943).

5 *Kenkoku daigaku juku geppō.*

6 More than 200 students of mostly the second entering class were drafted in the fall of 1943 when the Japanese government terminated the deferment of draft for male students enrolled in higher education institutions.

7 Japanese historian Fumiaki Shishida briefly mentions *Kenkoku* and *Juku Monthly* in his book, but does not examine their contents.

8 Editors for *Kenkoku* and *Juku Monthly* changed over time.

9 An exception to this wide representation were Taiwanese students. In all four periodicals, there is no entry that clearly identifies its author as Taiwanese. A number of entries that were published under pen names probably include some of the Taiwanese students' works, but unfortunately, there is no way to identify them.

10 "Editors' Notes," *Juku Monthly*, no. 1 (June 15, 1942), 5.

11 Aimaimokoo (pen name), "Shinnen, tettei, ikkan [Coherent commitment to one's belief]," *Reimei*, no. 5 (1940), 13–14, 13.

12 Ibid., 13.

13 Dong Liao, "Fu yu zi [father and son]," *Kenkoku* 2 (August 15, 1941), 95–101, 101.

14 Yang Liufeng, "Xie gei M [Letter to M]," *Kenkoku* 2 (August 15, 1941), 34–7, 35.

15 Ibid., 36.

16 Kazuo Terada, "Manchu *haiku* ron [Discussion on Manchurian *haiku*]," *Kenkoku* 1 (August 15, 1940), 89–96, 96.

17 Ibid., 96.

18 Jingxiang Shan, "Dengta: manzhou wenxue jiantao [Lighthouse: examination of the Manchukuo literature]," *Kenkoku* 1 (August 15, 1940), 97–101, 98.

19 Ibid., 98.

20 Ibid., 98.

21 Ziwo Yu, "Zhongguo shehui de guanjian [My personal views on the Chinese society]," *Kenkoku* 2 (August 15, 1941), 72–80.

22 Ibid., 76.

23 Ibid., 79.

24 Fengjun Kang, "Zhanzheng de biranxing yu bixuxing [The inevitability and necessity of wars]," *Kenkoku* 2 (August 15, 1941), 16–27.

25 Ibid., 24.

26 Ibid., 25.

27 Tingchao Yan, "Hanyu de xinwenzi yundong [The movement to reform the Chinese characters]," *Kenkoku* 3 (April 15, 1943), 101–7.

28 Ibid., 107.

29 Kōshō Tokuyama, "Kitan hōsei no kenkyū [Research on the Khitan legal system]," *Kenkoku* 3 (April 15, 1943), 32–41.

30 Ibid., 39–40.

31 Ibid., 41.

32 Jakkenshō (pen name), "Zuisō hutatsu [Two random thoughts]," *Juku Monthly*, no. 7 (November 20, 1943), 36–7.

33 Ibid., 37.

34 Ibid., 37.

35 Tōa dōbun shoin, a Japanese private research centre and college founded in Shanghai in 1901 and closed in 1946, concentrated on Sinology. But, the institution enrolled mostly Japanese students. From 1920 to 1934, the school had a division for Chinese students; however, its curriculum concentrated on Japanese language instruction and practical training useful for China–Japan trade.

36 For more on Ishiwara's vision of an East Asian League, his proposals for Kendai's curriculum and his uneasy relationship with the school's planning committee, see the sections "Forging an East Asian League to prepare for the Final War: Ishiwara Kanji's perception of Pan-Asianism" and "Visions of Pan-Asianist education: Ishiwara Kanji, Planning Committee, and the four professors" in Chapter 2.

37 For more details on Ehara and his fellow *jukutō* who also resigned, see Chapter 2, note 97.

38 "Zadankai," 70–85.

39 Fushinosuke Ehara, letter to student, *Kenkoku* 1 (August 15, 1940), 65.

40 Naifeng Guan, "Yashiya fuxing zhi genben wenti [Fundamental issues of Asian revival]," *Kenkoku* 1 (August 15, 1940), 15–26.

41 Ibid., 19–22.

42 Ibid., 22.

43 Ibid., 23.

44 Ibid., 23.

45 Yasuji Imamura, "Kitashi bekken [A glance at the Northern China]," *Kenkoku* 3 (April 15, 1943), 162–76. He made the two-week group field trip in July 1942.

46 Ibid., 175.

47 Ibid., 176.

48 Seredkin, "Manshū teikokunai ni okeru hakkei roshiya seinen no shimei [The mission of the white Russian youths in Manchukuo]," *Kenkoku* 3 (April 15, 1943), 53–6. Kendai's records list the names of Russian students only by their surnames.

49 Ibid., 55.

50 Ibid., 53.

51 Mengheboyan, "Mōkojin to tōa [The Mongolian people and East Asia]," *Kenkoku* 1 (August 15, 1940), 27–30.

52 Here, Mengheboyan is referring to the Mongolian People's Republic, which was established in 1924 and maintained close ties with the Soviet Union.

53 Mengheboyan, 28.

54 Ibid., 30.

55 Ibid., 30.

56 Ibid., 30.

57 Yūtarō Bandō, "'Gakusei' sonona ni yobigun wo sōki seshimuru nakare [Do not see students as reserve troops]," *Juku Geppō*, no. 1 (June 15, 1942), 4.

58 Ibid., 4.

59 Masuo Arashida, "Tōa no tami [The people of East Asia]," *Juku Geppō*, no. 2 (August 15, 1942), 4.

60 Ibid., 4.

61 Ibid., 4.

62 Kōgen Hiranuma, "Sekai [The world]," *Juku Geppō*, no. 2 (August 15, 1942), 3.

63 Ibid., 3.

64 Ibid., 3.

65 Ibid., 3.

66 Dobuchinbarajuru, "Daitōa kyōeiken to mōko [The Greater East Asia and Mongolia]," *Kenkoku* 3 (April 15, 1943), 44–8. The essay was written in September 1942 but was published in April 1943. The author's name was written only in the Japanese *katakana* in *Kenkoku* periodical and other institutional records. Because of this, I was not able to find out the conventional transliteration of his name.

67 Ibid., 46.

68 Ibid., 46.

69 Ibid., 48.

70 Di Liu, "Dongya qingshi he jiandasheng de fanxing [The situation of East Asia and Kendai students' introspection]," *Juku Geppō,* no. 2 (August 15, 1942), 5.

71 Ibid., 5.

72 Ibid., 5.

73 Shintarō Hayashi, "Minzoku kyōwa shokan [My perspective on the ethnic harmony]," *Juku Geppō,* no. 3 (January 15, 1943), 4.

74 Ibid., 4.

75 Ibid., 4.

76 Editors, "Ji [Some words by the editors]," *Kenkoku* 1 (August 15, 1940).

77 Yuge, "Henshū kōki [Editorial notes]," *Kenkoku* 1 (August 15, 1940), 170.

78 Hiroshi Matsumoto, "Heinen no michi—shinnyūsei shokun ni atau [The way of youths: my message to the new students]," *Juku Geppō,* no. 1 (June 15, 1942), 3.

79 Ibid., 3.

80 Arashida, *Juku Geppō,* no. 2 (August 15, 1942), 4.

81 Ibid., 4.

82 Ibid., 4.

83 Peiquan Liu, "Sanyan liangyu [My few words]," *Reimei,* no. 1 (1940), 4.

84 Er'yu (pen name), "Suixiang [Random thoughts]," *Juku Geppō,* no. 3 (January 15, 1943), 7.

85 Ibid., 7.

86 Shize Liu, 35.

87 Kōichirō Sano, "Kokoro to kotoba [The heart and words]," *Reimei,* no. 2 (1940), 11–12.

88 Ibid., 11.

89 Tetsuya Kamemura, "Hihan to shidō [Criticism and leadership]," *Kenkoku* 3 (April 15, 1943), 152–6, 156.

90 Ibid., 153.

91 Hiroshi Aizawa, "Zatsugo [Idle talk]," *Kenkoku* 3 (April 15, 1943), 117–19, 119.

92 Ibid., 119.

93 Ibid., 118.

94 For instance, a Japanese student Matsumura Aritomo (third entering class) writes about his long-standing struggle over the fact that he cannot wholeheartedly believe in Shinto deities. A Korean student Kim Cheol-Jong (third entering class) discloses that he does not have faith in any religion. Aritomo Matsumura, "Kansō [My impressions]," *Reimei,* no. 2 (1940), 13–14; Cheol-Jong Kim, "Boku no nikkichō yori [Excerpts from my diary]," *Reimei,* no. 2 (1940), 19–20.

95 Munemoto Ōtsuka, "Teiso no hōkō [The direction of the cornerstones that we should lay]," *Kenkoku* 3 (April 15, 1943), 58–67, 63.

96 Ibid., 63.

97 Ibid., 60.

98 Ibid., 61.

99 Seikei (pen name), "Tachiagaru mono [The one that rises]," *Kenkoku* 1 (August 15, 1940), 151–60.

100 Ibid., 155.

101 Ibid., 155–6.

102 Ibid., 156.

103 Ibid., 157.

104 Ibid., 156–7.

105 Ibid., 156.

106 Ibid., 159–60.

107 Ibid., 160.

108 Ibid., 160.

109 Ximing Zhang, "Shuyou [*Juku*-mates]," *Kenkoku* 1 (August 15, 1940), 114–17, 115.

110 Ibid., 115.

111 Ibid., 116.

112 Gunji Kobayashi, "Daiichi mokuhyō: meirō kattatsu sekinin kansui [Our first set of goals: upbeat and freehearted and completion of our responsibility]," *Juku Geppō*, no. 4 (May 15, 1943), 1.

113 "Zadankai," 70–85. The first entering class started at 150 (141 in some records) in May 1938. In that sense, at the lowest point in the spring of 1940, nearly half of the original members were either taking leave of absence or had withdrawn from school. In June 1943, 105 members graduated.

114 Takeo Aki, "Tomoni [To my friend]," *Kanki* (no page number).

115 Ibid.

116 Ibid.

117 Mōja (pen name), "Orini hurete: mōsō [Random thoughts: delusions],"*Reimei*, no. 5 (1940), 22–3.

118 Ibid., 22.

119 Ibid., 23.

120 Haruki Minaguchi, *Ōinaru gen'ei: manshū kenkoku daigaku [The great illusion: Nation Building University in Manchuria]* (Tokyo: Kōyō Shuppansha, 1998), 18.

121 Ibid., 19.

122 As noted earlier in the chapter, the *juku* periodicals do not include entries that are clearly identified with Taiwanese students. But, we have seen in Li Shuiqing's book-length memoir that this Taiwanese student was strongly committed to Ishiwara's concept of an East Asian League.

Chapter 7

1 On certain topics, I rely heavily on historian Eriko Miyazawa's brief discussion of Kendai alumni's post-1945 lives.

2   The Kendai administration ordered these non-Japanese students to return to campus on August 14. By that time, however, many of them had absconded.

3   Sōsuke Nishimoto in Yuji, 534–5, 534.

4   Yamada, 173–4.

5   The chronological timetable of Kenkoku University in Manchuria indicates that Kendai's closing ceremony was held on campus on August 23, 1945. However, there are other accounts that suggest different dates: August 9, 17, and 19.

6   Yamada, 205–16.

7   Kazuo Tanaka in *Hakki kaishi [Bulletin of the eighth entering class]* in Yuji, 561.

8   Sōsuke Nishimoto, "Kenkoku daigaku no shūmatsu zengo: kaku minzoku no dōkō [The situation of Kenkoku University around the time of its dissolution: the activities of each nationalities]," in *Kendaishi shiryō 2*, 20–3, 22; Nishimoto in Yuji, 555.

9   Ibid.

10 Ibid.

11 Both contemporary records produced by the Kendai administration and the alumni rosters compiled by the alumni association in Japan list Russian students by their surnames, omitting first names.

12 Ibid.

13 Ibid.

14 Yamada, 229–36.

15 For instance, Yamada introduces another case, Ueda Yoshihisa (eighth entering class), who returned to Japan with Li Chunshan (first entering class)'s help. Yamada, 231–2.

16 Miyazawa, 251–2.

17 *Kenkoku daigaku dōsōkai nihon deno ayumi [Foundation and activities of the Kenkoku University Alumni Association in Japan]* (Tokyo: Nihon kenkoku daigaku dōsōkai, 2007), 2–3. Hereafter, I call this source *Ayumi*.

18 Ibid., 1.

19 Miyazawa, 250.

20 *Kenkoku daigaku dōsōkai nihon deno ayumi [Foundation and activities of the Kenkoku University Alumni Association in Japan]* (Tokyo: Nihon kenkoku daigaku dōsōkai, 2007), 1–2. The very first alumni association was established on October 9, 1943, a few months after the first entering class graduated. Nevertheless, the association, named by Vice President Suetaka Kamezō as Isshinkai, or Association of One Mind, did not have any meaningful activities because virtually all its members were soon drafted. No significant records about Isshinkai have survived.

21 Even before the official foundation of the alumni association in May 1954, about eighty members gathered in Tokyo in January 1953, which sometimes is seen as the beginning of the alumni association.

22 *Ayumi*, 3–4.

23 After Sakuta resigned his post in 1973, succeeding presidents were all selected from former students.

24 *Ayumi*, 8–9.

25 *Kenkoku daigaku dōsōkai meibo [Kenkoku University Alumni Association Roster]* (Tokyo: Kenkoku daigaku dōsōkai, 2003).

26 The 2003 alumni roster has one former Mongolian student who currently resided in Mongolia. It is unknown if this person really is the only Kendai alumnus living in Mongolia after the establishment of the PRC.

27 *Ayumi*, 42.

28 Miyazawa, 252.

29 Ibid., 257. Footnote.

30 *Ayumi*, 120–1.

31 Ibid., 108.

32 Ibid., 118–20, 130.

33 Miyazawa, 252–3.

34 Cheusov, "Shimi jimi to kotoba ni ienai shiawase [Joy that cannot be expressed in words]," speech at Kenkoku University Alumni Association Annual Meeting on May 20, 1988, cited in Miyazawa, 254–5.

35 Miyazawa, 255.

36 *Kenkoku daigaku dōsōkai meibo [Kenkoku University Alumni Association Roster]* (Tokyo: Kenkoku daigaku dōsōkai, 1955). Hereafter I call this source the 1955 alumni roster.

37 *Ayumi*, 10–15.

38 Ibid., 12.

39 Ibid., 13.

40 Besides these members I mention here, I received warm words of encouragement from other Kendai alumni members whom I encountered in Osaka and Tokyo.

41 Besides the interactions with the alumni living in Taiwan, South Korea and the PRC, which I will discuss here, some Japanese alumni and their classmates residing in Outer Mongolia, Kazakhstan, the Soviet Union and later Russia, visited each other.

42 Ibid., 67.

43 Ibid., 69.

44 Ibid., 81.

45 Ibid., 108.

46 Ibid., 81.

47 Ibid., 171.

48 I do not have records about the date of foundation and other details of the alumni association in South Korea. The association must have been established before 1986, as it published collections of essays by the former Korean students in 1986 and 1988.

49 Akito Kuwahara in *Ayumi*, 54.

50 The Tokyo War Crimes Tribunal (1946–48) left out Japan's responsibility for its aggression during colonial rule in Korea such as the violent suppression of the independence movement of 1919. As colonial powers themselves, prosecutors from the Allied Powers felt reluctant in bringing up the matters related to Japan's colonial rule. Moreover, under the intensifying situation of the Cold War in East Asia, SCAP shifted its focus from dealing with Japan's military past to making the country a reliable ally. As a result, the second and third trials, which had originally been planned, were cancelled, and the Tokyo War Crimes Tribunal was closed in 1948.

51 The exact number of Japanese participants is reported in the alumni association's publications differently. One reports it as thirty-nine, and the other thirty-four.

52 Kuwahara in *Ayumi*, 160.

53 Ibid., 164–5, 128.

54 *Kankirei* (Tokyo: Kenkoku University Allumni Association, 1980), 79.

55 Yūtarō Bandō, "Netsurui saikai kenkoku daigaku no dōsōsei [Tearful reunion of Kenkoku University alumni]," *Nihon Keizai Shimbun*, September 10, 1980. (Reprinted in *Kankirei*, 33.)

56 Ibid.

57 Chinese participants in reunions held in 1992 were seventy-seven in Changchun, fifty-three in Beijing, thirteen in Dalian, twenty-nine in Shenyang, twenty-three in Harbin, and fourteen in Hohhut, the capital of the Inner Mongolian Autonomous Region. *Dōgaku reankan [Alumni's reunion]* (Tokyo: Kenkoku University Alumni Association, 1993), 196–204.

58 Chinese participants in reunions held in 1997 were fifty-one in Changchun, eighteen in Beijing, six in Dalian, twelve in Shenyang, and fifteen in Hohhut. *Ayumi*, 49–50.

59 *Ayumi*, 127, 217.

60 Chen Jian (seventh entering class), who had some position at the Jilin Province, and Wen Jianshen (fourth entering class), Professor of Foreign Languages at Changchun City Education Academy, were also involved in the project.

61 Later, Nagashima Kiyoshi (second entering class), who had been Professor at Osaka Prefecture University, joined the project.

62 Kazu Dodo in *Ayumi*, 59–61.

63 Ibid., 60.

64 Ibid.

65 Ibid., 61.

66 1 million yen in the late 1980s was about 6,700 USD.

67 Ibid., 59–61.

68 Ibid., 27.

69 Ibid., 25–40, 173.

Bibliography

Secondary Sources

Abe, Hiroyuki. "Ishiwara Kanji no shōgai [The life of Ishiwara Kanji]." In *Ishiwara Kanji to Manshū teikoku [Ishiwara Kanji and the empire of Manchukuo]*, edited by Rekishi dokuhon Henshūbu, 45–109. Tokyo: Shin jinbutsu ōraisha, 2010.

Allen, Chizuko T. "Northeast Asia Centered around Korea: Ch'oe Namson's View of History." *The Journal of Asian Studies* 49, no. 4 (1990): 787–806.

Amano, Ikuo. *Gakureki no shakaishi: kyōiku to nihon no kindai [Social history of students: education in modern Japan]*. Tokyo: Heibonsha, 2005.

Aydin, Cemil. *The Politics of Anti-Westernism in Asia: Visions of World Order in Pan-Islamic and Pan-Asian Thought*. New York: Columbia University Press, 2007.

Beasley, William G. *Japanese Imperialism 1894–1945*. Oxford: Oxford University Press, 1989.

Brown, Roger H. "Visions of a Virtuous Manifest Destiny: Yasuoka Masahiro and Japan's Kingly Way." In *Pan-Asianism in Modern Japanese History: Colonialism, Regionalism and Borders*, edited by Sven Saaler and J. Victor Koschmann, 133–50. New York: Routledge, 2007.

Bruun, Ole and Li Narangoa, ed. *Mongols from Country to City: Floating Boundaries, Pastoralism and City Life in the Mongol Lands*. Copenhagen: NIAS Press, 2006.

Cai, Huiyu. *Taiwan in Japan's Empire-Building: An Institutional Approach to Colonial Engineering*. New York: Routledge, 2009.

Caprio, Mark E. *Japanese Assimilation Policies in Colonial Korea, 1910–1945*. Seattle: University of Washington Press, 2009.

Chen, Edward I-te. "The Attempt to Integrate the Empire: Legal Perspectives." In *The Japanese Colonial Empire, 1895–1945*, edited by Ramon H. Myers and Mark R. Peattie, 240–74. Princeton, NJ: Princeton University Press, 1984.

Chien, Sechin Y. S. and John Fitzgerald, ed. *The Dignity of Nations: Equality, Competition, and Honor in East Asian Nationalism*. Hong Kong: Hong Kong University Press, 2006.

Chin, Gi-Wook and Michael Robinson, ed. *Colonial Modernity in Korea*. Cambridge, MA: Harvard University Asia Center, 1999.

Ching, Leo T. S. *Becoming "Japanese": Colonial Taiwan and the Politics of Identity Formation*. Berkeley: University of California Press, 2001.

Chou, Wan-yao. "The *Kōminka* Movement: Taiwan under Wartime Japan, 1937–1945." Ph.D. diss., Yale University, 1991.

Colonna, Fanny. "Educating Conformity in French Colonial Algeria." Translated by
   Barbara Harshav. In *Tensions of Empire: Colonial Cultures in a Bourgeois World*,
   edited by Frederick Cooper and Ann Laura Stoler, 346–70. Berkeley: University of
   California Press, 1997.

Coox, Alvin D. "The Kwantung Army Dimension." In *The Japanese Informal Empire
   in China, 1895–1937*, edited by Peter Duus, Ramon H. Myers, and Mark R. Peattie,
   133–57. Princeton, NJ: Princeton University Press, c.1989.

Cribb, Robert and Narangoa Li, ed. *Imperial Japan and National Identities in Asia,
   1895–1945*. London, New York: Routledge, 2003.

Cutts, Robert. *An Empire of Schools: Japan's Universities and the Molding of a National
   Power Elite*. New York: M. E. Sharpe, c.1997.

Doak, Kevin M. *A History of Nationalism in Modern Japan: Placing the People*. Leiden:
   Brill, 2007.

Doak, Kevin M. "Building National Identity through Ethnicity: Ethnology in Wartime
   Japan and After." *Journal of Japanese Studies* 27, no. 1 (2001): 1–39.

Dower, John W. *Empire and Aftermath: Yoshida Shigeru and the Japanese Experience,
   1878–1954*. Boston, MA: Harvard University Asia Center, 1988.

Dower, John W. *War without Mercy: Race and Power in the Pacific War*. New York:
   Pantheon Books, 1986.

Duara, Prasenjit. *Sovereignty and Authenticity: Manchukuo and the East Asian Modern*.
   Lanham, MD: Rowman & Littlefield Publishers, 2003.

Duus, Peter. *The Abacus and the Sword: The Japanese Penetration of Korea, 1895–1910*.
   Berkeley: University of California Press, c.1995.

Duus, Peter, Ramon H. Myers, and Mark R. Peattie, ed. *Japanese Informal Empire in
   China, 1895–1937*. Princeton, NJ: Princeton University Press, c.1989.

Eckert, Carter J. *Offspring of Empire: The Koch'ang Kims and the Colonial Origins of
   Korean Capitalism*. Seattle: University of Washington Press, 1991.

Egler, David George. *Japanese Mass Organizations in Manchuria, 1928–1945
   [microform]: The Ideology of Racial Harmony*, 1977.

Elliott, Mark and Motokazu Matsutani. "Manchu Studies in Europe and the United
   States: Past, Present, and Future." *Tōyō bunka kenkyū* 10 (2008): 309–25.

Fogel, Joshua A. *Nakae Ushikichi in China: The Mourning of Spirit*. Cambridge, MA:
   Harvard University Press, 1989.

Fogel, Joshua A. *Politics and Sinology: The Case of Naitō Konan, 1866–1934*. Cambridge,
   MA: Harvard University Press, 1984.

Fogel, Joshua A. *The Literature of Travel in the Japanese Rediscovery of China,
   1862–1945*. Stanford, CA: Stanford University Press, 1996.

Fujiwara, Akira and Mitsuyoshi Himeda, ed. *Nicchū sensō-ka chūgoku ni okeru nihonjin
   no hansen katsudō [Japanese anti-war activities during the Sino–Japanese War]*.
   Tokyo Aoki Shoten, 1999.

Fujitani, Takashi. *Race for Empire: Koreans as Japanese and Japanese as Americans
   during World War II*. Berkeley: University of California Press, 2011.

Furukawa, Nobuko. "Shokuminchi kindai shakai ni okeru shotō kyōiku kōzō: chōsen ni okeru higimusei to gakkō 'fukyū' mondai [Primary education system in the modern colonial society: voluntary enrolment and the problem of the popularization of schools in Korea]." In *Teikoku to gakkō [Empires and schools]*, edited by Takeshi Komagome and Nobuya Hashimoto, 129–64. Kyoto: Shōwadō, 2007.

Gann, Lewis H. "Western and Japanese Colonialism: Some Preliminary Comparisons." In *The Japanese Colonial Empire, 1895–1945*, edited by Ramon H. Myers and Mark R. Peattie, 497–525. Princeton, NJ: Princeton University Press, 1984.

Hall, Andrew Reed. "Constructing a 'Manchurian' Identity: Japanese Education in Manchukuo, 1931–1945." Ph.D. diss., University of Pittsburgh, 2003.

Han, Suk-Jung. "The Problem of Sovereignty: Manchukuo, 1932–1937." *Positions: East Asia Cultures Critique* 12, no. 2 (2004): 457–78.

Hara, Masatoshi, Takao Tsukinoki, and Toshihiko Saito. *Sōryoku senka ni okeru "Manshūkoku" no kyōiku, kagaku gijutsu seisaku no kenkyū [Research on the policy of education and science and technology in "Manchukuo" during the all-out war]*. Tokyo: Gakūshuin Daigaku Tōyō Bunka Kenkyūjo, 1990.

Hasebe, Shigeru. "Report on a Research Trip in Search of Materials Relating to Taiwan and Manchuria." *Takushoku daigaku hyakunenshi kenkyū* 10 (2002): 72–90.

Hasebe, Shigeru. "Reports: A General Summary of the Investigation into, and Compilation of Materials Relating to 'Manchuria.'" *Takushoku daigaku hyakunenshi kenkyū* 8 (2001): 111–33.

Hirano, Kenichirō. *The Japanese in Manchuria, 1906–1931 [microform]: A Study of the Historical Background of Manchukuo*. Ph.D. diss., Harvard University, 1982.

Horio, Teruhisa. *Educational Thought and Ideology in Modern Japan: State Authority and Intellectual Freedom*. Tokyo: University of Tokyo Press, c.1988.

Horne, Gerald. *Race War! White Supremacy and the Japanese Attack on the British Empire*. New York, London: New York University Press, 2004.

Hotta, Eri. *Pan-Asianism and Japan's War 1931–1945*. New York: Palgrave Macmillan, 2007.

Howland, D. R. *Borders of Chinese Civilization: Geography and History at Empire's End*. Durham, MD: Duke University Press, 1996.

Hsu, Shu-his. "Manchurian Backgrounds II." *Pacific Affairs* 5, no. 2 (1932): 131–50.

Hunter, Janet, ed. *Aspects of Pan-Asianism*. (Papers by W. G. Beasley, J. Y. Wong, and Masaki Miyake). London: Suntory Toyota International Centre for Economics and Related Disciplines, London School of Economics and Political Science, 1987.

Hwang, In K. *The Korean Reform Movement of the 1880s: A Study of Transition in Intra-Asian Relations*. Cambridge, MA: Schenkman Pub. Co., c.1978.

Hwang, Kyung Moon. *A History of Korea*. 2nd ed. New York: Palgrave Macmillan, 2017.

Ikeda, Hiroshi, ed. *Dai tōa kyōeiken no bunka kensetsu [The creation of culture in the Great East Asia Co-Prosperity Sphere]*. Kyōto: Jinbun shoin, 2007.

Imai, Takeo. *Nitchū wahei kōsaku: kaisō to shōgen, 1937–1947 [A peace overture between Japan and China: recollections and testimonies, 1937–1947]*. Tokyo: Misuzu Shobō, 2009.

Inaba, Shūji. "1929nen chūso honsō no 'shōgeki': manshū jihen chokuzen ni okeru nihon rikugun no soren gun nin: shiki [The impact of the warfare between China and the Soviet Union in 1929: the Japanese Army's knowledge about the Soviet Union in the eve of the Manchurian Incident]." *Gunji shigaku* 42, no. 1 (2006): 94–115.

Iriye, Akira. *Across the Pacific: An Inner History of American–East Asian Relations.* Revised Edition. Chicago, IL: Imprint Publications, 1967, 1992.

Iriye, Akira. *Cultural Internationalism and World Order.* Baltimore, MD: Johns Hopkins University Press, 1997.

Iriye, Akira. "Culture and International History." In *Explaining the History of American Foreign Relations*, 2nd ed., edited by Michael J. Hogan and Thomas G. Paterson, 241–56. Cambridge: Cambridge University Press, 2004.

Ji, Myeong-Gwan. "Sin Chae-Ho shigaku to Choe Nam-Seon shigaku [Sin Chae-Ho's views of history and Choe Nam-Seon's views of history]." *Annals of the Institute for Comparative Studies of Culture, Tokyo Woman's Christian University* 48 (1987): 135–60.

Kamachi, Noriko. *Reform in China: Huang Tsun-hsien and the Japanese Model.* Cambridge, MA: Harvard University Press, 1981.

Kan, Dokusan. *Chōsenjin gakuto shutsujin—mou hitotsu no wadatsumi no koe.* Tokyo: Iwanami shoten, 1997.

Kankōkai, Manshū kokushi Hensan, ed. [Society for compiling and publishing Manchukuo history]. *Manshū kokushi kakuron [History of Manchukuo: itemized discussion]*. Tokyo: Manmō dōhō engokai, 1970.

Kankōkai, Manshū kokushi Hensan, ed. [Society for compiling and publishing Manchukuo history]. *Manshū kokushi sōron [History of Manchukuo: general discussion]*. Tokyo: Manmō dōhō engokai, 1970.

Karasawa, Tomitarō. *Gakusei no rekishi: gakusei seikatsu no shakaishiteki kōsatsu [History of students: social history of student life]*. Tokyo: Sōbunsha, 1955.

Karl, Rebecca E. "Creating Asia: China in the World at the Beginning of the Twentieth Century." *American Historical Review* 103, no. 4 (1998): 1096–118.

Karl, Rebecca E. *Staging the World: Chinese Nationalism at the Turn of the Twentieth Century.* Durham, NC: Duke University Press, 2002.

Kawashima, Makoto. "Chūgoku Taiwan ni okeru tōan shiryō no jōkyō: kōkai jōkyō, bunsho gyōsei, shiryōteki igi [The condition of public records in China and Taiwan: accessibility, administrative control, and the significance of the public records]." *Nihonshi kenkyūkai shigatsu reikai* (2006).

Kawata, Hiroshi. *Manshū Kenkoku Daigaku monogatari: jidai o hikiukeyoito shita wakamonotachi [A story of Nation-Building University in Manchuria: the youth who sought to shoulder the time]*. Tokyo: Hara Shobo, 2002.

Kim, John Namjun. "The Temporality of Empire: The Imperial Cosmopolitanism of Miki Kiyoshi and Tanabe Hajime." In *Pan-Asianism in Modern Japanese History: Colonialism, Regionalism and Borders*, edited by Sven Saaler and J. Victor Koschmann, 151–67. New York: Routledge, 2007.

Kimura, Kenji, Jun Uchida, Jae-Won Sun, and Louise Young. "Japanese Settler Colonialism and Capitalism in Japan: Advancing into Korea, Settling Down, and Returning to Japan, 1905–1950." In *Occasional Papers in Japanese Studies*. Harvard University Edwin O. Reischauer Institute of Japanese Studies. No. 2002-3. 2002.

Komagome, Takeshi and Nobuya Hashimoto, ed. *Teikoku to gakko [The empire and schools]*. Kyoto: Shōwadō, 2007.

Kubo, Yoshizō. *Shōwa kyōikushi: tennōsei to kyōiku no shiteki tenkai [Educational history of the Shōwa era: the relations between the imperial system and education]*. Tokyo: Tōshindō, 2006.

Kurihara, Chūdō. *Shinkyō no chizu: chōshun kaisōki [The map of Shinkyō: recollection of Changchun]*. Tokyo: Keizai Ōraisha, 1982.

Lamley, Harry J. "Assimilation Efforts in Colonial Taiwan: The Fate of the 1914 Movement." *Monumenta Serica* 29 (1970-71): 496–520.

Lary, Diana. *China's Civil War: A Social History, 1945-1949*. Cambridge: Cambridge University Press, 2015.

Lebra-Chapman, Joyce. *Japanese-trained Armies in Southeast Asia: Independence and Volunteer Forces in World War II*. New York: Columbia University Press, 1977.

Lee, Hoon K. "Korean Migrants in Manchuria." *Geographical Review* 22, no. 2 (1932): 196–204.

Li, Lincoln. *The China Factor in Modern Japanese Thought: The Case of Tachibana Shiraki, 1881-1945*. New York: State University of New York Press, 1996.

Li, Maojie. "Chian kikan [The organizations for the public order]." In *Nicchū kyōdō kenkyū: "Manshūkoku" towa nandatta noka [The Chinese–Japanese collaborative research: what was "Manchukuo"?]*, edited by Shokuminchi Bunka Gakkai, 70-3. Tokyo: Shokuminchi bunka gakkai, 2008.

Li, Maojie. "Chian no jittai [The reality of the maintenance of the public order]." In *Nicchū kyōdō kenkyū: "Manshūkoku" towa nandatta noka [The Chinese–Japanese collaborative research: what was "Manchukuo"?]*, edited by Shokuminchi Bunka Gakkai, 73–82. Tokyo: Shokuminchi bunka gakkai, 2008.

Li, Narangoa. "Japanese Geopolitics and the Mongol Lands, 1915-1945." *EJEAS* 3, no. 1 (2004): 45–67.

Li, Narangoa. "Universal Values and Pan-Asianism: The Vision of Omotokyo." In *Pan-Asianism in Modern Japanese History: Colonialism, Regionalism and Borders*, edited by Sven Saaler and J. Victor Koschmann, 52–66. New York: Routledge, 2007.

Maekawa, Keiji. *Kikyō: manshū kenkoku daigaku chōsenjin gakuto seishun to sensō [Returning home: Korean students at Nation-Building University in Manchuria and the war]*. Tokyo: Sanichi shobō, 2008.

Marshall, Byron K. *Academic Freedom and the Japanese Imperial University, 1868-1939*. Berkeley: University of California Press, c.1992.

Marshall, Byron K. *Learning to Be Modern: Japanese Political Discourse on Education*. Boulder, CO: Westview Press, 1994.

Matsumoto, Ken'ichi. *Shōwa ni shisu—Morisaki Minato to Ozawa Kaisaku [Dying in the Showa era: Morisaki Minato and Ozawa Kaisaku]*. Tokyo: Shinchō-sha, 1988.

Matsumoto, Takenori. "Komento: 'shokuminchi kindai' wo meguru kinnen no kenkyū dōkō ni tsuite [Comment: regarding the recent trend in the research about 'modern colonialism']." *Tōyō bunka kenkyū* 10 (2008): 303–6.

Matsusaka, Yoshihisa Tak. *The Making of Japanese Manchuria, 1904–1932*. Cambridge, MA: Harvard University Asia Center, 2001.

Matsutani, Motokazu. "A New Perspective on the 'Name-Changing Policy' in Korea." In *Gender and Law in the Japanese Imperium*, edited by Susan L. Burns and Barbara J. Brooks, 240–66. Honolulu: University of Hawaii Press, 2014.

Matsuura, Masataka. *"Dai tōa sensō" wa naze okita no ka: han ajia shugi no seiji keizaishi [Why did the "Great East Asia War" occur? The political and economic history of Pan-Asianism]*. Nagoya: Nagoya Daigaku Shuppankai, 2010.

Matthiessen, Sven. *Japanese Pan-Asianism and the Philippines from the Late 19th Century to the End of World War II*. Leiden: Brill, 2016.

McClain, James L. *Japan: A Modern History*. New York: W.W. Norton & Company, 2002.

McCoy, Alfred W., ed. *Southeast Asia under Japanese Occupation*. New Haven, CT: Yale University Southeast Asia Studies, c.1980.

McNamara, Dennis L. *The Colonial Origins of Korean Enterprise, 1910–1945*. London: Cambridge University Press, 1990.

Memmi, Albert. *The Colonizer and the Colonized*. Boston, MA: Beacon Press, 1991.

Mitter, Rana. *The Manchurian Myth: Nationalism, Resistance, and Collaboration in Modern China*. Berkeley: University of California Press, 2000.

Miura, Hideyuki. *Goshoku no niji: manshū kenkoku daigaku sotugyōsei tachi no sengo [Five-color rainbow: postwar experiences of Manchukuo Kenkoku University alumni]*. Shūeisha: Tokyo, 2015.

Miura, Hideyuki. "Minzoku kyōwa no yume, jisedai e: Manshū Kenkoku Daigaku saigo no dōsōkai [Passing down the dream of 'ethnic harmony' to the next generation: the final reunion meeting of Manchukuo Kenkoku University]." *Asahi Shinbun [Asahi Newspaper]*, June 9, 2010.

Miyazawa, Eriko. *Kenkoku daigaku to minzoku kyōwa [Nation-Building University in Manchuria and the ideal of ethnic harmony]*. Tokyo: Kazama shobo, 1997.

Miyazawa, Eriko. "Manshūkoku ni okeru seinen soshiki to kenkoku daigaku no sōsetsu [Organizations of youth and the founding of Nation-Building University in Manchukuo]." *Ajia bunka kenkyū* 21 (1995): 55–66.

Miyoshi, Masao. *As We Saw Them: The First Japanese Embassy to the United States (1860)*. Berkeley: University of California Press, 1979.

Mizuno, Naoki. *Sōshi kaimei: nihon no chosen shihai no nakade [Sōshi kaimei in Korea under Japanese rule]*. Tokyo: Iwanami shinsho, 2008.

Myers, Ramon H. "Japanese Imperialism in Manchuria: The South Manchuria Railway Company, 1906–1933." In *The Japanese Informal Empire in China, 1895–1937*, edited by Peter Duus, Ramon H. Myers, and Mark R. Peattie, 101–32. Princeton, NJ: Princeton University Press, c.1989.

Myers, Ramon H. and Mark R. Peattie, ed. *The Japanese Colonial Empire, 1895–1945*. Princeton, NJ: Princeton University Press, 1984.

Nakagane, Katsuji. "Manchukuo and Economic Development." In *The Japanese Informal Empire in China, 1895–1937*, edited by Peter Duus, Ramon H. Myers, and Mark R. Peattie, 133–57. Princeton, NJ: Princeton University Press, *c*.1989.

Nanman kyōiku, zaiman kyōiku kenkyū [Research on education in southern Manchuria and Manchuria in general]. Tokyo: Nihon Tosho Senta, 1994.

O'Dwyer, Emer. *Significant Soil: Settler Colonialism and Japan's Urban Empire in Manchuria*. Cambridge, MA: Harvard University Press, 2015.

Ohnuki-Tierney, Emiko. *Kamikaze, Cherry Blossoms, and Nationalisms: The Militarization of Aesthetics in Japanese History*. Chicago, IL: The University of Chicago Press, 2002.

Ohnuki-Tierney, Emiko. *Kamikaze Diaries: Reflections of Japanese Student Soldiers*. Chicago, IL: The University of Chicago Press, 2006.

Okada, Hideki. "Jūni ten sanzero jiken to kenkoku daigakusei [The December Thirtieth Incident and Nation-Building University students]." *Hōsho gekkan* 179 (August 2000): 33–5.

Onegian, Svetlana V. "The Resettlement of Soviet Citizens from Manchuria in 1935 – 36: A Research Note." *Europe-Asia Studies* 47, no. 6 (1995): 1043–50.

Osterhammel, Jurgen. *Colonialism: A Theoretical Overview*. Translated by Shelley L. Frisch. Princeton, NJ: Markus Wiener Publishers, 1995, 1997.

Palmer, Brandon. *Fighting for the Enemy: Koreans in Japan's War, 1937–1945*. Seattle: University of Washington Press, 2013.

Park, Hyun Ok. *Two Dreams in One Bed: Empire, Social Life, and the Origins of the North Korean Revolution in Manchuria*. Durham, NC: Duke University Press, 2005.

Peattie, Mark R. "Japanese Attitude toward Colonialism, 1895–1945." In *The Japanese Colonial Empire, 1895–1945*, edited by Ramon H. Myers and Mark R. Peattie, 80–127. Princeton, NJ: Princeton University Press, 1984.

Peattie, Mark R. "The Japanese Colonial Empire." In *The Cambridge History of Japan Vol. 6*, edited by Peter Duus, 217–70. New York: Cambridge University Press, 1989–1999.

Peattie, Mark R. *Ishiwara Kanji and Japan's Confrontation with the West*. Princeton, NJ: Princeton University Press, 1975.

Porter, Ran Ying. "Education in Manzhouguo 1932–1945: Japan's Cultural Invasion in Chinese Manchuria." Ph.D. diss., University of Hawaii at Manoa, 2001.

Qi, Hongshen. *"Manshū" ōraru hisutorī: "doreika kyōiku" ni kōshite [Oral history of "Manchuria": resistance against the "education of enslavement"]*. Translated by Ken'ichi Takenaka. Tokyo: Kōseisha, 2004.

Rhee, M. J. *The Doomed Empire: Japan in Colonial Korea*. Aldershot: Ashgate, *c*.1997.

Roden, Donald. *Schooldays in Imperial Japan: A Study in the Culture of a Student Elite*. Berkeley: University of California Press, 1980.

Satō, Hideo. *Kyōiku no bunkashi [Cultural history of education]*. Kyōto: Aunsha, 2004, 2005.

Scharping, Thomas. "Minorities, Majorities and National Expansion: The History and Politics of Population Development in Manchuria 1610–1993." Cologne China Studies Online: Working Papers on Chinese Politics, Economy and Society No.1 (1998).

Schneider, Michael A. "Were Women Pan-Asianists the Worst? Internationalism and Pan-Asianism in the Careers of Inoue Hideko and Inoue Masaji." In *Pan-Asianism in Modern Japanese History: Colonialism, Regionalism and Borders*, edited by Sven Saaler and J. Victor Koschmann, 115–29. New York: Routledge, 2007.

Sewell, Bill. "Reconsidering the Modern in Japanese History: Modernity in the Service of the Prewar Japanese Empire." *Japan Review* 16 (2004): 213–58.

Shao, Dan. *Remote Homeland, Recovered Borderland: Manchus, Manchukuo, and Manchuria, 1907–1985*. Honolulu: University of Hawai'i Press, 2011.

"Shinpojiumu shokuminchi kyōikushi kenkyū ima, naniga mondai ka—shinshiryō, tachibasei, sōgō kōryū wo kangaeru [Symposium: What are the issues in the current research about colonial education? Thinking about historical records, subjectivity, and mutual exchange]." *Shokuminchi kyōikushi kenkyū nenpō* 8 (2005): 5–42.

Shishida, Fumiaki. "Kenkoku daigaku to Ishiwara Kanji [Nation-Building University and Ishiwara Kanji]." *Waseda daigaku ningen kagaku kenkyū* 16, no. 1 (1993): 109–23.

Shishida, Fumiaki. *Budō no kyōikuryoku: manshūkoku kenkoku daigaku ni okeru budō kyōiku [The educational value of Japanese budō (martial arts): the budō training at Nation-Building University in Manchukuo]*. Tokyo: Nihon Tosho Senta, 2005.

Shokuminchi bunka Gakkai, ed. *Nicchū kyōdō kenkyū: Manshūkoku towa nandattanoka [Collaborative research by Japan and China: what was Manchukuo?]*. Tokyo: shōgakkan, 2008.

Smith, Andrea. *Colonial Memory in Postcolonial Europe: Maltese Settlers in Algeria and France*. Bloomington: Indiana University Press, 2006.

Smith, Henry DeWitt. *Japan's First Student Radicals*. Cambridge, MA: Harvard University Press, 1972.

Smith, Norman. *Resisting Manchukuo: Chinese Women Writers and the Japanese Occupation*. Vancouver: UBC Press, 2007.

Song, Enrong, Zixia Yu, and Bihong Cao, et al., ed. *Riben qinhua jiaoyu quanshi [General history of Japanese colonial education]*. Beijing: Renmin jiaoyu chuban she, 2005.

Spence, Jonathan D. *The Search for Modern China*. New York: W.W. Norton & Company, 1999.

Suleski, Ronald. "Northeast China under Japanese Control: The Role of the Manchurian Youth Corps, 1934–1945." *Modern China* 7, no. 3 (1981): 351–77.

Suleski, Ronald Stanley. *The Modernization of Manchuria: An Annotated Bibliography*. Hong Kong: The Chinese University Press, c.1994.

Szpilman, Christopher W. A. "Between Pan-Asianism and Nationalism: Mitsukawa Kametaro and His Campaign to Reform Japan and Liberate Asia." In *Pan-Asianism in Modern Japanese History: Colonialism, Regionalism and Borders*, edited by Sven Saaler and J. Victor Koschmann, 85–100. New York: Routledge, 2007.

Takeda, Rieko. *Gakureki, kaikyū, guntai: kōgakureki heishitachi no yūutsu na nichijō [Academic credentials, social statuses, and military: depressive everyday lives of elite students]*. Tokyo: Chūō Kōron Shinsha, 2008.

Takenaka, Ken'ichi. *"Manshū" ni okeru kyōiku no kisoteki kenkyū [Basic research about education in 'Manchuria']*. vol. 1–5. Tokyo: Kashiwa shobō, 2000.

Takeuchi, Zensaku. "Meiji makki ni okeru chūnichi kakumei undō no kōryū [Late Meiji interactions between Chinese and Japanese revolutionary movements]." *Chugoku-kenkyu*. 5 (1948): 74–95.

Tamanoi, Mariko Asano, ed. *Crossed Histories: Manchuria in the Age of Empire*. Honolulu: Association for Asian Studies: University of Hawaii Press, 2005.

Tamanoi, Mariko Asano. "Knowledge, Power, and Racial Classifications: The 'Japanese' in 'Manchuria.'" *Journal of Asian Studies* 59, no. 2 (May 2000): 248–76.

Tamanoi, Mariko Asano. "Pan-Asianism in the Diary of Morisaki Minato (1924–1945), and the Suicide of Mishima Yukio (1925–1970)." In *Crossed Histories: Manchuria in the Age of Empire*, edited by Mariko Asano Tamanoi, 184–206. Honolulu: Association for Asian Studies and University of Hawaii Press, 2005.

Tamanoi, Mariko Asano. *Memory Maps: the State and Manchuria in Postwar Japan*. Honolulu: University of Hawai'i Press, 2009.

Tamura, Norio. "Iguchi Ichirō to kenkoku daigaku no dōryō tachi: ōdō rakudo ka nihon dasshutsu ka [Iguchi Ichirō and his colleagues at Nation-Building University: kingly way utopia or escape from Japan]." *Komyunikeshon kagaku* 31 (2010): 37–47.

Tamura, Norio. "Kenkoku daigaku jidai no Iguchi Ichirō [Iguchi Ichirō at Nation-Building University]." *Tokyo keizai daigaku junbun shizen kagaku ronshū* 127 (2009): 127–42.

Tanaka, Hiroshi. "Kenkoku daigaku ni okeru rinen to jissō: kōdōshugi kyōiku shisō to sono gengo seisakuron wo megutte [Principles and reality at Nation-Building University: ideas of imperial education and policy debate on language]." *Shokuminchi kyōikushi kenkyū nenpō* 4 (2001): 144–95.

Tanaka, Ryūichi. *Manshūkoku to nihon no teikoku shihai [Imperialist rule of Manchukuo and Japan]*. Tokyo: Yūshisha, 2007.

Tanaka, Stefan. *Japan's Orient: Rendering Pasts into History*. Berkeley, CA: University of California Press, 1993.

Tierney, Robert Thomas. *Tropics of Savagery: The Culture of Japanese Empire in Comparative Frame*. Berkeley: University of California Press, 2010.

Toby, Ronald. "Education in Korea under the Japanese: Attitudes and Manifestations." *Occasional Papers on Korea* No. 1 (April 1974): 55–64.

Townsend, Susan C. *Miki Kiyoshi (1897–1945): Japan's Itinerant Philosopher*. Leiden, Boston: Brill, 2009.

Tsuchida, Akio. "1929 nen no chūso hunsō to nihon [The warfare between China and the Soviet Union of 1929 and Japan]." *Chūō Daigaku ronshū* 22 (2001): 17–27.

Tsukase, Susumu. *Manshūkoku: "minzoku kyōwa" no jitsuzo [Manchukuo: the reality of "ethnic harmony"]*. Tokyo: Yoshikawa Hirobumi kan, 1998.

Tsurumi, Patricia E. "Colonial Education in Korea and Taiwan." In *The Japanese Colonial Empire, 1895–1945*, edited by Ramon H. Myers and Mark R. Peattie, 275–311. Princeton, NJ: Princeton University Press, 1984.

Tsurumi, Patricia E. *Japanese Colonial Education in Taiwan, 1895–1945*. Cambridge, MA: Harvard University Press, 1977.

Tsuzuki, Mizuo. "Iwama Tokuya to 'manshu' no chūgokujin kyōiku [Iwama Tokuya and the education for Chinese in 'Manchuria']." *Kokuritsu kyōiku kenkyūjo kiyō* 115 (1988): 115–28.

Tsuzuki, Mizuo. "Shiryō shōkai: 'zaiman gakkō kankeisha shuki mokuroku' sakusei ni tsuite [Introducing sources: regarding the preparation for 'bibliography of memoirs by people who were involved in the schools in Manchuria']." *Shokuminchi kyōikushi kenkyū nenpō* 7 (2004): 228–50.

Tucker, David Vance. "Building 'Our Manchukuo': Japanese City Planning, Architecture, and Nation-Building in Occupied Northeast China, 1931–1945." Ph.D. diss., The University of Iowa, 1999.

Tucker, David Vance. "Colonial Sovereignty in Manchuria and Manchukuo." In *The State of Sovereignty: Territories, Laws, Populations*, edited by Douglas Howland and Luise White, 75–93. Bloomington: Indiana University Press, 2009.

Uchida, Jun. "Brokers of Empire: Japanese and Korean Business Elites in Colonial Korea." In *Settler Colonialism in the Twentieth Century: Projects, Practices, Legacies*, edited by Caroline Elkins and Susan Pederson, 153–70. New York: Routledge, 2005.

Vlastos, Stephen, ed. *Mirror of Modernity: Invented Traditions of Modern Japan*. Berkeley: University of California Press, 1998.

Watt, Lori. "Imperial Remnants: The Repatriates in Postwar Japan," In *Settler Colonialism in the Twentieth Century: Projects, Practices, Legacies*, edited by Caroline Elkins and Susan Pedersen, 243–57. New York: Taylor and Francis, 2005.

Watt, Lori. *When Empire Comes Home: Repatriation and Reintegration in Postwar Japan*. Cambridge, MA: Harvard University Press, 2009.

Wu, Wen-Hsing, Shun-Fen Chen, and Chen-Tsou Wu. "The Development of Higher Education in Taiwan." *Higher Education* 18, no. 1 "From Dependency to Autonomy: The Development of Asian Universities" (1989): 117–36.

Yamamuro, Shin'ichi. *Kimera: Manshūkoku no shōzō [Chimera: the Portrait of Manchukuo]*. Tokyo: Chuko shinsho, 1993.

Yamamuro, Shin'ichi. *Manchuria under Japanese Dominion*. Translated by Joshua A. Fogel. Philadelphia: University of Pennsylvania Press, 2006.

Yamane, Yukio. "Chūgokujin gakusei kara mita giman kenkoku daigaku no kaioku [The memory of bogus Manchuria Nation-Building University from former Chinese students' perspectives]." *Tōhō [Eastern book review]* 207 (1998): 32–4.

Yamane, Yukio. "Kenkoku daigaku kankei shiryō no juzō [Donating the sources regarding Nation-Building University]." *Tōyō bunko shohō* 31 (1991): 31–6.

Yamane, Yukio. *Kenkoku daigaku no kenkyū : nihon teikoku shugi no ichi danmen [Research about Nation-Building University: one aspect of Japanese imperialism].* Tokyo: Kyuko Shoin, 2003.

Yamashita, Samuel Hideo. *Leaves from an Autumn of Emergencies: Selections from the Wartime Diaries of Ordinary Japanese.* Honolulu: The University of Hawai'i Press, 2005.

Yasuhiko, Yoshikazu. *Manga de egakō to shita tairiku to nihon seinen [The Japanese youth whom I attempted to portray in my comic books].* Nagoya: Arumu, 2007.

Yonetani, Masafumi. *Ajia/nihon: shikō no furonteia [Asia/Japan: frontier of philosophy].* Tokyo: Iwanami shoten, 2006.

Yosano, Akiko. *Travels in Manchuria and Mongolia: A Feminist Poet from Japan Encounters Prewar China.* New York: Columbia University Press, c.2001.

Young, Louise. *Japan's Total Empire: Manchuria and the Culture of Wartime Imperialism.* Berkeley: University of California Press, 1998.

Yu, Miin-ling L. "Sun Yat-sen University in Moscow, 1925–1930." Ph.D. diss., New York University, 1995.

Zhang, Ziwen, Guo Qizhuan, and Lin Weizhou, ed. *Taiwan lishi renwu xiaozhuan: ming qing ji rijushiqi [Brief biography of historical figures in Taiwan: Ming, Qing, through the era of Japanese occupation].* Taipei: Guojia tushuguan, 2006.

Zheng, Liling. "Senjiki taihoku teikoku daigaku no 'gakusei seikatsu chōsa' ['investigation on student life' conducted at Taihoku Imperial University during wartime]." *Empire and the Higher Education in East Asia* 42 (2013): 173–93.

Zheng, Liling. *Yakudōsuru seishun: nihon tōchika Taiwan no gakusei seikatsu [Vibrant youths: student life in Taiwan under Japanese rule].* Translated by Naoe Kawamoto. Osaka: Sōgensha, 2017.

Zheng, Min. "Rōmu shin taisei [The new labor system]." In *Nicchū kyōdō kenkyū: Manshūkoku towa nandattanoka [Collaborative research by Japan and China: what was Manchukuo?],* edited by Shokuminchi bunka Gakkai, 140–50. Tokyo: shōgakkan, 2008.

Primary Sources

An, Gwang-Ho. "Byōbō sanzen ri [In the remote past, at a great distance]." In *Kankirei—manshū kenkoku daigaku zaikan dōsō bunshū [Kankirei: collection of memoirs written by alumni in Korea].* Translated by Eun-Suk Kim and Yoshikazu Kusano, 101–7. Kenkoku University Alumni Association, 2004.

An, Gwang-Ho. "Manshū kenkoku daigaku [Nation-Building University]." In *Kankirei—manshū kenkoku daigaku zaikan dōsō bunshū [Kankirei: collection of memoirs written by alumni in Korea].* Translated by Eun-Suk Kim and Yoshikazu Kusano, 1–5. Kenkoku University Alumni Association, 2004.

An, In-Geon. "Kendaisei wa sabishiku nai [Kendai students know no loneliness]." In *Kankirei—manshū kenkoku daigaku zaikan dōsō bunshū [Kankirei: collection of memoirs written by alumni in Korea]*. Translated by Eun-Suk Kim and Yoshikazu Kusano, 77–82. Kenkoku University Alumni Association, 2004.

Bak, Hui-Seong. "Kendai seikatsu no kaiko [Recollection of my student life at Kendai]." In *Kankirei—manshū kenkoku daigaku zaikan dōsō bunshū [Kankirei: collection of memoirs written by alumni in Korea]*. Translated by Eun-Suk Kim and Yoshikazu Kusano, 63–70. Kenkoku University Alumni Association, 2004.

Bandō, Yūtarō. "Netsurui saikai kenkoku daigaku no dōsōsei [Tearful reunion of Kenkoku University alumni]." *Nihon Keizai Shimbun*, September 10, 1980. (Reprinted in *Kankirei*, 33.)

Bang, Hui. "Kenkoku daigaku to gaikōkan [Nation-Building University and my career as a diplomat]." In *Kankirei—manshū kenkoku daigaku zaikan dōsō bunshū [Kankirei: collection of memoirs written by alumni in Korea]*. Translated by Eun-Suk Kim and Yoshikazu Kusano, 34–9. Kenkoku University Alumni Association, 2004.

Chang, Cheng. "Guanyu Zhang Jinghui he Weigao Guicang [About Zhang Jinghui and Suetaka Kamezō]." In *Huiyi weiman jianguo daxue [Remembering Bogus Manchukuo Nation-Building University]*, 52–5. Changchun: Changchun City Government's Chinese People's Political Consultative Committee, Historical Record Committee, 1997.

Choe, Heung-Cheol. "Kendai no seikatsu wo kangaeru [Regarding the life at Kendai]." In *Kankirei—manshū kenkoku daigaku zaikan dōsō bunshū [Kankirei: collection of memoirs written by alumni in Korea]*. Translated by Eun-Suk Kim and Yoshikazu Kusano, 71–6. Kenkoku University Alumni Association, 2004.

Choe, Nam-Seon. "Sui no kami [The god of *sui*]." *KURIMJ* 9 (May 1941): 3.

Choe, Nam-Seon. *Tōhō kominzoku no shinsei kan'nen ni tsuite [Regarding the ancient eastern peoples' conception of divinity]*. Shinkyō: Kenkoku daigaku kenkyūin, 1939.

Dōgaku reankan [Alumni's reunion]. Tokyo: Kenkoku University Alumni Association, 1993.

Doroyanagi: Kenkoku daigaku yonkisei kaishi [Japanese poplar: bulletin of Nation-Building University's fourth entering class]. Vol. 23. Edited by Kunio Kitahara et al. 1992.

Fujimori, Kōichi. *Jukusei nisshi [Daily log of a juku student]*. In Yuji.

Fujimori, Kōichi and Shōjirō Suzuki. *Kenkoku daigaku nenpyō yōran [The chronological timetable of Nation-Building University in Manchuria]*. Tokyo: Kenkoku University Alumni Association, 2007.

Gang, Yeong-Hun. "Kioku ni nokoru onshi rokudō sensei no ohanashi [Memorable talk of my former teacher Rokudō]." In *Kankirei—manshū kenkoku daigaku zaikan dōsō bunshū [Kankirei: collection of memoirs written by alumni in Korea]*. Translated by Eun-Suk Kim and Yoshikazu Kusano, 40–3. Kenkoku University Alumni Association, 2004.

Gang, Yeong-Hun. "Kenkoku daigaku no gakufū ni tsuiteno ichi kōsatsu [Discussion of the academic culture of Kenkoku University]." In *Kankirei—manshū kenkoku daigaku zaikan dōsō bunshū [Kankirei: collection of memoirs written by alumni in Korea].* Translated by Eun-Suk Kim and Yoshikazu Kusano, 112–15. Kenkoku University Alumni Association, 2004.

Gao, Ke. "Weiman jianda fanman kangri huodong ji qi fazhan [The activities of anti-Manchukuo and anti-Japanese aggression and their development at Bogus Manchukuo Kendai]." In *Huiyi weiman jianguo daxue [Remembering Bogus Manchukuo Nation-Building University],* 86–116. Changchun: Changchun City Government's Chinese People's Political Consultative Committee, Historical Record Committee, 1997.

Gu, Xueqian. "Shenghuo zai minzu maodun zhi zhong [Living under the paradox of ethnic harmony]." In *Huiyi weiman jianguo daxue [Remembering Bogus Manchukuo Nation-Building University],* 268–73. Changchun: Changchun City Government's Chinese People's Political Consultative Committee, Historical Record Committee, 1997.

Hakki [Eight flags]. Kendai seventh and eighth classes' bulletin no. 80. Edited by Yoshihisa Ueda et al. 1985.

Han, Weiping. "Shūsen zengo no ashioto [The footsteps around the war's end]." Translated by Yoshihisa Ueda. In *Hakki [Eight flags].* Kendai seventh and eighth classes' bulletin no. 80. Edited by Yoshihisa Ueda et al. 1985, 21–5.

Hong, Chun-Sik. "Seishun hōkō ki [The record of my youthful days]." In *Kankirei— manshū kenkoku daigaku zaikan dōsō bunshū [Kankirei: collection of memoirs written by alumni in Korea].* Translated by Eun-Suk Kim and Yoshikazu Kusano, 26–9. Kenkoku University Alumni Association, 2004.

Hong, Chun-Sik. *Hankyore no sekai: aa nihon [The world of my countrymen: Ah, Japan].* Ansan, 1999.

Huiyi weiman jianguo daxue [Remembering Bogus Manchukuo Nation-Building University]. Changchun: Changchun City Government's Chinese People's Political Consultative Committee, Historical Record Committee, 1997.

I, Jong-Hang. "Itsu-ga no mizu wa imammo nagarete irudaro! [The water must still be flowing in the Yitong River!]." In *Kankirei—manshū kenkoku daigaku zaikan dōsō bunshū [Kankirei: collection of memoirs written by alumni in Korea].* Translated by Eun-Suk Kim and Yoshikazu Kusano, 6–11. Kenkoku University Alumni Association, 2004.

Im, Seon-Jun. "Manshū Kendai nyūgaku no michi [My experience before matriculating at Kendai in Manchuria]." In *Kankirei—manshū kenkoku daigaku zaikan dōsō bunshū [Kankirei: collection of memoirs written by alumni in Korea].* Translated by Eun-Suk Kim and Yoshikazu Kusano, 90–2. Kenkoku University Alumni Association, 2004.

Ishiwara, Kanji. "Kantō-gun shireikan no manshūkoku naimen shidō tekkai ni tsuite [Proposal to stop Kwantung Army commander's intervention in Manchukuo]." In *Ishiwara Kanji shiryō* edited by Jun Tsunoda. In Yuji, Manzō. *Kenkoku daigaku nenpyō [The chronological timetable of Nation-Building University in Manchuria].* Tokyo: Kenkoku University Alumni Association, 1981, 113–14.

Ishiwara, Kanji. "Manshū kenkoku to shina jihen [The establishment of Manchukuo and the Shina incident]" (1940). In *Ishiwara Kanji senshū 6*, edited by Yoshiichirō Tamai, 161–94. Kanagawa: Tamairaba, 1993.

Ishiwara, Kanji. *Ishiwara Kanji senshū (zen 10-kan) gapponban [Selected works by Ishiwara Kanji]*. Vol. 1–10. Tokyo: Tamairabo, 1993.

Ishiwara, Kanji. *Kokubō seijiron [Political theory of national defense]* (1942). In *Ishiwara Kanji senshū 5*, edited by Yoshiichirō Tamai, 9–173. Kanagawa: Tamairaba, 1993.

Izumi, Santarō. "Editor's Note." In Morisaki Minato, *Isho [The Will]*, 236–42. Tokyo: Tosho shuppansha, 1971.

Jeong, Gi-Su. "Kankirei no yume [The dream about the Kankirei]." In *Kankirei— manshū kenkoku daigaku zaikan dōsō bunshū [Kankirei: collection of memoirs written by alumni in Korea]*. Translated by Eun-Suk Kim and Yoshikazu Kusano, 93–100. Kenkoku University Alumni Association, 2004.

Jin, Won-Jung. "Kaiko to sekkei [Recollection and construction]." In *Kankirei—manshū kenkoku daigaku zaikan dōsō bunshū [Kankirei: collection of memoirs written by alumni in Korea]*. Translated by Eun-Suk Kim and Yoshikazu Kusano, 108–11. Kenkoku University Alumni Association, 2004.

Jukusei kokoroe [Rules and regulations at juku]. Shinkyō: Kenkoku Daigaku, March 1943.

Kanki [Joy] (June 1940).

Kankirei haruka [Kankirei, far and away]. Vol. 1–2. Tokyo: Kenkoku University Alumni Association, 1991.

Kankirei. Tokyo: Kenkoku University Alumni Association, 1980.

Kankirei—manshū kenkoku daigaku zaikan dōsō bunshū [Kankirei: collection of memoirs written by alumni in Korea]. Translated by Eun-Suk Kim and Yoshikazu Kusano. Kenkoku University Alumni Association, 2004.

"Kendai gakusei shinkyō chaku [Kendai students arrive in Shinkyō]." *Tokyo Asahi Shinbun [Tokyo Asahi Newspaper]*, April 26, 1938.

Kendaishi shiryō [Sources on the history of Kendai]. Vol. 1–3. Tokyo: Kenkoku University Alumni Association, 1966–1967.

Kenkoku daigaku dōsōkai nihon deno ayumi [Foundation and activities of the Kenkoku University Alumni Association in Japan]. Tokyo: Nihon kenkoku daigaku dōsōkai, 2007.

Kenkoku daigaku gakuto shutsujin kashū [Nation-Building University student soldiers' poems composed upon the departure to the warfront]. Shinkyō: Manshū yūgaikaku, 1944.

Kenkoku daigaku juku geppō [Kenkoku University Juku Monthly] Issue 1 to 7 (1942–1943).

Kenkoku daigaku kenkyū kihō [Periodical report by Kenkoku University Research Institute]. Vol. 1–5, 1941–1943.

Kenkoku daigaku kenkyūin geppō [Kenkoku University Research Institute monthly journal] (KURIMJ). Vol. 1–45 (with several missing volumes). Shinkyō: Kenkokou daigaku kenkyūin, 1940–1945.

"Kenkoku daigaku ni pekin kara ryōhakase [Two professors join Nationa Building University]." *Tokyo Asahi Shinbun [Tokyo Asahi Newspaper]*, April 15, 1937.

Kenkoku daigaku sanki sei kaishi [Bulletin of the 3rd entering class of Nation-Building University]. Vol. 15. 1968. In Yuji.

"Kenkoku Daigaku sōsetsu yōkō [Guidelines for the Establishment of Nation-Building University]" (August 5, 1937).

"Kenkoku Daigaku sōsetsu yōkō [Guidelines for the Establishment of Nation-Building University]" (August 5, 1937). In Yuji, 52.

Kenkoku daigaku tosho tokushu mokuroku [Kenkoku University library special catalogues]. Shinkyō: Kenkoku Daigaku Toshokan, March and December 1941.

"Kenkoku daigaku yoka daiikki seito senbatsu yōkō an [The resolution of guidelines for admission of applicants for 1st entering class of the preparatory course at Nation-Building University]" (June 9, 1937). In Yuji, 26–7.

"Kenkoku Daigaku yōran [Directory of Nation-Building University]." Shinkyō: Kenkoku daigaku kenkyūin, 1941.

Kenkoku: kenkoku daigaku juku zasshi [Nation-Building: Kenkoku University Juku Journal]. Vol. 1 (August 20, 1940), Vol. 2 (August 20, 1941), and Vol. 3 (April 20, 1943).

Kim, Jae-Jin. "Tsuioku no Kendai [Kendai in memory]." In *Kankirei—manshū kenkoku daigaku zaikan dōsō bunshū [Kankirei: collection of memoirs written by alumni in Korea]*. Translated by Eun-Suk Kim and Yoshikazu Kusano, 60–2. Kenkoku University Alumni Association, 2004.

Kim, Jong-Cheol. "Kankirei jidai no dansō [My scattered memories about the time I spent at Kenkirei]." In *Kankirei—manshū kenkoku daigaku zaikan dōsō bunshū [Kankirei: collection of memoirs written by alumni in Korea]*. Translated by Eun-Suk Kim and Yoshikazu Kusano, 30–3. Kenkoku University Alumni Association, 2004.

Kim, Sang-Gyu. "Ninen han no kaisō [Recollection of the two and a half year]." In *Kankirei—manshū kenkoku daigaku zaikan dōsō bunshū [Kankirei: collection of memoirs written by alumni in Korea]*. Translated by Eun-Suk Kim and Yoshikazu Kusano, 57–9. Kenkoku University Alumni Association, 2004.

Kim, Yeong-Rok. "Kamakiri no yume [The dream about Kenkirei]." In *Kankirei—manshū kenkoku daigaku zaikan dōsō bunshū [Kankirei: collection of memoirs written by alumni in Korea]*. Translated by Eun-Suk Kim and Yoshikazu Kusano, 12–25. Kenkoku University Alumni Association, 2004.

Kim, Yong-Hui. "Kenkoku daigaku seikatsu no kaiko [Recollection of my student life at Nation-Building University]." In *Kankirei—manshū kenkoku daigaku zaikan dōsō bunshū [Kankirei: collection of memoirs written by alumni in Korea]*. Translated by Eun-Suk Kim and Yoshikazu Kusano, 86–9. Kenkoku University Alumni Association, 2004.

Li, Shuiqing. *Dongbei banian huigulu [Memory about the eight years that I lived in Dongbei]*. Translated by Kenzō Takazawa. Tokyo: Kenkoku University Alumni Association, 2007.

Li, Songwu. "Duri de jingguo yu ganxiang [The report and impressions on my trip to Japan]." *KURIMJ* 8 (April 1941): 6.

Li, Songwu. "Manzhou wenhua sixiang shi [Cultural and intellectual history of Manchuria]." *KURIMJ* 36 (December 1943): 17–33.

Liu, Chengren. "Lingming qian de kanzheng [Struggle before the dawn]." In *Huiyi weiman jianguo daxue [Remembering Bogus Manchukuo Nation-Building University]*, 63–6. Changchun: Changchun City Government's Chinese People's Political Consultative Committee, Historical Record Committee, 1997.

Liu, Diqian. "Wo suo liaojie de weiman jianguo daxue [What I know about Bogus Manchukuo Nation-Building University]" (1985). Republished in Chunxi Shuikou, *"Jianguo daxue" de huanying [The illusion at "Nation-Building University"]*, 146–95. Translated by Bingyue Dong. Beijing: Kunlun chubanshe, 2004.

Liu, Shize. "Weiman jianguo daxue jishu [The summary of Bogus Manchukuo Nation-Building University]." In *Huiyi weiman jianguo daxue [Remembering Bogus Manchukuo Nation-Building University]*, 28–41.Changchun: Changchun City Government's Chinese People's Political Consultative Committee, Historical Record Committee, 1997.

Manshūkoku kenkoku daigaku seito boshū kōkoku [Official announcement of student recruitment for Nation-Building University in Manchukuo] (August 10, 1937). In Yuji, 56–9.

Matsuyama, Shigejirō. *Daitōa kensetsu no sekaishi teki haikei [The background of the establishment of the Great East Asia in the context of world history]*. 4th ed. Shinkyō: Manshū teikoku kyōwakai, 1942.

Min, Gi-Sik. "Kenkoku daigaku to shikikan [Nation-Building University and my career as Commander]." In *Kankirei—manshū kenkoku daigaku zaikan dōsō bunshū [Kankirei: collection of memoirs written by alumni in Korea]*. Translated by Eun-Suk Kim and Yoshikazu Kusano, 44–9. Kenkoku University Alumni Association, 2004.

Minaguchi, Haruki. *Ōinaru genei: manshū kenkoku daigaku [The great illusion: Nation-Building University in Manchuria]*. Tokyo: Kōyō Shuppansha, 1998.

Mishina, Takayuki. "Ishiwara shōgun no Kendai ni kansuru rinen to kōsō [General Ishiwara's idea and vision of Kendai]." In *Manshūkokushi sōron*. In Yuji, 18–19.

Mori, Katsumi. *Daitōa kyōeiken no rekishisei [Historicity of the Great East Asia Co-Prosperity Sphere]*. 9th ed. Shinkyō: Manshū teikoku kyōwakai, 1942.

Morisaki, Minato. *Isho [The Will]*. Tokyo: Tosho shuppansha, 1971.

Murai, Tōjūrō. *Daitōa kyōeiken no kōiki hōchitsujo [Broad law and order in the Great East Asia Co-Prosperity Sphere]*. 10th ed. Shinkyo: Manshūkoku kyōwakai, 1942.

Nagano, Tadaomi. *Jukusei nisshi [Daily log of a juku student]*. In Yuji.

Nakano, Sei'ichi. "Manshūkoku minzoku seisaku eno shoyōsei [Requests for ethnic policies in Manchukuo]." *Kenkyū kihō* 1 (1941): 3–65.

Nie, Changlin. *Maboroshi no gakuen kenkoku daigaku: ichichūgokujin gakusei no shōgen [Nation-Building University, the school of illusions: testimony of a Chinese student]*.

Translated by Hiroshi Iwasaki. Tokyo: Kenkoku University Alumni Association, 1997.

Nishi, Shin'ichirō. "Kenkoku seishin to ōdō [The nation-building spirit and the Kingly Way]." *Kenkyū kihō* 3 (1942): 57–87.

Nishimura, Jūrō. *Rakugaki: manshū kenkoku daigaku waga gakusei jidai no omoide [Scribbles: recollection of my student life at Nation-Building University in Manchuria].* Kobe-shi: Tosho Shuppan Marodosha, 1991.

Ono, Kazuhito. "Manshū kenkoku to nippon: nippon no taiman kōdō ni kansuru jakkan no rekishiteki kaiko [Nation-building in Manchukuo and Japan: some historical reflections on Japan's attitudes toward Manchuria]." *Kenkyū kihō* 3 (1942): 153–236.

Pei, Rong. "Dushu yu fan dushu de huodong [The activities of reading books and the suppression of them]." In *Huiyi weiman jianguo daxue [Remembering Bogus Manchukuo Nation-Building University]*, 243–8. Changchun: Changchun City Government's Chinese People's Political Consultative Committee, Historical Record Committee, 1997.

"Qianyan [Preface]." In *Huiyi weiman jianguo daxue [Remembering Bogus Manchukuo Nation-Building University]*. Changchun: Changchun City Government's Chinese People's Political Consultative Committee, Historical Record Committee, 1997.

Reimei: Kenkoku daigaku dai jūyon juku juku zasshi [Dawn: Kenkoku University the 14th juku periodical]. Issues 1–5 (1940).

Sakuta, Sōchi. *Manshū kenkoku no genri oyobi hongi [The principles and the core meanings of the founding of Manchukuo].* Edited by Tōjūrō Murai. Shinkyō: Manshū tomiyama bo, 1944.

Sakuta, Sōchi. *Shūshin dōtoku [Shushin morarity].* Shinkyō: Kenkoku daigaku kenkyūin, 1941.

Sakuta, Sōchi. *Wakaremi no kōchiku [The construction of wakaremi].* Edited by Shōji Yamada. Ōita: Hōsei insatsu, 1990.

Seihu kōhō (Shinkyō). In *Weimanzhouguo zhengfu gongbao.* Shenyang: Liaoshen shushe, 1990.

Shashinshū kenkoku daigaku [Photograph collection: Nation-Building University]. Tokyo: Kenkoku University Alumni Association, 1986.

Song, Shaoying. "Qianye da taowang [The great escape in the night before]." In *Huiyi weiman jianguo daxue [Remembering Bogus Manchukuo Nation-Building University]*, 73–6. Changchun: Changchun City Government's Chinese People's Political Consultative Committee, Historical Record Committee, 1997.

Suzuki, Shōjirō. *Kenkoku daigaku kyōshokuin roku [Record on Kenkoku University faculty and staff].* Tokyo: Kenkoku University Alumni Association, 2007.

Tae, In-Seon. "Kenkoku daigaku to watashi [Nation-Building University and myself]." In *Kankirei—manshū kenkoku daigaku zaikan dōsō bunshū [Kankirei: collection of memoirs written by alumni in Korea].* Translated by Eun-Suk Kim and Yoshikazu Kusano, 50–6. Kenkoku University Alumni Association, 2004.

Tsutsui, Kiyohiko. *Hoki [supplemental memos for the Chronology]*. In Yuji, 41.

Tsutsui, Ryūta. "Tōhatsu nagakeredo gankō mijikashi [Wearing her hair long, while fixing her eyes near]." In *Hakki [Eight flags]*. Kendai seventh and eighth classes' bulletin no. 80. Edited by Yoshihisa Ueda et al. 1985, 46–9.

Wang, Yeping. "Chongpo laolong ren niao fei [Quickly breaking the prison, birds flew away]." In *Huiyi weiman jianguo daxue [Remembering Bogus Manchukuo Nation-Building University]*, 77–85. Changchun: Changchun City Government's Chinese People's Political Consultative Committee, Historical Record Committee, 1997.

Xue, Wen. "Ji 'ba yi wu' qianhou de ririyeye [Note about the days around 'August 15']." In *Huiyi weiman jianguo daxue [Remembering Bogus Manchukuo Nation-Building University]*, 67–72. Changchun: Changchun City Government's Chinese People's Political Consultative Committee, Historical Record Committee, 1997.

Yamada, Shōji. *Kōbō no arashi: mansū kenkoku daigaku hōkai no shuki [The rise and fall in storm: memoir about the dissolution of Nation-Building University in Manchurial]*. 1980.

Yamashita, Kōichi. *Jukusei nisshi [Daily log of a juku student]*. In Yuji.

Yan, Defan. "Weiman jianda renwu sumiao [Sketch of people at Bogus Manchukuo Kendai]." In *Huiyi weiman jianguo daxue [Remembering Bogus Manchukuo Nation-Building University]*, 56–62. Changchun: Changchun City Government's Chinese People's Political Consultative Committee, Historical Record Committee, 1997.

Yan, Tingqiao. "Weiman jianguo daxue shimou zhaiji [A general note on Bogus Manchukuo Nation-Building University]." In *Huiyi weiman jianguo daxue [Remembering Bogus Manchukuo Nation-Building University]*, 21–7. Changchun: Changchun City Government's Chinese People's Political Consultative Committee, Historical Record Committee, 1997.

Yimen Zhang, "Zai zhimin tongzhixiade xuexi shenghuo [Student Life under Colonial Rule]" In *Huiyi weiman jianguo daxue [Remembering Bogus Manchukuo Nation-Building University]*, 282–8. Changchun: Changchun City Government's Chinese People's Political Consultative Committee, Historical Record Committee, 1997.

Yu, Jiaqi. "Weiman jianguo daxue ji qi pouxi [Analysis of Bogus Manchukuo Nation-Building University]." In *Huiyi weiman jianguo daxue [Remembering Bogus Manchukuo Nation-Building University]*, 1–20. Changchun: Changchun City Government's Chinese People's Political Consultative Committee, Historical Record Committee, 1997.

Yue, Yishi. "Wo likai jianda dao Chongqing [I left Kendai to go to Chongqing]." In *Huiyi weiman jianguo daxue [Remembering Bogus Manchukuo Nation-Building University]*, 117–19. Changchun: Changchun City Government's Chinese People's Political Consultative Committee, Historical Record Committee, 1997.

Yuji, Manzō. *Kenkoku daigaku nenpyō [The chronological timetable of Nation-Building University in Manchuria]*. Tokyo: Kenkoku University Alumni Association, 1981.

"Zadankai: gonenkan no juku seikatsu [Talk: five years of juku life]." In Yuji, 122.

Zhang, Tailu. "Kenkoku daigaku de mananda hibi [The days I spent at Nation-Building University]." Translated by Yoshihisa Ueda. In *Hakki [Eight flags]*. Kendai seventh and eighth classes' bulletin no. 80. Edited by Yoshihisa Ueda et al. 1985, 43–6.

Zhang, Wensheng. "Jianda xianxiang [Kendai phenomenon]." In *Huiyi weiman jianguo daxue [Remembering Bogus Manchukuo Nation-Building University]*, 264–7. Changchun: Changchun City Government's Chinese People's Political Consultative Committee, Historical Record Committee, 1997.

Zhao, Hong. "Wo de kongsu: 1954 nian shenpan riben zhanfan shi de kongsu shu [My accusation: my letter of appeal to the Japanese war crime tribunal in 1954]." In *Huiyi weiman jianguo daxue [Remembering Bogus Manchukuo Nation-Building University]*, 154–63. Changchun: Changchun City Government's Chinese People's Political Consultative Committee, Historical Record Committee, 1997. (Originally published as part of vol. 8 of *Riben diguo zhuyi qinhua dangan ziliao xuanbian dibaquan: dongbei lici dacanan [The selected archival records about Japanese imperial encroachment in China: the tragedy in the Northeast]* (Beijing: Zhonghua shuju, 1989).)

Index